BUILDING PROFESSIONAL WEB SITES WITH THE RIGHT TOOLS

ISBN 0-13-084317-2

90000

9 780130 843173

Hewlett-Packard® Professional Books

Atchison	Object-Oriented Test & Management Software Development in C++
Blinn	Portable Shell Programming
Blommers	Architecting Enterprise Solutions with UNIX Networking
Blommers	Practical Planning for Network Growth
Caruso	Power Programming in HP OpenView
Chew	The Java/C++ Cross-Reference Handbook
Cook	Building Enterprise Information Architectures
Costa	Planning and Designing High Speed Networks
Crane	A Simplified Approach to Image Processing
Day	The Color Scanning Handbook
Derickson	Fiber Optic Test and Measurement
Eisenmann and Eisenmann	Machinery Malfunction Diagnosis and Correction
Fernandez	Configuring the Common Desktop Environment
Fristrup	USENET: Netnews for Everyone
Fristrup	The Essential Web Surfer Survival Guide
Gann	Desktop Scanners: Image Quality
Grady	Practical Software Metrics for Project Management and Process Improvement
Greenberg	A Methodology for Developing and Deploying Internet and Intranet Solutions
Greenberg, Lakeland	Building Professional Web Sites with the Right Tools
Grosvenor, Ichiro, O'Brien	Mainframe Downsizing to Upsize Your Business: IT-Preneuring
Gunn	A Guide to NetWare® for UNIX®
Helsel	Graphical Programming: A Tutorial for HP VEE
Helsel	Visual Programming with HP VEE, Third Edition
Holman, Lund	Instant JavaScript
Kane	PA-RISC 2.0 Architecture
Ketkar	Working with Netscape® Server on HP-UX
Knouse	Practical DCE Programming
Lee	The ISDN Consultant
Lewis	The Art & Science of Smalltalk
Lichtenbelt, Crane, Naqvi	Introduction to Volume Rendering
Loomis	Object Databases in Practice
Lucke	Designing and Implementing Computer Workgroups
Lund	Integrating UNIX® and PC Network Operating Systems
Madell	Disk and File Management Tasks on HP-UX
Mahoney	High-Mix Low-Volume Manufacturing
Malan, Letsinger, Coleman	Object-Oriented Development at Work: Fusion In the Real World
McFarland	X Windows on the World
McMinds/Whitty	Writing Your Own OSF/Motif Widgets
Norton, DiPasquale	Thread Time: The Multithreaded Programming Guide
Orzessek, Sommer	ATM: & MPEG-2: A Practical Guide to Computer Security
Phaal	LAN Traffic Management
Pipkin	Halting the Hacker: A Practical Guide to Computer Security
Poniatowski	HP-UX 11.x System Administration Handbook and Toolkit
Poniatowski	HP-UX 11.x System Administration "How To" Book, Second Edition
Poniatowski	HP NetServer Guide for Windows NT®
Poniatowski	HP-UX System Administration Handbook and Toolkit
Poniatowski	HP-UX 10.x System Administration "How To" Book
Poniatowski	Learning the HP-UX Operating System
Poniatowski	Windows NT® and HP-UX System Administrator's "How To" Book
Ryan	Distributed Object Technology: Concepts and Applications
Sauers/Weygant	HP-UX Tuning and Performance
Simmons	Software Measurement: A Visualization Toolkit
Sperley	Enterprise Data Warehouse, Volume 1: Planning, Building, and Implementation
Thomas	Cable Television Proof-of-Performance
Thomas, Edgington	Digital Basics for Cable Television Systems
Thornburgh	Fibre Channel for Mass Storage
Weygant	Clusters for High Availability: A Primer of HP-UX Solutions
Witte	Electronic Test Instruments
Yawn, Stachnick, Sellars	The Legacy Continues: Using the HP 3000 with HP-UX and Windows NT

BUILDING PROFESSIONAL WEB SITES WITH THE RIGHT TOOLS

Jeff Greenberg
J.R. Lakeland
http://www.hp.com/go/retailbooks

Prentice Hall PTR
Upper Saddle River, NJ 07458
http://www.phptr.com

Library of Congress Cataloging-in-Publication Data

Greenberg, Jeff R.

    Building professional Web sites with the right tools / Jeff Greenberg, J.R. Lakeland.

      p.   cm.

    ISBN 0-13-084317-2

    1. Web sites--Design. I. Lakeland, J.R. II. Title.

TK5105.888.G72   1999

005.7'2--dc21   99-38304

                                                  CIP

Editorial/production supervision: *Vincent Janoski*
Acquisitions editor: *Jill Pisoni*
Marketing manager: *Lisa Konzelmann*
Manufacturing manager: *Alexis R. Heydt*
Editorial assistant: *Linda Ramagnano*
Cover design director: *Jerry Votta*
Manager, Hewlett-Packard Retail Book Publishing: *Patricia Pekary*
Editor, Hewlett-Packard Professional Books: *Susan Wright*

©1999 by Hewlett-Packard Company

Published by Prentice Hall PTR
Prentice-Hall, Inc.
Upper Saddle River, NJ 07458

Prentice Hall books are widely used by corporations and government agencies
for training, marketing, and resale.

The publisher offers discounts on this book when ordered in bulk quantities.
For more information, contact: Corporate Sales Department, Phone: 800-382-3419;
Fax: 201-236-7141; E-mail: corpsales@prenhall.com; or write: Prentice Hall PTR,
Corp. Sales Dept., One Lake Street, Upper Saddle River, NJ 07458.

TRADEMARKS: Puddleduck Press and The Blowhole are trademarks of Puddleduck Press Inc. Paint Shop Pro, Copyright
©1991-1999 Jasc Software, Inc. All Rights Reserved. Dynamic Billboard Java Applet by Robert Temple. Windows NT,
FrontPage, Windows, Visual Basic, Visual J++, Visual C++, JScript, Visual FoxPro, and Visual Studio and Visual
Interdev are either registered trademarks or trademarks of Microsoft Corporation in the United States and/or other countries.
Java and JavaScript are trademarks or registered trademarks of Sun Microsystems, Inc. in the United States and other countries.
Netscape and Netscape Navigator are registered trademarks of Netscape Communications Corporation in the United States and
other countries. Oracle is a registered trademark of Oracle Corporation.

All products or services mentioned in this book are the trademarks or service marks of their respective companies or
organizations. Screen shots reprinted by permission from Microsoft Corporation.

Screen shots using PaintShop Pro are reprinted by permission of Jasc Software, Inc.

Printed in the United States of America
10 9 8 7 6 5 4 3 2 1

ISBN   0-13-084317-2

Prentice-Hall International (UK) Limited, *London*
Prentice-Hall of Australia Pty. Limited, *Sydney*
Prentice-Hall Canada Inc., *Toronto*
Prentice-Hall Hispanoamericana, S.A., *Mexico*
Prentice-Hall of India Private Limited, *New Delhi*
Prentice-Hall of Japan, Inc., *Tokyo*
Prentice-Hall Singapore Pte. Ltd., *Singapore*
Editora Prentice-Hall do Brasil, Ltda., *Rio de Janeiro*

This book is dedicated to my mother, Betty, who never said "no" when I wanted to read, and who always says "yes" when others want to learn to.

Contents

List of Figures

Preface

One byte.

If you were to ask a dozen long-time programmers to name a single industry event that impacted their profession in the most far-reaching manner, you would receive at least ten unique answers (or more likely 10.25, considering the audience). I've pondered this question at length and have zeroed in on *my* answer. There's a story, hopefully an interesting one, behind it, so I'll keep you waiting for my answer just a while.

I joined the computer industry in 1977, an amazing period of technological beginnings after what seemed a long, relatively stagnant period. I was fortunate to learn a large breadth of programming languages, some still in use, some now lost in antiquity: BASIC, FOCAL, COBOL, FORTRAN, ALGOL, APL, Assembler, PL/1, SPL and RPG; C and C++ came later. The fortune from this knowledge was an intimate understanding through comparison of what makes a compiler tick, and as a result an understanding of how better to create an application.

I was also fortunate to make use of these programming languages, and dozens of variations of development tools and middleware, on several different computer systems. At the time, dominance in the marketplace was held by the mainframe.

I programmed an IBM 370 mainframe. I used an IBM 029 alphanumeric card-punch machine to create the cards that made up both the source code and the Job Control Language the machine required to compile and execute programs. I suppose these cards now exist mainly in computer museums, so for those of you who never saw one, each card had 80 columns (see Figure P-1). Columns 1-6 were reserved for line numbers (we were too lazy to number our cards — a decision which would haunt you if you were ever to drop your deck of, on average, 200 cards and have to put them back in order). Column 7 was only used if the card were a continuation of the card that preceded it. Columns 8 through 72 were used for the actual COBOL instructions, a styling used today despite the fact that the days of punch cards are long gone. OS/JCL was something that, once mastered, stayed with you. I can still rattle it off:

Figure P-1   A standard Hollerith card. Card courtesy of the
Computer Museum of America

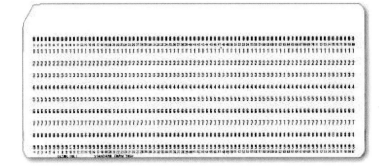

```
//MYPROG EXEC
//SYSOUT DD SYSOUT=A
//SYS005 DD UNIT=TAPE, LRECL=80, BLKSIZE=240, DISP=(,KEEP)
//SYSIN DD *
/*
//
```

Eventually we were able to do data entry with a teletype and with one of the first CRT's (Cathode Ray Tube) to hit the market. The teletype was always a mystery; you could tell where in the processing cycle the system was by the way the print ball would stop, pop up and down, and rotate. The CRT was a blessing. It still required the same 80-column format, but at least there was a backspace.

Another system at the high end was an IBM 1103. This was considered to be a minicomputer at the time. It also used cards, and the card reader was so slow that you could see it sucking the cards through one by one. When designing applications for these beasts, you only had to remember that the input was limited to 80 columns, and the output to 132 columns. There were columnar pads in both sizes that we stocked to facilitate designing reports and input files around the column parameters.

At the low end I entered the PC market before the first PC. I wrote my first applications on a Canon programmable calculator. It was precisely that, a large desktop calculator with thermal paper tape. It could handle 200 instructions or 2,000 bytes of data at a time. Connected to it was an 8" hard-sectored floppy drive, and an IBM Selectric typewriter that had a RS232 port. After executing 200 instructions, you would fetch more by issuing the command

```
I/O 7
6
I/O 9
0
I/O 9
0
I/O 9
2
0
0
I/O 9
1
0
0

Σm

2 0
RM
2 0
I/O 9
I/O a
```

So really, there were only 200 instructions less those 20 available. Entire applications were written by using functions still on calculators: Store Memory, Recall Memory and Accumulate Memory (M+).

What a debugging nightmare! If the users needed to enter alpha characters, they had to press a completely nonintuitive series of keystrokes, then press the character keys (on a calculator keyboard that didn't resemble a typewriter keyboard in the slightest), and another series of keys when they had finished.

About 1978 my Canon was replaced with an Ohio Scientific computer. Once we got the device drivers working, we had a working microcomputer with a boot choice of three internal chips: the Z80, the 8080A, and the 6502. With this micro came BASIC. This version of BASIC allowed computed GOTO and GOSUB statements, which led to debugging nightmares like:

```
10 GOSUB VAL(LEFT$(Y$,3))
```

but it didn't have RENUM command, so I had to write one. This machine also made it possible to present the user with a menu because the screen supported the ASCII codes 10 through 13, which allowed the cursor to be moved in a nondestructive manner. The file I/O was challenging and fun because it was direct, so functions had to be written to place the file cursor at the right point prior to reading or writing.

The microcomputer allowed the 132-column output format to be broken to some extent, because it did provide a means of sending output to the screen. However, despite its allowing the cursor to be moved, the cursor could not be absolutely placed. That is, if I wanted to put the cursor in the 25th column of the 15th screen row, I had to do this by starting at a given point and have the cursor move one position at a time relative to that point. This is still the way that many UI screens are drawn, but the positioning is not accomplished via a loop in a BASIC program. So full UIs were still just conceptual.

At the middle of the market was Hewlett-Packard's HP3000. I wasn't working with the original model (the Series CX), but close: a Series II, the third in the line. A large difference here was that I could touch the system, start it, shut it down, and communicate interactively with it. There was actually some *comfort* in the immediacy and the machine's "willingness to converse" with me.

The communications were via a terminal, the HP 2640, one of the finest terminals ever made. And this terminal brings me, finally, to my answer to the question I posed. The single industry event that impacted my profession in the most far-reaching manner.

One byte.

And that one byte is the escape character, ASCII 27.

You see, the escape character was used to get the attention of the terminal. The receipt of that character told the terminal that there was going to be a string of characters following the escape character, an "escape sequence," and that every character received after the escape character up until an uppercase character would be a request for the terminal to provide a specific service. These services could include resetting, performing a self-test, performing tape functions (for the 2645 models that supported an internal tape drive), and, germane to this discussion, formatting.

Oh the bliss. With a sequence of Esc &dA, I could make text blink. With Esc &dD, I could underline the text. And with the wonderful Esc &dJ, I could reverse the video (bright background, dark foreground) of characters. If I specified a column and row combination, then ended sequence with 'Y,' I could move the cursor to any absolute address on the screen, and with a different terminating character move the cursor in a relative manner. This was my first opportunity to code a UI. I could highlight fields to draw the user's attention, even put a status line at the bottom of the screen. If the user typed something erroneous, instead of trying to stop them in mid-flow I could wait until they requested the screen to be accepted, pop an error into the status line, highlight the erroneous entry, and move the cursor to the offending field. Wow!

Most of what I've coded since then has been an exercise in improving the UI. That's what receives the majority of my consideration when coding desktop applications and creating Web sites. There is one all-important facet to providing users with a visual interface: draw the users in and make them comfortable enough to stay awhile. This requires a well-designed interface to a well-designed application. They balance each other, and if either is insufficient, the users will either not use the application, or, if they have no choice, use it under protest.

Certainly the presentation to the user is only one part of what's required for a Web site, but let's face it, there's no sense in having the rest of it if there's nothing for the user to see. And always remember, they might be coming to your site for the information, but if that information isn't presented in an appealing manner they won't be back! And for the programmer, what a joy to see that drop-down list drop down, that button respond to the mouse click, that text field change when the radio button is clicked. The feeling is even better when you see the page counter incrementing from the people visiting the Web site that you created.

Figure P-2   HP 2640B Terminal

Building Professional Web Sites with the Right Tools takes you through one of many approaches to the entire process of creating a fully functional Web site. I've taken the approach and tools I think provides the best compromise; with Web development *everything* is compromise.

Instead of the usual reference book type of approach where every nuance of each technology is covered, often with little or no flow, you'll be walked through only as much technology as you need to fully understand each step of the process: obtaining and installing the tools, creating the graphics, designing and developing the database, Web pages and their elements, coding the applications and publishing to the Web.

Alternative tools and technologies that accommodate the creation of a Web site will be mentioned throughout the book. It's not implied, and no inference should be made that the tools, technologies and methods chosen represent the best or only choice — the way the industry is moving at bullet-train speed a different tool might make more sense next week — but those chosen *are* good, industry-leading tools. Since much time will be spent taking you step-by-step through *why* certain things are done, and just as importantly, why some *aren't*, you will ultimately decide whether the approach is good.

If you want to be able to absorb the facets of Web development and view them in a component-like manner, so that you develop the knowledge to develop your own sites, then *Building Professional Web Sites with the Right Tools* is the book for you!

Jeff Greenberg
Atlanta, 1998

Acknowledgments

A number of people have been instrumental in making this book a reality. I hope I've remembered you all. My thanks to:

Lindsay, Daniel, and Megan for not moving away when I announced I'd be writing another book.

My parents, in-laws, friends and colleagues for their encouragement.

Bill Hewlett, the late Dave Packard, and the folks at HP for a laptop that never failed me, and for helping make this happen, especially Gary England, Whit Matteson, Laurie Clough and Susan Wright.

Michael Zoellner for his time, friendship, buying my beer and feeding my fish.

The folks at Puddleduck Press for their Web pages and graphics.

The gang at The Blowhole for a great opportunity.

The folks at Adobe® for FrameMaker®.

J.R. Lakeland, another?!

The folks at Prentice Hall for their talents and encouragement, and especially Jill Pisoni, Jeffrey Pepper, Linda Ramagnano, Vincent Janoski, Camille Trentacoste and Lisa Iarkowski.

The Computer Museum of America for popping some Hollerith cards from their collection in the mail to a stranger.

Introduction

You can develop a Web site. *You* can do it! Yes, YOU! Whether you're new to programming or an experienced programmer new to Web development, you can develop a Web site from start to finish. I'm going to show you how, and instead of showing you *everything* there is to know (whether you need to know it or not), instead of dumping everything into chapters for you to search through, I'm going to lead you through just enough to create a fully functional site. If you later feel that you need to know more about a certain topic, you'll at least know where to look. Best of all, you're going to have fun!

This book has been designed to be an easy, interesting read, and if you read it cover to cover, you will know how to develop a fully functional Web site. There is at least one big difference between a novel and a book like this beyond one being fiction and the other nonfiction. In reading a novel, a work of fiction, you suspend your disbelief long enough for a good author to hook you. You do this without regard to the direction in which the author wants to lead you, so long as you're well led. With a nonfiction text, you want to know where you're being led, and why.

Why the Web?

There are two good reasons, among others, for paying attention to the Web: ease of development and ease of access. When developing for the Web, unless the content being developed requires advanced functionality, the code can be written once and run on many different platforms. This is because the browser does the work of interfacing with the services of the operating system such as graphics and typeface manipulation. Thus the screen display from a browser on one platform looks virtually identical to the output on another platform. As long as the development is done using a standard that the browser understands, the code can be ported without any issues, can display graphics and send email consistently without regard to API's or other machine-specific issues. Once the code is up and running, anyone with a browser and access to the Web can run the application.

For example, it used to be that if an application needed to be available to users on both a mainframe and a personal computer, the application would be written in COBOL (COmmon Business-Oriented Language) with CICS® calls to paint an IBM 3270® terminal screen for the former. For the latter, the application might have been written in C with calls to the MS Windows® APIs. What a programming and support nightmare! Now, with the browser providing the glue to the services of the machine on which it runs, Web pages can be developed to run on any machine that has a supporting browser.

Which Script?

Where the functionality in our Web site calls for some programming, we'll be using Microsoft VBScript, a subset of Visual Basic, for server-side scripting, and Java-Script for client-side scripting. Why?

Currently only two development technologies provide all the tools needed to construct the varied programmatic functionality needed on the Web page: Java (along with JavaScript and Java applets) and Visual Basic (along with VBScript and ActiveX). Why don't we use only one? If we want to do client-side scripting for things like form editing, and want Netscape Communicator *and* Internet Explorer users to be able to make use of it, we need to use JavaScript as VBScript is not currently supported by Netscape. On the other hand, VBScript is much easier to use and seems to work better on a Microsoft server than JavaScript, so when it comes to server-side scripting, where the code will be executed on the server, we'll use VBScript.

This is a learning book, and hopefully a fun learning book at that. While it certainly can be referenced when needed, it isn't meant to be a reference manual and is not laid out that way. *Building Professional Web Sites with the Right Tools* is a beginning-to-end learning guide on, well, crafting an Internet Web site. Actually, it's more than that. Here is a partial list of what *you* will be able to do after reading this book:

- use VBScript, JavaScript, Visual InterDev, Active Data Objects (ADO) and Active Server Pages (ASP) to provide rich server-side and client-side application functionality for a Web page
- use Cascading Style Sheets (CSS) to enrich the look and functionality of Web pages
- create buttons, rules, banners, image maps and other Web graphics using Paint Shop Pro and Image Composer
- install and configure the tools needed for development
- create the functional and detailed design for the Web site
- produce development standards
- design the data model and produce a database from it
- make images ready for Web use
- incorporate a Java applet in your Web page

Whew! Bet it was tiring just reading that list. So, what's it all mean? Well, have you been to sites like Yahoo (www.yahoo.com), where you can follow links to other sites? These are called "Web Portals," and that's what we're going to create.

I hope you can avoid the temptation to jump around and just pick things out that look important. I realize there are a lot of pages to read, but there are a lot of illustrations, and certainly you can follow along with the lessons using your PC. We often tend to learn only what we need to know to resolve a specific problem, an approach that leaves gaps in our knowledge. *Building Professional Web Sites with the Right Tools* is laid out almost like a diary, using a plausible business case to move systematically from defining a need through to a production Internet site. Following is a summary of what you will find in each chapter.

Chapter 1 — Defining the Need

Behind every great application is a need, the fulfillment of which drives the application's creation. The Web site and applications to be developed in this book are no exception. The phases of a software development cycle are reviewed. The business drivers are identified, and from them the requirements are generated. Finally, a high-level (functional) design is derived.

Chapter 2 — Untangling the Technology

This chapter will provide a primer on the technologies to be used in the solution. Also discussed will be the issues involved in using them based on their current implementation and the state of the applications that embrace them. The technologies include HTML, CSS, DHTML, ASP, ADO, CGI, JavaScript and VBScript.

Chapter 3 — The Solution

With an understanding of the business issues, the goal and the technology available, the architecture decisions are made regarding the targeted hardware platforms and the development tools. The low-level design is developed to define the big picture.

Chapter 4 — The DIY Store

This chapter will cover obtaining the tools you'll be using throughout the book, installing and configuring them.

Chapter 5 — Standards

Even if no one else but the author will ever need to maintain the Web site, defining and adhering to standards for coding, HTML, comments, variable names, and error handling will make the job easier.

Chapter 6 — The Database

In this chapter we create the database in seven steps: the design, normalization, the tables, access, queries, updates and reporting.

Chapter 6 — The Database

In this chapter we create the Microsoft Access database that we'll use throughout our Web site. We'll also create an ODBC Data Source Name so that the database can be accessed from the Web site.

Chapter 7 — Graphics

With the design document in hand, the coding, or construction, can begin. This chapter concentrates on creating the graphics that will be used on the Web site. Issues such as dimensions, file size, resolution, quality loss, color palette, transparency and format are considered. We'll create application graphics such as icons, buttons, the logo, and Web graphics for the Web application, such as buttons, horizontal rule, background, logo, and clipart.

Chapter 8 — The Environment

In this chapter we establish the development environment by creating a FrontPage project, a Visual Interdev solution and a data connection to our database.

Chapter 9 — Home

This is where the coding begins, and where better to start than at home, the "home page" that is. We'll create its frame structure here.

Chapter 10 — The Utility Pages

We have a number of pages that provide certain utility, namely the *Copyright* page, the *Ad* page, the *Web Rings* page and the *Awards* page. We'll create them in this chapter.

Chapter 11 — Home Again

We created the frame structure of the home page in Chapter 9. Now we'll put the code and elements in to support each of the frames on this powerful page. Once the page is complete, we'll use its image to create the *About* page.

Chapter 12 — Feedback

This suite of pages will have us code functionality that we haven't used before, as well as using existing routines in a different setting.

Chapter 13 — HELP!

We'll create a page that the site visitor can use to explain how the main page works.

Chapter 14 — This is Only A Test

Testing can be a complicated phase, especially when trying to debug Web applications. This chapter proceeds through testing the Web site, and contains tips for debugging.

Chapter 15 — Going Live

We'll be busy in this chapter discussing various to-market loose ends that we need to tie up, such as selecting an ISP and a Web Hoster, obtaining a domain, publishing your site and marketing it.

Chapter 16 — Epilogue

This chapter covers functionality that is planned for the next version of the Web site — things that will make it more valuable and robust, but that couldn't be worked into the initial time requirement.

Appendix A — What's At the Web Site

Along with this book, you've purchased the right to access a Web site that contains complementary materials.

Appendix B — Source code for Dynamic Billboard

One of the elements used widely in this book is a Java applet, the source code for which is listed here.

Throughout the book you will find informational icons in the outside margin of the page. These icons are used as follows:

Note — Information worth noting

Caution — This information is worth your close attention

Yikes — Don't let this happen to you Something you want to avoid

Well, enough of the administration, there's a long, fun road ahead of us. See you in Chapter 1, which, for the sake of convenience, is located just a page away.

Defining the Need

Measure twice,
Cut once.
-Norm Abrams
Master Carpenter

*D*on't jump!!!

If you've ever been a programmer, project manager, woodworker or sailor, you're familiar with the urge of the uninitiated to jump right in and code, implement, cut wood or sail. If you've ever given into that temptation, odds are you're also familiar with spaghetti code, over-budget projects, wasted wood and the word "Mayday!"

Unfortunately, we creative types often need to be efficient, proficient, or both, and thus must plan *before* we do. Planning certainly requires more patience than doing. It's a particularly hard sell in a PC environment. It was one thing when a mistake caused by a lack of planning meant that after three hours you received back your deck of punch cards and a printout with an error. In a PC environment where you have an immediate compile before your eyes, where you're not impacting anyone else's compute cycles and aren't being charged for them — there's not much reason to plan first. Still, all things being equal, the planner is moving on to a new project while the doer is trying to mop up the mess.

Since my goal with this book is to walk you *successfully* through the steps in developing a Web site, I'm going to lead you through the stages of planning on the front end. Stick with me and you'll receive an enjoyable learning experience; one that will prepare you to leap some of the hurdles you'll find later, instead of stumbling over them.

At this point, we're at the very beginning. At the beginning of any software development project, whether a simple program or a Web site, there is a defining need, a business case, which should justify the investment necessary to produce the solution. Let's take a look at the underlying need that interests us. We're not going to make a big deal out of it, but the learning experience is always augmented by knowing *why* you're doing something.

1.1 The Business Case

Let's create a company. The Blowhole will be a "mom & pop" company based in Atlanta, Georgia. I could invent all kinds of historical information about The Blowhole, but most of it would be unimportant fluff, so I'll just give you the highlights.

The Blowhole is a Web start-up business. Unlike businesses that use the Internet as part of a sales and marketing strategy, The Blowhole will use the Internet for its business in general, as it will be a niche Web portal[1] site much like Yahoo or Excite, but focusing on "all things marine."

At the last executive meeting, the CIO, Shauna Hill laid out her vision of the initiative needed to launch The Blowhole. The CEO, Megan Casteel, and most of the other staff members, including Caitlin Brookton, the Creative Director, supported Shauna's ideas. A minute or two of kudos was followed by some practical questions, such as "where would the core site information, the links, come from?" Would this be another "spider walk," a reference to the programs that some portals use, which gather site information by "crawling" through the Web at night. The implication was that this would not be acceptable; many people feel that the results of a search from such an index provides a high percentage of nonapplicable links. Shauna and the marketing staff had thought this through beforehand. The information, she said, would be provided in part by research staff, and in part by representatives of applicable sites submitting their information, much as they would to a search engine—after all, being listed on a portal is free advertising.

Shauna received the okay. The development will be done by another Atlanta "mom & pop shop," Puddleduck Press, and so it's time for us to move on to the requirements for this project, which has been named *Trade Winds*.

1.2 The Software Development Cycle

There is no shortage of software development methodologies. For this project we're going to borrow one from the Software Services Outsourcing Program (SSOP) of HP Consulting.[2] The methodology is called TSSP: Team Structure Software Process, as shown in Figure 1-1.

The major phases of the methodology are:

- Scoping—the requirements, the basic needs that must be fulfilled for the application to resolve the business issue(s) that justified its creation — are gathered and documented.

- High-Level (Functional) Design — the functions that are needed to account for the requirements are enumerated and described at a high level. The Platform Design, the hardware, software and networking tools necessary to develop, implement and support the application are chosen and documented.

---

1.   A "Web Portal" is a site on the World Wide Web that is used as a launching point to other sites, like a subject card catalog at a library.

2.   HP Consulting is a division of the Hewlett-Packard Company.

The Detailed Design, the layouts and detailed logic of the functions in the High-Level Design. The design of the database and the test plans.

- Infrastructure Ramp-up — The hardware and software components necessary for the solution development are installed.
- Construction — The applications are coded and unit tested.
- Testing — End-to-end system testing is performed, and if applicable (it isn't in this case), user-acceptance testing.
- Support Design — A design is created for the support environment and services that will be needed. In our case this doesn't apply, as the ISP (Internet Service Provider) will provide the support.
- Implementation — The tasks necessary to bring the solution on-line are executed.

Figure 1-1   TSSP Methodology

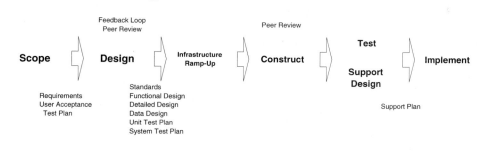

1.3 Requirements – What *They* Want It To Do

Puddleduck Press is going to be doing the Web design and has subcontracted the development to the Software Services Outsourcing Program of Hewlett-Packard Consulting. The project lead for HP SSOP, Daniel Pratt, met with Shauna Hill and Caitlin Brookton over dinner to discuss the requirements for the Web site, and there are a number that need to be satisfied in *Trade Wind*.

You'll want to make sure when creating the design that all functionality is derived from the requirements, and that all requirements are satisfied by the functionality; that there are no orphan requirements. Some requirements might not be satisfied until the Low-Level Design, because they're a level below the Functional Design.

The Requirements Phase is the most significant phase other than Implementation. The design is based on the requirements, and the construction is based on the design, so the requirements are the foundation for the entire project. It's not unusual to see a one-to-many relationship between the requirements and the Functional Design, and a one-to-many relationship between the Functional Design and the Detailed Design. Another example of this type of relationship structure is a family tree that shows the descendants of an initial couple. Imagine the impact to the tree, if after several generations we discover that an early generation had an additional member. If a requirement is incorrect, so too will be the result.

There are rules we're going to attach to the requirements to ensure that they're good requirements. Each requirement must:

- Be Well-Defined. The requirement must be well-defined and unambiguous to derive a design from it and base the user's acceptance on it being fulfilled. Care should be taken in the wording to avoid general adjectives and adverbs and to allow for only one reasonable interpretation.
- Be Achievable. The requirement must be achievable using ordinary means unless extraordinary means are part of the requirements. There's no sense taking on a requirement that can't be accomplished. For example, a requirement that a user receive a full Web page in two seconds is one that, if able to be fulfilled, can only be achieved using extraordinary means.
- Be Measurable and Testable. There needs to be a way of determining whether the requirement has been fulfilled. If the requirement states "all functions should be easy to use," there is no clear measure. If, however, the requirement calls for the user to need to execute no more than two mouse clicks per function, the requirement would then be measurable. Does it work as desired? It's important to be able to determine this, especially if the payment for your effort depends on some form of acceptance testing. The Unit and System testing will tie to the design, but the User Acceptance Testing will be tied directly to the requirements, so each requirement needs to be testable on its own or in combination with other requirements.

So, we'll keep an eye on the requirements to make certain the rules cover them.

1.3.1   Requirements

All requirements listed below refer to actions initiated by a visitor to the Web site. The system shall have:

1. The presentation of an initial list of categories, providing the ability to navigate down through subsequent levels of subcategory with one mouse click per change in level.
2. The ability to navigate from any level of subcategories up towards the initial list, one level at a time, with one mouse click per change in level, or up to the initial category list with a single click.
3. Category level changes accomplished and presented without repainting the entire window.

4. The selection of a (sub)category resulting in the display of related links and advertising in addition to the display of the next level of subcategory.
5. A means for the visitor to provide feedback of the following types:
   - General comments
   - Suggested links to be added
   - A broken link (a bad link or a link to a page that no longer exists)
   - Suggested categories to be added
   - Award nominations
6. An ODBC database (preferably Microsoft Access) on the server to house the categories, links and ad information.
7. Two advertisement banners on the Web page that support click-through, and a page that describes the ad policy.
8. Background information about The Blowhole with information on using the site.
9. An awards page, where sites of distinction are highlighted.
10. An overall design in keeping with the company's image, a subjective, non-measurable but important requirement.
11. The ability to search for and be presented with a list of categories.
12. The description of copyright ownership for site elements.
13. A display of the functional banners of the Web rings to which The Blowhole belongs.

And that's it! Not too bad, huh? Well, after all, we have only a few hundred pages in which to get this baby up and running, so it can't be *too* complicated. Actually, requirements in the real world might be more lengthy and complex than this, but we can limit our focus to what's germane to the book. With the requirements laid out, we can move on to a functional design.

1.4 High-Level Design – *What* It Will Do

There are many differing opinions on what constitutes a high-level, or functional, design, and how it differs from a low-level, or detailed, design. Never being short on opinion, I feel that a functional design should tell you what you can do, while the detailed design defines how it will be done and what it will look like. Functionality is what it's all about—the purpose of the application is for the user to use it, and they can't use it unless it's functional, right? We're going to "map" a path from what the requirements dictate to what functionality will fulfill those requirements.

I'm a pictorial kind of guy. I like being able to see the big picture, which is probably why I prefer piles on my desk instead of everything being hidden away in files. So, I'll begin with a function diagram in Figure 1-2.

Figure 1-2   Web Site Function Map

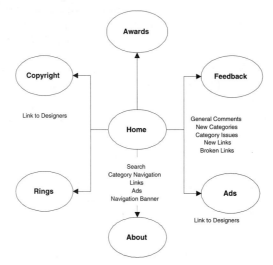

Okay, lovely illustration. It lays out the functions that will be available in this system. These are the things the visitor will be able to do. Being able to click on a link when viewing a Web page is a function. Being able to change the zoom percentage when using a word processor is a function. In fact, a functional diagram of all the functions in a word processor wouldn't fit on one piece of paper; even the functions available on the toolbar would be too much for one viewing. In our case, the applications are not complex, the function count not very large. That is by design. It's not my goal to impress you with what a great application I can write — but to use a small, complete application to teach you the things I think you need to know, via a small number of function points. Following is an explanation of each of them.

How is a "home page" invoked? It's worth a look. Figure 1-3 on page 8 shows the sequence of events.

When a user connects to a Web site using a browser, the address the user types in is something in the form of:

```
http://www.justanexample.com
```

Let's take a quick look at the structure of a Web address, or, as it's more properly called, a Universal Resource Locator (URL). A commercial site, a site involved in some form of commerce, is represented by 'com.' If you have a personal Web page, you're probably not engaged in commerce, but the company providing you the Web space is. Examples of other domain types are given in Table 1-1.

A domain name such as 'justanexample' acts like a telephone book entry. In this telephone book, the Domain Name Server (DNS), an address pointing to the computer that hosts the domain (several domains can be on one computer) is provided. The browser then asks for a connection to that address.

Upon establishing that connection, the 'www' server, the HyperText Transfer Protocol server (HTTP) on that machine will transmit the default Web page, normally index.html, to the browser. The default page is transmitted, because in this case no specific page was requested (no page name was present in the URL). A Web page is a file of HyperText Markup Language (HTML) information that tells the visitor's browser how the information contained in the file, and the images referenced in the file, should be displayed on the visitor's screen. With all that in mind, let's move on to dividing the functionality into separate Web pages, and the functionality of the pages themselves. This will make up our Functional Design. We'll assign each function a number and use them to match to the requirements.

Table 1-1   Typical Domain Suffixes

Domain Suffix	Meaning
.com	Commercial
.gov	Government Organization
.edu	Educational Institution
.org	Non-Profit Organization
.net	Network Provider

1.4.1   The Home Page

(1) The 'home page' is the page that acts as a focal point for the rest of the site. The home page will provide a launching board to the information, and the other locations at the Web site via clickable links. The home page to the visitor is like a recognizable landmark in an otherwise strange place, somewhere to return to and get one's bearings (like Cinderella's Castle in Disney's Magic Kingdom).

(2) Categories will be organized in a hierarchical fashion, and (3) displayed on the page grouped by their position, level, in that hierarchy, much like a multi-town phone book being organized alphabetically by name within each town's section. (4) The categories will be presented in such a way that the visitor can choose one, and then be presented with the ads and links associated with that category, as well as (5) the level of categories below the one chosen. Alternatively, the visitor can choose (6) to access the next "page" of categories, (7) move up through the category list, or (8) return to the primary category list.

Figure 1-3   From Request to Web Page

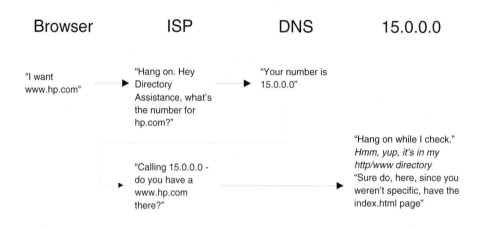

(9) Links associated with a selected category will be presented along with a description of the linked site, if available.

(10) A text box and any other necessary elements will support a search function to search for categories. (11) The resulting match(es) will be presented like a level of categories.

(12) Categories may have associated banner advertisements. Clicking on a banner advertisement will take the visitor to the advertiser's site.

(13) There will be a logo banner with (14) elements that allow the visitor to move to any other pages on the site with one mouse click.

(15) The data on the page will be kept in a database on the server.

1.4.2   The Feedback Page

(16) The visitor to complete that requires the entry of a name and email address — a formatting validation being performed on the email address.

The visitor will have the option of sending (17) general feedback, (18) category or link feedback, or (19) award nominations.

(20) If the visitor desires to provide category feedback, he will have the option to select a category from a current list to identify it as the category being discussed or the intended parent of a new category.

If the visitor desires to provide a new link or information on a broken link, he should be able to (21) navigate to the appropriate category to which the new link would be attached, or (22) to select the broken link which then becomes part of the feedback.

(23) The visitor should be able to indicate a desire to be contacted once the action they've requested has been taken.

1.4.3 The Awards Page

The page will display the four awards that will be available to other Web sites from The Blowhole, and a description of each:

(24) Presentation Excellence based on the site's visual appeal

(25) Research Merit based on the informational value of the site

(26) Coolness, based on the relative amount of the same

(27) An award for overall excellence when all of the above apply

1.4.4 The About Page

(28) A page that provides background information on The Blowhole and (29) instructional information regarding the use of the main page.

1.4.5 The Ads Page

(30) A page that describes the site advertising strategy and (31) the types of available ads. The page will also (32) provide a link to the home page of the company that can provide graphic design services for advertisers not having an existing banner ad. (33) The ads will be in the form of two ad banners on the home page. (34) The ad banners will support the ability to click on an ad and have a browser window open to the advertiser's site.

1.4.6 The Rings Page

The Blowhole will be a member of many Web rings (see side bar), and (35) this page will provide access to the rings for the visitor. The graphics and code for the page will be provided by the ring owners.

1.4.7 The Copyright Page

(36) This page will define the copyright information for the site, and (37) links to other sites by the same Web designer.

Web Rings?

Web rings are alliances of Web sites that are based on similar topics. The Web surfer can move from site to site, typically by means of a banner, without having to know what sites are members.

That's about it for the Web site functionality. Now we should go back to the requirements and ensure that those that can be addressed in the Functional Design have been. The items in the functional specification that apply to the requirements will be noted at the end of each requirement. Many of these items will be further defined in the detailed specification.

1. Being presented an initial list of categories, the ability to navigate down through subsequent levels of subcategory with one mouse click per change in level. (1) (2) (3)

2. The ability to navigate from any level of subcategories up towards the initial list, one level at a time, with one mouse click per change in level, or up to the initial category list with a single click. (7) (8)

3. When a level contains more categories than can be displayed at one time, the ability to 'page' forward or backward through the remaining categories. (6) (14)

4. Category level changes should be accomplished and presented without repainting the entire window. (accounted for in the detailed design)

5. The selection of a (sub)category resulting in the display of related links and advertising and the displaying of the next level of subcategory. (4) (5) (9)

6. A means for the visitor to provide feedback of the following types
   • General comments
   • Suggested links to be added
   • A broken link (a bad link or a link to a page that no longer exists)
   • Suggested categories to be added. (16) (17) (18) (19) (20) (21) (22) (23)

7. An ODBC database (preferably Microsoft Access) on the server to house the categories, links and ad information. (15)

8. Two rotating advertisement banners on the Web page that support click-through (12) (13) (14), and a page that describes the ad policy. (30) (31) (32) (33) (34)

9. Background information about The Blowhole with information on using the site. (28) (29)

10. An awards page, where sites of distinction will be highlighted. (24) (25) (26) (27)

11. An overall design in keeping with the company's image. (This will be addressed in the Detailed Design.)

12. The ability to search for and be presented with a list of categories. (10) (11)

13. The description of copyright ownership for site elements. (36) (37)

14. A display of the functional banners of the Web rings to which The Blowhole belongs. (35)

So, that's pretty much it for this chapter. Let's summarize what we've accomplished and then move on to the next chapter, which introduces many of the technologies we'll touch in the course of this book.

1.5 Summary

We looked at the business case that drove our need to create this system. After a brief introduction to some terminology, we took the business case and used it to develop a list of requirements. We then derived a high-level design highlighting the functions that will be available to visitors from the requirements. We also verified that the functions in the design fulfill the requirements.

To summarize our summary, what we've accomplished is understanding *what* we're going to do, and why we need to do it. We'll now move on to deciding on technologies and platform, and then define *how* we do it.

Untangling the Technology

We're off to a great start. You might not think that we've accomplished much, but we have, because we now have a checklist from which to work. Checklists are very handy things to have. They will be used in different forms throughout the book. Here are a few examples of their use:

- Project managers use project plans, which are a form of checklist.
- Pilots use a preflight equipment checklist.
- Boy Scouts use a checklist to pack their camping gear.
- Mortgage companies use them to navigate through a closing.
- My wife uses checklists to keep track of her checklists.

Why do people like to use checklists? Because they provide a simple, manageable method of ensuring that nothing is forgotten. So long as every item is listed, there is an easy means of verifying that each item was addressed. We started with a checklist in the form of a requirements list. We then moved to a functional design—a wordier checklist. With our functional checklist we're almost positioned to move on to a detailed design, which is a blueprint for our Web site and application—we just need to consider one more thing.

Part of developing the blueprint is understanding what options are available. For example, you need to know that you have a two-story house, and how the hallways of the two stories will be aligned, before you can decide what staircase to use.

We need to know what development technologies we will be using so that we can design the details of the functionality to complement them. Now, you could force the design of a house around a particular staircase you want, like a spiral staircase. Likewise, we could select specific technology to suit facets of an application. In this instance the functionality of the application can be provided by many technologies, so we'll select the technologies that best suit this book.

Some of the technologies will *drive* the development and production platform, or hardware/software, selection. That is, we'll select from the hardware and software that will support the technologies we want. Some technology choices will be *driven by* the platform selection. That is, if the hardware is already selected or in place, we could be limited to certain choices of technology to avoid having to purchase and support a new platform. Here we're in a terrific position. Shauna has told Daniel that the technology choices are open. Let's take a look at some of the choices.

2.1 HTML

Originally, users of the Internet could send text to each other, much like sending email. This was nice, but had limited utility. The primary users of the Internet at that time were scientists. They wanted to be able to share scientific stuff, not just email. But how would they accomplish this? How, for example, could they transmit "H_2O" when they could only send text? They couldn't. They *could* make an agreement though. What if they agreed that whenever "<sub>" appeared in a document that whatever came after it should be subscripted. Likewise, to state when the subscripting should stop, we could put another _{, but that could be confusing because you might lose track — so how about putting}? That works. So, if I were to read:

```
H<sub>2</sub>O
```

I would know it should be formatted as:

```
H2O
```

Think of the possibilities! If I saw <b> it would be bold. But if I wanted to emphasize the "2" in H_2O, I would see:

```
H<sub><b>2</b></sub>O
```

on the screen. And if I wanted the "2" to be blue and large, the resulting text would become even more unwieldy.

Formatting of text was made possible by the use of a mark-up language, a language that put tags around the portions of text to be formatted, or that linked the reader to another page of text when clicked. The language was named Hypertext Mark-up Language (HTML), and if you look at a Web page's source code, it looks as awful as the example above. However, one additional piece was added to the puzzle: a browser.

The browser is an application that can do a few things essential to providing access to Internet sites. It can navigate to a Universal Resource Locator (URL) address. It can decipher an HTTP header. More importantly, it knows how to use the graphical services of the computer on which it is running. That is, it knows how to draw underlined text, to create margins, to subscript. So when it receives a transmission with ₂, instead of displaying the tags, it displays a subscripted "2."

Capabilities and Limitations

HTML provides the contents of a basic Web page:

- text with selectable color, weight, style and relative size
- rectangular graphics (JPEG and GIF)
- hyperlinks, which when clicked take the user to another place
- image maps (server-side and client-side), which act as graphic hyperlinks
- tables, for tabular data as well as for aligning various page elements

For teachers, students and scientists, the original users of the Internet, this capability was sufficient. Then commerce hit the Internet and things were never going to be the same—it was a quick lesson in how the suitability of an item is only as static as the intended use!

The requests for more capability came in fast and furious. "Tables are fine, but we need to be able to give cells background images." "How about changing the color of the text?" "Why can't tables be side by side?" "Text needs to be able to wrap around an image." "We need a way to show more than one page simultaneously within frames."

With such an outspoken commercial response, the browser makers hurried to respond. They had two viable options: take the long-term route of lobbying to get all the enhancements into the HTML standard, or introduce the enhancements as extensions beyond the standard as quickly as they could turn them out.

The former alternative might seem to be the logical choice since a standard would be maintained—but the Internet was now out of the hands of academia and in the hands of software vendors whose primary interest is market share. Enhancements buy market share, and out they came—a slew of them.

There was a downside to this approach. Remember that HTML does nothing, that it is a method of encoding a request to the browser, which displays it to provide a degree of formatting. Since each browser developer was determining the enhancements for their own product, the competing browsers would not necessarily recognize the HTML that requested the formatting for those enhancements, nor be able to provide such formatting. The default action for browsers is to ignore any tag it doesn't understand instead of raising an error.

For example, if a browser understands that <RBL> indicates subsequent text should be formatted as a list item with rectangular bullets. Another browser that does not understand that tag would format the same code differently.

A question then is "how do you create a Web page that can be displayed in the same fashion by either browser?" There are two possibilities: avoid any of the HTML extensions, or, at the point when the page is to be displayed, determine which browser is displaying it and pass it HTML it understands. Neither solution is elegant, and choosing the latter route means maintaining multiple versions, but those continue to be the choices. Luckily, the commonality of functionality continues to grow larger.

There is another downside to extended HTML. In the event that a tag is understood by more than one browser, the implementation of that tag might be different. Similarly, the formatting that would result from a particular tag might be supported by each browser, but using a different tag or tag options, such as one browser supporting text color and another typeface.

The largest complaints are:

- the inability to do anything useful with form data beyond mailing it
- the inability to dynamically change page content without having to reload the page (for example, if the page says "Hello," there is no way for HTML to change it to say "Goodbye" without loading a new page)
- the fact that the pages didn't *do* anything but "sit there"

These issues have led to the explosion of technologies that have been bolted on to HTML.

2.2 Common Gateway Interface (CGI)

CGI is one of the most misunderstood areas of Internet content. CGI is *not* a programming language, and *not* a mysterious black hole. It's simply a gateway, which allows a Web page to transfer control outside the HTML environment. Application developers can think of it as a user exit.

To understand CGI, an understanding of the architecture of a Web site is needed. When someone surfing the Web enters a Universal Resource Locator (URL), such as http://www.puddleduck.com, what happens? A Web page appears, or a screen indicating a 404 error because the page doesn't exist, but what is happening under the covers? Following is a step-by-step look.

A link is clicked or a URL entered—the user's server asks its Domain Name Server (DNS) to find the new site. The browser probably has a status message saying "Searching for puddleduck.com."

The user's DNS contains an entry, supplied by InterNIC, which maintains the catalog of domain names, for the domain name requested (puddleduck.com). It provides an Internet Protocol (IP) address to the remote DNS, which services the requested domain.

The remote DNS provides the IP address of the requested site, which is the IP address of the server on which that site resides. The browser has a status message saying "Connecting to xxx.xxx.xxx.xxx"—the IP address.

An IP connection is made to the remote server, the machine on which the desired Web site resides. The browser has a status message saying "Connected—waiting for response."

The remote server maps the requested domain (puddleduck.com) to a directory in its file system (e.g. /wwwshare/puddleduck/www), and since no specific page was requested, the server will transmit a page based on the site default (usually either default or index .htm or .html). The user's server receives the HTTP transmission and relays it to the client, the browser, which displays it.

A typical directory in a Web account is cgi-bin. It is in this directory that CGI binaries will reside. A CGI binary can be an application written in any language such as Java, C or C++. It can also be a script, typically written in PERL or PERL5.

Why transfer control to an application? Typically to manipulate data. One use would be sorting through the mess transmitted when a user fills in a form and then submits it. A form can be coded to email the user data, and you would think that the email would be meaningful and readable.

If coded to do so, the submission invokes an application and makes available to it the data from the form. Invoking a CGI application is as simple as having a parameter in a form tag like the one below:

```
<FORM ACTION="/cgi-bin/my-app.exe" METHOD="POST">
```

This tag will invoke the application my-app and pass it the data from the form. The response from the CGI application is fairly simple as well. Once the application has opened an output stream, it outputs the HTTP protocol entries, and then outputs the equivalent of an HTML file, which results in a page being displayed to the user.

That data stream is far from user-friendly though, since it contains one long string of characters. Formatting it would be a good start for the application. Once the data is formatted and usable, the application might perform acceptance edits and then provide feedback to the user by transmitting a new page to the user's browser. A CGI application can do more than just reformat data. It can access other structures on the server, such as a database.

This opens up several possibilities. One would be to accept an order from a Web page and post that order to a database, responding to the user with a confirmation number. Another would be to provide information to the user from a database, such as the prices of items that fluctuate too often to make hard-coding them into a Web page viable, such as bullion prices.

CGI is available with UNIX and NT servers, although on NT platforms, depending on the programming language used it can be a bit tricky accessing the data stream. CGI programming doesn't need to be accomplished through an application; it can be a script, or command file, written in a scripting language like PERL, which would allow the program to be ported between dissimilar platforms more easily than using, for example, Visual Basic.

If the server on which the Web site resides is an NT server, another method of having the server perform background processing is by using Active Server Pages.

2.3 ASP

Active Server Page technology is a repackaging of Microsoft's OLE technology. An

Active Server Page is a Web page with an extension of .ASP instead of .HTM.

In addition to the HTML contained in the page, the file contains either JavaScript or VBScript (discussed later). The script in the file is executed by the server when the page is invoked. Typically, the script will perform some processing and generate HTML statements. What makes ASP great is that the only thing passed to the user is the resulting HTML — there is no visibility into the script code, not even if the user looks at the source code with the browser. The reason is that despite invoking, for example, myfile.asp, the user never sees that file. The resulting HTML is presented to the user as myfile.htm.

An example of the usefulness of ASP is the processing of a form. Instead of invoking a CGI program, the form data can be provided to an ASP file. That file can then process the data, mail it in a formatted message, and generate an acknowledgment page.

The largest drawback to ASP currently is that it's only fully supported running on Microsoft NT or Windows 95, Windows 98 or Windows 2000 servers. Any client on any browser can access Active Server Pages, because the only thing to reach the client is HTML, but most Internet Service Providers (ISP) are using servers which don't use the Microsoft operating systems.

We're going to use ASP for a number of reasons. It's easy, not requiring much in the way of programming expertise. As such, it's easy to maintain. It's interpreted instead of being compiled, which means we can make quick changes when debugging by using a text editor. Also, it provides server-side script capability, and since we don't control what architecture the users have and thus don't know what will run on their client (it's whatever browser and computer they want to use), we need to do most of the script activity on the server. Also, ASP support is built write into NT server, so the system administrator doesn't need to install anything for us, and that makes all of us very happy.

2.4 Java

The Java programming language was developed by Sun Microsystems. What makes Java unique is the fact that instead of being compiled into machine-dependent code, it is compiled into an intermediate "P code," which is identical from platform to platform. On each platform is a machine-dependent Java engine that can run this "P code."

Java resembles C++. It is an object-oriented programming language with many of the confusing aspects of C++ removed. There's nothing specific about Java that makes it better to develop CGI applications than another language, but because of its portability it's possible to use it to provide Web pages with rich content.

There are still concerns that the architecture of Java brings with it potential security breaches. It is interesting then, that on the other end of the spectrum, the Internet application technology considered to be very secure is the Java applet.

Microsoft has its own implementation of the Java language, Visual J++. They recently announced that they planned on moving in their own direction with regards to its capabilities, and will no longer follow the Sun standard. We won't use Java because it's difficult to program and not quite as architecture independent as we'd like it to be.

2.5 Java Applets

Applet is a cute name for a small application—and a small application is precisely what a Java applet is. Applets are secure because their architecture prevents them from touching anything outside themselves, such as files and memory, except for the creation of a "cookie," a controlled data element managed by the user's browser that is stored in a directory on the user's system.

The typical use of an applet is for a small self-contained graphical element on the Web page. The most familiar example of such an element is the ad banner, that rectangle of cycling advertisements. We'll be using just such a Java applet.

2.6 JavaScript and VBScript

JavaScript and VBScript are script languages built on a subset of Java and Visual Basic respectively. Script languages allow programming statements to be executed without having to compile. The process is accomplished by an engine, which supports the script language, being built into the browser. Because the instructions are being executed by the browser, the script is running on the client, unlike CGI and ASP, which run on the server. This is a good thing, because client code typically runs faster than server code; this is a bad thing, because the user has to sit and wait while the client code downloads along with the Web page.

Why would you want to execute code on the client? If there's a database to access, it will be on the server. If a new Web page is to be accessed or generated, it will come from the server. What does having code execute on the client buy you? Local processing, with no need to go to the server. An example of the utility of this is performing edits on a form. If there is a field that should have a date, and the user enters the date incorrectly, it would be nice to let the user know without his having to wait until the form is submitted.

JavaScript comes in two flavors, Netscape and Microsoft (called Jscript). The two have many syntactical differences, different capabilities, and even conflicting bugs. Also, it runs differently on each version of the same browser as the bug fixes were only applied to the version current at the time. Because the code runs on the client, the type of server is immaterial. VBScript currently is supported only with Microsoft's Internet Explorer.

Luckily, script code is encased in a comment block. Browsers that don't recognize script code will ignore it, thinking it a comment. Testing is more immediate because it can be executed on the client without having to be uploaded to the server.

We'll be making extensive use of VBScript for our ASP code. It's easier to write than JavaScript, and since we can control what architecture the server has, we can make certain that our Web site is put on a server that supports VBScript. As for the client scripting that we'll need for local editing, we'll use JavaScript because it's supported on the major browsers, so it doesn't matter which browser is being used. That's a good thing, because we can't control which browser is being used.

2.7 CSS

Cascading Style Sheets introduce the ability to apply more style control than HTML provides. Style sheets can be applied to a page element, a class of elements, or elements on multiple pages in a Web site, without having to code the style instructions repetitively.

It used to be tedious to add formatting to similar elements in a page. For example, if after coding a page of paragraph headings

```
<H2>This is item one
<H2>This is item two
<H2>This is item three
```

a decision is made to make the text in the list items blue, the old way to accomplish this was to change every heading

```
<H2><TEXT COLOR="BLUE">This is item one</TEXT>
<H2><TEXT COLOR="BLUE">This is item two</TEXT>
<H2><TEXT COLOR="BLUE">This is item three</TEXT>
```

but with CSS, styling can be applied to the tag element

```
<STYLE> <!-- H2 {text color:blue;} --> </STYLE>
```

every heading of type H2 will appear with blue text. The same result can be obtained through JavaScript by treating the H2 tag as an object.

```
<STYLE TYPE="text/javascript">
tags.H1.color = "blue";
</STYLE>
```

Styling can also be applied to a class

```
.clscool { text-decoration:underline;
  letter-spacing:2pt; text-align:center; }
```

then any tag that specifies a CLASS="cool" will have that formatting. A global style sheet can be set up so that every page on the site shares similar formatting. CSS provides the ability to format margins, typeface, spacing and other facets of layout. CSS is currently supported primarily by Internet Explorer 4, although Netscape is catching up. The specification for CSS-2 has been released, and offers much more control than the first release, but it will be a while before all browsers support it.

We'll use CSS because it can easily give all our pages a similar look and feel.

2.8 DHTML

Dynamic HTML (DHTML) takes CSS a step further. DHTML is made up of three parts:

- Cascading Style Sheets
- Positioning HTML
- Downloadable Fonts

The CSS portion of DHTML is as discussed in the section on CSS. By using styles, the visual aspects (color, size, spacing) of the Web page can be defined and controlled.

Positioning HTML is the next part of DHTML. Page elements can be positioned absolutely, a specific location on the page, or relatively, as the position relates to other elements.

The third part of DHTML is downloadable fonts, which remove the need to depend on Times Roman, Helvetica and Courier as the typefaces used on a page. Although a font would only need to be downloaded if it were not already present on the client, it can certainly add significant download time to a page when that happens. Therefore, this facility might only be appropriate for intranets, where groups within a company need the font to be able to view documents, forms, etc.

There is a very significant drawback to DHTML, and that is that Netscape and Microsoft have gone in very different directions in its implementation.

Microsoft has taken the route of opening the entire Web page. Every item on the page and every aspect of the item is available to be referencedvia the Common Object Model (COM). This then finally allows an ability that users have been screaming for — the ability to dynamically change text without having to resend the entire page. Before this, presentation aspects of the text could be changed, but not the text itself. Now, even the URLs behind the hyperlinks on a page can be altered.

Netscape chose not to open up the Web elements to the same degree. Instead, Netscape is providing the ability to specify page and element layers. By altering the Z-order of layers, the order in which they're stacked, a different version of page elements can be displayed. This method does not easily apply itself to the dynamic alteration of text.

The two methods are so different, it was difficult to define a standard. Netscape finally decided to support COM; however, this won't be fully realized outside of version 5 or better of their browser. Since most people are using an earlier version, IE, we feel that we'll exclude too many people by using DHTML. It would be great in an intranet environment where we have control over the client architecture, but we'll pass on using it on our site aside from some minor special effects that we'll add, which will be viewable by people using IE, but won't cause any problem to people using Netscape.

2.9 ADO

We are going to be using a database with our site. There will be a large amount of data available to be retrieved in small groupings by a search, and this lends itself to database technology. The standard today is SQL. There are other data technologies, but SQL is the main one, whether it be Oracle, Informix, Sybase or Microsoft SQL Server. Since we'll be using Microsoft server technology, it would make sense to use whatever database technology is native to it. Microsoft seems to come out with a different technology every year. The latest is called ActiveX Data Objects, or ADO. It relies on OLE (Object Linking and Embedding). It works very well and aside from some initial defining calls, it works just like SQL. We'll use it. We could use MS SQL Server as the database, but since we'll want to be able to easily upload a new database over our old one whenever we want, and since we're not expecting tremendously heavy traffic, we can use MS Access.

The Solution

We're ready to do the detailed planning of our site, so that we have a blueprint before we start coding. Some people would prefer to just start coding. If nothing else, a detailed design can be considered to be a checklist that will allow you to make sure all the requirements have been incorporated.

The content of detailed designs varies. Some are screen layouts and detailed descriptions of functionality, while others go down to the level of pseudo-code, a narrative of the programming statements that will later be coded. In our case, we'll follow the middle road. Our design will contain screen layouts, functionality description and logic flowcharts.

Let's take a look at the list of what we need to include in our design. Each item in the list will be a section in this chapter unless otherwise noted:

- development platform architecture
- application architecture
- production (operational) platform architecture
- the database (Chapter 6)
- feedback pages
- awards page
- about page
- advertising page
- copyright page
- rings page
- home (main) page

Okay, a lot of stuff. Normally a detailed design would be turned over to programmers to code from, but I'm the designer *and* the programmer — so why have the design? There are at least two viewpoints from which to consider the need for a detailed design — mine and yours. From mine, it will give me a blueprint from which to continue the development process, so that after months of writing, I don't find out that I mentioned something early on that wasn't accounted for in the final product. From your side, I would suggest that it provides a frame of reference to the things I will be presenting — you'll know where I'm trying to get to, so that the pieces make sense as they fall into place. And now, whether you bought that or not, it's time for the detailed design.

3.1 Development Platform Architecture

Our application is going to be a Web application, in the form of a Web site. By the World Wide Web's very nature, the application will thus be client-server. Since I'm developing in a team of one, and therefore don't have a need to share the code with other developers, I'll be using one PC as both the client *and* the server; this saves on expense and complexity. In later testing, when I'll need connectivity to other Web sites, I'll use an ISP's (Internet Service Provider) system as the server. Figure 3-1 shows the various pieces of the development platform architecture. The application will be written to accommodate any client, but since it will be resident on only one server, a decision had to be made as to what technology was wanted and what server it runs on. That will be NT technology as it will allow scripting to be written in the easy-to-use and feature-rich FrontPage and Active Server Pages.

Figure 3-1   Development Technologies

Internet Explorer 4.1	Netscape Navigator 4
ADO	
MS Access	
Visual InterDev 1	Visual InterDev 6
MS FrontPage 98	
ASP 2.0	
Pers. Web Server	
TCP/IP	
MS Windows 98	

3.1.1   Windows 98

We'll be using Windows 98 as the operating system, primarily because that's what I have on my system. Windows 95 or NT Workstation 4 will work too, although different versions of some applications might be necessary.

I've been asked if it's worth the upgrade from Win95 to Win98. I feel that it was. Although Win98 has bugs in it too, considering the number they fixed in Win95, I understand why it's much more stable than Win95 — I almost never lock up or face the "blue screen of death." I *have* run into an issue when using Visual Studio 6, Internet Explorer 4.1 and Win98 together, and that is that one of them has a memory leak. When applications create objects (dynamic arrays, lists, etc.), they ask for memory. They're supposed to give the memory back when they destroy the object. If they don't, the memory is lost at least until the application ends, and sometimes until you reboot. The symptoms are the system becoming slower and slower until it locks up or you receive messages saying that there's insufficient memory to do what you've asked. However, even with the memory leak, I find Win98 to be faster, better with memory in general (I can run more applications concurrently), and the drivers for my devices are much more up-to-date.

3.1.2   TCP/IP

Since the Internet runs over TCP/IP as a network protocol, we'll need that installed and configured. TCP/IP comes with the operating system.

As I mentioned, I'll be using the client as a server too. Since I won't be dialing into an ISP to connect to the Internet, I need HTTP services provided so that I can enter a URL in the browser, a URL that points to a page on my client, and have it served up to me. That functionality is achieved by turning my client into a Web server, and the easiest way to do that is to install Personal Web Server.

3.1.3   Active Server Pages

There will be server-side functionality in the application, scripts that execute on the server. Since we'll be using NT technology, we can use Active Server Pages to provide the script processing.

3.1.4   FrontPage

We need a way to configure the Web site and keep it updated. We could just create the directory structure on the "server," and eventually on the ISP's server, and transfer files using the FTP utility. However, we can avoid having to remember which files we modified and need to transfer. We do that by setting up the site with FrontPage, then using FrontPage to track which pages have changed and publish those changed pages from the development area to the site directory. FrontPage also provides a WYSIWYG (what you see is what you get) HTML editor. We'll be using FrontPage '98, but FrontPage '97 would work too.

3.1.5   Visual Interdev

We're also going to be using VI (Visual Interdev). Like FrontPage, VI provides a WYSIWYG environment. However, it also provides a rich Web page debugging environment and a framework for doing database access from within server script, and we *will* be doing database access. I'll point out now that there are some incompatibilities between VI and FrontPage, so we'll have to remember to use only one product or the other to access a particular page.

Ah, one other thing. We'll be using Visual Interdev versions 1 and 6. These are sequential versions despite the gap in the version numbers. Visual Interdev 1 has a wonderful set of wizards, or application generators, for creating Web pages for database maintenance. Visual Interdev 6 does not. I asked Microsoft why these wizards were not in their most recent version. The answer is that the wizards were to be supplied by a third party or parties, and either they didn't deliver on time or they were accidentally omitted. The wizards will be in the next version of VI, although I think they might be hidden somewhere on the version 6 CD. As to why we don't just use VI 1, it doesn't have the robust debugging functionality found in version 6.

3.1.6   Access

Our database will be MS Access. The database will reside on the server, and since the server will be NT, and since Access is also a Microsoft technology, it seems like a fit. The other nice thing is that Access runs on the client, and since we'll be using the client as the server too, this is a good thing. Also, it's fairly simple to make changes to the database structure or contents and then upload the changed file to the server. With all the other complexities, some ease is a good thing too.

There are a number of different ways to access a database. The middleware necessary for the access, such as RDO, ADO, DAO, ODBC, is built into the environment, but we need to make a choice. Caitlin Brookton and Daniel Pratt debated the selection for awhile. Caitlin convinced Daniel that ADO is the most recent, seems to be very stable, works with an Access database, and will be the selection.

3.1.7   Netscape Communicator / Internet Explorer

The final decision in our development architecture is the browser with which to test. The majority of the market is using either Microsoft Internet Explorer or Netscape Navigator, so to make sure the Web pages work with both, we'll use both. We'll use the most recent stable version of each, 4.x. Many people use version 3.x, but we'll be using features that aren't compatible with those versions, and hey, the upgrades are free. Version 5 of IE is available, but it hasn't been out long enough for me to consider it viable.

3.2 Application Architecture

Now that we have the platform architecture, let's take a look at the technologies that will make up the application architecture. Sure, some were mentioned above, such as ADO, because it's an explicit technology. However, some of the technologies are present on a Web page or contained within the code of a Web page without representing platform decisions. Figure 3-2 shows the application architecture pieces that will be used throughout the site. Not all pages on the Web site will contain all technologies.

Figure 3-2   Application Architecture

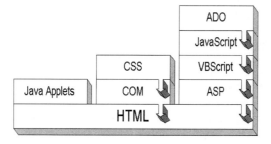

3.2.1   HTML

The code for every page on the Web site will have HTML, since a minimum of HTML is needed for it to qualify as a Web page. Following is a minimal Web page.

```
<HTML>
<HEAD>
<TITLE>My Page</title>
</head>
<BODY>
Here is some text
</body>
</html>
```

There's not all that much to it, but it *is* HTML, and there will be at *least* that much on every page, but typically much more. The layout directives for each page will be HTML, for things such as tables, frames and text.

3.2.2   ASP

Active Server Page technology will allow us to provide behind-the-scenes programmatic processing on the server, either before a page is displayed to the user or after the user has submitted a form.

3.2.3   VBScript

A subset of Visual Basic, VBScript will be the language used to create the server-side script that forms the server portion of an ASP page. Currently, VBScript is only supported on NT servers, but since we'll be picking the development server and the server that hosts the Web site, and since the code we create with the VBScript will only be running on the server, that shouldn't be a problem.

3.2.4   JavaScript

Why would we want to use JavaScript if we're going to be using VBScript? Well, again, VBScript is only supported on NT servers. What about any scripts we need executed on the client? VBScript is supported on Internet Explorer, but not Netscape Communicator. Since we don't want to exclude those who use the Netscape browser, we need to use a technology that's supported on both—which is JavaScript.

3.2.5   ADO

ActiveX Data Objects (ADO) is an automation-based interface for accessing data. ADO uses the OLE DB interface to access a broad range of data sources, including but not limited to data provided via ODBC. As it's the most current connectivity method available, is stable and meets our needs, we'll use it.

3.2.6   DHTML

Originally the thought was to use Dynamic HTML to provide additional functionality. However, although Netscape has committed to supporting the Common Object Model in the future, they're not there yet. This means that using DHTML would require the page to have a Netscape version and a separate IE version, since DHTML in IE makes use of COM.

3.2.7   COM

The Common Object Model is an extensible model that opens up every element on the Web page to direct reference. We'll be using COM with JavaScript to provide client-side editing, such as in the case of form processing.

3.2.8   CSS

Cascading Style Sheet functionality allows us to alter the presentation of Web elements in a manner not achievable through standard HTML. We'll be making use of this quite often. Because of current discrepancies between the way the two major browsers implement CSS, we're going to use CSS as style directives with IE, and as JavaScript directives with Netscape, and even then, there will be some slight differences in the way a page appears on each browser.

3.2.9   Java Applets

We're going to be using Java applet technology for our rotating ad banners. The purpose of a rotating ad banner is to rotate through a series of graphic advertisements, and should the viewer have their interest piqued by an ad and click it, to take the viewer to a Web site with more information. Typically this type of ad is revenue generating, although our Web site will include a non-profit banner ad too.

Microsoft FrontPage includes a banner ad control, so why are we going to use a Java applet and introduce yet another technology into our architecture? Well, forgive me for being somewhat blunt, but the Microsoft control has a functional design flaw: whether you're displaying one or twenty ads, only one destination (in the event of a click) can be defined for the entire group. Well, I don't know about you, but I can't think of one page I could design that would make sense out of ending up there regardless of what ad had been clicked.

3.3 Production Platform Architecture

Since we'll have no control over the client (someone sitting at home or office), the only platform we need to be concerned with is the server. The server will belong to a Web-hosting company, so we won't have control over the details, but there is a baseline we can require.

- Windows NT — The application architecture in our design requires an NT server, because many of the pieces are not yet available on UNIX.
- IIS — Microsoft's Internet Information Server, the software that allows the NT box to act as a Web server, comes with support for the relevant pieces of our architecture.
- FrontPage Extensions — The FrontPage product has server extensions that need to be installed for FrontPage-specific technology to be supported.
- ASP — As we're going to make heavy use of ASP functionality, the server needs to support it.
- ODBC (Open DataBase Connectivity) — This is the standard we'll be using for accessing our database, so we need it too. This goes hand-in-hand with Windows NT, so having it available shouldn't be an issue.

3.4 Application Map

An aid to comprehending the "big picture" is a map of the Web site, with each Web page being enumerated. The purpose of the map is to identify each page on the Web site, and to show the navigation that leads to a given page. Technically, most pages are interconnected because there will be a navigational banner at the top of each page from which a visitor to the site can move to almost any other page. There would, however, be no point in a map that has lines connecting every page to every other page, so we won't do that.

In looking at the map (see Figure 3-3), note that each box is a Web page. The box presents the page title as well as the name of the file that provides the page. In the event of framed pages, those pages that are subdivided on the screen with one page controlling the divisions and each division containing a separate Web page, the function of each page is listed in the box on the map as well.

There are lines connecting boxes to other boxes. The arrowheads on the lines indicate flow direction. I'll refer to the end of the line without the arrowhead as the origin, and the end *with* the arrowhead as the destination. The line indicates that the destination

Web page is reached from the originating Web page. If the line is solid, the movement from the origin to the source is controlled by the visitor, typically by clicking text or image link, or by submitting a form. A broken line indicates that the movement to the destination Web page is a function of the Web site not controlled by the user, such as a Web page being loaded into a frame when the visitor arrives on the page.

Figure 3-3   Site Map

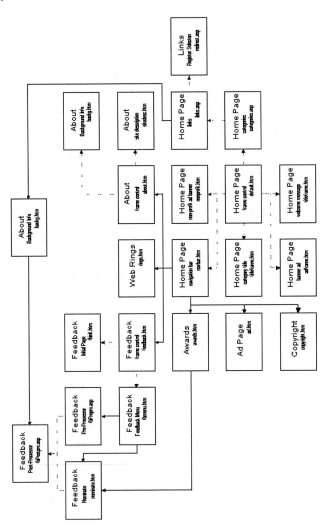

3.5 Feedback Pages

Okay, enough of the boring stuff. Let's get on with designing the Web site. There are numerous ways of presenting a design, and of course, often the method you want to use is different than the method your customer wants you to use. Daniel ran into this with Caitlin, who had her own idea of what she wanted to see, and soon convinced him.

Table 3-1   Design Icons

Icon	Meaning	Icon	Meaning
	Button		Check Box
TEXT	Caption/Text		Check Box (selected)
COMBO	Combo Box		Frame (a corner)
	Image	J	Java Applet
LINK	Text Link	LISTBOX ▼	List Box
This is a multi-line text box	Multi-Line Text Box		Radio Button
	Radio Button (selected)		Table (corner)
Text Box	Text Box	LINK	Image Link

Each page will be presented with numbered icons representing various screen elements, and a description below the page of each of those elements. Normally in a detailed design the actual intended content would be shown instead of place-holders, but like in our case there are occasionally reasons to do it differently:

- The specifics of the content might not be ready.
- The design illustrations would look just like the Web page.

3.5.1   The Feedback Frames

This first page can be seen in Figure 3-4. It's not a particularly complex page, but does have some attributes worth covering. The page that's initially loaded is *feedback.htm*. This page is a frame page, so its only responsibility is apportioning and presenting the frames, and identifying the source from which they will initially be loaded.

The frames will not have a border. Table 3-2 gives the specifications for each frame. These specifications will be used to generate the HTML for these frames later on.

Table 3-2   Feedback Frames

Characteristic	Left Frame	Right Frame
Name	fmMain	fmMenu
Width	600 pixels	remainder
Border	None	None
Resize	No	No
Scrolling	Yes	Yes
Marginwidth	5 pixels	5 pixels
Marginheight	0 pixels	0 pixels

The frame *fmMain* will be used to provide information to the visitor, and to receive information from the visitor. It will initially be loaded from the file *fbInit.htm*. As can be seen in the page layout, *fbinit.htm* consists of a graphic in the top left corner, some text, and a text link. The graphic (1) will actually be a modified version of the navigational banner, the original not being used because the original, used on the home page, depends on its being in its own frame, which this banner will not. The text (2) will thank the visitor for taking the time to provide feedback, and offer the visitor the alternative of simply sending an email message. A link (3) will be provided, which, when clicked will allow the user to send an email to the site.

The frame *fmMenu* presents a title (4) centered in the frame, followed by centered text links (5-9) that will, when clicked, cause a specific feedback page to be loaded in *fmMain*. Table 3-3 lays out each link.

We'll use the table data during construction to create the HTML link information. The *HREF* column shows the file that will be loaded. The *Target Frame* column shows the frame in which the file will be loaded. In this case it will always be the left-hand *fmMain* frame. The *Get Parms* column shows the parameters, if any, that will be passed to the invoked file as part of the HREF line.

Figure 3-4   Feedback Frame Layout

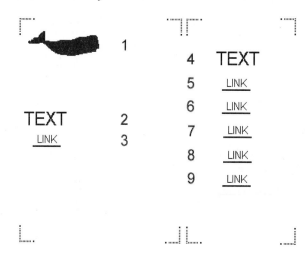

All forms of feedback with the exception of award nominations invoke the same .asp file. We could have each link invoke a separate page, but much of the information that will be requested of the visitor to complete is the same, and since we can programmatically control the design of the form the visitor receives, it will be easier to have one program determine what to present to the visitor based on the type of feedback they wish to provide. The presentation for award nominations is sufficiently different to warrant a separate page.

Table 3-3   fbMenu links

Functionality	HREF	Get Parms	Target Frame
General Comments	fbPrepro.asp	feedbackcode=general	fmMain
New Category	fbPrepro.asp	feedbackcode=newcategory	fmMain
Category Comments	fbPrepro.asp	feedbackcode=category	fmMain
New Link	fbPrepro.asp	feedbackcode=newlink	fmMain
Award Nomination	nominate.htm		fmMain

3.5.2   Feedback Pre-Processor

The Feedback Pre-processor, *fbPrepro.asp*, is the first of the site applications for us to discuss. The general functionality of the application is the same for all forms of feedback, as shown in Figure 3-5.

The heart of the pre-processor consists of the settings made, which later determines which fields will appear on the form presented to the visitor. The feedback form will be constructed from these fields, and should a given field appear on the form, it will be in the same order with regards to the other fields. The decision as to whether each field shall be used always occurs in the same sequence without regard to the feedback type. The form settings can be found in Table 3-4, and the field properties in Table 3-5.

There are parameters that remain the same regardless of the form type, and these are handled during the initiation of and completion of the form. Each of these global form parameters are as follows:

- Method — the form method will be POST so that the passed parameters won't be visible to the provider of the feedback
- Name — fFeedback
- OnSubmit — there will be client validation editing done in a routine named fFeedback_Validator, and the form will be submitted as a result of the return value
- Width — 330 pixels
- Border — none
- Action — the receiving .asp for the form will be *feedback.asp*

Figure 3-5   Feedback PreProcessor

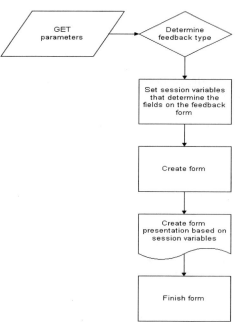

The first field on the form will be a hidden field named *feedbackcode*. The purpose of this field is to provide a means of notifying the post-processor what type of feedback is contained in the form data.

After the main body of the form we'll have a submit button for the feedback provider to use to submit the information. The field name will be *Submit*. We'll set the tab index to 99, so that no matter how many fields we have on the form (there will always be less than 99) the submit button, which will be located at the bottom of the form, will always be last in the tab order.

Let's take a look at what each of the elements in Table 3-4 mean if set to true.

- m_tfCategories — results in the presentation of a categories tree, with each category having a radio button alongside so that the appropriate category can be selected
- m_tfInstructionsCategory — results in instructional text describing how to select a category
- m_tfInstructionsParent — results in instructional text describing how to select a category parent
- m_tfInstructionsLinkParent — results in instructional text describing how

to select a link parent

- m_tfName — results in a text box and caption for the feedback provider's name
- m_tfEmail — results in a text box and caption for the feedback provider's email
- m_tfNewCategory — results in a text box and caption for the feedback provider to name the category be added
- m_tfNewLink — results in a text box and caption for the feedback provider to name the link be added
- m_tfURL — results in a text box and caption for the feedback provider to identify the URL to be used should the new link be clicked
- m_tfDescription — results in a multi-line text box and caption for the feedback provider to include a description for the new link
- m_tfComment — results in a multi-line text box and caption for additional comments
- m_tfContact — results in a check box to be checked if the feedback provider desires to be contacted

Table 3-4   Feedback Pre-processor Settings

	General Comments	Category Feedback	New Category	New Link
m_tfCategories	False	True	True	True
m_tfInstructionsCategory	False	True	False	False
m_tfInstructionsParent	False	False	True	False
m_tfInstructionsLinkParent	False	False	False	True
m_tfName	True	True	True	True
m_tfEmail	True	True	True	True
m_tfNewCategory	False	False	True	False
m_tfNewLink	False	False	False	True
m_tfURL	False	False	False	True
m_tfDescription	False	False	False	True
m_tfComment	True	True	True	True
m_tfContact	True	True	True	True

The logic for the category tree will be the same as on the categories page, so we'll define it there.

Let's take a look at each of the feedback types and what the form is intended to look like. It *is* up to the application to "draw" the form, but laying out the design will provide us with something to refer back to when we're coding and testing.

3.5.3   New Category Request

The purpose of this page is to allow the visitor to request that a new category be added to the category list. For this addition to be complete, we'll want to know where in the current category tree the requestor envisions the new category. We'll capture this information by having the requestor tell us what the parent category should be — what category will need to be clicked for the resulting list to include the new category.

We could simply provide a text box and depend on the visitor's memory of the category tree to identify the parent category, but we then risk having a parent category named that doesn't exist. A better way would be to present the category tree, and let the visitor select the category from it.

The layout for this page can be seen in Figure 3-6. The page will reside in a frame, and comprises of a small area above a large table consisting of one row, and two columns. The small area at the top of the page contains the banner logo navigation bar (1) and text explaining the use of the page (2).

The left-hand column will contain the category information. The top of the cell will have a caption with an image link (3), which when clicked will cause the categories to be listed from the beginning. Below them will be a caption with an image map (4), which when clicked will cause the previous or next page of categories at the current level to be listed. This functionality is explained in more detail in the design of the Category page. Below the navigational icons will be a list of categories, displayed a page (six) at a time. Each category can be a link, and this functionality is also discussed on the Category page design. Beside each category are radio buttons (5-10), any of which can be used to identify the adjacent category as the parent of the new category being suggested.

Figure 3-6   New Category Page

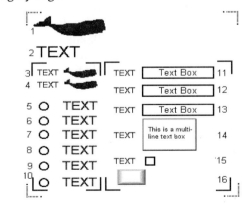

The right-hand column contains the remainder of information needed. The fields have all been defined in Table 3-5. They are, in the order in which they appear:

- name (11)
- email (12)
- newcategory (13)
- comment (14)
- contactme (15)

The final element on the page is the submit button (16). When clicked, the field edits are performed. If the fields pass the edits, the form data is submitted to the post-processor *fbPostpro.asp* for final processing.

3.5.4   Category Comments

The purpose of this page is to allow the visitor to provide feedback on an existing category. This page has a need to display the current category tree, just as the on the New Category page, so that the applicable category can be selected.

The layout for this page is almost identical to the New Category page, and can be seen in Figure 3-7. The page contents will reside in a frame, and consists of a small area above a large table consisting of one row, and two columns. The small area at the top of the page contains the banner logo navigation bar (1) and text explaining the use of the page (2).

The left-hand column will contain the category information. The top of the cell will have a caption with an image link (3), which when clicked will cause the categories to be listed from the beginning. Below them will be a caption with an image map (4), which when clicked will cause the previous or next page of categories at the current level to be listed. This functionality is explained in more detail in the design of the Category page. Below the navigational icons will be a list of categories, displayed a page (six) at a time. Each category can be a link, and this functionality is also discussed on the Category page design. Beside each category are radio buttons (5-10), any of which can be used to identify the adjacent category as the category being commented upon.

The right-hand column contains the fields to hold the remainder of needed information. The fields have all been defined in Table 3-5. They are, in the order in which they appear:

- name (11)
- email (12)
- comment (13)
- contactme (14)

The final element on the page is the submit button (15). When clicked, the field edits are performed. If the fields pass the edits, the form data is submitted to the post-processor *fbPostpro.asp* for final processing.

Table 3-5   Field Specifications

Field Name	Field Type	Caption	Width	Tab	Req	Min Width	Lines	Checked
name	textbox	Name:	20	1	Y			
email	textbox	Email:	20	2	Y	7		
newcate-gory	textbox	New Category:	20	3	Y	2		
newlink	textbox	New Link:	20	4	Y	2		
url	textbox	URL:	40	5	Y	2		
description	multi-line	Description:	40	6	N		4	
comment	multi-line	Comment:	40	7	Y	1	4	
contactme	checkbox	Please contact me:		8				N

3.5.5   New Link Page

This page allows the visitor to submit a new link. Because links are presented within the context of a category, this page has a need to know about the current category tree just as the on the two prior pages, so that the applicable category can be selected.

Figure 3-7   Category Feedback Page

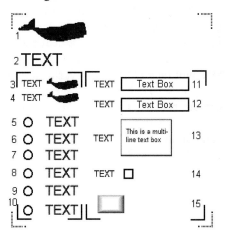

The layout for this page can be seen in Figure 3-8. The page contents will reside in a frame, and comprises a small area above a large table consisting of one row, and two columns. The small area at the top of the page contains the banner logo navigation bar (1) and text explaining the use of the page (2).

Figure 3-8   New Link Page

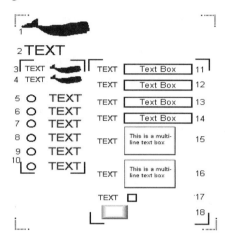

The left-hand column will contain the category information. The top of the cell will have a caption with an image link (3), which when clicked will cause the categories to be listed from the beginning. Below them will be a caption with an image map (4), which when clicked will cause the previous or next page of categories at the current level to be listed. This functionality is explained in more detail in the design of the Category page. Below the navigational icons will be a list of categories, displayed a page (six) at a time. Each category can be a link, and this functionality is also discussed on the Category page design. Beside each category are radio buttons (5-10), any of which can be used to identify the adjacent category as the category with which the new link is associated.

The right-hand column contains fields to hold the remainder of information needed. The fields have all been defined in Table 3-5. They are, in the order in which they appear:

- name (11)
- email (12)
- newlink (13)
- url (14)
- description (15)
- comment (16)
- contactme (17)

The *newlink* field contains the name of the link, and the *url* field contains the Web address of the link. The final element on the page is the submit button (18). When clicked, the field edits are performed. If the fields pass the edits, the form data is submitted to the post-processor *fbPostpro.asp* for final processing.

3.5.6   General Comments Page

This page allows the visitor to submit feedback that doesn't apply to the earlier topics. Unlike the other pages in the feedback suite, the information needed to process this page does not include categories, so the page itself is fairly simple.

The layout for this page can be seen in Figure 3-9. The page contents will reside in a frame, and consist of one large area. The top of the page contains the banner logo navigation bar (1).

Below the navigational icons will be fields to hold the remainder of needed information. The fields have all been defined in Table 3-5. They are, in the order in which they appear:

- name (2)
- email (3)
- comment (4)
- contactme (5)

The final element on the page is the submit button (6). When clicked, the field edits are performed. If the fields pass the edits, the form data is submitted to the post-processor *fbPostpro.asp* for final processing.

Figure 3-9   General Comments Page

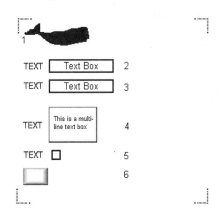

3.5.7   Award Nomination Page

The Blowhole Web site gives awards to Web sites in four different categories. Nominations can be made either by The Blowhole staff who find the page, or by a visitor to The Blowhole Web site who nominate their favorite sites.

This page allows the visitor to submit an award nomination. The layout for this page can be seen in Figure 3-10. The page contents will reside in a frame, and consist of a small area atop a table. The top of the page contains the banner logo navigation bar (1) and some text describing the use of the page (2). The table has one row with two columns.

Figure 3-10   Award Nomination Page

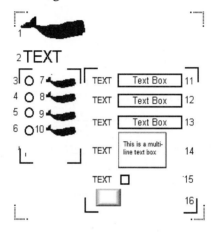

The left-hand column will contain four images, each representing an award (7-10), each with a radio button aside it (3-6) to designate the award for the entire site is being nominated. Radio buttons are used instead of check boxes because only one award can be selected per nomination.

The right-hand column will contain fields to hold the remainder of needed information. The fields have all been defined in Table 3-5. They are, in the order in which they appear:

- name (11)
- email (12)
- url (13)
- comment (14)
- contactme (15)

The final element on the page is the submit button (16). When clicked, the field edits are performed. If the fields pass the edits, the form data is submitted to the post-processor *fbPostpro.asp* for final processing.

As can be seen on the site map, an alternative path to this page is the Awards page.

Figure 3-11   Post-Processor Flow

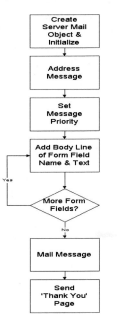

3.5.8   Feedback Post-Processor

The Feedback Post-processor (*fbPostpro.asp*) is an active server page that processes the form data from any of the feedback forms we've just covered. Just as we had a number of standard Web elements from which we selected for the feedback pages, we will also have a standard way of processing each of the form items passed to this page. Let's take a look at a flowchart for the post-processor (see Figure 3-11) to get some idea of its flow.

The method for creating and initializing a mail message will depend on the mail system used by the Web-hosting company that hosts the Web site. At this point that company hasn't been selected, so we're not certain what the mail object or its methods will look like. This isn't an obstacle though, because all mail objects work fairly much the same, so we'll just put some placeholders in the logic.

First we'll create, or instantiate, a mail object. Then we'll perform whatever object initialization that's required by that mail system. With that done, we'll do what you'd expect in sending an email message:

- address the message
- create the body text

• mail the message

The form data from the Feedback Pre-processor is received in the ASP request form variables. By looping through each field in the request variable, we will create a line of body text consisting of the field name and the associated data.

Having clicked on the submit button in the Feedback Pre-processor, the feedback provider is still waiting for some evidence that something has happened as a result. We'll take care of that by sending a page back that says "thank you."

3.6 Awards Page

The Awards page (*awards.htm*) is very simple and straightforward compared to the Feedback pages. The first indication of this is in the design layout for the page, as seen in Figure 3-12.

The page has our navigation banner at the top (1), with text below it in the form of a heading and a description of the page (2). Beneath them are the four award images (3,5,7,9), with a description of each award (4,6,8,10). At the bottom of the page is a text hyperlink (11) that leads to the Award Nomination feedback page.

Figure 3-12   Awards Page

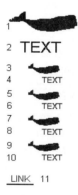

3.7 About Page

The purpose of the About page (*about.htm*) is to provide some background information on The Blowhole, and a description of how best to use the site. We're going to use some special effects on this page, and they don't translate well to a layout. However, you might think otherwise, so let's take a look at it first in Figure 3-13.

Figure 3-13   About Page

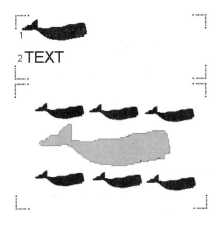

Well, how's that for a meaningful layout? If we were doing a thoroughly detailed design, aside from boring you to death and filling half the book, we might also be able to account for states on a page. For example, on pages where holding the mouse over an element causes the element to change, how would we capture that on a layout? Well, in the world of needing to depend on thorough and complete detail for contractual protection, we'd have to find a way, but since we're not there let's not bother.

The top frame of the page will have the navigation banner (1) and text describing The Blowhole (2). The lower frame will have an image that's a copy of the home page, but instead of being an image placed on the page by way of an <IMG> tag, it will be the frame background. The reason for this is that we're going to place some transparent graphics throughout the frame, and if the banner were presented as an image it wouldn't be possible to have it overlapped by these transparent graphics unless we were using DHTML, and DHTML were properly supported by both browsers. The reason we need the transparent graphics is that whenever the visitor's mouse cursor passes over one of the elements in the background that we want to describe, a transparent graphic will be replaced by a description of the element, until the mouse is moved again.

3.8 Advertising Page

The Advertising page (*ads.htm*) will be used to describe the various types of ads available at the site. The page will have two tables to present information, and the page will have a layout as shown in Figure 3-14.

The page will have a navigation banner (1) and text describing the advertising opportunities on the site (2). The first table (5) will have information about each ad type as well as examples, one of which will be an actual ad banner in the form of a Java applet (3), another as an image (4).

The first table will be followed by text explaining the ad pricing policy (6), and then a second table (7), which will contain the ad pricing. The final element on the page will be a link (8) leading to Puddleduck Press, the vendor The Blowhole will use to create banners for those wishing to advertise but not having a banner.

Figure 3-14   Ads Page

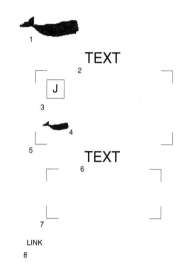

3.9 Copyright Page

The Copyright page (*copyrite.htm*) will be provided by Puddleduck Press, the site developers. We'll take a look at the code later in the book, but since we won't be designing it, we won't cover it here. Essentially, it will have copyright statements applying to the site and page elements, and a table of banners of the other sites created by or maintained by Puddleduck Press, and links leading to them.

3.10 Rings Page

Rings are affiliations of Web sites dealing with a particular topic. For example, there might be an Elbonian Web Developers Web ring. It would have a site that manages the Web ring and provides the graphics and code for it. A site wanting to join the ring sends a message to the Web ring manager. The manager reviews the applicant's Web site to make sure it's appropriate, and then sends an email to the new site with a ring member number.

After putting the code and graphics in place, and replacing place-holder strings in the code, such as "your-member-number-goes-here," the site is now part of the ring. A ring template typically allows a visitor to click and proceed either to the next Web site in the ring, the previous site in the ring, or a random site in the ring.

The Rings page (*rings.htm*) will contain the panels for each of the rings to which The Blowhole will belong.

3.11 Home (Main) Page

I've saved the most complex for last. The home page consists of nine tightly integrated pages, and two others that are core to the functionality, but are more loosely integrated as they are always present.

Nine pages! Wow, how can that be? Simple really: the "home page" is actually one page that sets up seven frames (one frame has two possible source pages), each frame being a separate Web page.

The name of a home page typically depends on the system configuration of the server on which it resides. The Web server settings will dictate what the default home page name should be. You don't *have to* give your home page that name, but if your domain is www.mydomain.com and your home page isn't give the default name, people entering your domain name without entering the name of the page will receive an error in going to your site. We're not certain what the default will be as the Web hoster hasn't been selected yet, but *default.htm* is common, and we'll use it. Let's take a look at the frame make-up, and then we'll move on to each supporting Web page.

3.11.1   DEFAULT.HTM

The true "home page" is one that the users will never see. It's the page that does nothing but subdivide the browser display into frames, and load those frames with Web pages. In the following table we'll look at the information needed to configure those frames.

Table 3-6   Home Page Frames

No.	Name	Page	Location	Height	Width	Scroll	ReSize
1	banner	navbar.htm	r1 c1	138	375	no	no
2	fp_ad	forprofit.htm	r1 c2	*	*	no	no
3	np_ad	nonprofit.htm	r1 c3	*	*	no	no
4	title	titleframe.htm	r2 c1 r1	23	200	no	no
5	contents	categories.asp	r2 c1 r2	*	200	yes	no
6	ad	adframe.htm	r2 c2 r1	59	*	no	no
7	main	welcome.htm	r2 c2 r2	*	*	yes	no

In the table above, the column *Location* has entries by row (r) and column (c). Keep in mind that Web page tables don't have to be symmetric like those of a spreadsheet. Thus, for example, row 2 can be subdivided into two columns, and each of those into two rows, so r2 c1 r1 is a different row than r2 c2 r1. Figure 3-15 shows how the above frames appear on a page. The asterisks in the *Height* and *Width* columns indicate that that area uses whatever space is left over and does not have a specific dimension defined.

Figure 3-15   Home Page Frames

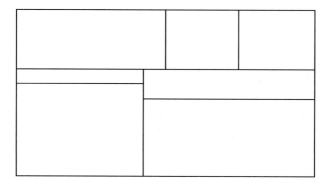

Most of the frames are set to not be scrollable, so that scroll bars do not appear in them. The frames containing the categories and links are an exception, because often the contents will exceed the starting dimensions, so a scroll bar will be necessary. The frames are not resizeable either, as a visitor changing the frame dimensions could end up making the page nonfunctional.

Let's take a look at each frame and the page(s) behind them individually.

3.11.2   Navigation Frame

The navigation frame will be similar in operation to the graphic being used on the About page. The frame will have a background defined, the image for which will be a banner logo, which we'll create in Chapter 7. Overlapping the banner logo will be a table with two rows, the first row having one column, and the second having six, as shown in Figure 3-16.

Column A will hold a completely transparent graphic the size of the column. Hold that thought for now. Columns B–G will have small graphics naming other locations on the site as follows:

- About
- Feedback
- Advertise
- Awards
- Rings
- Copyright

Figure 3-16   Navigation Frame Table

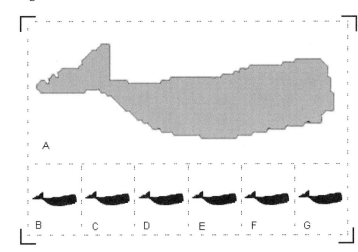

Each of these graphics are image links, which will take the visitor to the page they mention. In addition, when the visitor moves his mouse cursor over each image, a Java-Script routine will be executed that replaces the transparent graphic with a graphic providing a description of the linked page. When the visitor moves the mouse cursor away from the image link, the transparent image returns.

Why go through the trouble of revealing and hiding these descriptive images? Because they're unattractive, despite being functional. We don't want a bunch of graphics of words clogging up the Web page, so we'll make them "appear out of thin air" when we need them.

3.11.3   Title Frame

The Title frame is just that, a frame with a text title in it. The title is "Categories." Why should a frame be devoted to this instead of just having the title in the same frame as the categories themselves?

Any time a category is clicked, a new list of categories will be displayed, and to do that the categories frame will need to be repainted, which in the Web world can translate to disappearing for a few seconds. We're using frames instead of having everything on one page because it's much less distracting to have only part of the page repainted, likewise with the categories — the distraction will be less if the title remains static.

3.11.4   For-Profit Ad Frame

This frame holds an image that's an ad in the form of an image link. All ads in this frame will be 192 pixels wide by 96 pixels tall. The image to display is selected from the site database (specifics on the database are in Chapter 6).

By retrieving from the database, based on the date and the category, information detailing what ad should be displayed, the image is selected and presented in this frame as a static ad. If there is not a current advertiser, a default ad will be presented.

3.11.5 Non-Profit Ad Frame

This frame also holds ads in the form of an image link, but via a Java Applet that produces a rotating banner—a number of images are displayed for a period of time in rotation.

By retrieving from the database all information for non-profit ads, configuration information for the Java applet can be constructed. Following is a sample of the HTML needed to support the applet.

```
<APPLET code=DynamicBillboard.class _
  codeBase=java/ height=96 width=192>
<PARAM NAME="bill0" VALUE="images/
yourad.gif,ad.htm">
  <PARAM NAME="bill1" VALUE="images/pduckb.gif, _
  http://www.puddleduck.com/ad.htm">
<PARAM NAME="delay" VALUE="5000">
<PARAM NAME="billboards" VALUE="2">
<PARAM NAME="bgcolor" VALUE="#FFFFFF">
<PARAM NAME="transitions" VALUE="4,RotateTransi-
tion _
  ,FadeTransition,TearTransition,RotateTransition">
</APPLET>
```

Let's take a look at each of the parameters in the above example.

- code—the name of the application
- codeBase—the path to the application relative to the domain's root directory
- name—this applet expects the name to be "bill" with a sequential number suffix beginning with 0
- value (for 'name' parameter)—this parameter has two subparameters separated by a comma. The first is the image file name with a relative path, and the second is the URL the server should connect to if the image is clicked
- delay—the amount of time the applet should wait before cycling to the next image; the value is in milliseconds (1000 = 1 second)
- billboards—the number of images to be shown
- bgcolor—the RGB value for the background color (the color shown within the space occupied by the applet that exceeds the size of the image)

- transitions—the transition classes that will be used. Because of an apparent flaw in the coding, the first transition should be repeated as the last

3.11.6 For-Profit Rotating Ad Frame

This frame also loads ads for a rotating banner; the difference is that these will be selected by date and category. The frame will be invoked by the Categories frame each time the list of categories changes. Should there not be an advertiser for the current category, a random selection of all current ad images will be taken.

3.11.7 Categories Frame

The Categories frame is the most complex of all the frames and contains four sections. The reason the sections are all contained in one frame is that the category section appears above the others, and it is variable in height. Frame dimensions are fixed at the time the page is painted, and we don't want to repaint the entire page, nor do we want to live with the extra white space we'd have if we forced the category section to be a fixed size.

The four sections are summarized below, and will then be described in detail.

- Category—the first of four vertically aligned areas, used to present each list of categories
- Category Navigation—a band that contains icons, in varying states, to navigate through the category list
- Search—an area in which the visitor can search for a particular word in the category list instead of tunneling down through it
- Book—The Blowhole is an associate of Amazon.com, and visitors will be given the opportunity to purchase a recommended book on the current topic

3.11.7.1 Category

A category is a subject for which links will be presented, if there are any in the database. The categories are presented in a hierarchical order, with the highest-level, broadest sweeping ones being presented first. The details of the minimal information that will be kept with each category in the database (Chapter 6) are as follows:

- Category name—the subject
- Category number—a sequential value used for look-up
- Parent categories—up to two category numbers for categories that precede this one in the hierarchy (top-level categories have 0 as a parent)
- Amazon—the ISBN of a recommend book on this category, if any
- Amazon Image—'yes' or 'no' as to whether an image exists

When the page first loads, the first page (page size yet to be determined) of categories that have a parent of 0 are presented. Since this is going to be an iterative page (it will load itself subsequently), we'll need a way of knowing where we've come from and where we're going. If the page is loaded with no parameters attached to the URL, we'll assume it to be the initial load. If the page is loaded with a parameter requesting the categories with a parent of 0, we'll receive the same list. When we have a page call itself iteratively, its reload requires a new connection with the server.

One way we can "maintain state," retain information from one connection to the next, is to use session variables, which retain information until the session has ended or timed-out. This method works well—if you know what values you want to retain. In our case, the information we'll need to process when the page loads will depend on which category was clicked on the previous iteration.

We don't know what category will be clicked, and once it's been clicked we've lost control until the page is loaded again. So, the logical way to pass the data is to make it part of the link that causes the page to be loaded, that is, attach it to the link as a parameter on the URL that's loaded when the category is clicked.

The possible parameters to be passed on the URL are:

- Parent—the category number of the current category. The page of categories being displayed are all children of the current category, so it will be the parent of whatever category is clicked.
- Grandparent—the category number of the current category's parent, which will become the grandparent of whatever category is clicked. Passing this value helps retain the path through the categories that got us here. The reason is that once we've left the initial list of categories due to one being clicked, we'll display the name of the clicked category atop the new list of categories as a means of allowing the visitor to backtrack. We'll need to know the grandparent of the clicked category, because it will be inserted in the URL of this displayed clicked category name, so that if *it* is clicked we know what its parent is. This concept is displayed in Figure 3-17.

Figure 3-17   Sample Category Flow

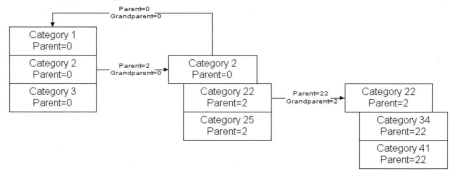

- Starting Category—If the categories in the current hierarchy level are more numerous than can be displayed on one page, we'll give the visitor the option of scrolling through each page. When we call the next iteration of the page, we know from where in the list to begin displaying by passing this value, the category number of the last category displayed on the current page, thus making it the first category displayed on the next page.

- Direction—There are numerous pages of categories to display at the current level, once we've displayed the first page, until we've displayed the final page. When that happens, we're in a position where there are pages prior to and subsequent to the one we're currently displaying. We want the visitor to be able to scroll in either direction, so we'll indicate the direction they've chosen by passing the direction as the P(revious) or N(ext) page.

- Find—When the visitor chooses not to browse through the category list, but instead to search for a topic, they enter a search value in a text box and click a button. In that case, we need to let ourselves know, for the next iteration, that we're not drawing the list of categories from our sequential position based on scrolling direction or parent, but instead from the result of a search.

Okay, so we now know from where to obtain the page of categories to display. Do we simply display them as a series of bullet items? No, we need to determine some additional things, because they will affect how we display the categories:

- Children—Determine whether a category has children by searching the database for category entries with this category being the parent. If children exist, then the category name will be displayed as a link and its name will be suffixed with "..." to indicate there is more information available.

- Links—determine whether a category has links associated with it by searching for links that point back to this category number. If there are links, then the category name will be displayed as a link.

- Book—Determine from database information associated with this category whether there is a book recommendation for it. If so, then display the category name as a link.

Should none of the above be true, then the category name will be displayed, but as text and not a hyperlink. If it *is* a hyperlink, the format of it will need to be as shown in Table 3-7. There needs to be a JavaScript routine to cause a hover reaction (a change of color when the mouse cursor hovers above the text) with the links.

The only thing else we need to discuss about the Category area is that upon loading, a meta tag must be included in the HTML code that will cause the Link and For-Profit Ad frames to reload. We need them to reload so that they can reflect the current set of categories, but there isn't a simple way to have the frames themselves cause their own reload as a result of the Category frame reloading—we must force the event.

Table 3-7   Hyperlink Parameters

Context	Parameter	Meaning
Category	parent=	parent of category
	start=	starting category in multi-page display
	gp=	parent of parent category
Home	parent=0	present initial list
Previous Page	direction=P	display previous page of categories
Next Page	direction=N	display next page of categories
Search	find=	search categories for this string

3.11.7.2 Category Navigation

I mentioned earlier that categories will be displayed a page at a time, and that we'll provide the visitor with the ability to navigate through the categories. The navigation will take the form of two icons (which we'll be developing in Chapter 7).

The first icon will be for 'home.' There will be two versions of the icon, one in color and one gray. The colored icon will be presented as an image link when displaying the initial level of categories is viable (i.e., any page without 0 for a parent is being displayed). When the initial level is being displayed, the image will be the gray icon, which will not be an image link.

The second icon will be an image map representing left and right, previous and next, arrows. When anything but the initial page of any level is being presented, there is a viable previous page to display, so the left arrow will be colored and clickable; otherwise it will be gray and static. The same approach will be taken with the right-hand arrow; if we're presenting anything but the final page of a level, this arrow will be colored and clickable.

The reason we have various states of icon is that it's far less confusing to the visitor if the icons are always present albeit in different states than if they're there sometimes and not others — much like toolbar icons and menu choices in most software applications.

3.11.7.3 Search

The search area will consist of a text box in which the visitor enters the search string. There will also need to be some minor artwork to clue the visitor in to the fact that the text box is for searching.

Search engine logic can become quite extensive, but in the first release of this application we will not be supporting compound items ("blue" "whale") or boolean expressions ("blue" AND "whale").

We *will* provide some minor functionality though, namely we'll remove quotation marks if the visitor uses them (many search engines encourage the use of quotation marks to denote a search for an exact phrase).

3.11.7.4 Book
There are three contexts for which we want to account when creating the functionality around the Amazon.com feature.

- Recommendation with image—If the category database record contains a value for ISBN *and* 'Yes' for a book image, the image will be displayed as an image link.
- Recommendation without image—If no book image exists for the recommended book, a logo will be presented with text indicating that clicking the logo will take the visitor to a recommended book on the current topic.
- No recommendation—A logo will be presented, and the text will indicate that clicking the logo will allow the visitor to search for a book on the current topic.

The code for the links will be provided by Amazon.com. One point to note is that we need to allow for recording whether each category will support the no-recommendation functionality. The reason is that some categories are much too broad to offer the visitor a search for a book on the topic. For example, the highest-level category under which resorts and vacation locations appear is titled "Destinations." This is far too general a topic on which to perform a search for a book.

3.12 Cascading Style Sheets

As we saw in Chapter 2, CSS is very useful for providing formatting beyond that which HTML provides. We're going to use a site-wide style sheet for just such advanced formatting. Below are the requirements for these styles. The styles will also be coded as JavaScript, because currently support for CSS in Netscape Navigator is not as thorough as it is in Internet Explorer.

```
Links (general)
      font-size:10
      color:maroon
      text-decoration:none
      font-family:"helv"
Links (specific)
      font-size:10
      color:navy
      text-decoration:none
      font-family:"helv"
Inactive Link
      font-size:10
      color:gray
      font-family:"helv"
```

```
            margin-left: 100em
Title
        font-size:10
        color:maroon
        font-family:"helv"
Navigation
        font-size:9
        color:white
        text-decoration:none
        font-family:"arial"
H3 (Heading 3)
        background-color: brown
        color: white
        font-family: arial
        font-size: 24px
        font-weight: bold
        text-align: center
H4
        background-color: wheat
H5
        background-color: powderblue
        color: black
        font-family: arial
        font-size: 14px
        font-weight: bold
        letter-spacing: 3px
        line-height: 4pt
        text-align: center
Body Text
        color: black
        font-family: Times New Roman
        font-size: 10pt
        text-indent: 0.25in
```

The DIY Store

*I*n this chapter we're going to install the applications and services that we need. It's always a somewhat simplistic approach to provide screen shots of software installation, because the screens can vary based on the version you're installing, the platform onto which you're installing it, and what you already have on your system. Nonetheless, I'm going to provide a narrative and screen shots for most of the architecture we'll be using:

- Paint Shop Pro version 5.01
- FrontPage '98
- Image Composer 1.5
- Personal Web Server 4
- Visual Interdev 6
- NT Server Extensions
- Visual Interdev Extensions

We won't be installing the operating system or the browser, as the former is far too involved and hardware architecture-specific, and there are new versions of the latter coming out every several months.

Note

Even if you're installing the same version as I am onto the same operating system that I have, it's possible the dialog windows you receive will be different and/or in a different order than those presented here.

4.1 Paint Shop Pro 5.01

Paint Shop Pro (PSP) is a shareware application. That means you can download a trial version, use it for a period of time, and then purchase it if you like it, or discard the version you downloaded if you don't. You can download it via the Web site for this book (see Appendix A). I'll be installing the retail version here.

Figure 4-1   Paint Shop Pro Setup Launch

Launching the setup program results in the menu screen shown in Figure 4-1. We'll select *Install* from the menu.

PSP warns you to exit other applications before continuing (see Figure 4-2). Most installs do the same thing. It's a good idea to heed the advice. I go as far as turning off all the applications in my system tray that aren't essential.

Figure 4-2   "Other Application Warning"

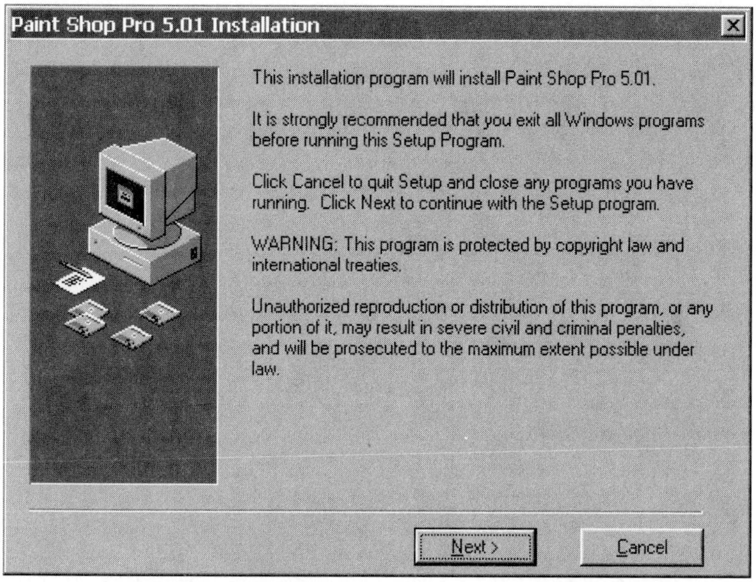

Like most installations, we're notified of the intended installation directory, and asked to change it if we desire (see Figure 4-3). There is a small amount of risk in changing the location, as occasionally the application has sections where the path was mistakenly hard-coded, and therefore the files being sought aren't found.

Figure 4-3   Selecting PSP Destination

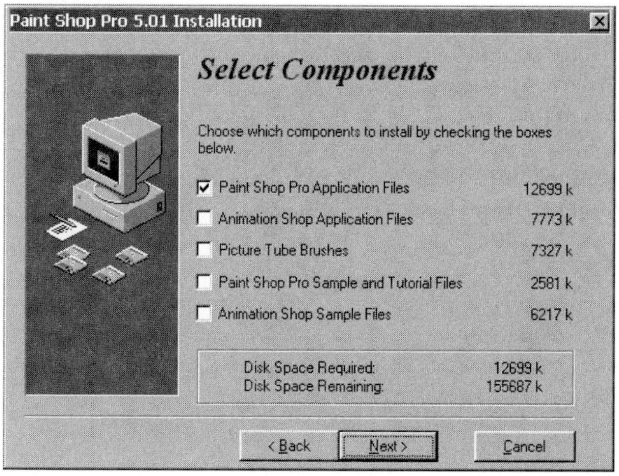

This screen also informs us of the the amout of disk space we'll have left following the install. Most applications will tell you if the available space is insufficient for the install, but it's good to view the numbers and decide for yourself before continuing.

We're given the opportunity to select the components we want to install (see Figure 4-4). The only necessary components are the application files, although you're certainly welcome to install any or all of them.

Figure 4-4   Selecting PSP Components

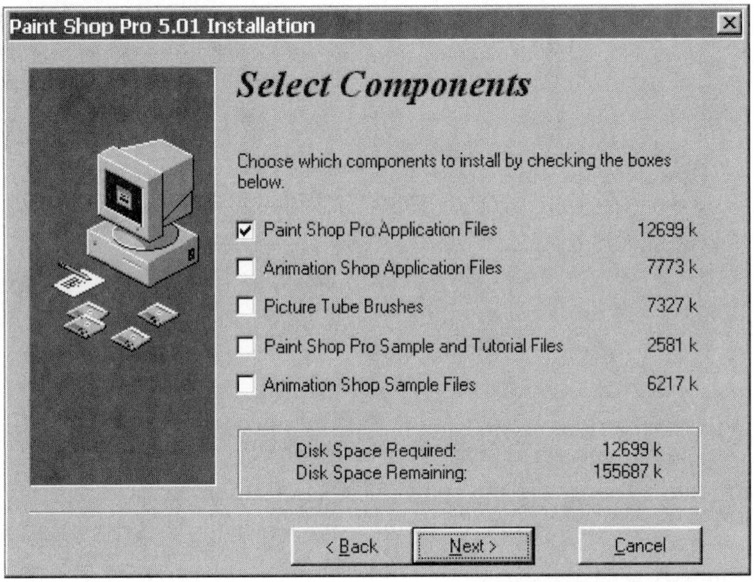

Once we make our selection, we're ready to install (see Figure 4-5). As Paint Shop Pro is installing, a progress meter shows the percentage complete (see Figure 4-6). No one is quite sure what these meters measure. It doesn't seem to be the elapsed time compared to the total required. Perhaps it's the total number of bytes or the total number of files.

Figure 4-5   Ready to Install

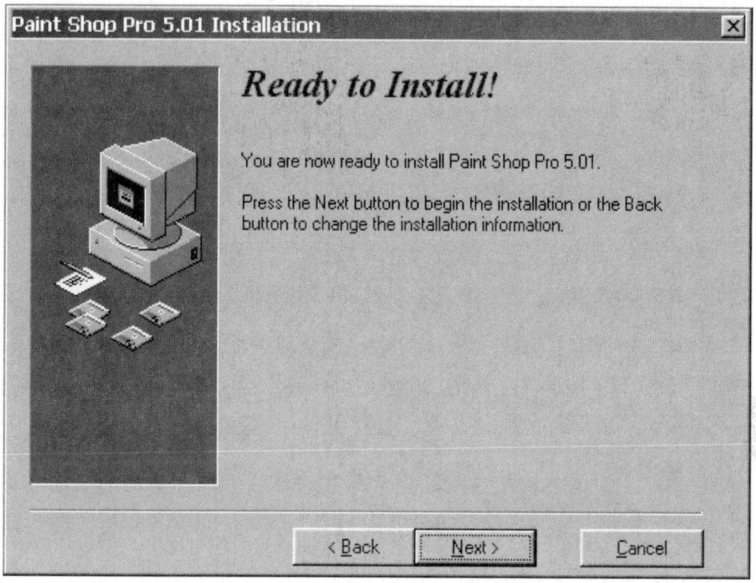

Figure 4-6   PSP Installation Progress Meter

Once we get to 100% the installation is complete, and we receive a dialog box congratulating us on our success (see Figure 4-7).

Figure 4-7   PSP Installation Completed

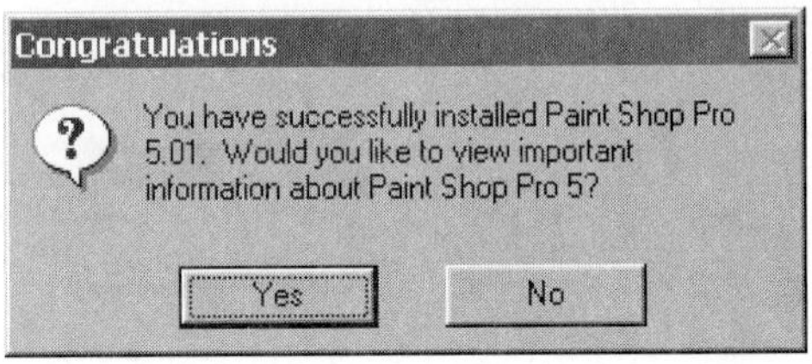

4.2 FrontPage '98

This installation can throw a few curves depending on your circumstances. I had one come up because I upgraded to FrontPage '98 from FrontPage '97. Having had bad experiences "writing over" earlier versions of software when upgrading in the past, I removed the '97 version first. The first thing '98 did was to search my system for evidence of my owning the previous version — the one I had just uninstalled. Unable to find it, of course, the installation terminated. Okay, so I reinstalled '97 and was then ready to install '98. The second hitch was that I had also uninstalled the Microsoft Personal Web Server for the same reason. Since this software is provided free, there was no upgrade problem, but as it turns out, FrontPage requires it to be present before it will install (see Figure 4-8).

Figure 4-8   Oops

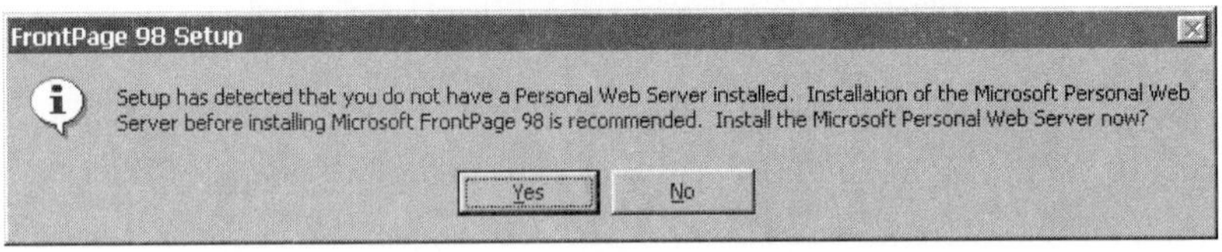

Next up is the obligatory Microsoft EULA — End-User License Agreement. You're not allowed to install the software unless you first agree to the license (see Figure 4-8). There's no middle road, no room for a conscientious objector — agree, or say "bye-bye".

Figure 4-9   EULA

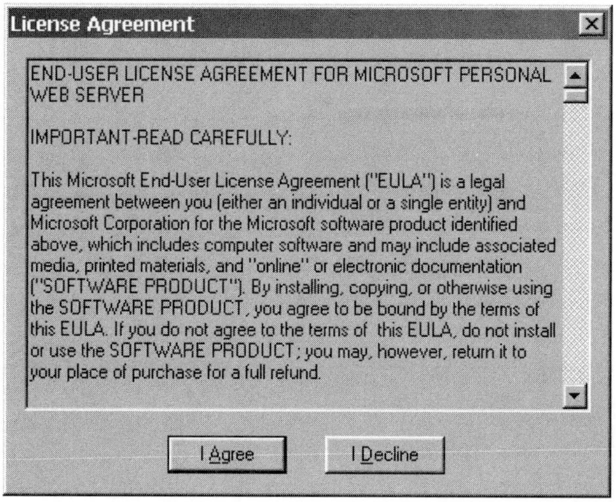

I'll agree to the terms of the agreement, and this will trigger the copying of the files to my hard drive (see Figure 4-10).

Figure 4-10   PWS Files Being Copied

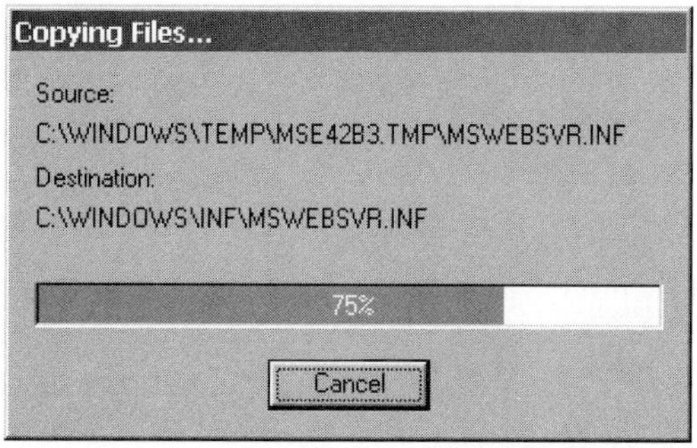

Once the files have all been copied, the installation program prompts us to restart the system (see Figure 4-11). Since I don't know what part of this application FrontPage searches for to satisfy itself that Personal Web Server (PWS) is installed, restarting is a good idea so that the application is fully installed.

When the system has completed rebooting, PWS is installed and we can move on to installing FrontPage.

Figure 4-11   PWS Prompts for Reboot

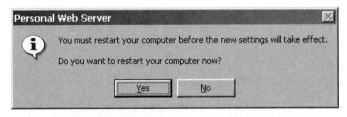

Figure 4-12   FrontPage Install Menu

Figure 4-13   InstallShield

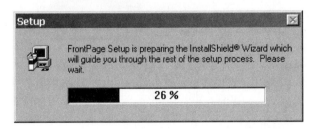

FrontPage will now find Personal Web Server, and, with this requirement being met, will proceed to the installation menu (see Figure 4-12). We'll select *Install FrontPage 98*.

FrontPage then launches the InstallShield. I have no idea what it's shielding us from (sometimes a successful install it would seem), but off it goes (see Figure 4-13).

You may receive the error message in Figure 4-14, depending on how your system's access is set up. It's not a concern at this point, since we won't be going online with our Web site.

FrontPage warns us about closing all other applications (see Figure 4-15) — again, I would strongly advise heeding its advice.

Figure 4-14   FrontPage Security Warning

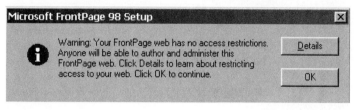

Figure 4-15   A Warning to Consider

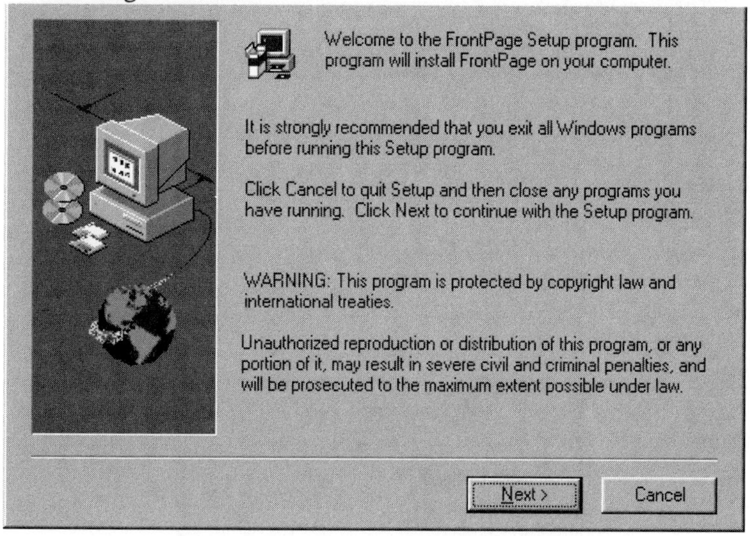

We'll need to enter some registration information (see Figure 4-16). A company name isn't mandatory, but your name is.

Figure 4-16   Registration Screen

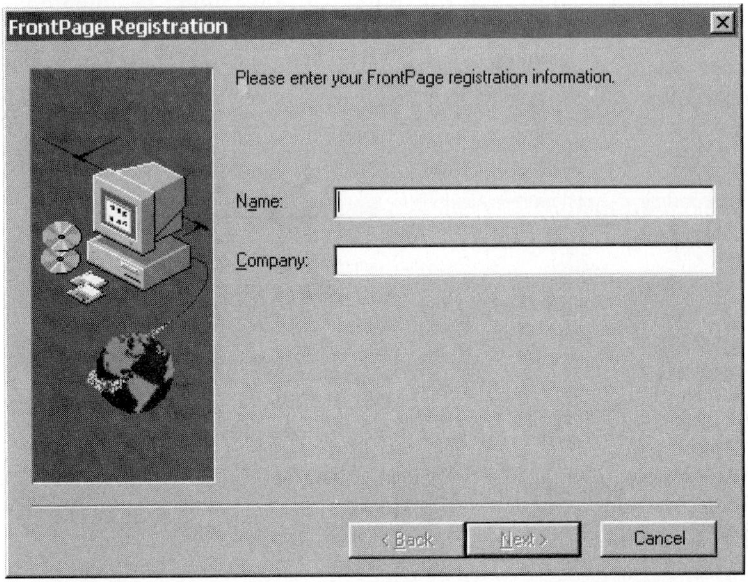

We're then asked to enter the CD key (Figure 4-17), which is the number on the sticker on the back of the CD jewel box. This doesn't stop anyone from pirating software, as it's fairly simple to stick a piece of masking tape on a bogus copy and write the CD key on it. However, the key and an algorithm result in a unique product ID, without which you can't receive support from Microsoft.

Figure 4-17   CD Key Dialog

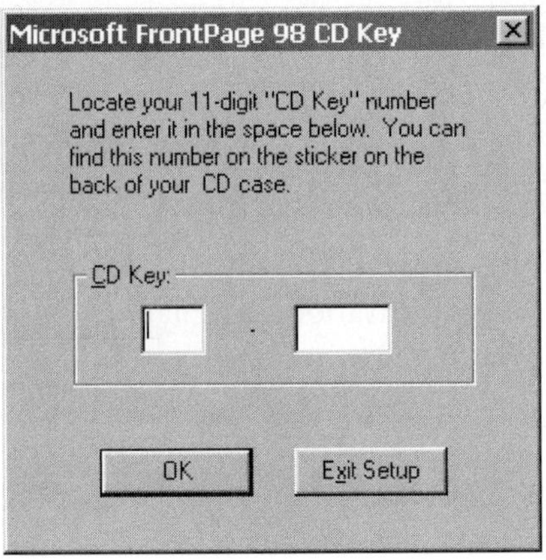

Figure 4-18 shows that "gotcha" I mentioned earlier. As long as you have the earlier version of the software you'll be able to continue.

When FrontPage finds what it's looking for, it moves us on to the next step—another EULA (see Figure 4-19)!

Figure 4-18   FrontPage Upgrade Gotcha

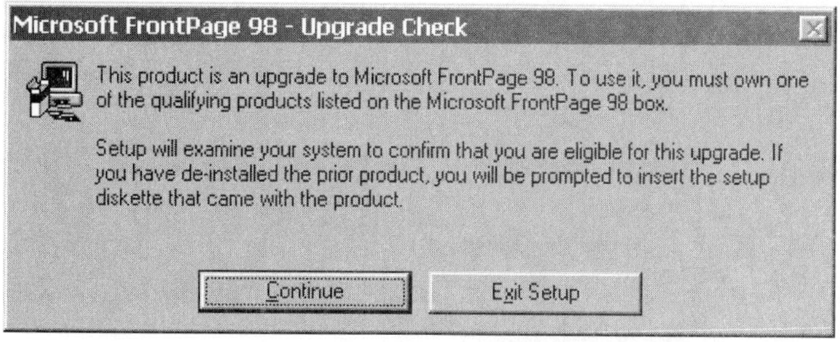

Figure 4-19   FrontPage EULA

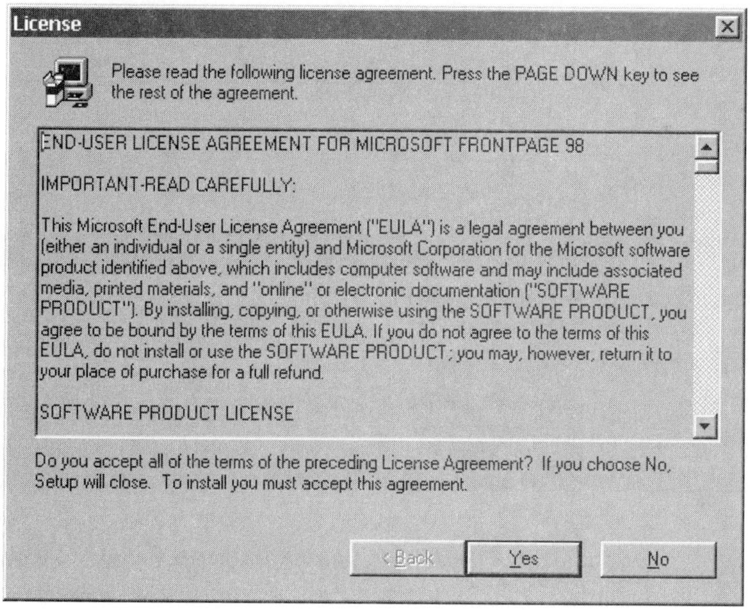

FrontPage asks us whether we want to decide what components to install, or whether we want to let FrontPage decide for us (see Figure 4-20). Sometimes I select the former, because usually I find something I want to install that the application would not have. This time we'll go with the typical installation.

Figure 4-20   Installation Preference

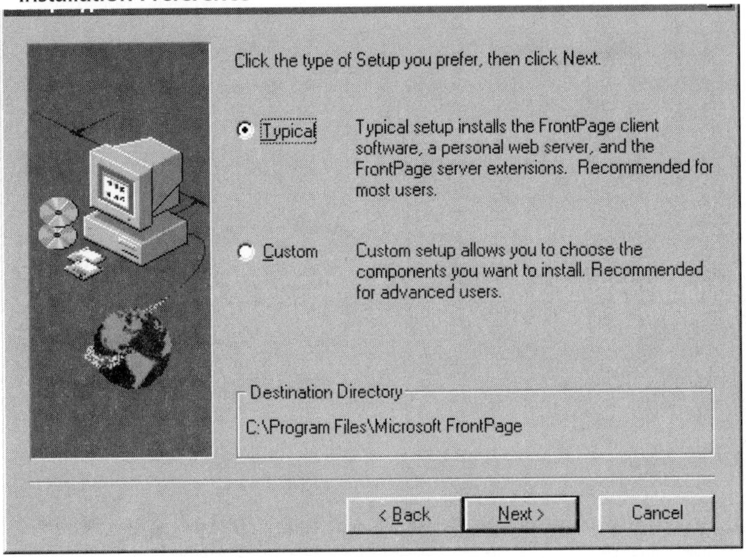

Figure 4-21   Copying the FrontPage Files

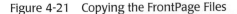

Finally, the transfer of files begins. Meters indicate the amount of progress and space available (see Figure 4-21).

And that's it for FrontPage, as you can see from the congratulatory dialog box in Figure 4-22. Let's move on to Image Composer. Leaving the box checked will cause FrontPage to launch when we exit, but we have more to install, so we'll clear it.

Figure 4-22   FrontPage Install Completes

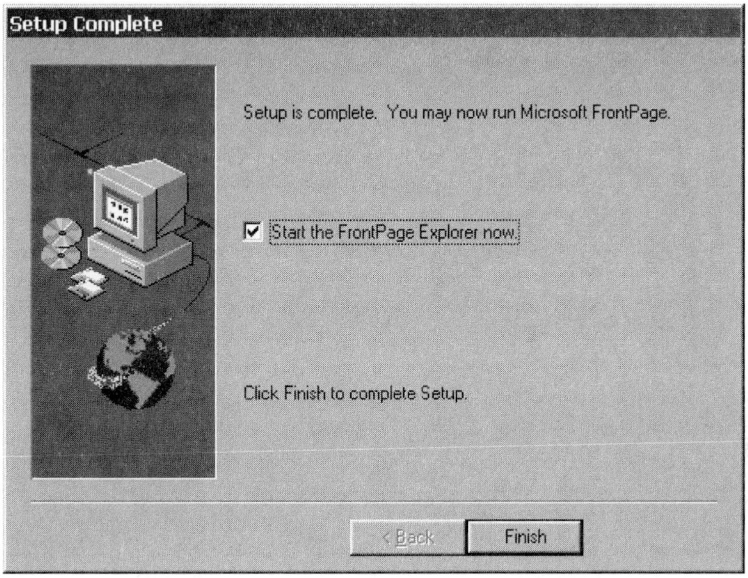

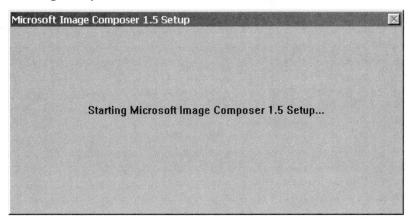

4.3 Image Composer 1.5

Clicking *Finish* from the FrontPage installation returns us to the installation menu. We'll select *Install Image Composer*, shown in Figure 4-23.

Figure 4-23   Image Composer Installation

Figure 4-24   Image Composer Warning

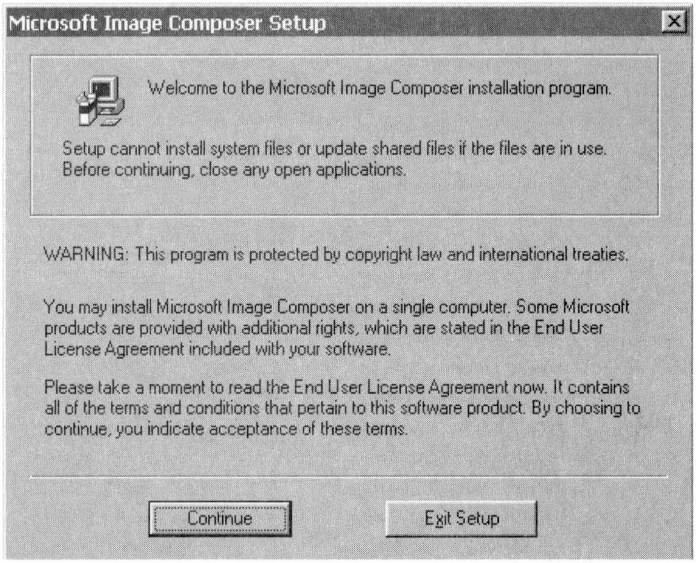

The setup begins with another warning to close all other running applications (see Figure 4-24).

Now, for some odd reason we need to register again (see Figure 4-25). Is it me? I mean, here we are installing the second application from the same CD, and it's asking us for our name again. Surely it stored it somewhere the first time and didn't toss it into write-only memory.

Figure 4-25   Image Composer Registration

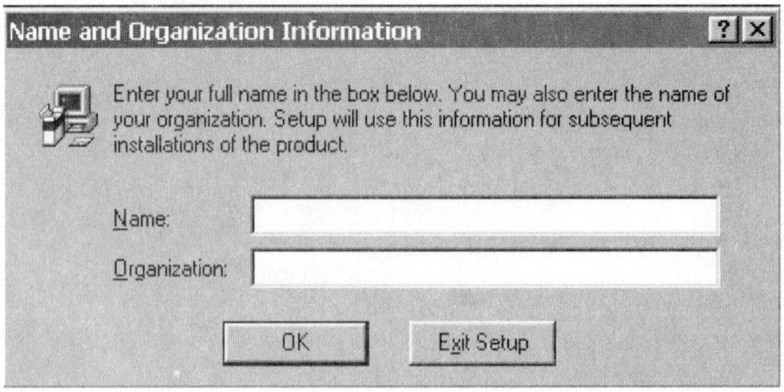

Figure 4-26   Image Composer Product ID

Image Composer presents us with our unique product ID number (see Figure 4-26), and then we're ready to install.

Well, almost ready. You didn't really think we'd get by without having to read and agree to another EULA, did you (see Figure 4-27)?

Figure 4-27   Image Composer EULA

Figure 4-28   Composer Setup Screen

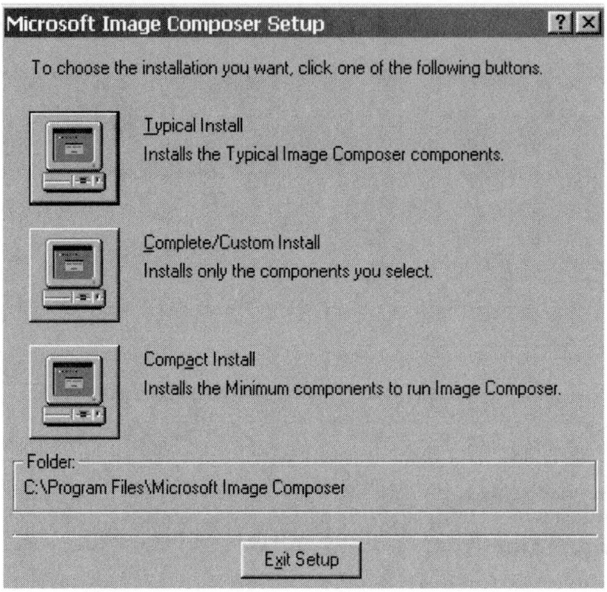

We're presented with the *Composer Setup Screen*, which gives us three options for installation (see Figure 4-28). We'll select *Custom*.

Funny thing for a graphics program that comes bundled with a Web publishing application — the option to install Web graphics samples is not a default (see Figure 4-29). We'll select it.

We're also prompted (see Figure 4-30) as to what program group we want the execution shortcuts to be located.

The file copying begins. We're given a progress meter to keep us occupied (see Figure 4-31). Once the copying is done, we'll hopefully receive a dialog box informing us of our success (see Figure 4-32).

Figure 4-29   Component Selection

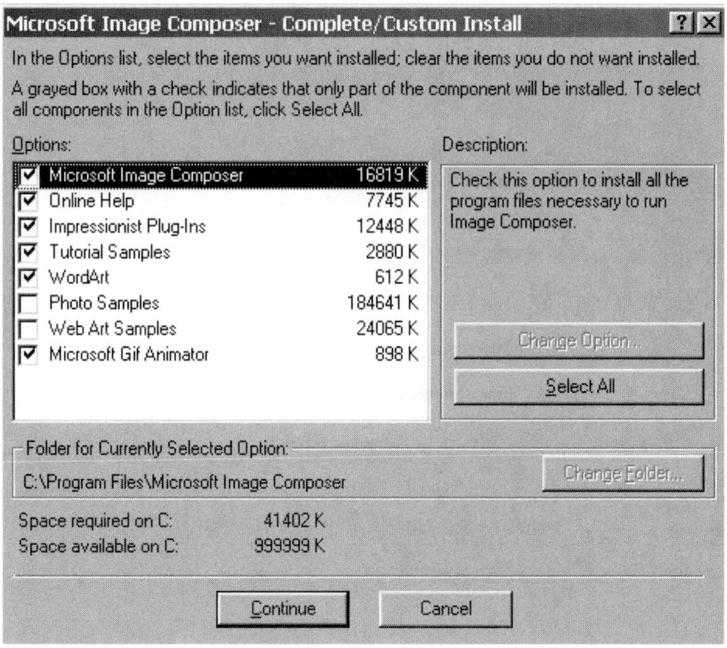

Figure 4-30   Program Group Selection

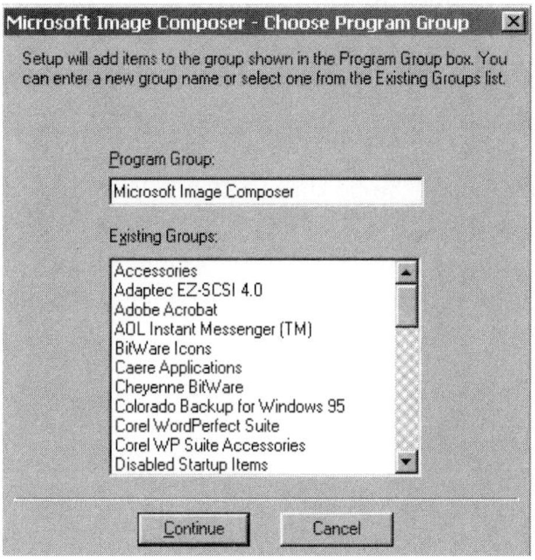

Figure 4-31   Image Composer File Copy

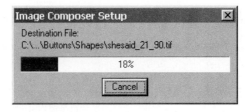

Figure 4-32   Image Composer Install Complete

4.4 Visual InterDev 6.0 & Servers

Visual Interdev (VI) is part of the Visual Studio suite. We're going to be installing the version of VI that comes with the Enterprise edition of Visual Studio. It's a three CD set, and we'll start with the first CD.

Loading it launches the install program for Visual Studio (see Figure 4-33). I had previously installed Visual Basic. Since that is also a Visual Studio application, I received the screen shown in Figure 4-34.

Clicking *Add/Remove* takes us to the component selection screen (see Figure 4-35). I'll clear all the check boxes and check the one for Visual InterDev.

Figure 4-33   Launching Visual Studio Installation

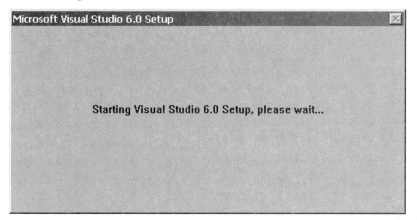

Figure 4-34   Visual Studio Installation Maintenance

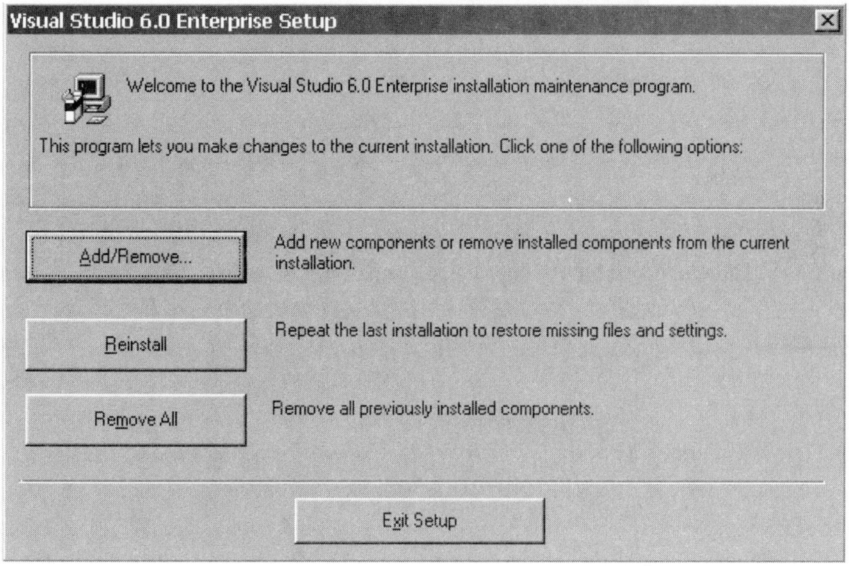

Figure 4-35   Visual Studio Component Selection

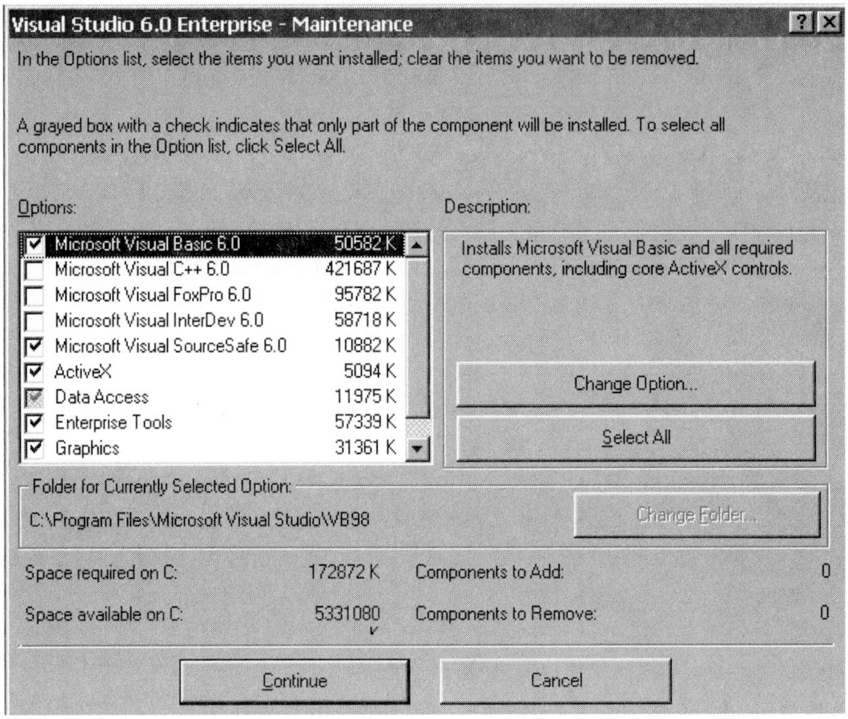

Figure 4-36   VI Files Being Copied

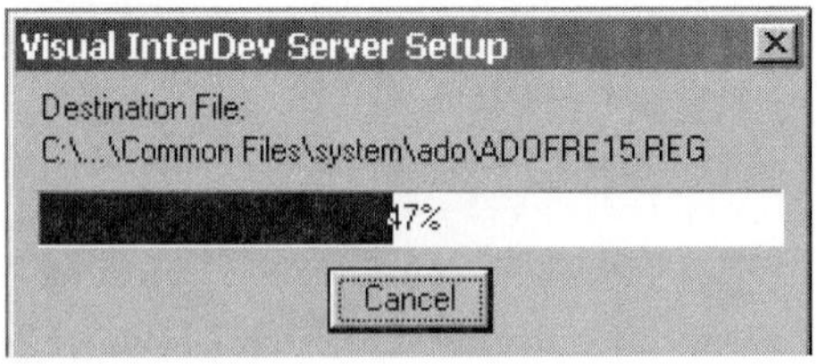

Having made our selection and clicked *Continue*, the copy of the files begins (see Figure 4-36).

Once all the files are copied, the installation program suggests restarting Windows see Figure 4-37). We don't need to do it right now, so long as we do it before trying to use VI.

Figure 4-37   VI Asking for a Restart

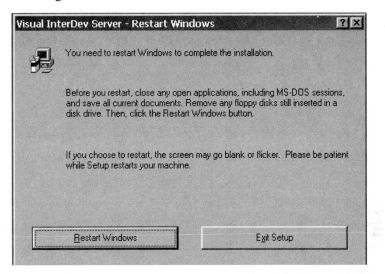

We'll choose to add components again from the Visual Studio installation program. There are a number of add-on components that we'll want in order to have the functionality that we want. We'll add the Server Setups one at a time (see Figure 4-38).

First we'll install the NT Option Pack. It provides us with Active Server Pages functionality among other things. We'll have to do a CD swap, because the software is on the second CD (see Figure 4-39).

If you currently have Microsoft's FTP program installed (you may, and not even know it), you will be notified that it's going to be removed (see Figure 4-40). This is nothing to be concerned with.

With that complete, we'll go on to installing the next component. We'll go back to the Servers screen and install the Microsoft Personal Web Server (see Figure 4-41). Yes, we already installed it when we installed FrontPage, but this is a newer version.

Personal Web Server allows us to use our system as a client *and* a server, so that we can bring pages up on our browser by using a Web address. This is a critical part of our architecture for development *and* testing.

The installation program has determined that it is upgrading an instance of PWS, and asks whether we want to upgrade on the components we currently have or perhaps add new components as well (see Figure 4-42). We'll choose the latter.

We're going to select *Upgrade Plus*. This results in a component screen for PWS. We want to make sure we're getting all the components we need, particularly the Data Access components. Let's highlight it and select *Show Subcomponents* (see Figure 4-43).

Figure 4-38   Preparing to Install NT Option Pack

Installation Wizard for Visual Studio 6.0 Enterprise Edition

Server Setups

To install one of the server tools listed below, select the setup you wish to run and click the "Install" button. If the server tool setup requires a reboot, you will return to this wizard page.

Server Components

NT Option Pack (for Windows9x)
FrontPage 98 Server Extensions
Data Access Components 2.0
Visual InterDev Server Components
Application Performance Explorer
Visual FoxPro Server Samples
Visual Source Safe Server
Visual Studio Analyzer

Install

Figure 4-39   A CD Swap

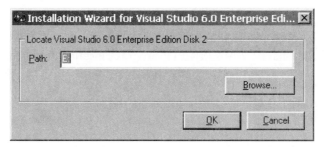

Installation Wizard for Visual Studio 6.0 Enterprise Edi... ☒

Locate Visual Studio 6.0 Enterprise Edition Disk 2

Path: E:

Browse...

OK   Cancel

Figure 4-40   FTP About to be 86'd

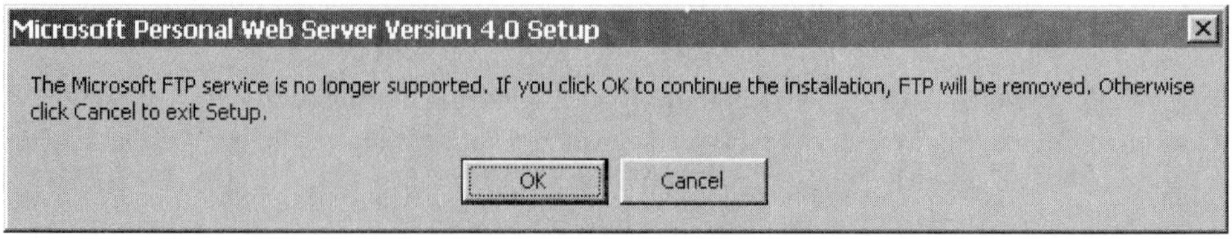

Microsoft Personal Web Server Version 4.0 Setup   ☒

The Microsoft FTP service is no longer supported. If you click OK to continue the installation, FTP will be removed. Otherwise click Cancel to exit Setup.

OK   Cancel

Figure 4-41   Launching PWS 4.0 Install

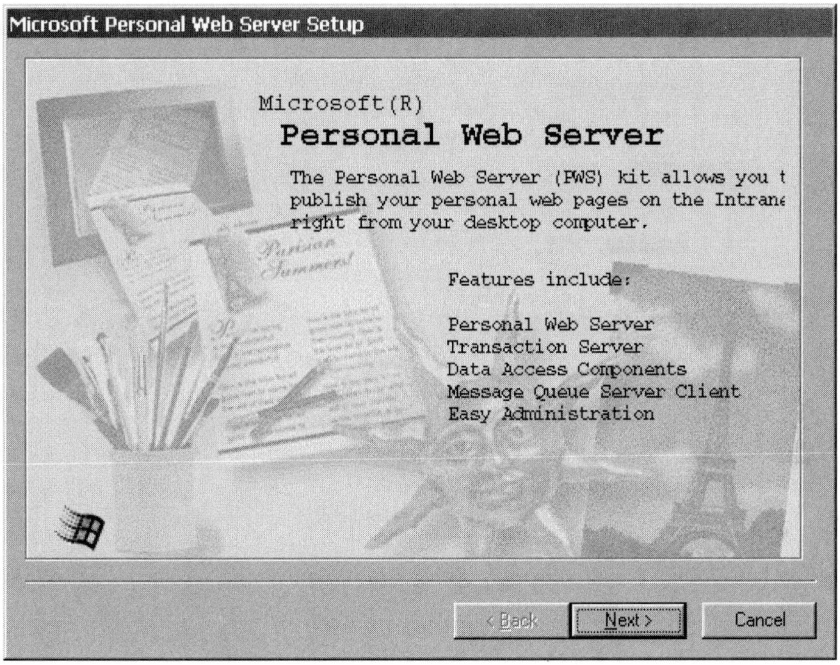

Figure 4-42   Select Installation Type

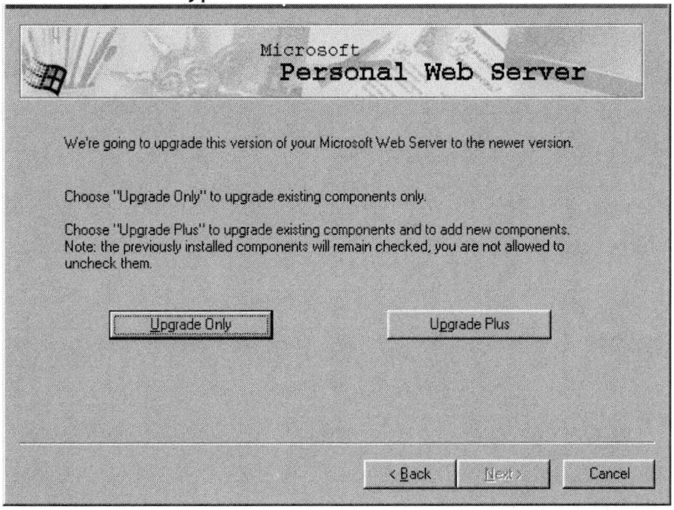

Figure 4-43   Selecting PWS Data Access Components

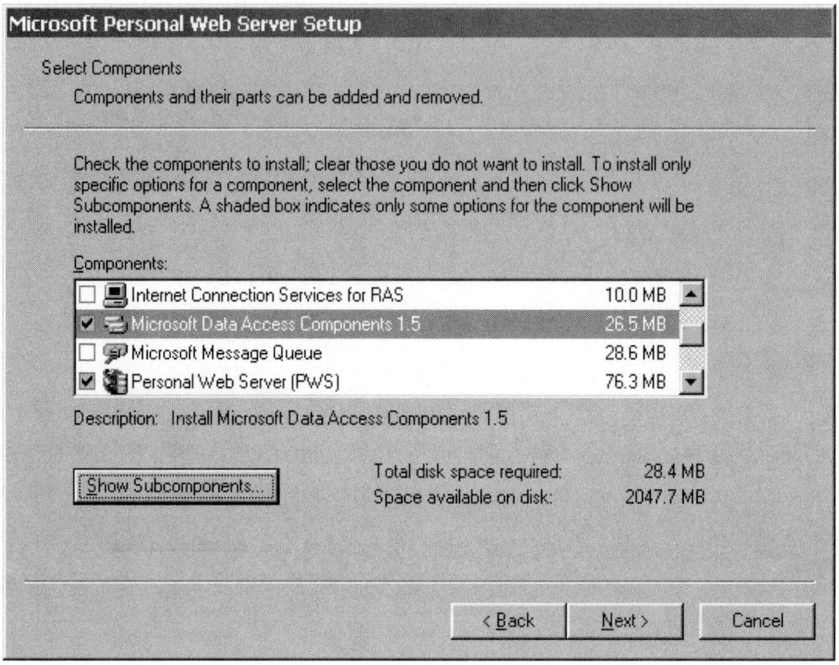

This will bring up yet another components screen. We want to focus on the ActiveX Data Objects (ADO) subcomponents, so we'll highlight them (see Figure 4-44) and click on *Show Subcomponents.*

Doing *show* brings up another selection window. It reveals that ADO would not have been selected (see Figure 4-45). Let's check the box, and click *OK* until we're back to the first components window, and we can then click *Next.* Of course there will be another EULA to review, but I'll spare you the graphic this time.

Figure 4-44 Hunting for ADO

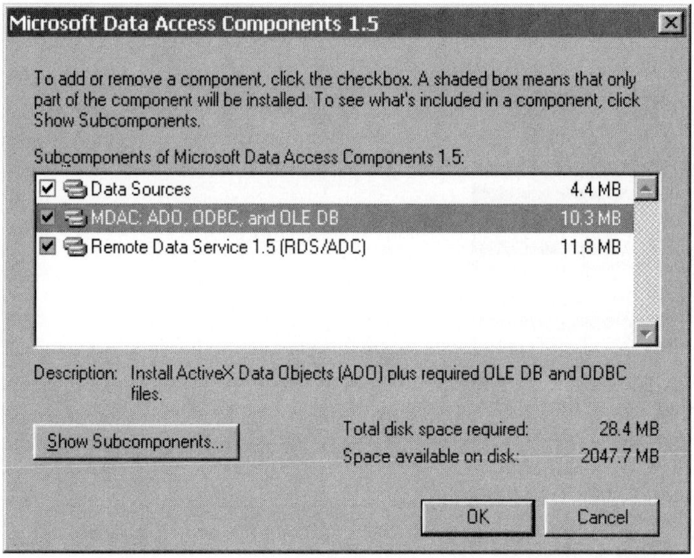

Figure 4-45 Selecting ADO

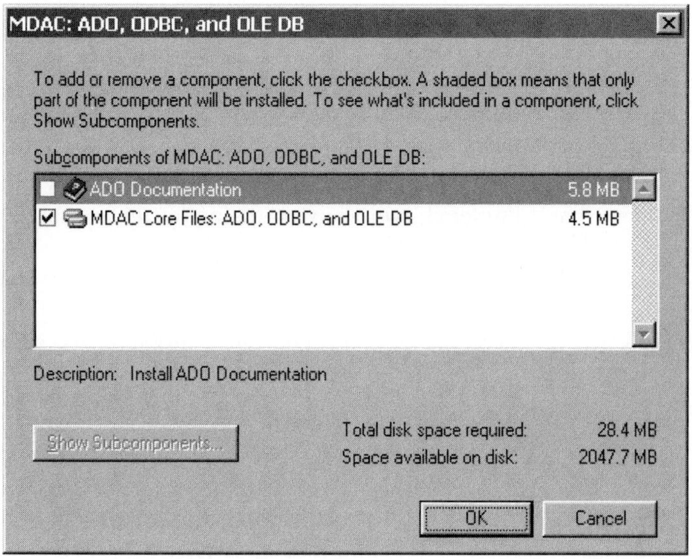

Figure 4-46   MTS as a Bonus

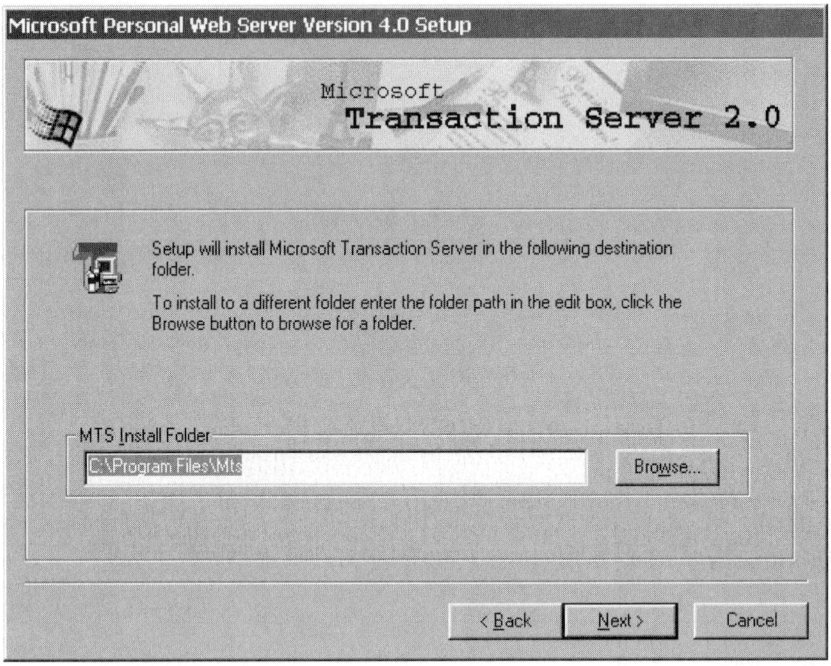

From the next screen (Figure 4-46) we can see that I didn't uncheck the Microsoft Transaction Server (MTS) box. No harm in this, we'll just let it install.

PWS is ready to install, and clicking *Next* starts the process shown in Figure 4-47. Once the file copying has completed, we receive a dialog letting us know that the PWS installation is complete (see Figure 4-48).

We are asked to reboot the system once again, as shown in Figure 4-49, but again, we don't need to do it at this time.

We'll go back to the Servers screen and choose FrontPage Server Extensions (see Figure 4-50). These extensions allow us to test FrontPage components in our Web pages. Without them we'd have to upload our pages to a server and test them there.

Figure 4-47   PWS Being Installed

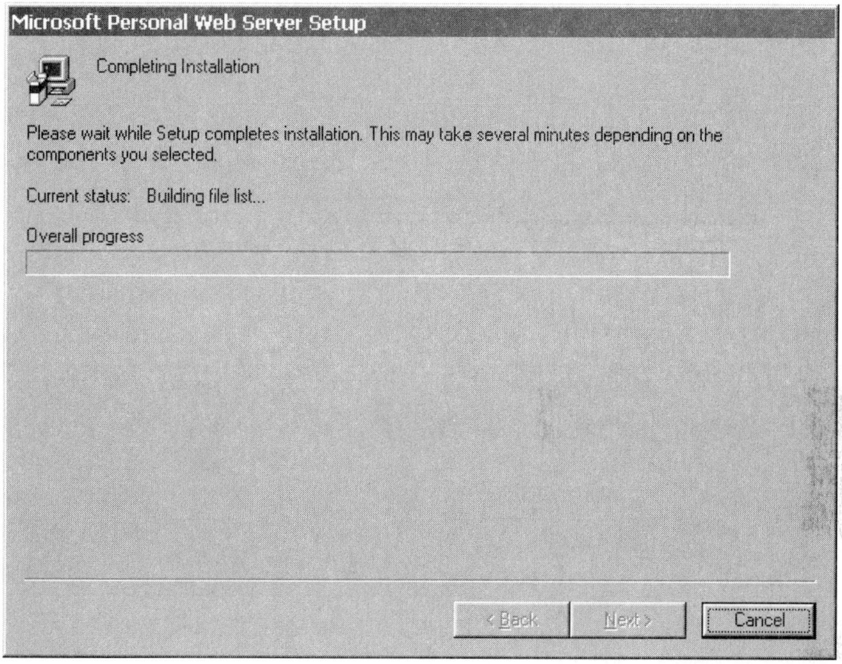

Figure 4-48   PWS Installation Completed

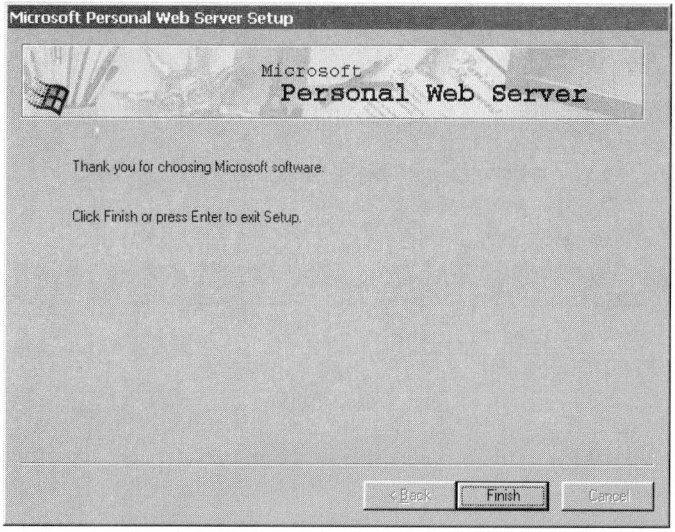

Figure 4-49   Reboot? No, Not Yet

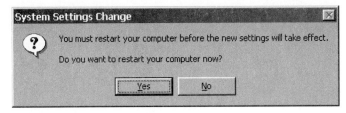

Figure 4-50   Installing FrontPage Server Components

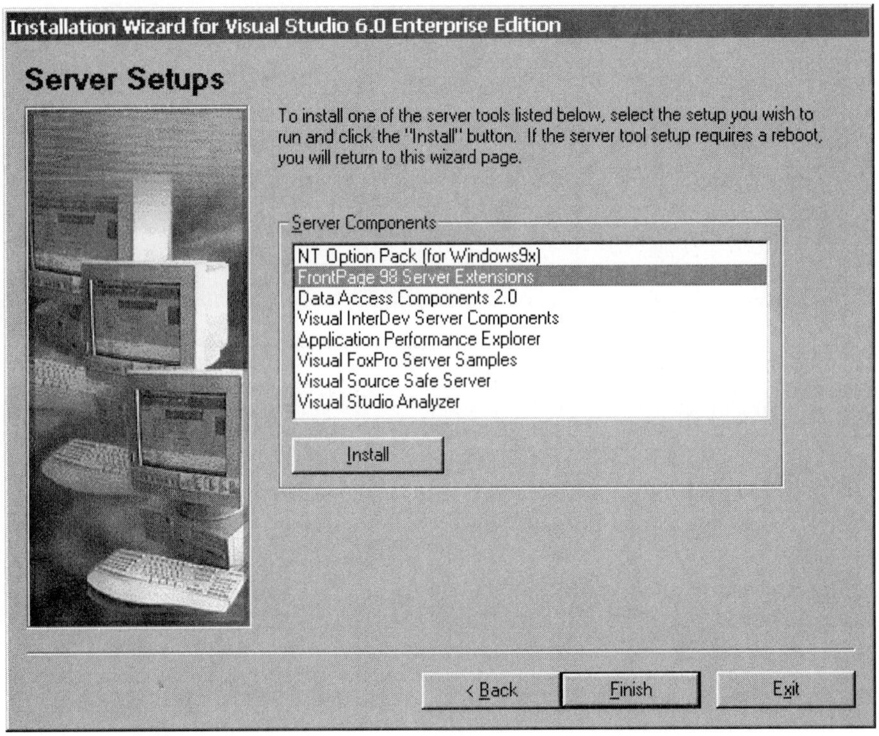

We already had FrontPage Server Extensions installed along with the FrontPage installation, but Visual InterDev 6.0 was released after FrontPage '98, so perhaps the version on it is newer. As shown in Figure 4-51, the installation program starts an InstallShield Wizard.

Figure 4-51   FrontPage Extensions InstallShield

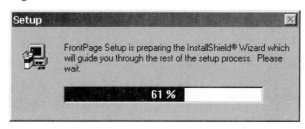

Figure 4-52   FrontPage Installation Program

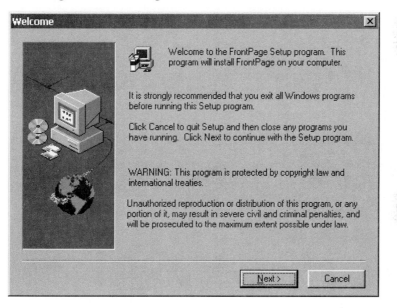

It then runs the FrontPage installation program (see Figure 4-52). Don't worry, we're not installing FrontPage again, just the server extensions.

When we click on *Next*, a copy of the server extensions begins (see Figure 4-53). This is our first confirmation that we're actually installing the extensions and not FrontPage itself.

Figure 4-53   Copying FP Server Extension Files

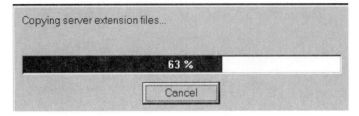

Figure 4-54   Installation of FP Extensions Completed

Once the files have been copied, we receive a message letting us know the installation is complete, but the message again refers to FrontPage and not the FrontPage Server Extensions (see Figure 4-54).

We're ready to move on now to the Data Access Components (see Figure 4-55). We're presented with yet another EULA, and once we agree to it, the preparation of the setup program occurs (see Figure 4-56).

We're given the option of choosing a standard or custom installation (see Figure 4-57 on page 88). We want to check the subcomponents again, so we'll choose custom.

Figure 4-55   Starting Data Access Components Installation

Figure 4-56   Setup Program Loads

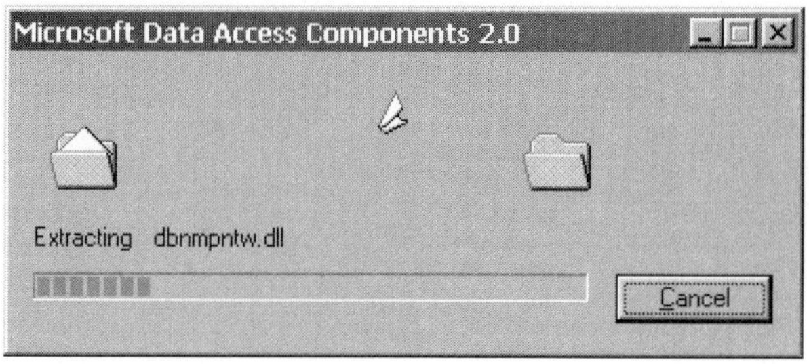

Figure 4-57   Installation Options

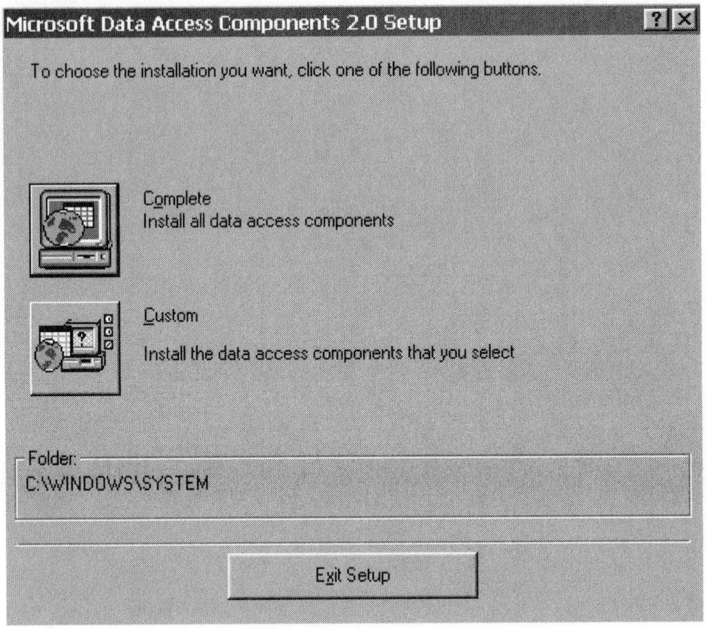

Figure 4-58   Data Access Components Selection

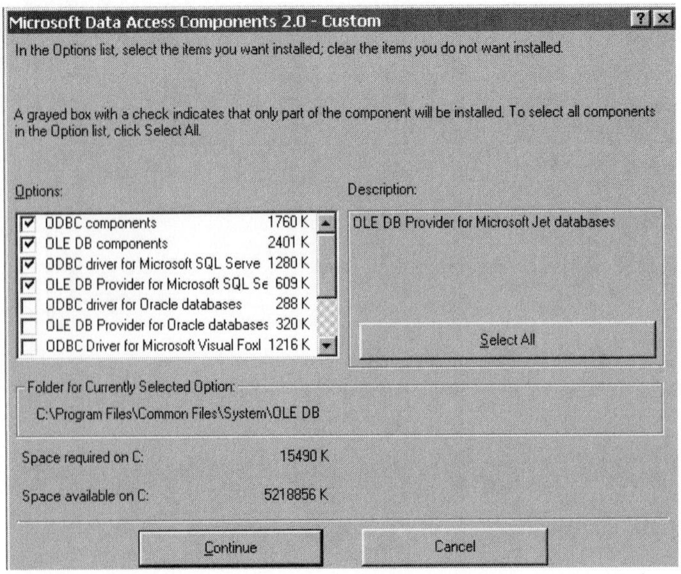

Figure 4-59   Copying Data Access Component Files

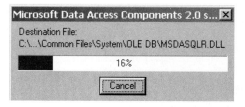

Figure 4-60   Data Access Components Install Complete

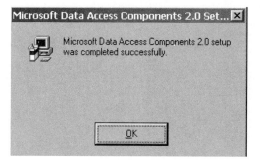

A list of the installable components is presented (see Figure 4-58). We don't need the components for Oracle and Visual FoxPro, so we'll uncheck those boxes.

Now that we've select the components, the file transfer will take place. We get a progress meter like before (see Figure 4-59).

Once the files have been transferred, we receive the dialog window in Figure 4-60 telling us that the installation is complete.

We have one last component to install, and that is the Visual InterDev Server. We'll select it from the components screen (see Figure 4-61).

Once we've clicked *Finish* and the software installation has completed, we're done with our software installs.

Figure 4-61   Installing the Visual InterDev Server

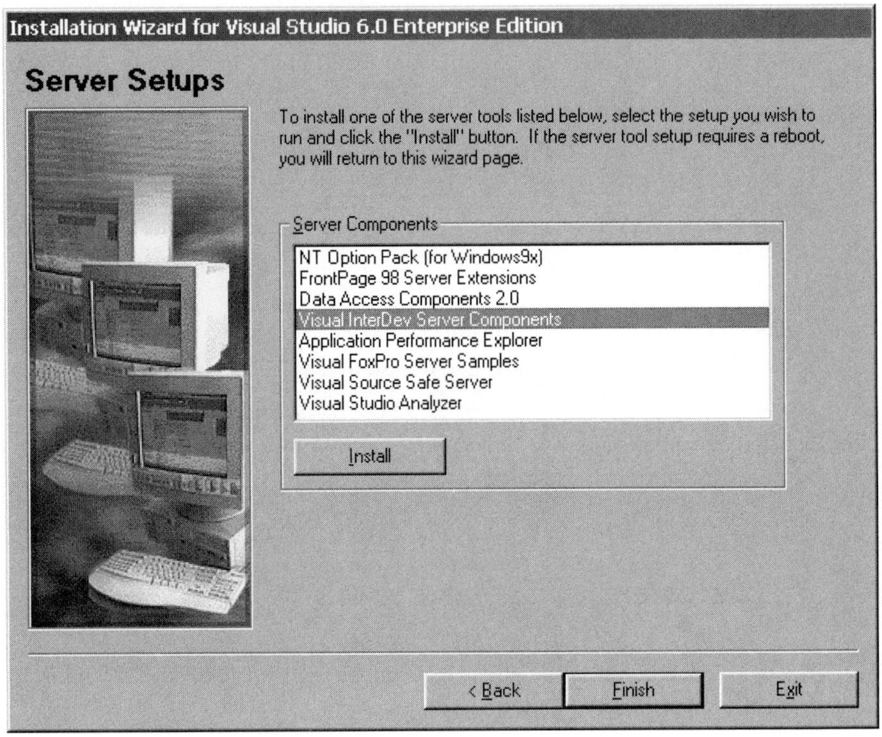

4.5 Enabling ASP

Personal Web Server doesn't default to enabling our web for use with Active Server Pages. If we were to enter a URL in our browser pointing to an ASP file on our web, we would receive a message indicating that we were about to download a file. Enabling the web to execute ASP script is trivial. Let's start by double-clicking on the Personal Web Server icon in the system tray, which results in the screen shown in Figure 4-62.

Figure 4-62   Preparing to Configure a Web

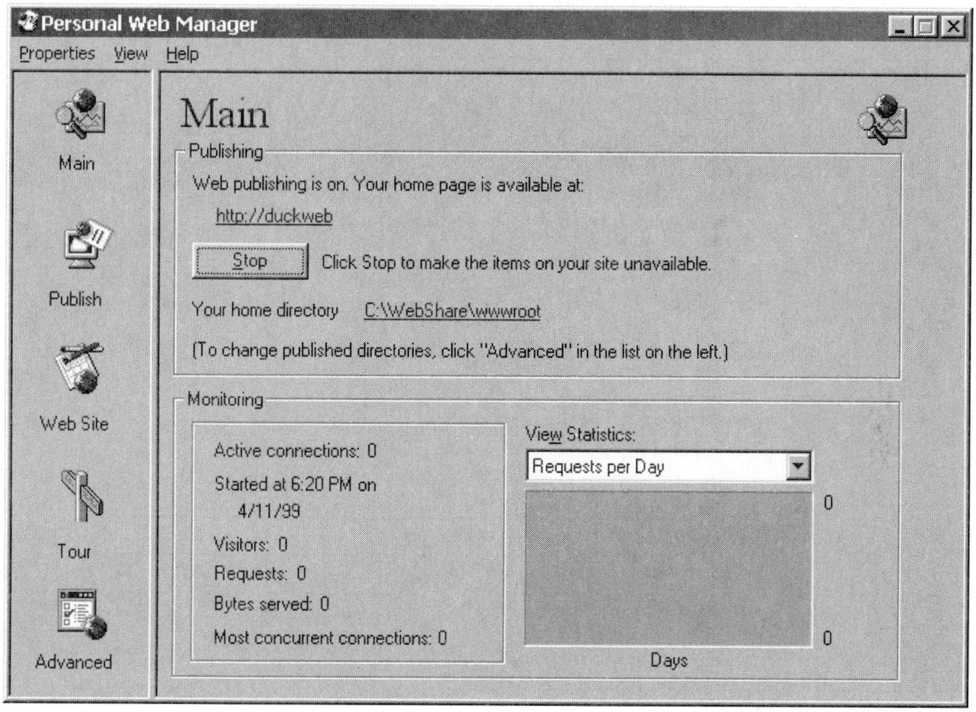

We'll click on the *Advanced* tab, which brings up the display shown in Figure 4-63. This is the place to define what our site will consider to be a default page. That is, if we enter a URL without a page name, the file names that the server will look for at that location. Right now we're looking for *default.htm* or *default.asp*, but we could change it to *index.htm* if we wanted to. It's best to set this to whatever your Web hosting service has set on their server.

We'll highlight the home directory and edit its properties. You'll see the default setting in Figure 4-64 on page 92. The *read* and *scripts* permission is set, but we need *execute* to run an ASP page, so let's check that box.

Figure 4-63   Advanced Web Site Options

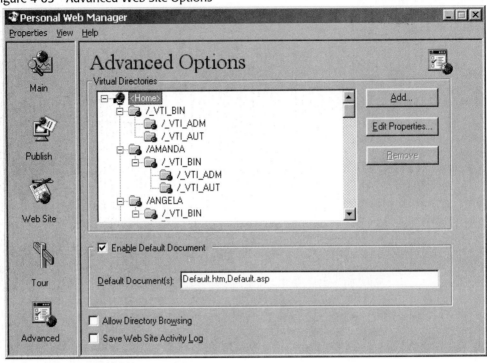

Figure 4-64   Enabling ASP

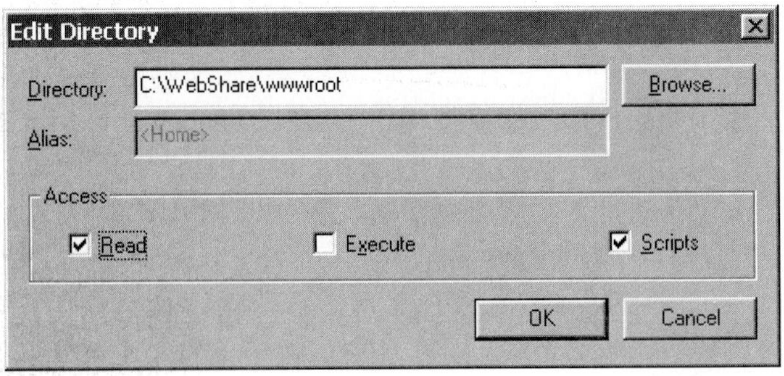

That ends our software installation. We also need the Java classes for our rotating banner ad. You'll find the code for that at our Web site (see Appendix A). It's in a self-extracting Zip file. All you need to do is create a "Java" directory off your Web directory, drop the file in it, and execute it.

Now that we have our architecture in place, we're ready to start coding. However, before we do that we ought to discuss standards, and that's just what we'll do in the next chapter.

CHAPTER 5

Standards

Lucky for us, our world is filled to the brim with standards. Imagine no standards for wall outlets, batteries, TV tuners, lumber sizes, etc. That helps explain the need for standards, but why would we want to spend a chunk of time on standards? I mean, if I'm going to be the only one maintaining the Web site?

Perhaps the site owner requires standards. Okay, what if I *am* the site owner? Why would I want standards for my own site? It's not like someone else is going to be doing any coding.

Well, one reason is memory. Try an experiment: the next four messages you take from people that you don't know, put the phone number on a scrap of paper with no other notation. After a few weeks, go back and look at the scraps of paper and see if you can remember what the numbers were for. You'll have about the same chance of success in going back to your own uncommented code with short, meaningless variable names and remembering what it's doing. Let's look at an example.

```
sub checkit(x)
r = FALSE
if len(x)>=4 then
y=right(x,4)
if isnumeric(y) then
if y/4=y\4 then
if y/100<>y\100 then
r=TRUE
else
if y/400=y\400 then r=TRUE
end if
end if
```

```
    end if
    end if
    checkit=r
    end sub
```

Yuck. I don't usually write code that looks as bad as that. It's painful to look at. So, do you know what it does? If you've been coding for awhile, you probably figured it out, but if you did, consider whether something less obvious would be as easily understood with coding like *that*. For those of you who don't know what the code is doing, let's apply some coding standards to it.

```
    sub a_iCheckForLeapYear(l_iYear)
    '********************************************
*
    '*  inputs:    l_strInDate - a date               *
    '*  outputs:   none                               *
    '*  returns:   TRUE or FALSE indicating whether   *
    '*               l_strInDate is a leap year, or a *
    '*               number indicating an error condition *
    '*  written:   12/13/1998 by jg                   *
    '*  modified:                                     *
    '********************************************
*
    '
    ' set the return value to FALSE that way we'll only
have to
    ' do TRUE or error assignments
    '
     l_iReturn = FALSE

    '
    ' first we'll check to make sure we have enough
characters
    '   in our input string to support a 4-digit year
    '
     if len(l_strInDate) >= 4 then
    '
    ' grab what should be the year, the last 4
    '   characters of the date
    '
        l_strTempvar = right(l_strInDate,4)
    '
    ' check to see if our substring is numeric
    '
```

```
      if isnumeric(l_strTempvar) then
'
' create a numeric value from the year
'
        l_iYear = val(l_strTempvar)
'
' 1st leap year test - evenly divisible by 4?
'
        if l_iYear / 4 = l_iYear \ 4 then
'
' passed first test
'   2nd leap year test - *not* evenly divisible by
100?
'
            if l_iYear / 100 <> l_iYear \ 100 then
'
' passed second test - we have a leap year
'
                l_iReturn = TRUE
            else 'l_iYear / 100 <> l_iYear \ 100
'
'   3rd leap year test - evenly divisible by 400
'
                if l_iYear / 400 = l_iYear \ 400 then
'
' passed third test - we have one
'
                    l_iReturn = TRUE
                end if  'l_iYear / 400 = l_iYear \ 400
            end if  'l_iYear / 100 <> l_iYear \ 100
        end if  'l_iYear / 4 = l_iYear \ 4
      end if  'isnumeric(l_strTempvar)
  end if  'len(l_strInDate) >= 4
'
' let's return the results to the sending line of
code
'
  checkit = l_iReturn
  end sub
```

Well, hopefully you agree that the second example is easier to comprehend. Yes, there are ways to improve it even more, but it will do. There are a number of elements that make this code easier to follow:

- concise, meaningful comments
- indentation
- meaningful variable names

Whoa Sea Biscuit! Meaningful variable names? All of those variable names look a bit strange — "x" is more normal looking. Ah, but there's a method to the madness— well, to the variable naming at least, and that might be a good place to start the definition of our standards.

5.1 Naming Standards

It's hard enough to pick up a piece of code after a hiatus and figure out what it's doing when you know what the variables hold, let alone when you don't. So, naming them in a way that makes understanding the reason for their existence more intuitive is a good beginning.

With an agreement in place to name in such a way, it's probably a good thing to make sure that the method of naming is consistent. Thus, we'll create naming standards to code from. You can use whatever conventions you want, but I'll put forth some suggestions, which I'll use throughout the book for variables, functions, subroutines and structures.

The key to naming conventions, aside from descriptive names, is to use a series of prefix and/or suffix components to describe architectural characteristics about the item being named. I tend to use prefixes to describe the scope of the item, whether it exists outside the scope of a function or module, and to describe the type of item, such as an integer. I use a suffix to specify whether the item is an element of something, such as a form or database record. Let's take a look at some examples in Table 5-1.

Figure 5-1   Variable Naming Convention

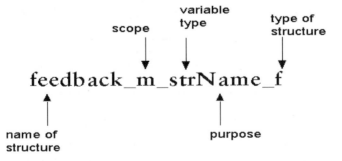

Much clearer now? Okay, somewhat clearer. Let's consider some examples so that we can further clarify. In the preceding code we saw the variable *l_iYear*. If we again look at Table 5-1, we see that this variable is an integer with local scope (see the side bar on Scope). This variable is meant to contain a number representing the year. Taking another example from the code, *l_strInDate*, this variable also has local scope, and is a string meant to contain an input date. One other piece to the naming standards is the prefacing of a standard name with a record name. For example, if we have a form on the page, and the form's name is "feedback," then a field on that form that contains a name might have the name of *feedback_m_strName_f*.

Table 5-1   Naming Conventions

Modifier	Position	Meaning
l_	prefix	local scope (function/ subroutine)
m_	prefix	module scope (Web page)
s_	prefix	session scope (Web site)
i	prefix	integer
tf	prefix	true-false
yn	prefix	yes-no
str	prefix	string
l	prefix	long
f	prefix	float
a_	prefix	array
_f	suffix	form
_db	suffix	database
_s	suffix	function/subprogram

The system makes sense. It's documentable and predictable. And with all that in mind, you might still hate it, but it will do for now. It might seem a bit awkward, but let's take a look at what a block of code might look like.

```
feedback_m_f
    feedback_m_iCustID_f     as integer
```

```
feedback_m_strName_f     as string*36
feedback_m_strAddress_f  as string*36
feedback_m_strCity_f     as string*16
feedback_m_strState_f    as string*2
feedback_m_strZip_f      as string*10
```

Hopefully that makes it look somewhat more meaningful. It might make names longer than you'd like, and you might find a convention that you prefer, but the important thing is that you can look through code you've never seen before and have some idea what the variables are doing. We'll also be able to tell which variable containing the customer's name is part of the database record, and which is part of a form.

SCOPE

When a variable is to be created, thought needs to be given to what access will be needed to the variable.

If the variable is for use within a function or subprogram only, then the variable should be created within the confines of that structure. It will then only be known to exist by that function or subprogram, and is said to have *module scope* – that is, it's only known locally.

If the variable needs to be accessible anywhere within a Web page, it should be created in the main body of the page, and is then said to have *application scope*. It can be accessed by any function and subprogram in the Web page code, as well as from within the main body of the code.

In non-Web programming, a variable can be created outside the confines of an application, and is said to have *session scope* because every program has access to it. In Web programming, each new page requires a reconnection to the Web site, resulting in a loss of state; all information is lost between pages. With Active Server Page (ASP) programming though, there are session variables available, and these variables are maintained for the life of a session – until the user leaves the site or the session times out.

Let's look at a code example.

```
<%
DIM m_iCounter
SUB IncrementCounter_s(l_iIncrementValue)
    m_iCounter = m_iCounter + l_iIncrementValue
    SESSION("s_iMaintainCounter") = m_iCounter
END SUB
%>
```

In the example above, the variable l_iIncrementValue has local scope, it doesn't exist outside the subprogram and is destroyed when the subprogram ends. The variable m_iCounter has module scope, and can be accessed from anywhere in the Web page code. Finally, the session variable s_iMaintainCounter will retain its value so long as the Web site visitor doesn't surf to a new site or time out.

5.2 Coding Standards

With what we covered in the previous section, we know that when we look at the code, we'll be able to decipher what the variables are for. That won't be enough. If the code is "spaghetti code," a big tangle, then we might know what the variables hold, but we won't know what they're being used for.

There are dozens of rules that would make sense for coding standards. Some are specific to the programming language being used and some are generic. I'm not going to cover everything, but let's take a look at those that are the most important and applicable to what we'll be doing:

- The GOTO verb will not be used.
- The preceding rule is inviolate.
- Each statement or group of functional statements will be commented.
- In the case of nested IF statements, each ELSE and END IF will have an inline comment that contains the text of the IF statement.
- Large chunks of code, typically more than 20 lines, should be meaningfully divided into functions or subprograms.
- Global variables should only be used when absolutely necessary.
- CASE statements will be used instead of large IF statements.
- A blank line will be used to separate each function and subprogram.
- Presentation logic and data logic will be segregated from other application logic.

These are only a subset of the coding standards that might be in effect, but they'll do to get the point across. Let's take a close look at each one, so that the importance becomes more evident.

The GOTO verb will not be used.

In code maintenance, there is nothing more aggravating than trying to follow the logic flow of code that has GOTOs in it, and more often than not that code will be uncommented. The GOTO statement causes a permanent transfer of control to another place, like a one-way ticket. I would call for the banning of the statement entirely, but for one thing: the error-handling framework of Visual Basic continues to require the GOTO statement. Aside from that, however, structured code and the GOTO statement should remain mutually exclusive.

The Preceding rule is inviolate.

This is somewhat self-explanatory, but indulge me for a moment. The fact is, it's much easier to use GOTOs — if you're doing the writing. Laying out code in a structured fashion in the form of subprograms and functions is quite a bit of work, but it's worth the investment!

Each statement or functional statement block will be commented.

Don't Trust Your Memory. Okay, someone out there is saying, "but I remember what I had for lunch every day in third grade." Great—then you're way too scary to be programming, so gently put down the book and go watch Jeopardy. For the rest of us, lines of code that are less than blatantly obvious will confound us after a few months, especially lines that we added to cover a hole in our original logic. Do yourself, and everyone who will ever touch the code, a favor and comment! Just think how simple it would have been to find all the lines of code that needed Y2K attention if they were well commented.

In the case of nested IF statements, each ELSE and END IF will have an inline comment that contains the text of the IF statement.

Nested IF statements are evil, but at times a necessary evil. The proper way to code one is to use indentation as shown below, and actually, that indentation should be one of the coding standards.

```
IF thisthing > thatthing THEN
    dosomething(thisthing)
    dosomething(thatthing)
ELSE
    IF thatthing > 10 THEN
        dosomethingelse(thatthing)
    ELSE
        dosomethingelse(thisthing)
    END IF
END IF
```

Those statements were fairly easy to follow, but what happens in real life is that the block of statements between each IF and ELSE, and between each ELSE and END IF can be fairly large (see next rule), and it becomes difficult to see which IF an ELSE belongs to, even with the indentation, so a standard that helps would have the code appear as follows, although we'd probably only use the standard for much longer passages:

```
IF thisthing > thatthing THEN
    dosomething(thisthing)
    dosomething(thatthing)
ELSE 'thisthing > thatthing
    IF thatthing > 10 THEN
        dosomethingelse(thatthing)
    ELSE 'thatthing > 10
        dosomethingelse(thisthing)
    END IF 'thatthing > 10
END IF 'thisthing > thatthing
```

Large chunks of code, typically more than 20 lines, should be meaningfully divided into functions or subprograms.

Imagine picking up the source for an application you've never seen before, looking at a section of 100 lines and trying to figure out what's going on. Then imagine looking at the same code, organized as follows:

```
IF thisimportanttest = TRUE THEN
    GetUserInput_s(...)
    ValidateUserInput_s(m_strField1)
    ValidateUserInput_s(m_strField2)
    FormatOutput_s(...)
    PresentOutput_s(...)
END IF
```

Each of those lines of code temporarily transfers control to a routine with a specific intent. In a few lines of code we can see what the flow is intended to be, and if we want to inspect any part of the functionality in more detail, we can look at that routine. In the real world it might not be this clear cut and easy. For example, we might end up calling a routine *ValidateUserInput* and have *it* make the iterative calls to validate each field.

"Meaningful" is key here. We don't want to create functions and subprograms just to divide the code into smaller chunks—the chunks need to revolve around one theme, one function or action, otherwise we have to look at all the lines in the function to determine what it's doing instead of just looking at the function's name.

Global variables should only be used when absolutely necessary.

Global variables are a scourge upon the earth. Well, maybe they're not that bad, but they can definitely be an evil thing. For one thing, if too many variables are thrown into global space you can run into stack problems, a memory allocation problem that can cause the application to abort. For another thing, if the variable can be accessed from anywhere without being passed, it can be changed from anywhere as well.

Active Server Page (ASP) programming prevents us from entirely abandoning global variables, because in order to maintain values while a user is changing pages, the values need to be kept in session variables, which are global. However, since session variables are all of the form *Session("variable name")*, it's easy to recognize them for what they are.

CASE statements will be used instead of large IF statements.

This standard applies to what would normally be large IF statements that exist to check a series of possible values. For example:

```
IF m_iRecordtype = 1 then
    dosomething
```

```
ELSE
   IF m_iRecordtype = 2 then
      dosomething
   ELSE
      IF m_iRecordtype = 3 then . . .
```

The structure is greatly simplified by using a CASE statement, such as:

```
SELECT CASE m_iRecordtype
   CASE 1:
      dosomething
   CASE 2:
      dosomething
   CASE 3: . . .
```

A blank line will be used to separate each function and subprogram.
Not a whole bunch of commentary is needed here. It's just easier for the eye to determine a beginning or end when there's a break in the blur of code. Another method is to have a structured comment block at the beginning of each routine.

Presentation logic and data logic will be segregated from other application logic. It's very confusing to follow code where data retrieval, presentation and business logic are being done all throughout. It might be easier to check some business rule and, based on the result, affect the presentation, but it's not easier to debug or maintain. Whenever a data or presentation requirement changes, the question of "which part of the code does that require me to change" typically has an answer of "possibly any part."

Maintaining the code will be much easier if the impact can be narrowed to a certain location or set of routines. The way to do this is, for example, to examine the business rules first, and transfer control to a routine that affects the presentation based on the results.

In defining and following a set of coding standards we can keep the code functional, easy to follow and maintainable. Let's move on to a similar but more focused topic, coding standards for HTML.

5.3 HTML Coding Standards

Why does HTML coding require its own standards? Because there are things that apply to HTML that don't apply to other coding. One reason is that it's very difficult to indent with HTML since the indentation white space would become part of the Web page.

- Individual elements, and elements in a series, such as list items and table cells, will each begin on their own line with the series tag appearing first, as follows:

```
<UL>
<LI>Item 1
<LI>Item 2
<LI>Item 3
</ul>
```

There aren't many standards needed for HTML. Keep in mind that there isn't really much HTML in an application Web page. Most of it is JavaScript or VBScript, in which case the standards that apply are coding standards.

5.4 Comments

Just a few comments about comments (sorry, I couldn't resist). Comments should be used liberally. In non-Web programming, there is no performance hit from lacing the source code with comments because the comments are discarded during compilation. However, HTML comments *are* downloaded to the client, which means that for every byte of comment there is an additional byte of Web page that needs to download. I suppose HTML could be changed so that the comments are ignored during download, but that would be disastrous, because comments are used in Web pages for something other than commenting; they're used to hide script and other non-HTML structures from browsers that don't support them. This is accomplished because, although comments are transmitted to the browser, they're not processed unless the browser sees something inside the comment block it understands, such as a script or style sheet.

Following are our comment format standards for HTML and VBScript:

```
<!--
     This is an HTML comment block. The characters in
the
     preceding line start a comment, and the charac-
ters
     in the following line end a comment.
  -->


  '
  ' This is a VBScript comment. An apostrophe not
within
  ' a string indicates a comment. It's best to put a
  ' blank comment line before and after a comment
block
  ' so that it's easy to spot the code between comment
  ' blocks
  '
```

Our routines will have blocks of comment code defining upcoming blocks of program code. In the event that the reason for a particular code statement is not evident, we will have a comment directly preceding that line of code. Any code added at a later date will be preceded by a comment identifying who added it and why.

5.5 Error Handling

HTML doesn't support error handling in the conventional sense, but there are nonfatal errors that need to be processed, specifically, user interaction errors.

- Wherever possible, data entry errors should be captured and processed on the client.
- Error messages should be provided in pop-up browser windows so that the user's input doesn't disappear by being taken to another page.
- Error messages should be meaningful and in plain language.
- The focus should be placed in the field that has the invalid contents.

So, there isn't all that much in the way of error-handling standards, but sometimes it's just a matter of making the user's life a little easier.

CHAPTER 6

The Database

Why on earth would we want or need a database? After all, this is a web site we're creating, not an inventory program. What possible connection can there be between a database and a web page?

The fact is that there *can* be a connection between a web page and a database, in the physical sense as well as the figurative. There *is* technology available that is relatively easy to use, which can allow us to connect a database to our web site. Okay, so why would we want to?

To give this question the consideration it's due, I'm going to provide some background on data management—for free! Before that, though, we should take a look at what we're going to accomplish.

In this chapter, we will:

1. learn why a database is important from the business standpoint
2. design the site database
3. create the site database
4. normalize the design — tweaking the design with a specific intent
5. create the tables
6. create a System Data Source Name (DSN)

6.1 Why A Database?

Databases are kept in a directory that is part of a web site, and accessed via CGI (Common Gateway Interface) or ASP programming. The database is typically relational, and the access typically some flavor of SQL (Structured Query Language), sometimes via ODBC (Open Database Connection), or OLE DB (Object Linking and Embedding).

Some uses of a database on a web site:

- search index
- yellow pages
- portfolio tracking
- product support information
- catalog ordering

All of the above examples require that data be retained and made available based upon specific requests. There are a number of different ways to approach this, but by far the most structured and straight-forward is the use of a database. A typical database scenario can be found in Figure 6-1.

Figure 6-1   Sample Database Transaction

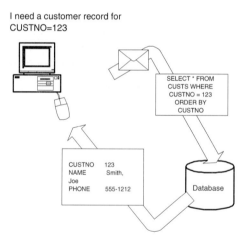

Microsoft Access uses a technology that makes the database a poor choice for large amounts of traffic, but the site isn't expecting a high level of concurrent traffic. However, our design won't be specific to Access, so should the need for a more robust database occur down the road, the design can be used as is with another technology.

6.2 Creating the Database

We'll use the user interface of Microsoft Access to create the database, and later to create the structures within it. You need Access for this because Visual Studio doesn't let you create or alter the database structure for an Access database yet, but hopefully it will in the next release.

So let's run Microsoft Access and begin the creation of our database. We won't do much at this point, but anything hands-on is probably welcome. We have actually reached a plateau, at which point we'll be doing quite a bit of hands-on from this point on.

After launching Access, we'll use the opening dialog (see Figure 6-2) to identify that we want to create a new blank database. We could use the Database Wizard to create the database, but we haven't yet made the decisions necessary to answer the Wizard's questions.

Figure 6-2   MS Access Opening Dialog

Having requested a the creation of a new database, we'll need to identify where we want the file to be placed and what we want to name it. I'm going to select our project directory and name the database after the site, *theblowhole* (see Figure 6-3).

Once we've saved the database (the complete file name is *theblowhole.mdb*), we're presented with a database window (Figure 6-4). From this window we'll later create our tables, but we can't do that until we've decided on the structure. So, putting Access aside for now, let's return to pencil and paper.

Figure 6-3   Saving the New Database

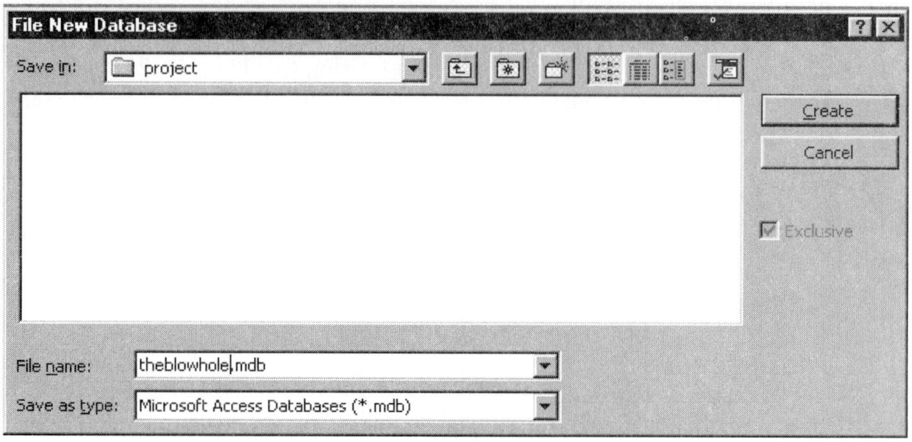

Figure 6-4   Database Window

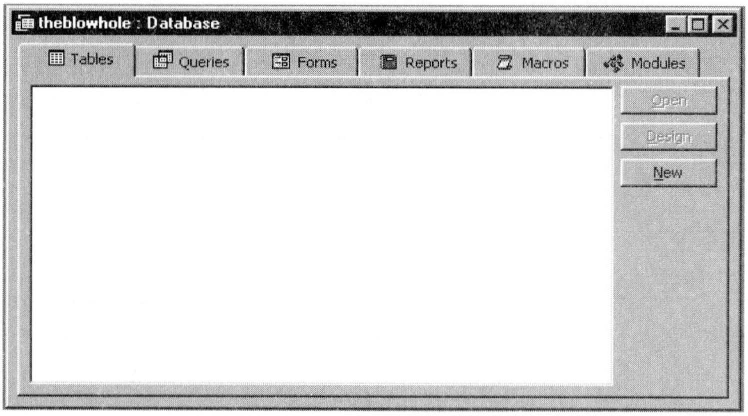

6.3 The Elements

The first step in designing a database is to decide what elements need to be stored in it. We can kill two (virtual) birds with one stone by dividing the elements up logically into tables. What is a table? It's an element of a database containing identically constructed groupings of data, differing only at the data level.

An example of a table is a collection of driver's license applications. Each application holds the same type of information, name, address, birth date and so on, with the data being different for each applicant. If the applications are stored in name order, it's very easy to find a particular application, and, since the application forms are identical, to find the needed information once we find the form. What we need to do is determine what information needs to be on each of our 'forms,' and then design them. First, let's take a look at the types of information that we'll be needing to retrieve based on our site design — often the fallout from this is a good start on tables. Let's start at the highest level of types of information and expand from there.

- categories
- links
- ads

Databases need to start somewhere, and in our case there isn't a tremendous amount that needs to be in it to start. As the site matures, more and more functionality will be added, and as a result more information will be kept in the database. Okay, we have the major types of information, let's move on to the data elements that need to be kept with each.

Table 6-1   Database Tables Draft

Categories	Links	Ads
Category Number	Link Number	Ad Number
Category Name	Link Title	Company
Parent Category	Site Description	Ad Type
Parent Category 2	URL	Image Name
ISBN	Email	URL
Offer Search?		
Book Image	Date Contacted	Email
	Category Number	Phone
	Category Name	Category Name
		Date Contacted
		Expiration Date
		Street Address 1
		Street Address 2
		City
		State/Province
		Country
		Zip/Post Code

6.3.1   Categories

Based on the detailed design we discussed in Chapter 3, we know that a category has a number for internal identification. It also has a name to use to identify it to the visitor. We further know that a category can have up to two parent categories for determining its backward path. And finally, a category can have a recommended book associated with it, and an indication whether there is an image of the book cover — if there is it will be in a predetermined directory, and have a file name the same as the ISBN. If there is no recommendation, an Amazon search will be offered if the search field is set to True.

6.3.2   Links

The links will also have a number for internal tracking and a name. They need to be associated with categories, so we'll need category information too. Also, there will be a description of the link. We'll need the URL of the site, so that when the link is clicked we can send the visitor there. Also, to let the site owner know that his site has been linked, we'll want an email address to which we'll send a notification, and record the date of the notice.

6.3.3   Ads

For each ad we need to know the company doing the advertising. Aside from the company, we need to have a contact, a phone number, an address, and, in this day and age, an email address.

We have three ad banners, and the only way to know which ad is for which banner is to track the type of ad (non-profit, static or rotating), and the category to which the ad applies. The ads aren't permanent, so we'll need to know when the ad ends. Oh yes, we'll also need to know the file name of the ad image.

Lastly, but most important—we'll need the URL of the site we're advertising, otherwise when the visitors click the ad, we won't know where to send them.

Now that we've given some thought to the pieces of data we need, let's create a diagram that shows our tables and their contents (Table 6-1).

In the next section, we will normalize the database, making sure that the tables are laid out to make the most sense in terms of retrieval and avoidance of data duplication. For now, let's assume that our field list is complete and move on to describing and naming each field. Oh, wait a second, it's good practice to record when a record was added as well as the last time it was altered, so we'll add two date fields to each record. Table 6-2 will lay out the attributes of each field.

Table 6-2   Database Field Properties

Field	Field Name	Field Type	Additional Information
Category Number	liCatNo_db	Numeric	Long Integer
Category Name	strCategory_db	Text	60 characters
Parent Category	liParentCatNo_db	Numeric	Long Integer
Parent Category 2	liParentCatNo2_db	Numeric	Long Integer
ISBN	strISBN_db	Text	12 characters
Offer Search?	ynOfferSearch_db	Yes/No	
Book Image	ynImage_db	Yes/No	
Link Number	liLinkNo_db	Numeric	Long Integer
Link Title	strLinkTitle_db	Text	60 characters
Site Description	strSiteDesc_db	Text	128 characters
URL	strURL_db	Text	64 characters
Email	strEmail_db	Text	50 characters
Date Contacted	dtContacted_db	Date/Time	mm/dd/yy
Ad Number	liAdNo_db	Automatic	
Company	strCompany_db	Text	60 characters
Ad Type	strAdType_db	Text	2 characters
Image Name	strImage_db	Text	50 character
Expiration Date	dtExpiration_db	Date/Time	mm/dd/yyyy
Street Address 1	strStreet_db	Text	50 characters
Street Address 2	strStreet2_db	Text	50 characters
City	strCity_db	Text	30 characters
State/Province	strState_db	Text	2 characters
Country	strCountry_db	Text	24 characters
Zip/Post Code	strZipPost_db	Text	10 characters
Date Added	dtCreated_db	Date/Time	mm/dd/yyyy hh:mm
Date Modified	dtModified_db	Date/Time	mm/dd/yyyy hh:mm

With a list of data elements in place, it's time to give some consideration to how we'll use them, and possibly arrange them in a more meaningful manner. Once we've done that, we can add the tables and their fields to the database and move on.

6.4 Normalizing

Let's take a look at a the key data retrieval processes we are likely to require and how they would look given our existing data model, and we can then determine if the model is okay as is.

We'll start with Categories. There are a number of processes that we'll be using with categories:

- retrieve a category based on its number (category listing)
- retrieve a category based on its name (search)
- add a category
- retrieve a category based on its parent's number (category listing)

We can look at this graphically in Figure 6-5. We can see that, regardless of what data item we use to look up one or more records in the database, we're expecting each category number/category name combination to be unique, that is, only one of each category number.

Figure 6-5   Categories Table Transactions

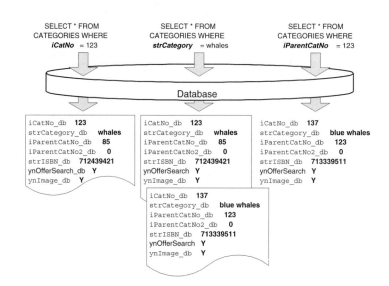

For each field we'll be using to determine a path through the records on the database, we'll want that field to be an index, with the field used in the most used path being a primary key into the table.

The result is that the Categories table is already normalized; there isn't any tweaking we'll need to do to it having identified the indexes.

Let's move on to the Links table. The processing of links has some different requirements than categories:

- retrieve a link based on a category number (link listing)
- add a link
- add a link that applies to more than one category

These processes are shown in Figure 6-6. Now here we run into an interesting situation. First, when we add a link, where does the category information come from? If we depend on the person adding the link to accurately enter category information already present in the category table, there could be data entry errors so that the category number or name is entered incorrectly.

Figure 6-6   Links Table Transactions

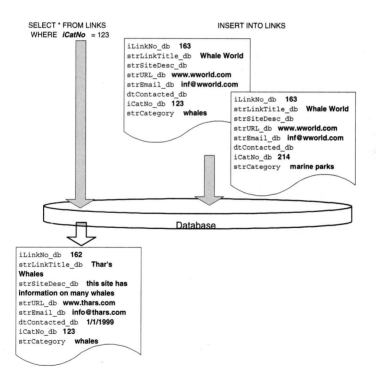

If we want to avoid this, we could possibly have the category information retrieved from the category table record and deposited in the link record. However, look what happens when we have two links applicable to the same category (see Figure 6-7) and one link applicable to two categories—in the former the category information is duplicated in each record, and in the latter the link information is duplicated in each record. This is a waste of space. Not only that, but if the name of a category or description of a link ever changes, instead of changing it in one location in the database we'd have to find every occurrence of it and change each one.

Figure 6-7   Too Much Data

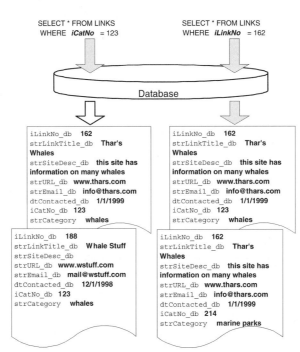

The way to avoid this is to normalize the current Link record by removing the category information from it. We can retrieve the category information from the category table. But then how would we know what category applies to a link? Would we just have a field on the link record in which we put a category number? No, because that would result in a new link record, with duplicated information, every time a link applies to more than one category (Figure 6-8).

Figure 6-8   A Bad Fix

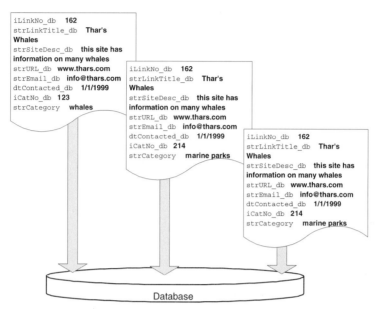

What if we were to have more than one category field on the link record? Well, how many is enough? Two, three, four? There could be many categories applicable to a link, such as a retail store that sells fish, aquariums, fishing tackle, etc. Not only would we use the space for all those fields on every record whether they were needed or not, but every one of those fields would need to be checked on every record on every search. For example, if we wanted a Link that applies to category 123, we would need to check all the category fields on a link record to see if any were equal to 123.

Another approach we could take is to have a bridging table. This is a table used to form a bridge between other tables while avoiding data duplication. In our case, we could create a table as shown in Figure 6-9 that contains only a link number and a category number. Thus, if a link applies to four categories, we would have four of these entries. If four different links applied to one category, four more records. These two scenarios are shown in Figure 6-10 and Figure 6-11.

This seems to work very well. One drawback is that there are additional database reads required, since this table provides our pathway through the Categories table and Links table when needing information from both, but the simplicity of it makes it well worth the additional overhead. We'll use this approach, call the table LinkCat, and set each field as an index.

Figure 6-9   Categories-Links Table

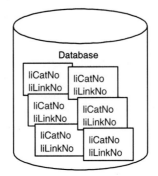

Figure 6-10   One Link : Four Categories

liCatNo   123
liLinkNo   345

  liCatNo   144
  liLinkNo   345

    liCatNo   218
    liLinkNo   345

      liCatNo   345
      liLinkNo   345

Figure 6-11   Four Links : One Category

liCatNo   123
liLinkNo   345

  liCatNo   123
  liLinkNo   1512

    liCatNo   218
    liLinkNo   22

      liCatNo   345
      liLinkNo   790

The resulting Link table is shown in Figure 6-12, and now we can safely decide that there only needs to be one entry per link, so that the link number with this table will be unique. Since there can be multiple LinkCat entries with the same link number, the relationship between the two tables is considered to be one-to-many. The same goes for the relationship between the Categories table and LinkCat.

We're down to the last table now — Ads. Looking back at the fields in this table, we see that we can face the same issue that we did with the Links table, that the contact and address information will be duplicated for any ad purchased by the same customer. So, it would seem that the direction to move in would be to separate the address from the table and put it in an Address table, and perhaps do the same thing with contact and company.

Figure 6-12   LinkCat Table

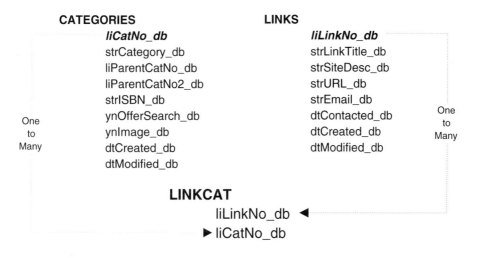

There is a trade-off when doing this, however. Daniel Pratt paid a visit to Caitlin Brookton's lead designer, Megan Bell, and laid out the issue to her. After listening to the options, Megan decided that in this case the economies of those efficiencies would be overshadowed by the coding necessary to maintain the relationships of the various tables. She has no desire to maintain the customer list at that level, what with the possibilities that two different ads can be purchased by different contacts at different locations of the same company.

Is our design for the ad table fine? No, there is one further complication. The current table design has a field to hold the category number. What if the ad is purchased for more than one category? Do we want duplicate ad records? No, that much inefficiency would be ridiculous.

We're going to create a bridging table here as well. This table contains the fields *liCatNo_db* and *liAdNo_db*. The resulting table, AdCat, can be seen in Figure 6-13.

With the Ads and AdCat tables out of the way, we've completed our normalizing activity. A map of the complete database appears in Figure 6-14. With this map, and the field definitions in Figure 6-2, we're prepared to go back to the client application of Microsoft Access and create the tables for our database.

Figure 6-13   AdCat Table

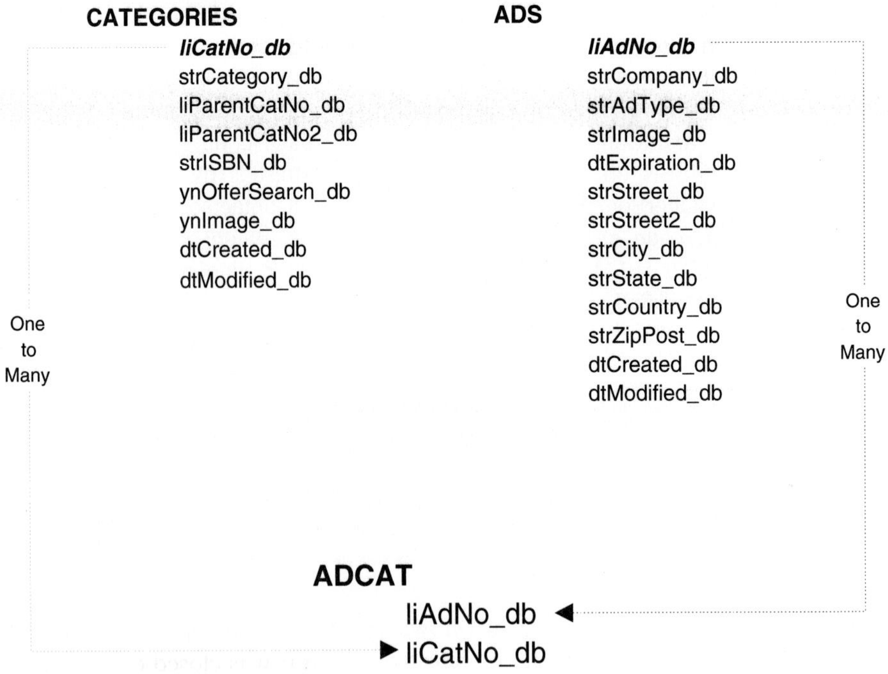

Figure 6-14   The Blowhole Database

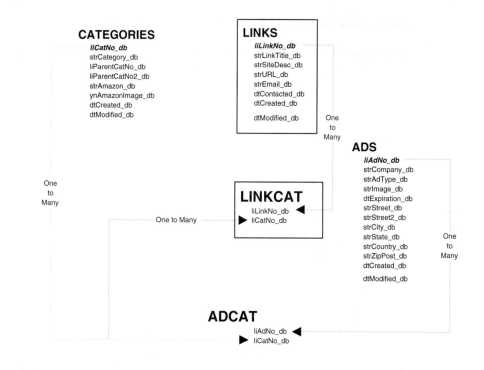

6.5 Creating the Database Tables

6.5.1   Categories

The first step in creating a new database table is to let Access know that we have a new tables to create. We'll want to reopen the database if it was closed earlier, and click the *Tables* tab on the database dialog. We'll then click on the *New* button (see Figure 6-15) and proceed to the next dialog—New Table.

From the New Table dialog (Figure 6-16) there are several choices. For someone who wants to drive the table definition from sample data, the *Datasheet View* might be good. For someone with little experience in creating a table, the *Table Wizard* could be the better choice. We'll select the *Design View*, since we have a chart that provides most of the information we need.

We'll now be presented with a blank table layout (see Figure 6-17). We'll go through this layout entering one field at a time. The *Field Name* column is where we name the data item, *liCatNo_db*, for example. The second column is *Data Type*, and it's

Figure 6-15   New Table

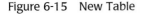

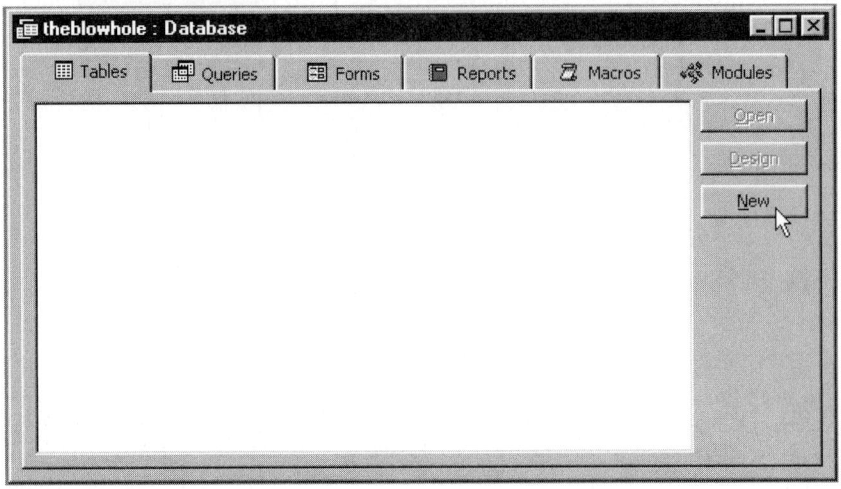

Figure 6-16   New Table Dialog

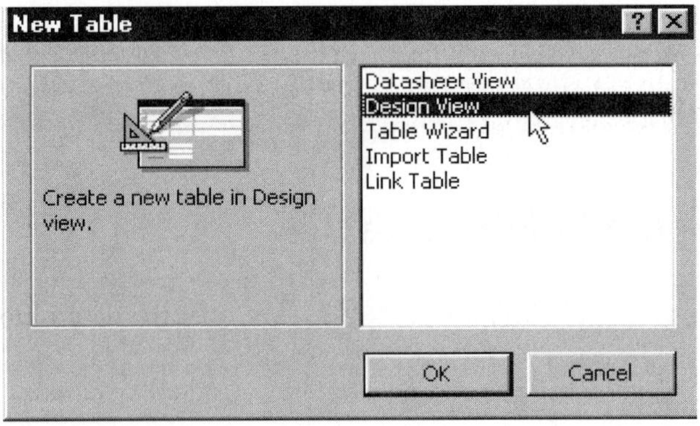

here that we define the field as being, for example, *text*, *numeric* or *date*. The final column is *Description*, and this entry is purely for documentation, typically a place to record what the intention is for the data item.

The tabbed dialogues on the bottom left provide the opportunity to define additional requirements and formatting information for the field. The dialog options vary for different field types, so we'll cover them as we get to them.

Figure 6-17   Table Definition

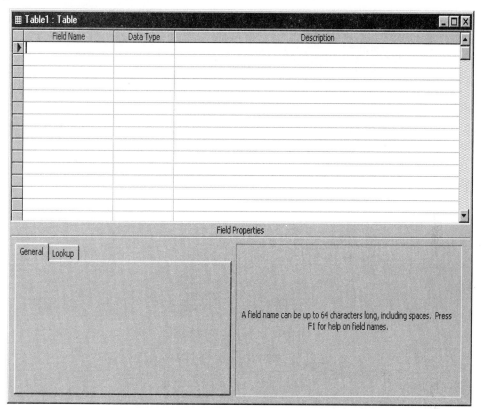

6.5.1.1   liCatNo_db

The first field we'll enter is *liCatNo_db*. From the *Field Type* list box we'll choose *Number*, since we'll be assigning numeric values to it. In the description field, we'll note that this is the primary key for our table.

Before we move to the tabbed dialog, we'll click the key icon on the toolbar at the top of the screen to select this field as a primary key by which we'll normally search this table. A primary key is an index, and we'll discuss the use of indexes a bit later.

Now, moving to the tabbed dialog, we see that it's changed to match the context of our current field type, *Number* (see Figure 6-18). In this dialog we will provide further information about *liCatNo_db*.

The first consideration is the *Field Size*, which in the context of a number is determined by the type of number we use. If we click the arrow on the list box and drop it down, we see a selection of types. Each type of number is stored differently internally, and thus will allow a different and distinct range of values to be kept. A discussion of each number type applicable to us can be found in Table 6-3.

Figure 6-18   Number Definition Context

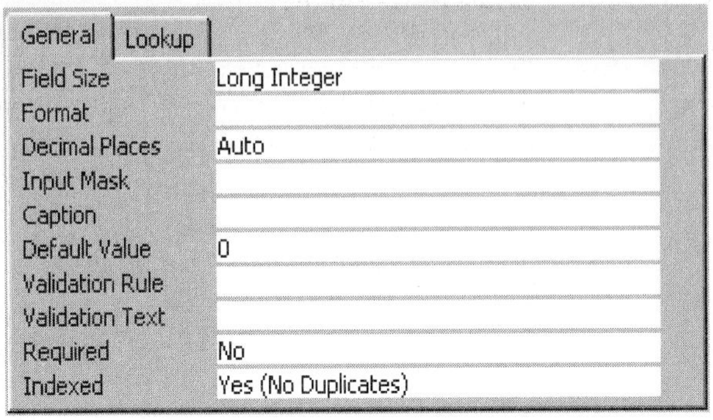

General	Lookup	
Field Size	Long Integer
Format	
Decimal Places	Auto
Input Mask	
Caption	
Default Value	0
Validation Rule	
Validation Text	
Required	No
Indexed	Yes (No Duplicates)

Table 6-3   Number Types

Number Type	Storage	Values
Byte	1 byte	0 to 255
Integer	2 bytes	-32,786 to 32,767
Long Integer	4 bytes	-2,147,483,648 to 2,147,483,647
Single (Floating Point)	4 bytes	-3.402823E38 to -1.401298E-45 for negative values 1.401298E-45 to 3.402823E38 for positive values
Double (Floating Point)	8 bytes	-1.79769313486232E308 to -4.94065645841247E-324 for negative values; 4.94065645841247E-324 to 1.79769313486232E308 for positive values

The category number will be an integer. As the site could eventually have well over 32,767 categories, we'll play it safe and define the field as being a *long integer*. The format will be *fixed*, in that all entries will have the same format. We'll be having only whole values, so we'll set *decimal places* to 0. We won't be using Access' GUI as part of the web site, so the next field in this dialog that interests us will be *Required*. Although we'll be providing validation within our web pages, better safe than sorry. We'll change this value to "Yes," and rest easy knowing that we'll receive a database error should we somehow try to add a record with no key. The final field, *Indexed,* was set for us when we clicked the key icon to name the field as being a primary key.

An index is a value usable in a search for records. The simplest way to conceptualize this is to consider this book. If I sent you to the book and, considering each page of the book to be a database record, asked you to provide me with the number of each record in which "database" is mentioned, you'd have two options: use the index, which names each key (a word or phrase) and its address (a page number), or read every page in the book looking for "database." If the key can appear on more than one page then we'll need to identify the index as "Yes (Duplicates OK)," otherwise we'd select "Yes (No Duplicates)."

Since we've normalized our database so that the Category table need only have one occurance of any category number/name pair, we'll leave it set to "Yes (No Duplicates)." Where would we want to use the other possibility? One example would be an order table. If one of the indexes is customer number, assuming we're not restricting our customers to only one order we'd define this index as allowing duplicates.

Note **An index that allows duplicate values can not be a primary key, which is why when we clicked the key icon Access set this field to "Yes (No Duplicates)."**

Okay, one down. The completed dialog can be seen in Figure 6-19. Let's move on to the next field.

Figure 6-19   liCatNo_db Settings

General	Lookup	
Field Size	Long Integer	
Format	Fixed	
Decimal Places	0	
Input Mask		
Caption		
Default Value	0	
Validation Rule		
Validation Text		
Required	Yes	
Indexed	Yes (No Duplicates)	

6.5.1.2 strCategory_db

This field will contain the name of the category, and thus we'll define it as being of type *Text.* On the tabbed dialog, we're going to make the field a size that will hold large category names, so 60 characters will do. We don't need to worry about format for a text field, so we can move down to *Required* and set it to "Yes." With a text field we have to consider whether we will allow an empty entry. Since the category name defines the category, we do not want empty entries, so we'll set *Allow Zero Length* to "No." The last consideration is whether this represents an index into the table. We will be searching by category name when the visitor uses the Find box, so this will be an index. Will duplicates be allowed? Actually, the answer is "Yes." The reason is that different category trees may have the same categories. For example, there might be a category for "Basic Education" as child under "Saltwater Aquariums" and under "Scuba Diving."

6.5.1.3 liParentCatNo_db and liParentCatNo2_db

Why do we have two parent catalog number fields? I just finished explaining that if we have two categories with the same name, they'll be different records. In that case, those category entries, and their associated links, have nothing in common except the name. Here, we're talking about the one category that can be navigated to in two different ways. For example, if we start with a category of "Wildlife", work our way down through "Fish" and end up at "Tahiti." We might also end up at the same place following a completely different path, but still want to know more about Tahiti. For that reason, we'll provide for the possibility of two paths. We could possibly need more, but again, Megan decided that she'd prefer to address the possibility and effort of a bridging table at a later date if necessary and simply allow for two paths at present.

The definition for these two fields is the same as the definition for *liCatNo_db*, except that we'll allow duplicates in the index and they're not primary keys. So let's plug that information in and move on to the next field.

6.5.1.4 strISBN_db

The ISBN for a book is 12 characters in length (including two hyphens) and alphanumeric in nature, so we'll define the field as being *Text*. We will not be performing a search based on the ISBN, so we do not need to make this field an index. Also, since not every category will have a recommended book, we will not make this field required.

6.5.1.5 ynOfferSearch_db

This is the first field of this type in our database. We will be using this field to record whether we want to offer the visitor a search of the Amazon.com database based on the category name — some categories are just too generic for this. So, all we need to know is: "Yea or nay." Access supports a data type that makes this easy for us. It holds one of two values, Yes (true) or No (false). After selecting *Yes/No* as the data type in the tabbed dialog, we just need to set the *Required* field to "Yes," and we're done. This field will not be an index.

6.5.1.6 ynImage_db

This field will inform us as to whether there is an image of the cover of the recommended book. If there is, the file name of the image will be the ISBN appended to ".gif". This field will be defined the same as *ynOfferSearch_db*.

6.5.1.7 dtCreated_db and dtModified_db

The final fields in our table will contain dates. One will indicate the date the record was created, the other the date on which the record was last changed. We'll start by defining the field as *Date/Time*. On the tabbed dialog, we'll define the format as *General Date*, which will hold an entry such as "6/10/99 5:20:19 PM."

For the *Default Value* we'll enter *Now()*. This will default to the two fields being equal to the current date and time when the record is created. We'll leave *Required* on these fields set to "No," since we'll let the system worry about filling them in. The completed tabbed dialog can be seen in Figure 6-20.

Figure 6-20   dtCreated_db and dtModified_db Settings

General	Lookup	
Format	General Date
Input Mask	
Caption	
Default Value	Now()
Validation Rule	
Validation Text	
Required	No
Indexed	No

The completed table is shown in Figure 6-21. The final thing we need to do is save the table. So, we choose *File* then *Save* from the menu, and name the table *Categories*. One down, three to go.

Figure 6-21   Categories Table

Field Name	Data Type	Description
liCatNo_db	Number	This field is our primary key
strCategory_db	Text	The name of the category
liParentCatNo_db	Number	Category that preceeds this one
liParentCatNo2_db	Number	Category that preceeds this one in alternate path
strISBN_db	Text	The ISBN of a recommended book on this category
ynOfferSearch_db	Yes/No	Should an Amazon.com search for this category be offered in the absence of an ISBN?
ynImage_db	Yes/No	Is there an image of the recommended book? If Yes, the name will be ISBN+.gif
dtCreated_db	Date/Time	Record creation date
dtModified_db	Date/Time	Record modified date

6.5.2 Links

We'll start this table the same way we did the Categories table, by selecting *New* from the database dialog, and then selecting *Design View*. Having done that we're ready to move on to defining each of the fields. Since we've gone over the considerations surrounding each of the data types, I'll summarize by providing a table (Table 6-4).

Table 6-4   Links Field Definitions

Field Name	Data Type	Field Size	Format	Dec Place	Req	Index
liLinkNo_db	Number	Long Int	Fixed	0	Y	Yes (No Dups)
strLinkTitle_db	Text	60			Y	No
strSiteDesc_db	Text	128			N	No
strURL_db	Text	64			Y	No
strEmail_db	Text	50			N	No
dtContacted_db	Date		General		N	No
dtCreated_db	Date		General		N	No
dt_Modified_db	Date		General		N	No

The field information for the Links table can be seen in Figure 6-22. The only thing worth mentioning from the above table is that the field *strURL_db* is required because a link is worthless unless it has a destination; the visitor would be clicking on it and going nowhere.

Figure 6-22   Links Table

Field Name	Data Type	Description
liLinkNo_db	Number	Identifying number for the link
strLinkTitle_db	Text	Title of site we're linking to
strSiteDesc_db	Text	Description of site
strURL_db	Text	URL of site
strEmail_db	Text	Email address of site contact
dtContacted_db	Date/Time	Date site was contacted about link
dtCreated_db	Date/Time	Date record was created
dtModified_db	Date/Time	Date record was last modified

6.5.3   LinkCat

The LinkCat table is the bridging table that we created to bridge the Categories and Links table. As we mentioned earlier, this table will have but two fields, *liCatNo_db* and *liLinkNo_db*. The two fields will be defined just as they were within the Categories and Links tables respectively.

Since neither field will hold a value that is unique to the table (there can be many records referring to the same category, as well as many occurrences of a link which applies to many categories), there will be no primary key, and both fields will be defined as indexes allowing duplicate values. Because of this, both need to be required values.

When we go to save this table as *LinkCat*, Access will warn us that no Primary Key is specified, and ask if we want to specify one. We'll select "No," and complete the save. The final table is shown in Figure 6-23.

Figure 6-23   LinkCat Table

Field Name	Data Type	Description
liCatNo	Number	Category number of the category that applies to this link
liLinkNo_db	Number	Identifying number for the link

6.5.4   Ads

The Ads table will hold the information related to a site advertisement. The field information is shown in Table 6-5, and the table dialog is shown in Figure 6-24, in which you can see that the ad number, *liAdNo_db* has been made the Primary Key.

6.5.5   AdCat

The final table in our database is another simple one. *AdCat* is the bridging table between the Ads table and the Categories table. It will look just like the LinkCat table, except that instead of having the field *liLinkNo_db* it has the field *liAdNo_db*.

6.5.6   Summary

We've finished creating our database. If we look at the database main window in Figure 6-25 we can now see the tables listed. There's only one problem now, and that's that when the user connects to our web site, they can only access files by URL, not by a typical PC path name. Databases cannot be accessed by URL, so how will the web page provide access to our database? The answer is in the next and final section of this chapter.

Table 6-5   Ads Field Definitions

Field Name	Data Type	Field Size	Format	Dec Place	Req	Index
liAdNo_db	Number	Long Int	Fixed	0	Y	Yes (No Dups)
strCompany_db	Text	60			Y	Yes (Dups OK)
strAdType_db	Text	2			Y	No
strImage_db	Text	50			Y	No
strURL_db	Text	64			Y	No
strEmail_db	Text	50			N	No
strPhone_db	Text	15			N	No
dtExpiration_db	Date		General		Y	No
strStreet_db	Text	50			N	No
strStreet2_db	Text	50			N	No
strCity_db	Text	30			N	No
strState_db	Text	2			N	No
strCountry_db	Text	24			N	No
strZipPost_db	Text	10			N	No
dtContacted_db	Date		General		N	No
dtCreated_db	Date		General		N	No
dtModified_db	Date		General		N	No

Figure 6-24   Ads Table

Field Name	Data Type	Description
liAdNo_db	Number	Identifying number for the ad
strCompany_db	Text	Company that owns the ad
strAdType_db	Text	Type of Ad: NP=non-profit FS=for-profit static FR=for-profit rotating
strImage_db	Text	Name and path of the ad image
strURL_db	Text	URL of Company
strEmail_db	Text	Email of Company contact
strPhone_db	Text	Phone number of Company contact
dtExpiration_db	Date/Time	Date and time that the ad expires
strStreet_db	Text	First line of Company's street address
strStreet2_db	Text	Second line of Company's street address
strCity_db	Text	Company City in address
strState_db	Text	State or Canadian province of Company
strCountry_db	Text	Country of Company
strZipPost_db	Text	Zip Code or Post Code of Company
dtContacted_db	Date/Time	Date Company was contacted
dtCreated_db	Date/Time	Date record was created
dtModified_db	Date/Time	Date record was last modified

Figure 6-25   Table List

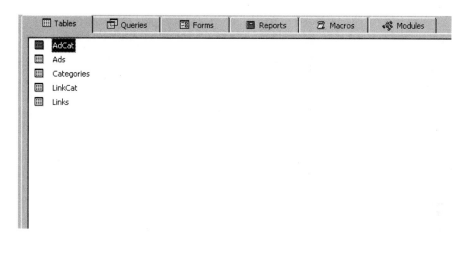

6.6 Creating the Data Source Name

A Data Source Name (DSN) is a name that can be referenced by a web page that points to a physical data structure on the host computer. Thereby, a web page can access a database, and can do it without having to know where the database is. We need to create a Data Source Name on our development system so that we can access our database. When the web site is actually put on a web hoster's server, the web hoster will need to create the DSN for us. The first step is to run the ODBC software found in the Control Panel (see Figure 6-26).

Once launched, we'll want to click on the *System DSN* tab on the initial dialog. We want the reference to this data source to be available system-wide (see Figure 6-27).

When we click on the *Add* button, we're presented with the *Create New Data Source* dialog (Figure 6-28). We're going to select *Microsoft Access Driver* from the list of potential data provider drivers, since our database is an Access database. In clicking the *Finish* button we're provided with the dialog for *ODBC Microsoft Access 97 Setup* (Figure 6-29).

We'll name our DSN *TheBlowHoleDSN*, and then click on the *Select* button to point the DSN to the actual database, in this case *C:\project\theblowhole.mdb*. Once we've done that we'll click on *OK* and have our DSN (Figure 6-30). That's it for this chapter. We've created the database and the tables inside it to hold the data needed for our web site, and created the Data Source Name so that we can access the database from our web pages. In the next chapter, we'll create the graphics we'll be using on our web pages.

Figure 6-26   Control Panel

Figure 6-27   System DSN

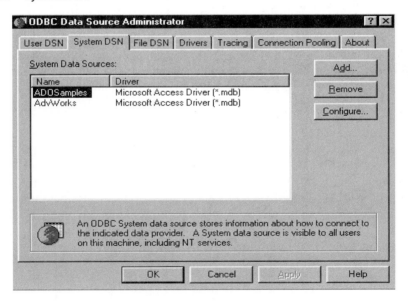

Figure 6-28   New Data Source Dialog

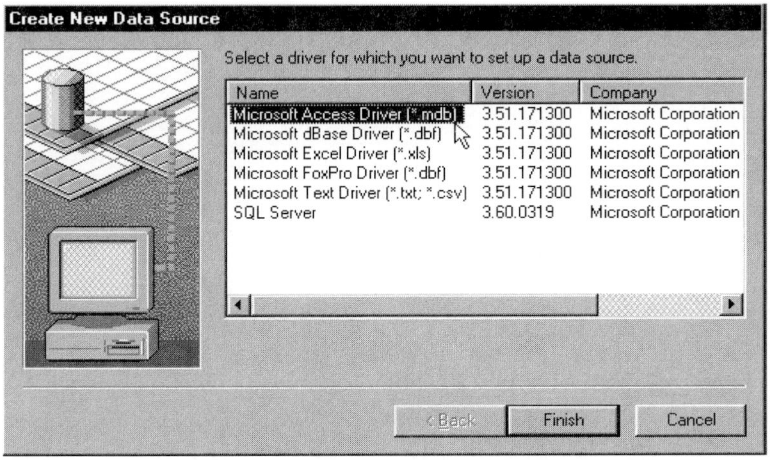

Figure 6-29   MS Access DSN Setup

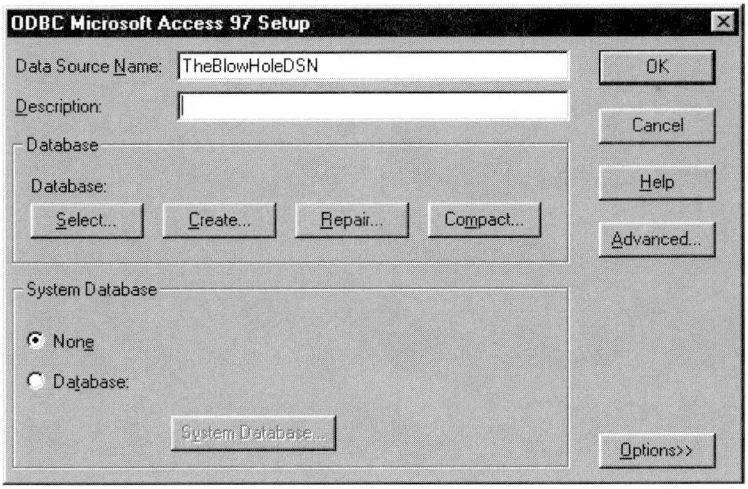

Figure 6-30   TheBlowHole DSN

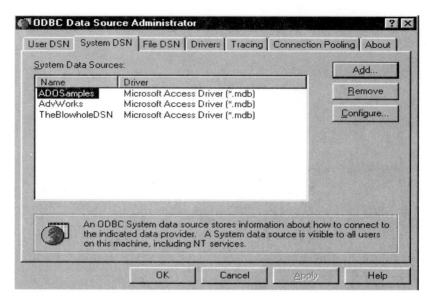

CHAPTER 7

The Graphics

*T*his chapter is going to be a ton of fun! Promise!! Why? Because we're going to create a number of different graphical elements for our pages. You might be wondering why I consider this activity to be fun. You might say, "I'm not an artist." That's okay, you don't need to be an artist. We'll be drawing very little from scratch. For the most part we'll be modifying existing graphics to suit our needs.

I consider this to be fun because there's virtually no debugging to be done when creating graphics — literally what you see is what you get — almost all the time.

Why are graphics important enough to warrant a chapter? If you're visually stimulated like most people, the Web sites you will respond to the most positively are those that are aesthetically pleasing. What affects the aesthetics of a Web page more than anything else are the graphical elements on the page.

Sure, there are other elements that contribute to the appearance of a Web page such as the text and all of its characteristics such as size and font. However, the graphics typically catch the visitor's eye first.

Let's create a list of graphics that we'll need for our site.

- a logo banner
- a "Find" button
- category navigation icons
- a banner ad

In this chapter we'll also use these applications for graphics manipulation:

- Paint Shop Pro
- Image Composer

Each has its uses, and while this chapter isn't going to be a complete reference manual, you will learn how to perform various functions with each of them.

> **Note** A big consideration in page design is download time, which increases with the number of graphics. Use graphics sparingly, take measures to reduce their Kb size, and make them look good.

7.1 Button It Up

I purposely selected this graphic to work on first because you will quickly see from the exercise that graphics aren't too hard if the tools are good. One of the function points on the home page is a button. When the user clicks the button, the character string that was entered in the text box beside the button is searched for on the Web site.

HTML has an input type of "button" that will create a button much like the one typically used to submit information on a Web form. So why don't we use one of those instead of creating a graphic? Figure 7-1 shows one of the reasons. It displays a Web page consisting of two buttons; one defined with a width of 10 pixels and a height of 5 pixels, the other with a width of 30 pixels and a height of 2 pixels by the following HTML code.

```
<INPUT TYPE="BUTTON" HEIGHT="10" WIDTH="5">
<INPUT TYPE="BUTTON" HEIGHT="30" WIDTH="2">
```

Figure 7-1   Button Problems

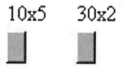

If you're thinking that the two buttons look similar, you're correct. In fact, they're identical. How can they be identical? Are the HTML statements incorrect? No, the syntax is fine. The reason for this is that HTML, or the browser itself, doesn't seem to tolerate buttons smaller than a certain size — and that size is larger than what we're asking for in both cases. The resulting buttons are thus the minimum size the browser will display. So, since we want a smaller button than what the browser is willing to give us, we'll have to create our own.

To do this we'll use Paint Shop Pro. The first thing we need to do is create a new image. Figure 7-2 shows the dialog box to accomplish this. We want the image to be 28 pixels wide by 15 pixels high. Pixels are the appropriate unit of measurement to work with, because items dimensioned in that way stay in proportion regardless of the screen density, whereas if a button were an inch wide on all screens, it would look quite different at 800x600 than it would at 1028x760. We'll set the resolution at 96 pixels/inch because that's the standard for screen display, and set the Image type to 16.7 million colors because an effect we'll be using later requires that the image be that type.

Figure 7-2   Creating an Image in Paint Shop Pro

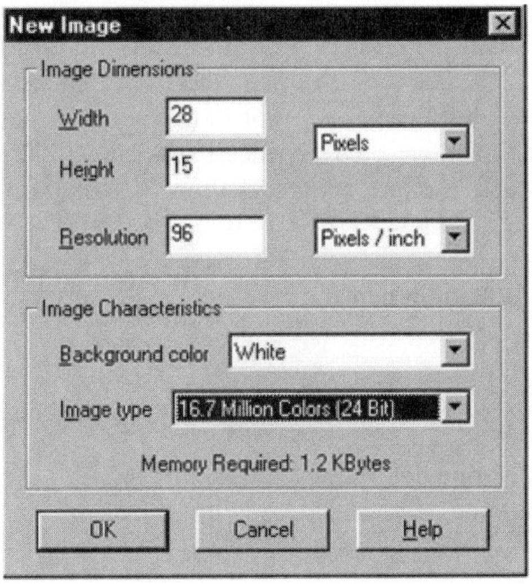

Once we click on the *OK* button we're presented with a new, blank image as shown in Figure 7-3. This is our blank palette on which to create our illustration. A white palette makes it easier to see any elements we draw, except of course if they're white, in which case we can either select a different color background when we create the image, or change it later.

Figure 7-3   New Paintshop Pro Image

The purpose of this button is to activate a search. So what do we have right now? It doesn't look much like a button, and if I were looking at it I'd have no clue that clicking it is going to activate a search. We need to do a few things to it. Normally, when creating a graphic that will have text superimposed on it, I would choose to use Image Composer because it allows each element of the graphic to be created as a separate layer, and these layers can be maintained in the event that editing is required at a later time. Most other paint programs merge any element added to the graphic into one large layer, making editing difficult later on. Paint Shop Pro supports its own implementation of layers, but I use Image Composer out of personal preference. What I'd typically do is create the background, in this case a button, and then add the text on top, but we're not going to be doing that here. The reason will become apparent.

The next thing we want to do is put a caption on the button. To do that we'll use the text tool (see Figure 7-4). The text tool provides us with a cross-hair cursor. I've never quite figured out where I should put the cursor in relation to where I want the text, but it doesn't matter because I can move the text once I create it. So I'm going to place the cursor about where I'd like the top left corner of the text to be and click (Figure 7-5) and click.

Figure 7-4   Selecting the Text Tool

Figure 7-5   The Text Cursor

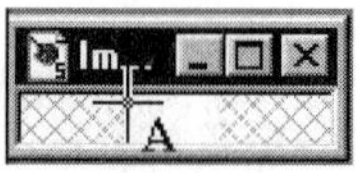

We're now presented with a dialog in which we'll define the text we want and its associated properties (Figure 7-6). I'm going to select "Arial" as the typeface. Arial is a sans-serif font, that is, a typeface that does not have fancy bits (serifs). A good example is the following letters, first in the serif typeface of this text, and then sans-serif.

q q J J

When reading text that is particularly small, such as the caption we'll have on our button, a sans-serif font is much easier to read because there's less detail to preserve in such small lettering. I'll choose *regular* as the style instead of *bold* or *italic* for the same reason. The size needs to be 8-point, because it's the largest size to fit the button well. I know that because I've already created the button, but normally it's trial and error; create text of one size, and if it's too big or small, delete it and create it in another size. I'll check the box next to Antialias. An item on the screen is composed of dots, and when the item's size is such that there is only room for a small number of dots to represent it, the appearance can start to become jagged — a prime example being a diagonal line. When a raster graphics object, an object drawn from an array of dots is resized, the introduction of these "jaggies" is called "aliasing." To prevent this phenomenon, "antialiasing" procedures fill in the spaces between jagged edges with a tonal color. If the item is black, gray will be used. Figure 7-7 shows an enlargement of two lines, one antialiased and one not, and shows the results of enlarging a character.

Figure 7-6   Entering the Text

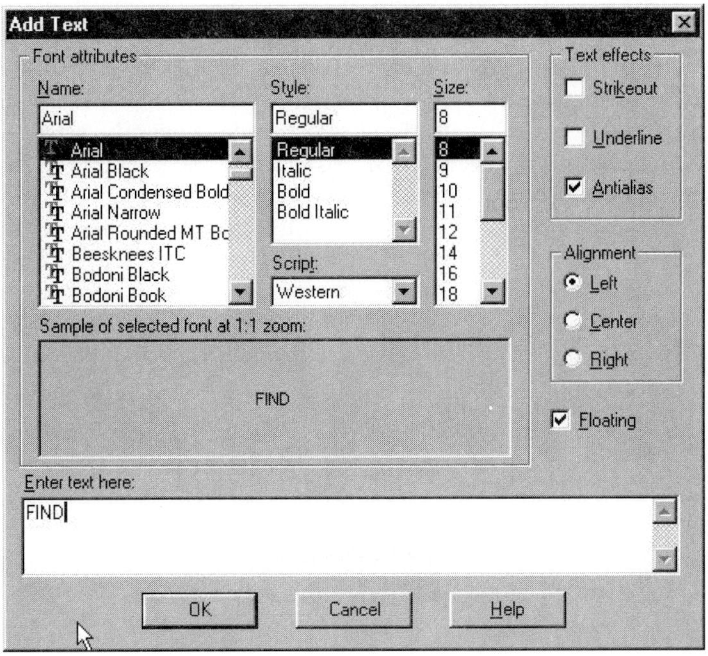

Figure 7-7   AntiAliasing

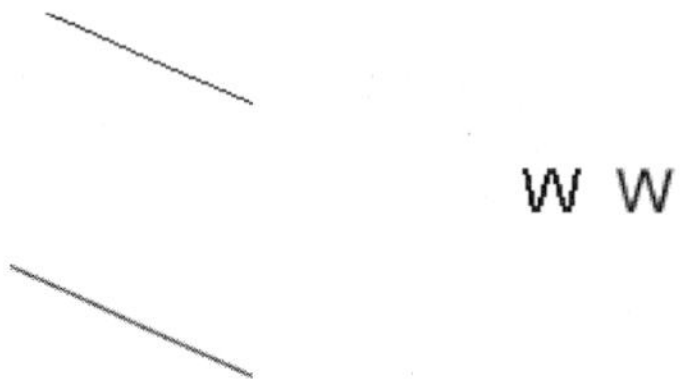

W W

    We'll choose antialiasing for our text because it will make it easier to read. Now, what should the caption say? The logical choice is *Search,* but on this small a button *Find* will allow us larger characters, so we'll type "FIND" in the *Enter Text here* box. Let's click on *OK* and see what we end up with. It doesn't look like much, but that's because the text is surrounded by a mask—a border that surrounds the imaginary rectangle around the text. The mask flickers and makes it hard to read the text, but right now what we want to do is move the text to the right place. While the text is selected, as indicated by there being a mask around it, move the cursor anywhere over the mask so that the cursor appears as compass arrows (Figure 7-8). Now is the time to click and drag the text so that it is centered within our "canvas." Once we've done that, we'll drop the mask around the text by clicking the *Selections* menu item, and then *Select none* as shown in Figure 7-9. Now we have a nice clean rectangle that says "FIND." It doesn't look like much of a button though, does it? Buttons are supposed to look fairly three-dimensional — time to do some magic to our graphic.

    The first thing we need to do is make sure that the background color of the button is the color we want to work with. To do this, we set the background color in Paint Shop Pro.

Figure 7-8   Moving the Text

Figure 7-9 Unmasking the Text

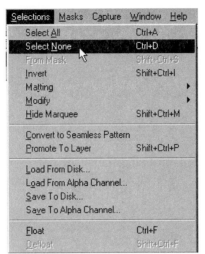

Changing the background color is fairly simple. First we want to click on the current background color. On the right-hand side of the screen, there are two rectangles, one partially covering the other. The rectangle on top is the foreground color, and the one behind the background color. To change the background color, we click on the background color rectangle. This will result in a dialog being displayed such as the one in Figure 7-10.

Figure 7-10 Changing Background Color

The color dialog represents a color wheel, which allows the selection of virtually any visible color. There are a number of items worth noting in this dialog:

- Basic Colors — the squares in this area of the dialog represent the colors that are standard in the palette with which you are working. Clicking on one of the squares will select the color
- Current Color — when a color is selected, its identification is presented using

three of the four common identification systems, which can also be used for data entry to select a color:

- RGB — the color based on its content of red, green and blue light, with each composite color content ranging from 0 to 255
- HSL — the color as represented by its hue (tint), saturation (shade) and luminance or light. The values range from 0 to 255.
- HTML Code — again, RGB, but represented with hexadecimal values (Base 16 instead of Base 10) for use within Web pages
- CMYK — the one system that's conspicuously absent, where RGB is the composition based on light, this is the composition based on pigments of Cyan, Magenta, Yellow and blacK. I mention it for completeness.

- Add Custom — this button will take the current color, as selected through clicking on a color or by data entry in one of the other fields, and add it to your color palette as a custom entry, so that it can be selected again at another time from one of the custom color squares.
- Color Wheel — the color wheel provides a way of selecting a color by Hue. Once the hue is selected, the square within the wheel or the dialog boxes can be used to select Saturation (left to right in the box) and Luminance (top to bottom).

We're going to use one of the standard palette colors. Before we select it, let's discuss the influence of software developers upon us. Think of a button, any button, anything you encounter in a normal day that's pressable, even a key on your keyboard. Now, how many of them are gray? Not many, if any. Yet, if you were expecting to encounter a clickable button on the screen, what color would it be? Yup, gray. I don't know why, but since we've been conditioned in this manner, I'll stick to it with our button. So in the Basic Colors boxes, I'll select light gray (Figure 7-11). When I click the square, the information about this color appears in the other dialog boxes. I'll click *OK*, and the background color square on the main screen will change to the newly selected light gray. Now it's time to turn that rectangle into a button. First stop — selection of the *Buttonize* menu option (Figure 7-12). In response to our click, we're given a dialog box to set the property values of our button (Figure 7-13). We're not going to change anything in this dialog, although of course you're free to experiment by changing settings.

Figure 7-11   Changing Background Color

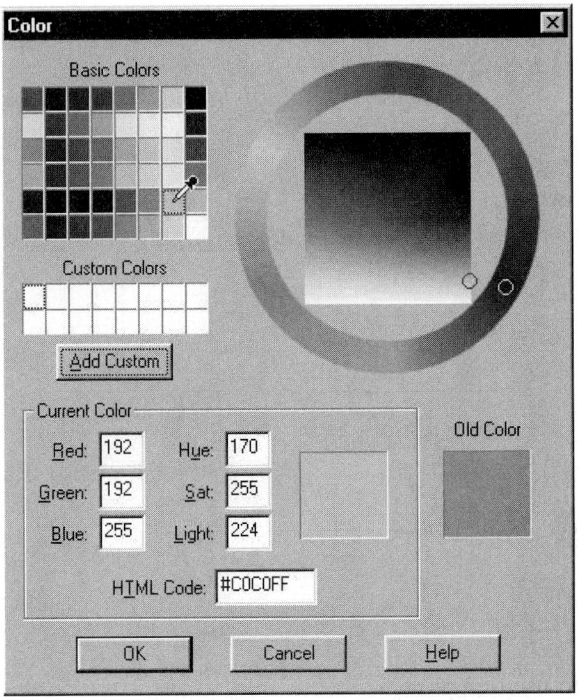

Figure 7-12   Buttonize

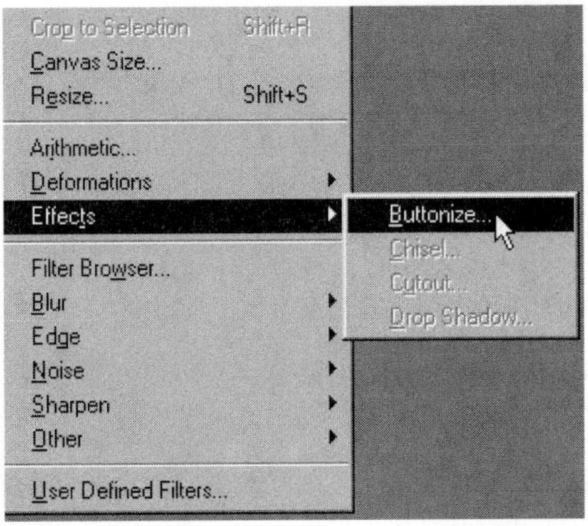

Figure 7-13   Buttonize Dialog

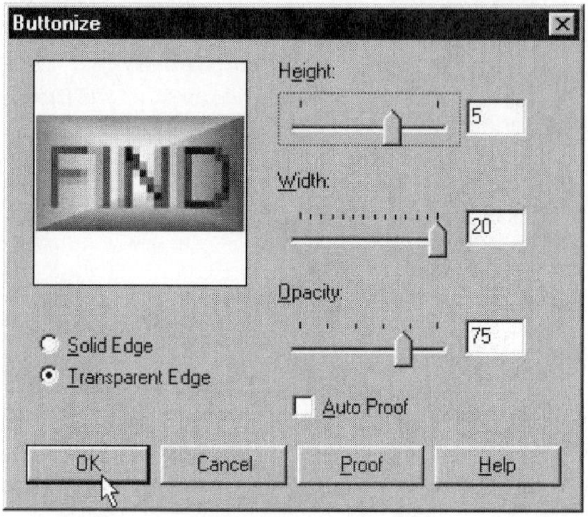

If you don't like the result, just use the Undo command on the Edit menu, and try again. So, we'll just click OK and relish the resulting button (Figure 7-14). It's time to save our button. Right now it's just a graphic, and so we'll have to instruct our Web page on how to use it, but not right now, because we're only interested in creating the graphics at this point. To save this graphic, we'll select *Save As* from the *Edit* menu. We choose *Save As* because *Save* is used when we don't need to change any of the file settings, and we do.

Figure 7-14   Our Find Button

The *Save As* dialog screen appears (Figure 7-15). We'll want to change the directory to the Images subdirectory of our Web project. We also want to change the left-hand portion of the file name to "find". The *Save as type* drop-down list box defaults to a Paint Shop Pro image, the native format for this application. We could use this format, but if we do, you won't ever see the graphic appear on the Web page, because the browsers can't display .psp images. However, if we had used layering with this graphic, we would want to save a .psp version of it so that the layering information would be retained, because as soon as we save the graphic as another format, this information, of use only to Paint Shop Pro, is lost. Currently, most browsers support two graphics formats, CompuServe's Graphical Interchange Format (.gif), and Joint Project Equipment Group (.jpg/ .jpeg). The two formats are described in the sidebar. We're going to save the image as a .gif file, the reason being that we don't require anywhere near the millions of colors the JPEG format supports. We'll choose Compuserve Graphics Interchange from the drop down list box, which will change the file extension in the file name box to *.gif*—then we click *OK* and we're done. Not very painful (I hope), and now we have a graphic suitable for framing, or at least suitable for a Web page. Well, one down, several more to go. No time for dawdling — spit spot!

JPG or GIF?

JPG is a file format based on 16 million colors, and GIF on 256 colors.

In general, JPG is used for photographs, or images with a large number of colors, while GIF is used for clip art, illustrations and black & white images (256 levels of gray are typically the most encountered).

Beyond that, GIF supports transparency – a color being defined as being transparent, which allows non-rectangular images, as well as animation through several images in one file.

JPG is a "lossy" format. It compresses by dropping "unimportant" information, so on each save of a JPEG image, more information is lost.

PNG, a new format from Microsoft, promises to provide color depth, support for transparency and animation, and no data loss. It currently is supported only with Internet Explorer 4.

7.2 Show Me the Way

When a category is chosen from the list on the main page for drilling down, the list is then replaced with the list at the subsequent level. This approach was taken instead of an expanding outline (like the directory list in the dialog in Windows Explorer) because there are so many categories that the visitor could become lost in the list. Well, that's fine, but how will the visitor navigate from a level 3 list of categories back to the category that got us there (level 2), or back to the initial list? Also, at each lower level list of categories, only the first six are displayed. The reason for this is a bit complex.

When the visitor clicks on a category, not only is a subsequent list of categories given, but any links attributed to the clicked category are displayed, as well as any ads. All of this information needs to be retrieved from the database when the category is clicked; the quantity of information is too large to send it all to the client initially and display portions of it via client-side scripting. Currently there is no way to trigger communication between the client and the server in a Web page without either repainting the entire page or using a technology not supported by all browsers.

Okay, so if we don't want the entire page repainted every time a category is clicked, what to do? The solution that our team agreed upon is to use frames. Most browsers support frames, which is the subdividing of a Web page into sections, each section containing a Web page. If a Web page in a frame is asked to interact with the server, only one frame need be repainted. Normally that frame is the one on which the clicked link appears, but the link can instruct the server to repaint one of the other frames.

Every facet of Web development has potential glitches. One that affects frames is that if the frame has more data in it than can be shown in the frame window, the frame will display either a horizontal scroll bar, or a vertical scroll bar, or both. This is very nasty looking showing up in the middle of a larger page, so we want to avoid it. The way to avoid it is to make sure the content to be displayed in the frame window *fits* in the frame window. Thus we're limiting the number of categories to six. This means that we need to provide the visitor a way in which to view the remaining categories. There are various approaches, and the one the team has selected is to provide graphical icons for requesting the next group of six, or the previous group of six. We'll actually need four icons for this; what and why will be discussed shortly, but first . . . .

7.2.1   Home Again, Home Again, Jiggity Jig

Our first navigational graphic will be the icon for "Home." This little button will reset the category list to the top level. We'll be drawing this and the rest of the navigational graphics. Don't worry, you still don't need to be artistic. We're going to be using Paint Shop Pro again, but different functions this time.

First step — a new graphic image. We're going to make this one smaller than the button we just finished. We'll bring up the *New Image* dialog either by clicking the blank page menu icon or by clicking on the *File* menu choice and then *New*. We're going to create an image much like the last one, except the size will be 18 pixels wide by 15 pixels high (Figure 7-16).

Figure 7-15   Saving the Find Button

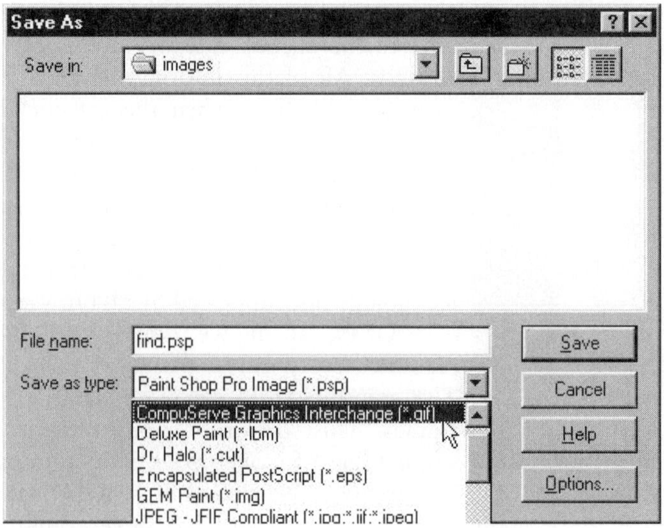

Figure 7-16   New Image for the Home Icon

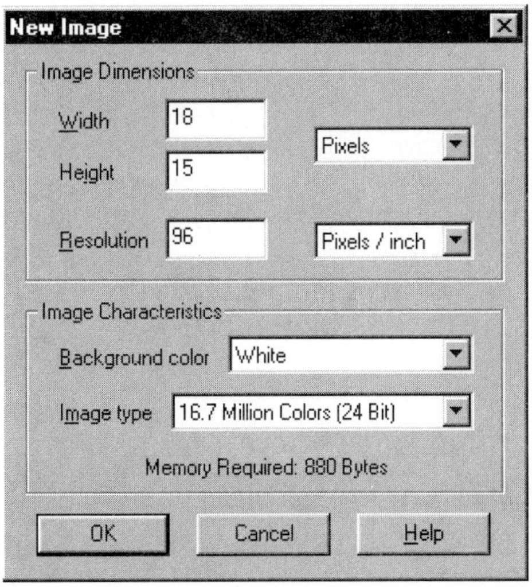

We need to perform some housekeeping functions before we begin creating the image. First, let's see if we need to set the foreground color. We want it to be black. To determine what color it is set for currently, hold the cursor over the square—the RGB values will appear below it. We want black, and since RGB is the value of light in the

Figure 7-17   Checking the Foreground Color

color, and black is the absence of all light, we're looking for a value of 0 for each component (Figure 7-17). If the foreground color is not currently black, we can change it by clicking on the foreground square and selecting black from the standard palette.

The other thing we're going to do is make the image easier to work with, because 18x15 is fairly tiny. We'll do this by clicking on the Magnify tool — the one that looks like a magnifying glass — then hold it over the image and click five times. As you can see in Figure 7-18, this gives us a larger view to work with. The actual size of the image has not changed, but the representation of each pixel is now larger, so we won't go cross-eyed while working on it.

Figure 7-18   Zooming In on the Image

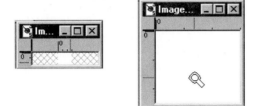

With that done, let us turn to drawing. Since I'm not much of an artist, the easiest way to draw the house is in sections. The first section is going to be the base, and since it's rectangular, we'll use the Shapes tool (Figure 7-19) to create it. Once we select the tool, we're presented with a control dialog for the shape tool. We're not interested in having a thick border, so we'll set the width to 1 pixel. We just want the outline for now, so we'll change the Style from *Filled* to *Outline*. This image will be distinct enough to remove any need for Antialiasing, so that box should not be checked. Figure 7-20 shows what the Controls window should look like when set properly. Once we've done that, it's time to draw the rectangle.

Figure 7-19   Selecting the Shapes Tool

Figure 7-20   Shapes Tool Settings

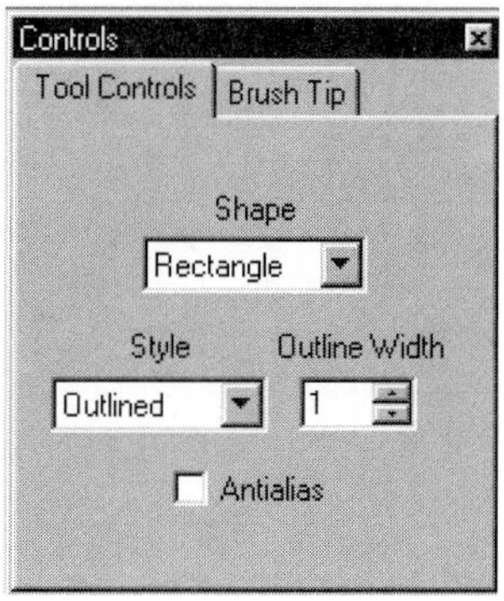

You might be wondering how big the rectangle should be, and how we draw it in the correct place. Well, if you'll move your mouse over the blank image, and look at the status bar at the bottom of the screen, you'll see that it displays the coordinates over which the mouse is hovering relative to the image. The coordinate system is a flip-flop of a normal XY graph. That is, the coordinates (0,0) are at the top left, and (17,14) at the bottom right. Why (17,14) and not (18,15), the size of the image? Because our counting is beginning at 0 and not 1. We're going to place our cursor at the coordinates (3,8), then while holding down the left mouse button, we'll drag the cursor to coordinates (14,14) and the release the button. Voilá — a rectangle (Figure 7-21). Not much of a house yet; let's put a roof on it. Paint Shop Pro like many graphics programs, does not have a tool for drawing a triangle, so we'll have to do it ourselves.

The shape tool won't help us here, so we'll trade it in for the Line tool (Figure 7-22). The Line tool has settings that appear in the Controls window, but we'll leave them as is. Let's place the cursor at the coordinates (0,8), hold the left mouse button down and drag the cursor to coordinates (8,0) as shown in Figure 7-23. We'll then place the cursor at (16,8) and drag it to the existing line-end we left at (8,0). There, a roof without messing with trusses. Yes, I know, it still doesn't look like a house, but we're not done yet! Let's add a couple of lines, and then we'll do some pixel editing.

Figure 7-21   A Rectangle

Figure 7-22   Selecting the Line Tool

Figure 7-23   Beginning the Roof

Figure 7-24   The Roof's On

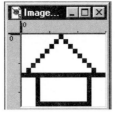

The two lines are horizontal. The first line will run from (14,8) to (17,8). The second line from (3,8) to (0,8). This will leave us with the drawing in Figure 7-24.

Next we'll switch back to the Shape tool again to draw one last rectangle. We'll click on (3,1) and drag to (5,5), which gives us what we see in Figure 7-25. As crazy as it

Figure 7-25   Chimney Added

may seem, we're now going to erase a line; not the line we just drew with the Line tool, but part of the rectangle we drew. It was a choice of drawing three lines or drawing a rectangle and erasing one line — I chose the latter. Erasing is just a matter of drawing with the background color. Make sure the background color is white by holding the cursor over it — white is R255 G255 B255, and we're ready to go.

When we drew lines and rectangles before, we used the left mouse button to draw with the foreground color. We're drawing with the background color now, so select the line tool and draw a line, using the right mouse button, from (4,8) to (13,8). This updates our drawing to look like Figure 7-26.

Figure 7-26   Line Removed

Figure 7-27   Paint Brushes Tool

That's about all we can do with shapes and lines, we'll have to do the rest by coloring individual pixels. To manipulate individual pixels, we'll use the Paint Brushes tool (Figure 7-27).

Selecting the Paint Brushes tool results in the presentation of the Paint Brushes controls. We want to select the *Brush Tip* tab, and make sure that the size of the paintbrush is set to 1 pixel (Figure 7-28), otherwise, every time we click the paintbrush we'll get a "drop of paint" more than one pixel wide. We want the width to be the same as what we'll be painting over, and all the lines we've drawn have been one pixel in width. Sometimes we use the paintbrush to change pixels to different colors, but here we will be using it to remove some remnants that we don't need.

Figure 7-28   Paint Brushes Tool Settings

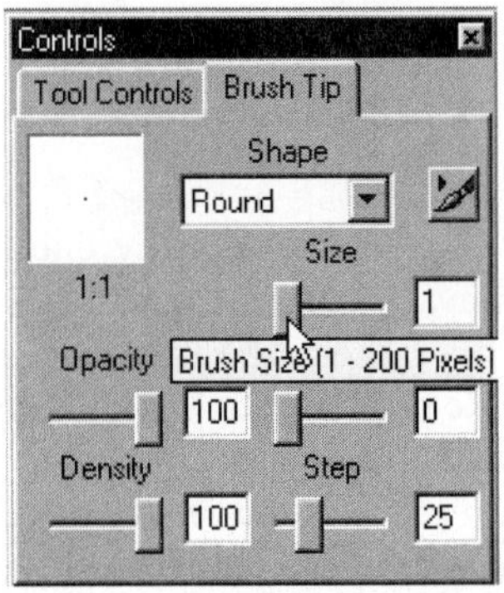

Take the paintbrush and right click it over each of the following coordinates: (4,5), (4,4), (5,5) and (5,4). This last touch-up leaves us with our house (Figure 7-29). Now all we have to do is paint it, and to do that, we'll "drop" a bucket of paint on it.

Figure 7-29   An Unpainted Home

First we'll click the Flood Fill tool (Figure 7-30). We'll also select a pale shade of yellow with which to paint our home. We'll do this by clicking on the Foreground Color square, and select the appropriate color (Figure 7-31). We'll hold the cross hairs of the Flood Fill bucket anywhere inside the house (but not over any of the lines) and left click, and our house is painted. We still have a white background around the house. Had there been a break in any of the lines in the drawing, the background in the illustration would have been flood-filled too.

We're going to turn the house into a button now, much like we did with the *Find* button, but we'll change some of the settings. First, we'll change the background color again. We're doing this because the background color is used to set the color of the button, and we don't want gray this time. Click on the background color square and set the RGB value to R-144, G-200, B-207. This will give us a nice shade of blue.

Figure 7-30   Flood Fill Tool

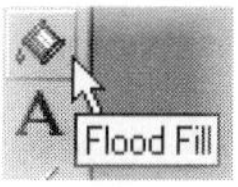

Figure 7-31   Selecting the "House Paint"

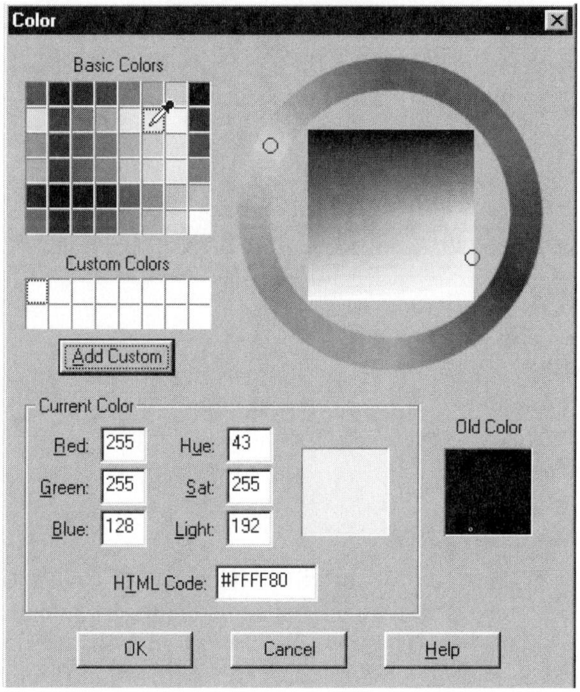

Next, we'll choose *Buttonize* from the *Effects* menu choice off the Image menu. We'll set the dialog as shown in Figure 7-32 and click *OK*.

With our button made, I'd like to see it at its normal size. If we select *Normal Viewing 1:1* from the *View* menu, this will set the presentation of the image back to it's actual size (i.e. zooms out), and we see our house as shown in Figure 7-33. The only thing left to do at this point is save the image. we'll use the *Save As* menu option on the *File* menu. Again, we'll choose *Graphical Interchange Format* as the type of file.

Figure 7-32   Selecting the "House Paint"

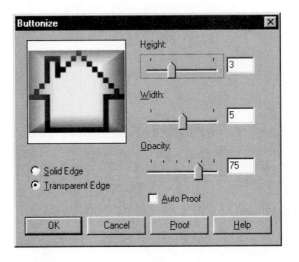

Figure 7-33   Our House

7.2.2   A Matter of Direction

We now have a "Home" icon that will provide a path back to the top of the list. There's another type of navigation we'll need to account for though. As stated earlier, categories are only displayed six at a time. We'll need an icon to help us move through that list. Actually, we'll need four icons to cover the following possibilities:

- a category list with six or less entries
- a category list with more than six entries, where the initial six are being displayed
- a category list with more than six entries, where the final six are being displayed
- a category list with more than six entries, where neither the initial six nor the final six are being displayed

The four icons are to cover the four states. These four possibilities offer the same states as a simple truth table. A truth table and these four statements are shown in Table 7-1 and Table 7-2. The topics aren't necessarily the same, but look at the pattern of true and false in the first table. Compare the possibilities to those in the second table and you'll see that the pattern is the same. It's a matter of the number of elements (two) and the number of possibilities for each (two), and then turning it over to the mathematics of combinations:

$$\text{Combinations} = E^O$$

where E=Number of elements and O=number of options

Table 7-1   Result Table

Statement A	Statement B
T	F
T	T
F	T
F	F

Table 7-2   Icon Truth Table

	Next list to display?	Previous list to display?
List Start, List Size >6	T	F
Not List Start, List Size >6	T	T
List End, List Size >6	F	T
List Size <=6	F	F

So in this case, since we have two elements and two options, there are four possibilities, and we'll need an icon for each. Once coded, only one icon will be presented to the visitor, and that icon will be selected based on the same criteria shown in the table.

The reason that there will be one icon for each possibility is that the icon will have an arrow pointing to the left for *Previous* and to the right for *Next*. The arrow will be presented with the appearance of a clickable button only if the situation requires it. For example, if the initial list of six categories is being presented, and if there are more than six at that level in total, then having the *Next* button activated makes sense, but not the *Previous* button. We'll create one image from scratch, and then modify it to create the other three images. The code that eventually will be added in support of the image will control the testing of the state of the list and the setting of the image as a result.

We'll begin by creating a new Paint Shop Pro image. This image will be 25 pixels wide by 16 pixels high. We'll be using the same tools that we did for the last image, except this time we'll be creating buttons the old-fashioned way.

Let's start by selecting the *Flood Fill* tool. We'll change the background to RGB value R-144, G-200, B-207 and fill the new image. Okay, next we'll need the line tool to draw a few lines. Let's set the foreground color to black (R-0 G-0 B-0), and draw a line from (24,0) to (24,15), from (24,15) to (0,15), and from (12,14) to (12,1). That should give us the image shown in Figure 7-34.

Figure 7-34   Step 1

Let's change the foreground to white (R-255 G-255 B-255). Now we'll draw lines from (0,14) to (0,0), (1,0) to (23,0), and (13,1) to (13,14). This gives us the image as shown in Figure 7-35.

Figure 7-35   Step 2

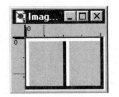

By this time you might be wondering what all these lines have to do with arrows. Not a thing, but they do have to do with creating the "buttons" around the arrows. So, let's change the forecolor again to Dark Gray (R-102 G-102 B-102). Let's draw a line from (23,1) to (23,14), (22,14) to (14,14), (11,1) to (11,14), and (10,14) to (1,14). You might start to have your eyes fooled with a 3-D effect with the results, shown in Figure 7-36.

Figure 7-36   Step 3

One more step and we're done with the "buttonizing." The foreground needs to be changed to Light Gray (R-204 G-204 B-204). The lines will be from (1,13) to (1,1), (2,1) to (10,1), (14,13) to (14,1), and (15,1) to (22,1). We now have complete buttons, although you won't really appreciate that until we zoom out and see them as shown in Figure 7-37.

Figure 7-37   Step 4

I'll understand if you're singularly unimpressed. These buttons aren't much use in their current form. Let's do something to them to remedy that. The buttons are to control paging forward and back. Our design team has given a lot of thought to how that would be represented in a figure on the buttons. The initial thought was to have the figure of a page of paper on each button with an arrow pointing forward on one and backward on the other. The problem is that the buttons are too small to support such a complex image. So there was a unanimous vote on a fairly unimpressive but functional arrow for each button.

We'll start with the left-hand, or "page back" arrow. Make sure the foreground color is black (R-0 G-0 B-0), and select the Line tool. Draw two lines, from (10,4) to (7,4), and (10,11) to (7,11). Then two smaller ones, from (7,3) to (7,2) and (7,12) to (7,13). Finally, two more from (7,2) to (2,7) and from (7,13) to (2,8). You should now have the image shown in Figure 7-38. If not, this would be a good time to tell you how to erase and start over.

One way is to select the *Undo* command from the *Edit* menu. This will allow you to backtrack to where you went wrong. Or, if you want a clean slate, choose the *Dropper* tool (see Figure 7-39), hold it over the button's background, and click with the right button. This will select the button's background color as the default background color. Then choose the *Selection* tool (see Figure 7-40). You're going to use this tool to draw a rectangle around the area you want to erase. So place the cursor at the top left corner of that area, hold down the left mouse button, and drag the mouse to the bottom right corner of the area, and then release the mouse button. The area you want to erase should now be enclosed in a rectangle. Press the DEL key, and you'll have a blank button again. This method will only work if you're willing to replace the entire contents of the rectangle with the background color, which in this case is just fine.

Figure 7-38   "Page Back" Arrow

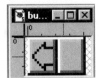

Figure 7-39   "Dropper" Tool

Figure 7-40   "Select" Tool

Okay, let's create a mirror-image arrow for the other button. Make sure that the background color is the same as the button's. Choose the Select tool and draw a rectangle around the entire arrow without including any of the button edging; the top left and bottom right coordinates of (2,2) and (11,13) should work — and zooming in to enlarge the image will help. Once the selection is made (Figure 7-41), choose the *Copy* command from the *Edit* menu, and then the *Select None* command from the *Selections* menu.

Figure 7-41   Selected

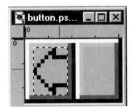

Now select the *Edit* menu, *Paste* command, and *As New Selection* option. Another arrow will appear in the image (Figure 7-42).

Figure 7-42   New Arrow

Move the cursor to the right-hand button so that the arrow is placed entirely in the blue background, and then click with the left button. A selection rectangle will appear around the arrow. Select the *Mirror* command from the *Image* menu. The arrow will reverse direction (Figure 7-43), but not the rest of the image, because only what is inside the selection mask is affected.

Figure 7-43   Reversed Arrow

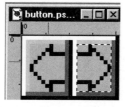

The last thing to do with this image is to give it a little color. Let's set the foreground color to red (R-255 G-0 B-0), select the Flood Fill tool, and click anywhere inside the left-hand arrow, but not on any of its bounding lines. Next, change the foreground color to green (R-0 G-255 B-0) and click inside the right-hand arrow. If we change the view to normal size, we'll see the completed image as shown in Figure 7-44. Let's save it as a GIF image named *lr_u.gif* (left and right arrows are up), and move on to the next.

Figure 7-44   lr_u.gif

The image as seen now will be used when both options are active, that is when we can scroll backwards or forwards. What about when there is no list to scroll backwards to? We could just remove the left button's ability to respond to a click. I don't like that solution though. If it looks like a duck I want it to act like a duck. So we'll change its look so that it is still recognizable as an arrow, but not a button.

First we'll select the Dropper tool and right-click on the light gray edge of either side of the button. This sets the background to that color. Then we'll left-click on the dark gray edge, which sets the foreground color. Now we'll select the Flood Fill tool. Take the cross-hairs and click in each blue quadrant surrounding the red arrowhead. Click on the dark gray border, and the red arrow. The sequence is as shown in Figure 7-45.

Figure 7-45   De-Buttonizing the Button

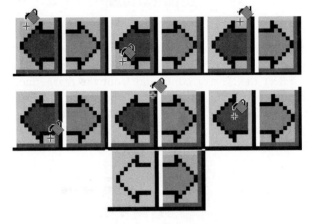

So, what have we accomplished here? I think Figure 7-46 shows it best. If you were to see this control on the screen, I hope you would not confuse the left-hand side for a clickable button, because I'm counting on the visitors not doing so. Of course, even if they do there will be no supporting code to process the click, but we don't want to aggravate them. Another option would be to hide the left-hand arrow completely when it is not active, but that isn't what the typical computer user has come to expect, because tools and menu icons don't typically disappear when they're not available in a particular context, instead they are "grayed out," as is our arrow. Okay, let's save this one as *r_u.gif*.

Figure 7-46   r_u.gif

We need a counterpart to this image for when there is a path to a previous page, but we're displaying the final page, so that there are no remaining pages. To do this we'll reopen *lr_u.gif* so that we have the color back on the left side. Then we'll do to the right side the same thing we had done to *r_u.gif*. The result is shown in Figure 7-47, and we'll save this as *l_u.gif*.

Figure 7-47   l_u.gif

The last image in this series is to cover the possibility of no page scrolling. This scenario will occur when the number of categories is less than or equal to six, the number that will be displayed at one time. In that case, all categories are displayed simultaneously, so there is no paging to be done, and thus there is no reason to have the "Next" or "Previous" arrows functioning.

We should still have *l_u.gif* and *r_u.gif* open. Let's select the *Zoom* tool and zoom in on both images by left-clicking each image twice. Then we'll put them side by side. Now we'll use the *Select* tool, and draw a bounding rectangle on *l_u.gif* from (13,0) to (25,16) as shown in Figure 7-48. Then we'll make a copy of that region by clicking on the copy icon (see Figure 7-49). Now, click on the title bar of *r_u.gif* to select that image to work with. Next, from the *Edit* menu, select the *Paste* command and the *As New Selection* option.

Figure 7-48   Select Region

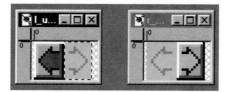

Figure 7-49   Copy

Move the arrow that appears until the coordinates show as (13,0). The original arrow and its border should be completely covered, so that the image looks as shown in Figure 7-50, and then left-click. If we now use the command *Select None* from the *Select* menu item, the mask will disappear from around the arrow and we'll be left with the image we want. This can be saved as *lr.gif*. Be careful to use the *Save As* command and not the *Save* command, otherwise you'll overwrite *r_u.gif*. This ends the design of our navigational icons. Before we move on to the more difficult (and more fun) stuff, let's take a look at what we've created.

Figure 7-50   Copying

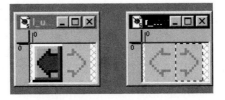

There are probably as many software packages out there to help you maintain your graphic images as there are graphic images to maintain. You'll find, though, that Paint Shop Pro has a very useful feature to handle this. If you select *Browse* from the file menu, and select the directory that contains your images, Paint Shop Pro will create a thumb-nail, a miniature version, of each image. This makes it much easier to select the proper image than doing it from a normal file listing.

7.3 A Name To Remember

Okay, let's take on the difficult one next — the logo banner. A logo banner is a graphic that gives identity to the Web site. It typically comprises the company logo (see Figure 7-51). We're going to use a different application for creating the banner, because the ability to retain individual objects in a graphic will be important to us, and that func-tionality is provided by Microsoft Image Composer. So, let's fire it up.

Figure 7-51   Logo

Image Composer launches with a blank canvas, so let's dirty it up by loading what will be our background onto it. We'll do that by selecting the *Insert* menu, and the *From File* menu choice. Let's navigate to the correct directory, and select the file *chart.gif*. As you'll see, it loads at the top left corner of our work area. It's a clip from a nautical chart.

Let's grab it with the mouse and move it so that it's centered on the screen. It's wider than our work area, so position it to extend past the edges relatively equally on the left and the right — as shown in Figure 7-52 — we can adjust the size of the canvas later if we need to.

The background is a bit busy. If we put the logo and other elements over it they will be lost in the detail. So, what we'll do is mask some of the detail in this graphic, much like a photograph where the background is visible but slightly out of focus.

To do this, we need the help of the *Shapes* tool (Figure 7-53). When we select it, its dialog box appears. The only change we need to make to the defaults is the *Opacity* setting — changing it to 40%. This setting controls how much of whatever is behind the object will show through the object. "What object?" you ask. The one we're about to make.

Figure 7-52   Original Background

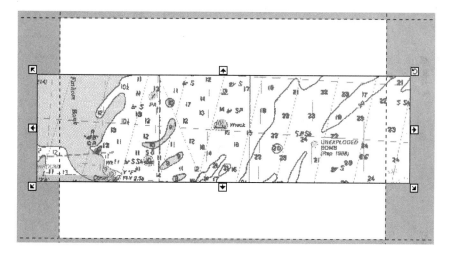

Figure 7-53   Shapes Tool

We'll click on the rectangle shape (Figure 7-54) and draw a rectangle mask over the background image. With the mask in place, click the *Create* button, and the background is masked (Figure 7-55). We haven't actually changed the background image. If you were to press the delete key right now, the rectangle object would be deleted, with the background looking as it did before.

Figure 7-54   Rectangle Shape

Figure 7-55   Masked Background

Figure 7-56   Logo on Background

Looks great! Okay, the next step is to add some content to the background, and the first thing we'll add is the company logo. So again, we'll insert from a file, this time *logo.gif*, and then move it over our background as shown in Figure 7-56.

That adds quite a bit to the banner, but there's still something missing. If these were the only elements we were going to have, some additional color would be needed, assuming that it wouldn't be added by the rest of the page. There's a whole lot of blue here, albeit different shades, but that's it. So, let's get to work and make it more interesting.

If you become a Web page designer, you'll spend more of your time searching the 'net and other sources for clipart than you will developing the pages. Right now there isn't a great way to search for clipart of a specific subject matter, but you can search for clip-art. Eventually, if you're lucky, you'll work your way to a royalty-free site that contains an image that you want, or one close to what you need that you can later modify. Another method is to create your own clipart. No, you don't need to draw it yourself. With a digital camera, you can photograph the object, transfer it to your computer, and use a graphics application to alter the image to render it as clipart, typically by reducing the number of colors in the palette from millions to 256.

We'll add a number of nautical images to our banner. Let's start with a ship's compass. Let's Insert from File and use the *scompass.gif* file. I'll move it below our banner, and point out that right now it's much larger than I want it to be (see Figure 7-57).

Figure 7-57   Compass Added

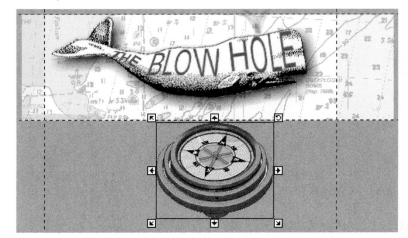

This is easy to fix. We simply need to resize the image. We can do it manually, but I can never remember the keystrokes for resizing an object while keeping aspect ration — keeping the width and height in the same proportion. In some applications you hold down the shift key while dragging one of the "handles" around the object, in other applications it's the control key, and in some it's both. Instead of doing this, I'll use one of the Image Composer tool palettes, the Arrange palette (Figure 7-58).

Figure 7-58   Arrange Palette

This will cause the Arrange Palette dialog to be shown. This dialog can be used to flip the image horizontally or vertically, to rotate it, crop it, warp it or align it with other images. We're going to use it to resize the image. The dialog (see Figure 7-59) defaults to the resizing units being pixels. If we know that we want the image to be a specific height or width, we can set that value and, since the *Keep aspect ratio* box is checked, the other dimension will change proportionately.

Figure 7-59   Arrange Dialog

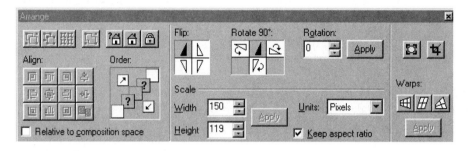

We don't know the specific size we want, but about half the size will do. We could do the math, but there's an easier way. The drop-down list box that contains *Pixels* can be changed to *Percentage*. Once we've done that, we can enter 50 for width, which will cause 50 to appear in the *height* box as well. Now click the *Apply* button, and the image will be resized. Now we can move the image into place. Figure 7-60 shows how the compass looks on our banner. There are two problems — although it's in the position I want it, it's covering the whale's face, and it's too visible. That is, it stands out too much. Luckily, there's an easy fix these problems too. We can get the compass off the whale's face (and make the whale much happier in the process) by changing the z-order of the items. "Z-order" is the relative position of the items on the z-axis, that is, which item is in front of which. The way we do this is by selecting *Send Backward* from the *Arrange* menu, resulting in what we see in Figure 7-61.

Figure 7-60   – This Won't Work

Figure 7-61   The Whale Can See Again

Our whale can see again! But what it sees is an extremely discordant composition in its path. Ah, but we've already laid the groundwork for fixing this — our translucent mask. We created that 60% translucent mask (40% opaque) in the form of a white rectangle to cover the chart. If we place the compass between the mask and the chart, it too will be softened. Since we know that we want the compass in behind everything except the chart, we'll select *Send to Back* on the *Arrange* menu, which will temporarily make the compass disappear from view since it is now behind the chart, and then select *Bring Forward* to promote it one layer. This gives us the results we want (Figure 7-62).

Figure 7-62   Compass Positioned

Next up is a starfish, to be found, coincidentally, in *starfish.gif*. This image is already sized correctly, so let's just place it where we want it, and move it to that translucent layer (Figure 7-63). We're getting so close I can taste it (*it* being completion — not the saltwater). Just two more additions.

Next up is the ship's wheel. This will be found in *wheelt.gif*. This image needs to be reduced by 50%. We're going to have it overlap the starfish a bit, so when we move it to the back, we'll then bring it forward two times, once to move in front of the chart, and then again to move in front of the starfish, but still remain behind the whale (it just got over having the compass on its face, we can't pin its tail too). This brings the image to the stage we see in Figure 7-64.

Figure 7-63   Starfish Positioned

Figure 7-64   Wheel Positioned

The final addition of content will be another nautical element, a sextant. We'll load this image from *sextant.gif*. It needs to be reduced by 50%, and then we'll place it, and deposit it in the same layer as the others — send it to the back and then bring it forward one layer. Okay, we can see the resulting image in Figure 7-65.

Figure 7-65   Sextant Positioned

The last thing we need to do before saving the final image is trim it. You see the vertical dashed lines on all four sides of the image. These can be grabbed with the mouse and moved, and we'll move them into place on our image. We'll be saving two versions of our banner logo. We'll save it in the Image Composer native format, .MIC, because this format retains all the separate layers, which comes in very handy if we want to make a change at another time. The other version will be a JPEG, .JPG, because it's the more color-rich format that can be viewed in a browser. When we save the latter format, only the portions of the image that fall inside these lines will be saved. So long as we save the .MIC version, we can use the canvas outside of those lines as a work area to hold other items, but we need to make certain that what we want as our banner on the Web page falls between those lines. Once we've done that, we can save the first copy using *Save As* from the *File* menu, with *Microsoft Image Composer* as the file type. We can then save the second copy with *JPEG* as the file type.

> Saving images from Image Composer with formats such as GIF and JPG requires the "flattening" of the image – all layers are merged and the layer data is lost. Therefore, save the .MIC version first.

We now have a beautiful banner logo (Figure 7-66). We're going to use it later on as part of a site navigation structure. We're ready to move on to the final elements for our home page — the banner ads.

Figure 7-66   Banner Logo

7.4 And Now a Word From Our Sponsors

We need to create four banner ads for the two ad banner controls that will be on the home page. One control will be for commercial advertisements, the other for non-profit site advertisements. We're going to work with Paint Shop Pro and Image Composer here, but will also be paying closer attention to color because when using advertisers' logos, we want to make sure we'll get accurate color reproduction (see the sidebar on Web-Safe Palettes for more information).

Let's start the first commercial banner by opening a new image in Image Composer. The dimensions of the image will be 400 pixels in width by 40 pixels in height, which we'll indicate in the New Image dialog.

We're going to work some magic on this image, but first we need something to work it on. The white canvas we see is actually just a place holder. We need to put something on it to work on. So we'll use the *Shapes* tool again and create a rectangle, but this time we want the opacity to be 100%, giving us a white rectangle. We'll click on the *Rectangle* tool on the dialog and drag the cursor from the top left of the image to the bottom right, or from coordinates (0,0) to (399,39). Then click *Apply* and we'll have a rectangle. It doesn't look any different than before, but now we can make changes to the rectangle.

The next thing we want to do is make use of the *Effects* tool (Figure 7-67). This tool gives us access to a large portfolio of graphical effects. From the *Effects* dialog, we want to select *Gradients* (Figure 7-68). The *Gradient* effect enables the user to select four colors between which a gradual transition will take place on the object.

We're going to click on the *Details* tab, which gives us access to the gradient settings. We could define a custom gradient here, but there's a stock effect that will suit us just fine. From the drop down menu we'll select Gold (Figure 7-69), make sure our rect-

Figure 7-67   Effects Tool

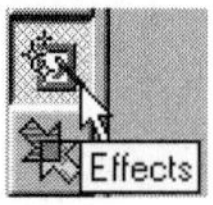

Figure 7-68   Gradient Effect

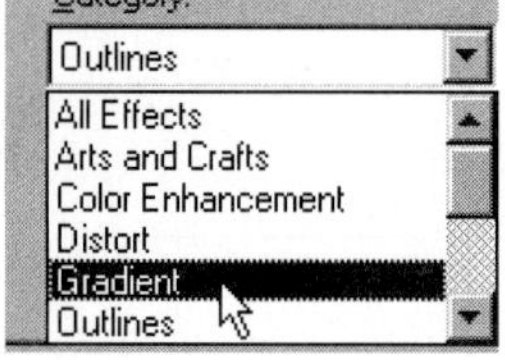

angle is selected, and then click *Apply.* Our rectangle is now a flat gold bar. We'll copy the image using *Copy* from the *Edit* menu. Okay, let's move on to Paint Shop Pro.

Figure 7-69   Gradient Effect

We're going to use Paint Shop Pro to create a button, because we want this first banner ad to have a 3-D effect. First we paste the image from the clipboard using the *Edit* menu and *Paste* command. Once pasted, we'll select the *Buttonize* command from the *Effects* choice of the *Image* menu. This results in the dialog shown in Figure 7-70, which also shows the settings we'll use to give the image a slightly raised look. We're going to want to take the new and improved image back to Image Composer, so we'll copy it back to the clipboard, move back to Image Composer, press the *Delete* key to delete the current image—the gold rectangle we created—and then paste from the clipboard. This gives us a canvas on which to put our ad.

Okay, back to Paint Shop Pro for awhile. We'll open the Puddleduck Press logo found in the file *pduck.gif,* which can be seen in Figure 7-71, and select *Save As* from the *File* menu, and save it as *temp.gif,* so that we don't inadvertently hurt the original.

We don't need the entire image; we're going to use only the head. We need to select the head with the *Selection* tool, drawing a rectangle so that there's as little selection aside from the head as possible. We'll end up with some of the logo text too, because of the way it's positioned (Figure 7-72). We need to get rid of the text remnant. The *Eraser* tool (Figure 7-73) will help us to do that. The tool changes any pixel that it touches to the current background color. We'll first select the *Dropper* tool and right click on the fluorescent green of the logo, which will set the background color. Then we'll select the *Eraser* tool, set the brush size to 1 pixel (Figure 7-74). We'll then "draw" over the text remnant and save it just as soon as we select *Set Palette Transparency* from the *Colors* menu and set the transparency to the background color.

The transparency will not be retained if the clipboard is used to transfer it to Image Composer instead of importing it in from a file.

Figure 7-70   Buttonize Dialog

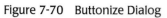

Figure 7-71   Puddleduck Press Logo

Figure 7-72   Selection

Figure 7-73   Eraser Tool

Figure 7-74   Eraser Dialog

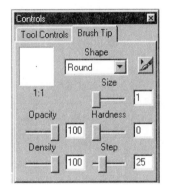

Back in Image Composer, we'll now choose *From File* from the *Insert* menu, and choose the image we just saved. You might be wondering why we went through the trouble of cropping the head in Paint Shop Pro. It's because Image Composer isn't a painting program, and doesn't provide for the kind of pixel editing we needed to remove the text remnants.

We'll place the image on one end of our banner (Figure 7-75). The remaining portions of this banner will involve text. We could create the text in Paint Shop Pro, but there is a drawback to doing that. Paint Shop Pro is a raster-based painting program that treats its "canvas" as a large bitmap. Once an item is drawn or dropped onto the canvas, it becomes part of that bitmap and loses its original identify. Therefore, should the text need to be changed at a later date, there would be no text to change; that is, the portion of the image that was once text would not be selectable as such, nor editable as such. Therefore, the only way at that point to change the text would be to create new text and cover the old text with it, which might require several additional steps to avoid remnants or the corruption of other items that had been positioned in front of the original text. So, with that in mind, we'll stay in Image Composer to create the text we need. First we select the *Text Tool* (Figure 7-76).

Figure 7-75   Duck head image added

Figure 7-76   Image Composer Text Tool

Let's fill in the dialog box. We want the text to be a deep maroon. Right now the color is set for black. So we'll click on the color swatch, which results in the *Color Picker* dialog window appearing. We'll set the color to R-80 G-0 B-0 (Figure 7-77) and click *OK*. We want the text to be Times Roman, 26 pt., bold and smoothed. The dialog settings are shown in Figure 7-78. Next, we'll click somewhere outside of the image and a text box appears. Since we're working with larger type, we'll need to increase the size of the text box so that our text will fit — Image Composer won't dynamically increase the size while we type. We increase the size by grabbing the middle handle on the right-hand side of the image and drag to the right. We then type the words "Puddleduck Press" (the advertiser), and click anywhere outside the text box to close it and create our "sprite," which is what the individual objects in an Image Composer composition are called (see Figure 7-79).

There's one more step. We want the text to stand out a bit from its background when we place it. The way we'll accomplish this is to outline the text in a lighter color. We'll select the *Effects Tool* again, the one we used to create the gold gradient. Instead of gradients this time, we'll select *Outlines* as the type of effect, and *Edge* as the type of outline (Figure 7-80).

Figure 7-77   Text Color Picker

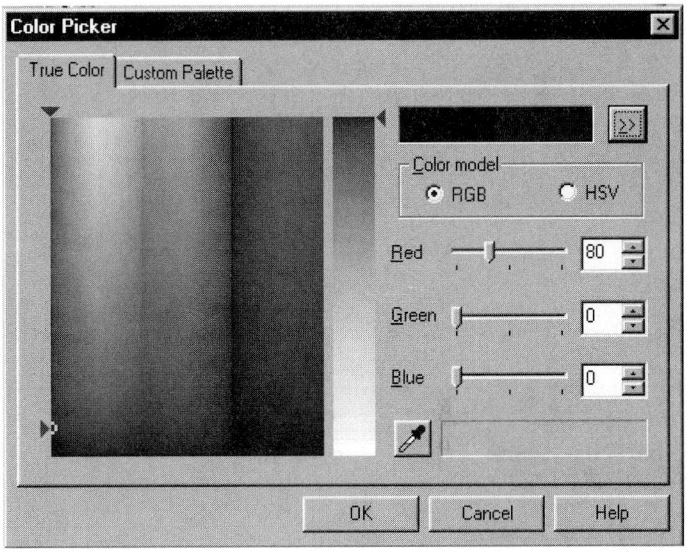

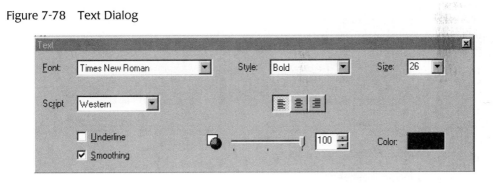

Figure 7-78   Text Dialog

We'll click on the *Details* tab and set the thickness to 1, the opacity to 75% and the color to white (R-255 G-255 B-255). Then we click *Apply*. The results can be seen in Figure 7-81. We'll take the text sprite and place it on our banner as shown in Figure 7-82. Let's move on to the next text sprite.

Figure 7-79   Created Text

Figure 7-80   Edge Effect

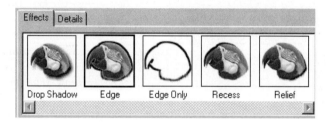

Figure 7-81   First Text Group in Place

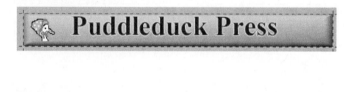

Figure 7-82   Washed-Out Text

Let's select the *Text Tool* again, and set the color to a deep turquoise, R-49 G-115 B-255. We'll set the typeface to *Arial* this time (or some other sans-serif font), bold, smoothing and 14 pt. The text we'll type in is "Web Page & Print Design Services." We'll position the text overlapping the bottom of the company name, as shown in Figure 7-82, and you'll see that although it's a bright color, it gets lost in the text behind it. We'll resolve this by once again outlining the text, but this time we'll outline it in black (R-0 G-

0 B-0), with a thickness of 2 and 100% opacity. When we click *Apply*, the text practically jumps out at us. We'll adjust the position just a little and run the ad by Lindsay Hardcastle, the art director of Puddleduck Press. She's happy with it, except that she wants more red in the lettering. So, we'll go back and double click on the lettering to edit the text. By choosing to edit the text, we'll lose all formatting we've done to it, namely the outline. We'll change the color to R-127 G-0 B-0, and then add the white outline again. The image is shown in Figure 7-83. The final thing we need to do is create a text sprite saying "click." You see, the purpose of an ad banner is to attract the visitor's attention to the point of clicking the ad, which then takes her to the Web side of the advertiser. Just in case the visitor doesn't know how the ad works, the "click" will provide instruction. We'll select the *Text Tool* again, and keep "Arial" as the typeface, but we'll set the size to 18 pt., the color to white (R-255 G-255 B-255), and the weight to "normal" instead of "bold." The text will simply say "Click." We're going to outline the text again, using the same color as we used for the company name (R-127 G-0 B-0), with the thickness set to 2 and the opacity at 80%. Then we'll click and hold the top right handle of the sprite, the handle that indicates rotation. We'll drag that handle counter-clockwise, and watch the status bar until it indicates that we've rotated -45 degrees. We'll then move the sprite over to the right-hand side of the banner (Figure 7-84). Then we'll save the file first as the native *.MIC* format, and finally as *pduckb.jpg*, and we're done. The reason we've saved it as a *.JPG* and not a *.GIF* is because the latter format only supports 256 color palettes, which won't retain the nuances of that true gold appearance that the gradient has given us.

Figure 7-83   Vivid Text

Figure 7-84   Puddleduck Ad Banner

The next banner ad is a generic ad to inform visitors to the site of the advertising opportunity — much like a billboard that says "Your Ad Here." In fact, let's have that as our ad. We'll start in Image Composer with a canvas of the same size as our other ad. In this instance, we'll set the background color to black. This is accomplished in *Composition Setup* as shown in Figure 7-85.

Figure 7-85   Composition Settings for a New Image

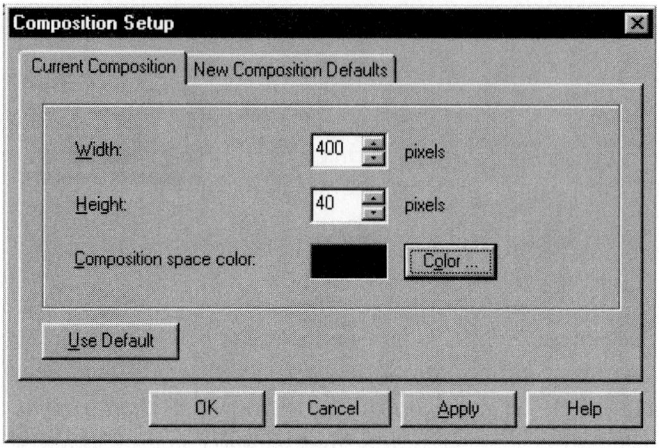

We're not going to do anything fancy in the way of "buttonizing" with this image; we'll leave it as a black rectangle, so we can go directly to the text. We *will* do some special formatting with the text so that it stands out. Ads are one of the few places that I advocate putting light-colored letters on a dark background. There are two things that won't change no matter how "cool" a dark page looks: dark text on a light background is easier to read and light text on a dark background looks awful when it's printed. Because ads are small they don't present much in the way of reading material, and are rarely printed, so they are a good place to experiment with different types of color schemes and backgrounds. We're going to use an informal typeface for this ad. You might not have the same typefaces on your computer, but any will do so long as it's easy on the eye. I'll use *Bradley Hand*. It's a great informal font. I'll click the *Text Tool* and set the font. Let's make the weight *bold*, the size 30-point — you'll actually have to type the size in since 30 points is not one of the choices in the list box — and make sure that the check box for *Smoothing* is checked (Figure 7-86).

The text frame we end up with is a bit too large to fit on the ad canvas, so we'll resize it. If we move the frame over the image and then click somewhere on the screen outside of the text frame and not on the ad canvas, the text frame will show in its final form. We can then hold down the *control* key and drag a corner handle of the frame. While we're dragging, there will be a white rectangle which shows the current size of the text (Figure 7-87). When that white rectangle fits within the ad, we can release the handle. The text will still look good *because* we selected that it be smoothed. If we hadn't, resizing could very well have left us with jagged edges.

Okay, time to add some pizazz. Right now the text looks like chalk on a blackboard, so let's liven it up a little. Let's select the *Effects Tool*, and select the *Outline* effect. We'll click on the *Details* tab of the dialog. I'm going to select a bright blue as the color (R-0 G-107 B-255), a thickness of 2 and an opacity of 80% (Figure 7-88), and then click

Apply. The resulting image (Figure 7-89) is definitely an eye-catcher without being overly flamboyant.

Figure 7-86   Font Settings

Figure 7-87   Resizing the Text Box

Figure 7-88   Setting Outline Details

Figure 7-89   Outlined Text

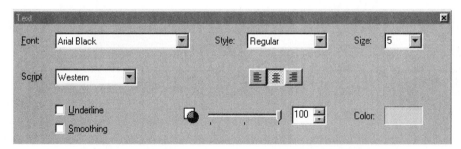

The final requirement on this banner is an indication to the reader that clicking will accomplish something. The word "click" is a great way of doing that. We don't want the word to detract from the message, so we'll set the text to a normal sans-serif font, *Arial*, the color to light gray (R-213 G-213 G-213), *Normal* style, centered and *Smoothing*. Let's grab the center handle on the top of the text box and stretch the text box so that it's tall. We'll then enter the word "Click" and hit the *Enter* key after each letter so that the word is vertical. Once we click somewhere else to have the text generated, we will grab a corner handle on the text box and resize it until it fits on our image. If we now double-click on the text, the dialog box will appear again (note that the text size will be different because we resized the text) as in Figure 7-90, and we'll turn *off* the *Smoothing* setting— as very small text is easier to read without the additional pixels that are used to "smooth" the image. That completes the banner, and we can see it in Figure 7-91.

Figure 7-90   "Click" Text Settings

Figure 7-91   "Your Ad Here" Banner

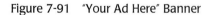

The next banner is for a non-profit organization. The Blowhole site will be providing no-charge advertising for non-profit organizations. The size of the banner will be different, 192x96. There are two banners to be created in this category. The first is for *Greenpeace.* They have provided one of their banners, but the size is wrong, so the exercise here is simply to resize the existing banner.

Resizing has to be done just right, otherwise the resulting image looks very bad compared to the original. There are various methods for resizing, and the one that works best with graphics is called "resampling."

The first step will be to bring the image into Paint Shop Pro. The original image is a .GIF file, so it has a 256-color palette. Resampling requires a full palette, so we'll select the *Increase Color Depth* command from the *Colors* menu choice (Figure 7-92). This will assign a full-color palette to the image. We can then choose *Resize* from the *Image* menu,

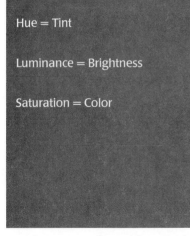

HLS

HLS stands for Hue, Luminance (or Lightness) and Saturation. With these three properties any color can be defined.

The meaning of each is sometimes unclear to those who don't regularly work with colors. I find the following formula, based on the settings on a standard television set, to be the easisest to understand.

Hue = Tint

Luminance = Brightness

Saturation = Color

and ask for it to be resized to 192 x 96. We'll have to uncheck the box for retaining the aspect ratio (ratio of height to width) as the shape of the original graphic can't be resized in ratio and still reach the size we want (Figure 7-93).

Figure 7-92   Increasing Color Depth

With the graphic now at the size we want, we'll need to convert the palette again. This time we'll select *Decrease Color Depth* from the *Colors* menu choice, and decrease the colors back to 256, the size supported by the .GIF format. We'll be given a choice of various methods for accomplishing the palette change (Figure 7-94), and we'll select the default. You'll see no visible difference in the graphic once the palette reduction has completed, since the original was using less than 256 colors, so all are contained in the resulting palette. The finished banner is shown in Figure 7-95.

That brings our chapter on Graphics to a close. We've learned how to manipulate graphics in several different ways, and to create a number of different items frequently found on a Web page. There are many no-royalty CDs available with thousands of clipart images, so that with a good piece of graphics software for manipulation, you should rarely have to resort to creating the elements from scratch.

Figure 7-93   Resampling

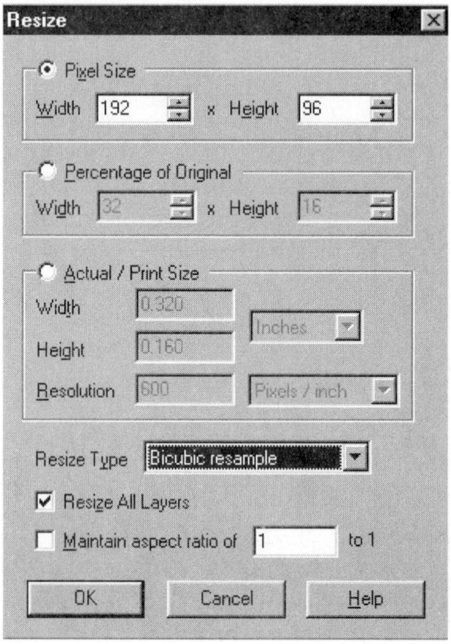

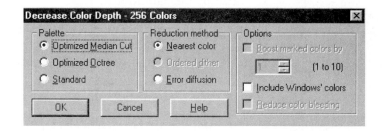

Figure 7-94   Decreasing Color Depth

Figure 7-95   Greenpeace Banner

The Environment

No, this isn't a chapter on acid rain and deforestation. We're going to create the environment from which we will construct our Web site. It's not a lot of work. We have but three objectives in this chapter:

- Create a FrontPage Web
- Create a Visual Interdev Solution
- Connect the solution to the Data Source Name (DSN)

8.1 The Blowhole Web

We'll be using Microsoft FrontPage for some development and as our tool to publish the local version of our Web site to a Web hoster's server. Since Visual Interdev provides a means for attaching its projects to existing FrontPage Webs, but not vice-versa, we'll create the FrontPage Web first.

We're using FrontPage '98 instead of FrontPage 2000 for one reason only — my Web hosting company does not yet support the FrontPage 2000 extensions. This is always an important consideration with the flood of new versions of tools that comes out each year — if by their use you're assuming your Web hoster or ISP will embrace them in beta or soon after release, I'd advise that you verify your assumptions. The first step is to launch FrontPage (see Figure 8-1).

Once in FrontPage, we'll begin our navigation through the new Web dialogues by using the *Create a New FrontPage Web* option from the opening dialog of the program (Figure 8-2).

This brings up a dialogue from which different Webs of specific utility can be created (Figure 8-3). We're not going to use the templates to create our Web as it doesn't match the more common types of functionality. So, instead of selecting *From Wizard or Template*, and instead of *Import An Existing Web*, since we don't have an existing Web to import, we'll select *One Page Web*.

Figure 8-1   Launching Microsoft FrontPage

Figure 8-2   Create a FrontPage Web

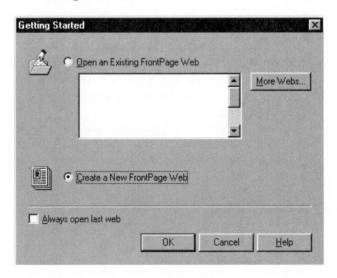

Figure 8-3   Web Creation Dialog

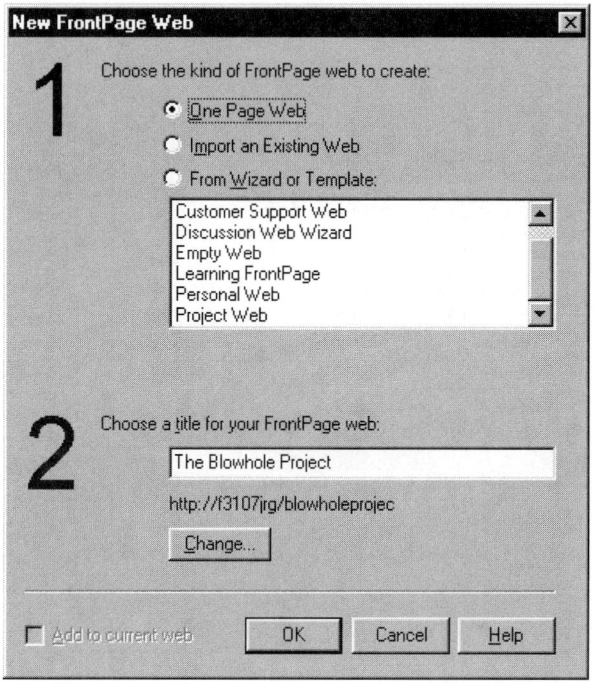

This option will create the directory structure FrontPage uses to manage "a Web" (this is a Web site—but since it may not be the actual Web site, just the content, they call it, simply, "a Web"). It will also create an empty HTML page with a name that matches the site setting for a default name, sometimes *index*, and in our case, *default*. This is also the place where we give our Web a name. I'll name it *The Blowhole Project*. As we can see, this causes FrontPage to select *blowholeprojec* as the directory to attach to our root directory to house this Web. Apparently the directory naming is limited to 14 characters, which leaves the name looking a bit odd. I'll click on the *Change* button and change the directory name to *blowholeproj* (Figure 8-4). When we click *OK*, FrontPage will create its environment in the directory we chose (Figure 8-5), and show us the directory structure in FrontPage Explorer (Figure 8-6).

An explanation of this directory structure is needed. Microsoft FrontPage defaults to creating a directory named *Webshare* to hold Web configuration information. One of the subdirectories off this directory is *wwwroot*, which acts as the Web site root directory. Our directory, *blowholeproj* is a subdirectory of *wwwroot*. On my machine, the machine name is f3107jrg — you can check yours by looking at the properties of your *Network Neighborhood*, specifically the *ID* tab. So in my case, if I run Netscape Communicator or

Figure 8-4   A Better Directory Name

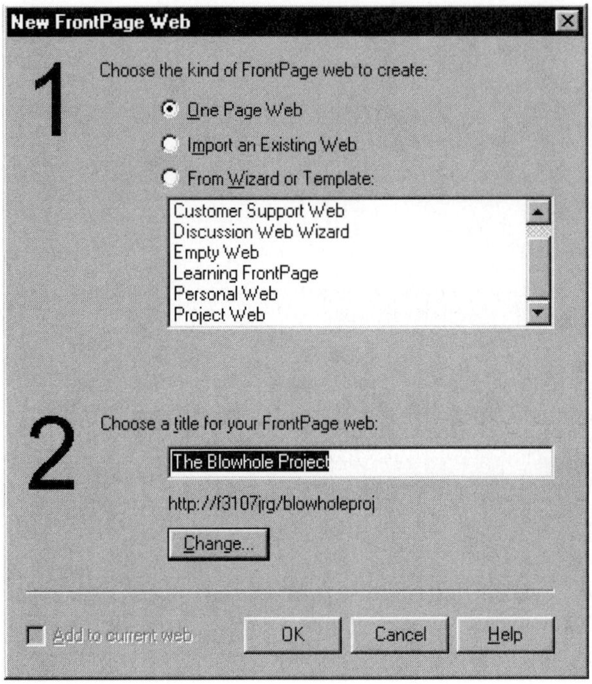

Internet Explorer and enter

```
http://f3107jrg/
```

as the Web address, the page that will be loaded is the default page in the directory

```
\Webshare\wwwroot
```

This means that on my computer, if I want to access the page *default.htm* of *blowholeproj*, I would enter

```
http://f3107jrg/blowholeproj/default.htm
```

as the address, since this directory is the root directory relative to the local Web site. If I had a directory that was mapped as *theblowhole.com* on a Web hoster's server, that directory would then be the root directory relative to the Web site. Moving *default.htm* from *blowholeproj* on my computer into that directory on the Web hoster's machine would then allow me to refer to it as

```
http://www.theblowhole.com/default.htm
```

on the Internet. On the Web hoster's server, the physical file will be in a directory too, and it might be named the same that it was on *my* computer. This can be very confusing, and it sometimes takes quite a while until people understand relative and absolute references, and in fact, sometimes the software doesn't understand them well enough, so you spend your time fixing broken links that weren't broken on your machine but become broken once you move everything to the Web hoster's machine.

Figure 8-5   FrontPage Creates the Web

Figure 8-6   Web Directory Structure

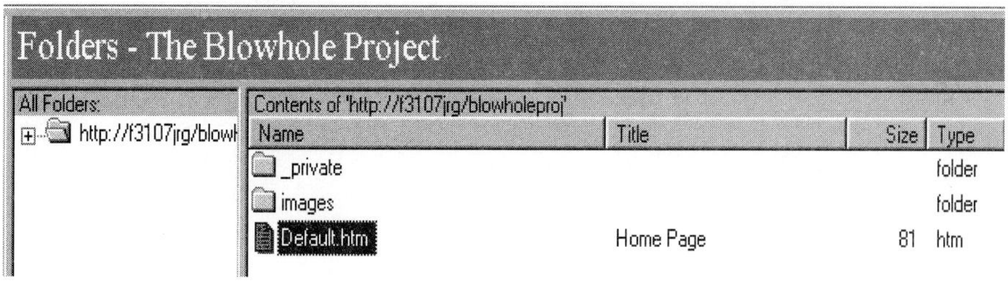

8.2 The Visual Interdev Solution

Visual Interdev is going to be our tool of choice for dealing with Active Server Pages (ASP). It provides the functionality of connecting the Web pages with a database, which of course interests us.

It's worth mentioning something about the VI syntax before we begin. The highest level unit of work in VI is the *solution*, which can comprise multiple *projects*. In our case we'll only have one project.

Okay, let's get our solution set up. I was going to start with an image of the splash screen like I did with FrontPage. Unfortunately, VI seems to take control of the system when it launches and doesn't release it until the splash screen is gone, so it's impossible to accomplish a screen capture of it. Thus, we'll start with an image of the VI environment as it looks upon start-up (Figure 8-7).

Figure 8-7   Visual Interdev Environment

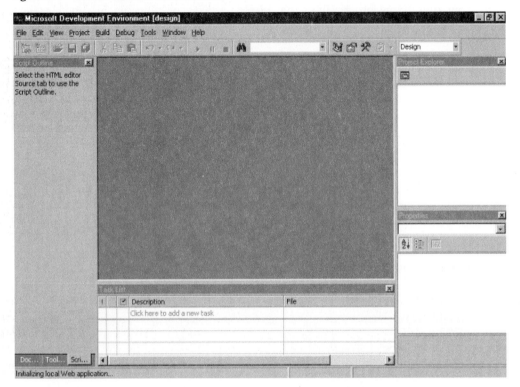

Like everywhere else, we're going to begin with the New option. In this case, it can be found in the *File* menu as the *New Project* command (Figure 8-8). There isn't actually a *New Solution* command. When you create a project and the VI environment isn't in a Solution context, a solution is automatically created and the project placed within it.

Okay, I jumped ahead just a bit. I left you hanging on the *File* menu. So, now we've clicked *New Project* and we receive the dialog shown in Figure 8-9. We'll click on *Visual Interdev* to select a new VI project. Next, we'll enter a project name, *The Blowhole Project*, and we'll accept the resulting directory choice.

Figure 8-8   Creating a New Project

Figure 8-9   New Project Dialog

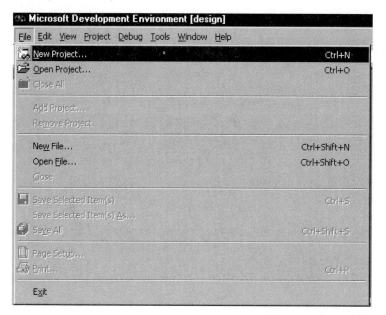

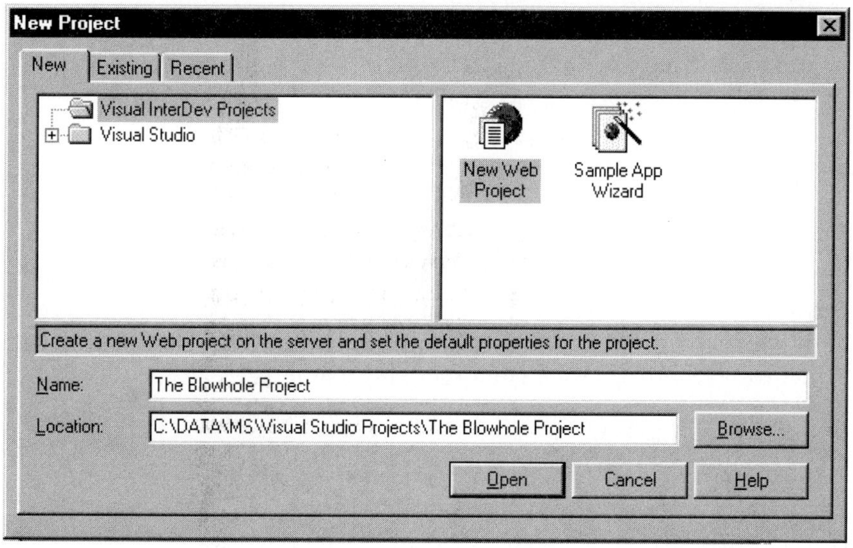

We'll now click the *Open* button, which will launch the Web Project Wizard. The Wizard has four screens, although we'll be using only two, and the first asks us to identify the appropriate server and working mode (Figure 8-10). The drop-down list box for Server might not have any entries in it. If not, simply enter your server name. This can be found in the properties of your *My Computer* icon.

Figure 8-10   Web Project Wizard Screen 1

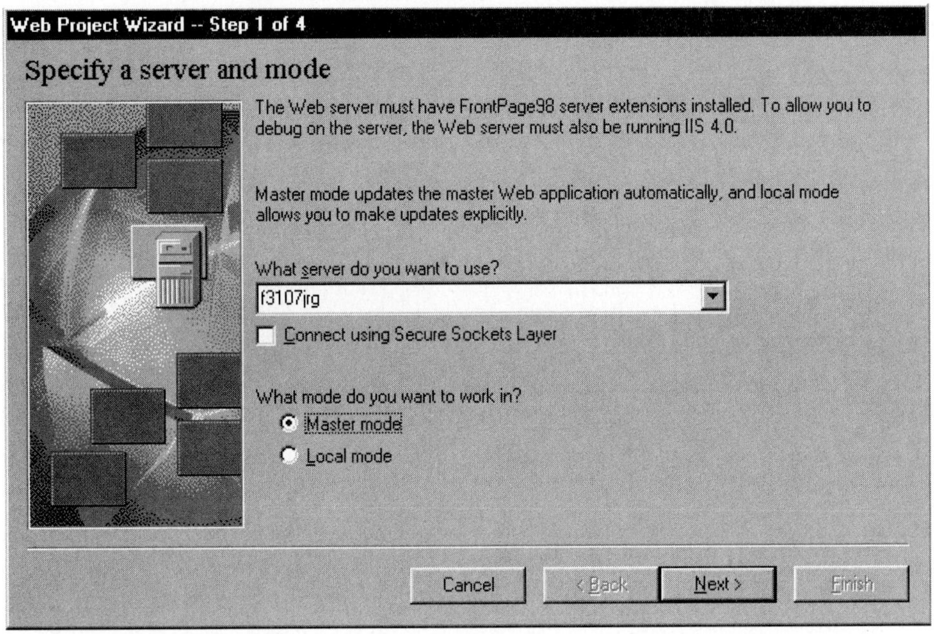

The working mode choices are *Local* and *Master.* Local means that when you want to touch a file, a local copy will be created from the master copy in the FrontPage directory. Master mode has you making the changes directly to the FrontPage version. Since we don't need to worry about anyone else touching our file, we'll choose Master mode.

The next Wizard panel (Figure 8-11) asks us to decide whether VI is to create a new project, or whether we'll be connecting to an existing project. Since we have created a Web project with FrontPage, we'll point the Wizard at it.

Figure 8-11   Finishing the Web Wizard

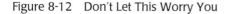

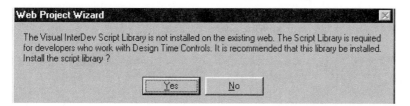

We can then click *Finish*, and VI will create the Web project. If your system is set up up like mine, you'll receive one or both of the following warnings about functionality that will not be available (Figures 8-12 and 8-13). Don't worry about them; they won't stop us from accomplishing what we need to. However, if you want to install the NT extensions so that server debugging can be done, please refer to the Visual Studio documentation.

Figure 8-12   Don't Let This Worry You

Figure 8-13   Same Goes for This One

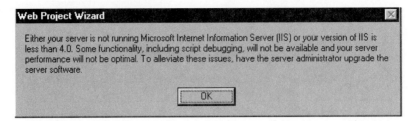

The project window in the VI environment shows that our project *and* solution have been created (Figure 8-14). The only other thing we need to do prior to making the data connection is save our project, and we can do this with the familiar *File->Save* command (Figure 8-15).

Figure 8-14   Our Web Project

8.3 Connecting a DSN

All right, our environment is up, which will allow us to create Web pages and ASP content, and we have a DSN defined, which will give us access to our database. What we need to do now is point our environment to the DSN.

We'll begin from our current VI work space by selecting the *Add Data Connection* command from the *Project* menu (Figure 8-16).

Figure 8-15   Saving the Project

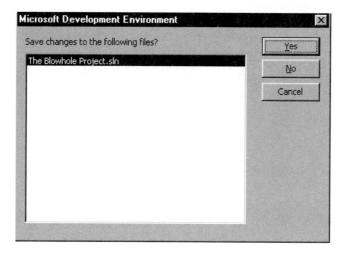

Figure 8-16   Add Data Connection

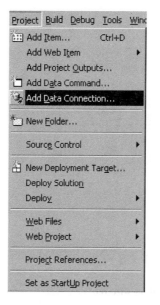

This menu choice acts a bit differently from others in that, as soon as we select it, VI changes our environment without providing us a cancel button. Oh, there *is* a way to undo it, but it's worth noting that VI immediately creates a reference to a generic data source in its Project Explorer window (Figure 8-17).

Figure 8-17   Add Data Connection

The window shows an entry for *Global.asa*. This file is a repository for script to be executed when an application on the Web site begins or ends execution. One of the pieces of script that is worth having is the script that defines the data connection. The *DataEnvironment* entry is a place-holder until we define our data source—which reminds me, we have more to do.

Aside from adding the entry in our Project Window, clicking the *Add Data Connection* command results in the presentation of the *Select Data Source* dialog (Figure 8-18).

Figure 8-18   File Data Sources

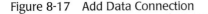

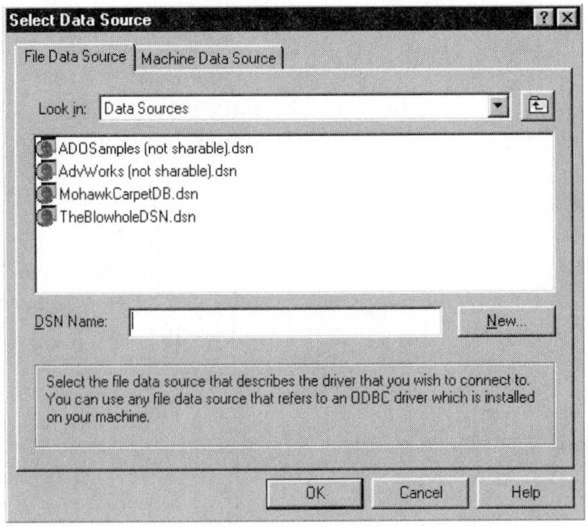

Figure 8-19   Machine Data Sources

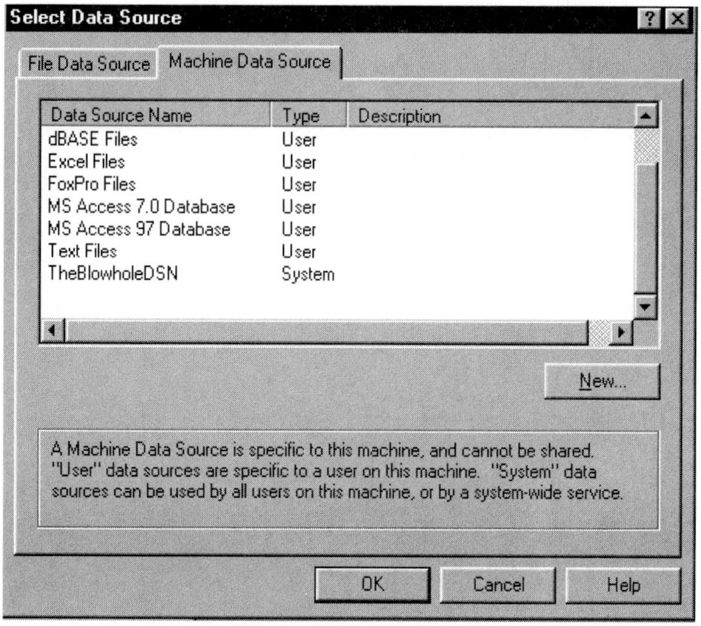

If we select *Data Sources* from the *Look In* list box, we see that among the lists is our DSN, *TheBlowholeDSN*. One thing that might escape your attention at first is that the DSN has an extension, .DSN. There's an extension because this is a file name, and if you look at the tab at the top of the panel you'll see that it says *File Data Source*. We do *not* want a File Data Source. Why? Because we want the connection to our database to be as if it were on the Internet and not as a file-to-file connection. We need to click on the *Machine Data Source* tab, which gives us a slightly different presentation (Figure 8-19). In this list we can see *TheBlowholeDSN* without an extension, and a notation that it is a System DSN. This is the one we want.

We'll select it by clicking on it (Figure 8-20), and then click *OK*. This will give us a new dialog with which to provide further information (Figure 8-23). You'll note on the dialog that we're being provided with a default name for the connection, and that this default name is now showing in our project window instead of *DataEnvironment* (Figure 8-21), and that we now have a *Data View* window that shows the database reference (Figure 8-22). Interestingly, the database is shown as a file reference, but rest assured that the connection is via the System DSN. This means that when we move our code to another machine, such as a Web hoster's, so long as a System DSN of the same name has been created on that machine our code will find the database no matter what directory it resides in.

Figure 8-20   Selecting a Data Source

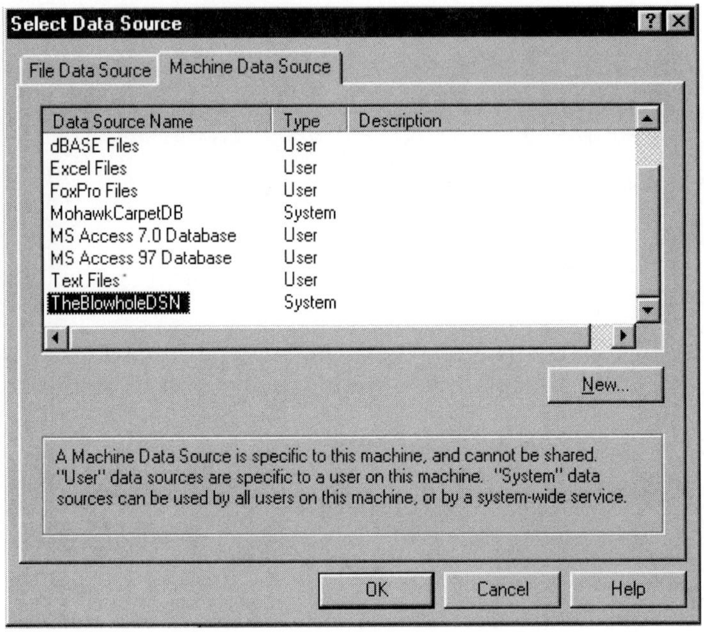

Figure 8-21   Default Connection

The name we choose for our connection will be used throughout our code, and although *Connection1* has utility, I'd prefer that not to be the name, perhaps just my sense of aesthetics. Instead, let's select *ODBC1* (Open Database Connection), as shown in Figure 8-24.

Figure 8-22   A Database Connection

Figure 8-23   Default Connection Name

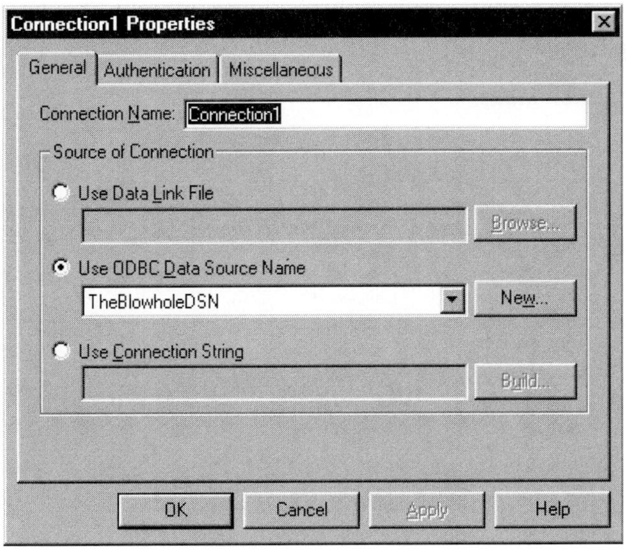

Figure 8-24   Our Connection Name

Figure 8-25   Connection Made

When we click *OK*, this results in our Data Connection name changing in our Project Explorer window (see Figure 8-25).

If we now click on the '+' symbol next to our database listing in the *Data View* window, it expands and we see that the we have a *Tables* entry (Figure 8-26). If we then click the '+' symbol next to it, we see the tables in our database listed (Figure 8-27). This provides us with the proof we need that our connection is working. If you click the '+' sym

Figure 8-26   Opening the Database

Figure 8-27   Our Database Tables

bol next to any of the table names, you'll be provided with a listing of the fields in the table.

This concludes the installation of our environment. We can now move on to the next chapter and creating the first of our Web pages.

Home

You've been patient through eight chapters, and now it's time to have even more fun than we did creating the graphics and database. We'll start with the easier pages and build up to a crescendo.

Well, almost every Web site has a "Home Page," and so shall The Blowhole. As we saw way back in Chapter 3, our Home Page comprises several frames, as shown in Figure 9-1.

The Home Page has no database requirement and no ASP code, so we'll use FrontPage to construct it. FrontPage's editor has a Frame Wizard that can be used to create frames pages, but only frames pages that have a standard layout. Our design (Figure 9-1) is not a standard layout, so using the Wizard will buy us nothing.

We'll begin in FrontPage Explorer, the program that appears when we launch FrontPage. Once we open our Web, *The Blowhole Project*, we see in the files window that there is already a file named *default.htm* (your default page might be *index.htm*). We'll double click on the file, and in so doing we'll launch the FrontPage Editor. When the editor begins, the screen will be blank (Figure 9-2) since we have not put any code in place that affects the display, but we'll change that soon enough. At the bottom left of the screen you will find three tabs for the three contexts available in FrontPage.

- Normal—the WYSIWYG (What You See Is What You Get) context, where the design version of the elements is shown
- HTML—the code window, where the lines of HTML and script code are shown
- Preview—a slimmed-down Internet Explorer context that will show most of the HTML elements just as they would be seen in a browser

Since there are no drag and drop frame elements, we'll be using the HTML context for this and coding it ourselves. If we click on the HTML tab, we'll find the basic HTML needed for a Web page.

Figure 9-1   Frame Layout for the Home Page

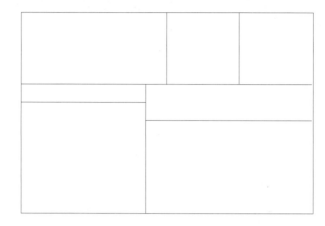

Where code will not fit on a single line, the line will be split with an under-score character at the end of the first line

```
<html>
<head>
<title>Home Page</title>
</head>
<body>
</body>
</html>
```

The first thing we'll do is change the title of the page. The title shows up in various places, typically in the browser's title bar and its Windows icon. We want the title to accurately reflect the page being viewed, so we'll change it as follows.

```
<title>The Blowhole Home</title>
```

Figure 9-2   FrontPage Editor Environment

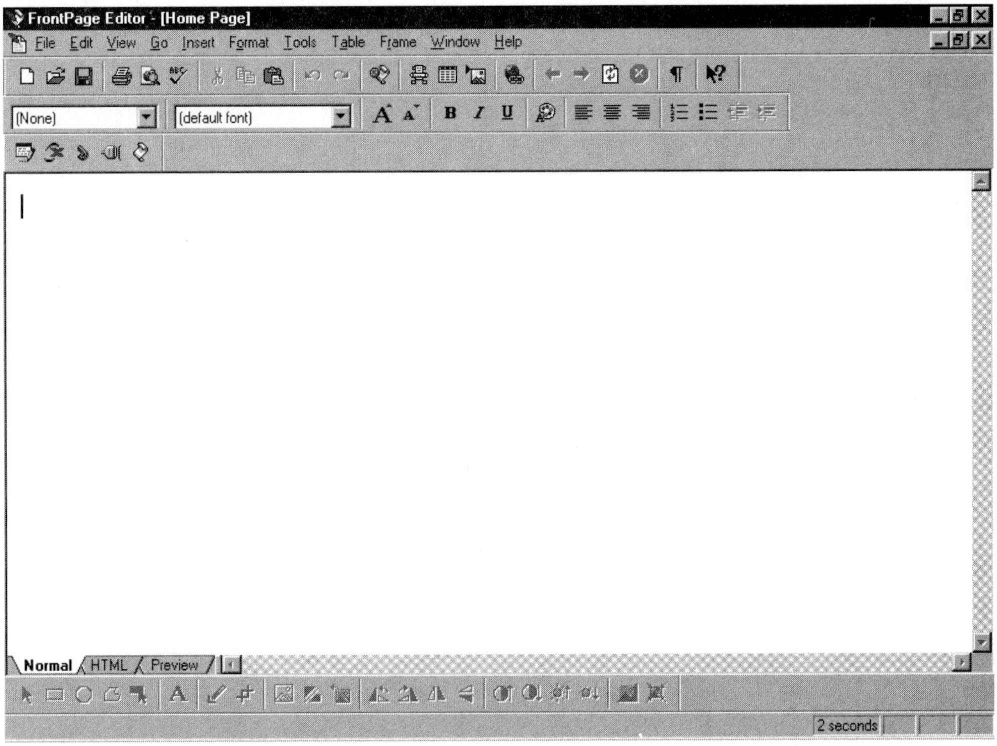

Let's begin work on the body of the page. We're going to divide the page into frames. Frames are subdivisions of a page in the form of rows and columns. If I take a rectangle, the page, and define a row of a certain size, then the remainder of the page is a second row if I define nothing else; there is no unused portion. So when we look back at Figure 9-1, we're not looking at seven individually defined rectangles, we're looking at what can best be considered a large plot of land that has been divided into large parcels, and those parcels subdivided into smaller parcels, and so on.

Some terminology: a *row* is a division that is oriented horizontally, and a *column* is oriented vertically. Figure 9-3 shows the steps we'll take to divide the page:

- two rows (outlined in heavy lines)
- the top row into three columns
- the bottom row into two columns
- the bottom left-hand column (light gray) into two rows
- the bottom right-hand column (dark gray) into two rows

Okay, let's do it. The first thing is to divide the page into two rows. In HTML, the division is defined using a *frameset* tag and is instantiated using a *frame* tag. So, in our code, after the </head> tag and before </html> we'll put the following:

```
<frameset frameborder="0" rows="138,*">
   <noframes>
      <body>
      <p>This page uses frames, but your browser
doesn't _
   support them.</p>
      </body>
   </noframes>
</frameset>
```

Figure 9-3   Home Page Subdivisions

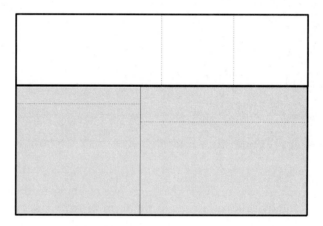

The *frameborder* parameter is set so that the frame has no border around it; it is invisible in terms of its boundaries. The *rows* setting says that the top row will be 138 pixels in height, and the bottom row will use whatever is left over, which, considering most monitors are 640x480 or better, should be at least 300 pixels (leaving room for window border, task bar icons, etc.).

The <noframes> tag provides a place for us to provide functionality for those persons using an old browser that doesn't support frames. The reason the paired *body* tags appear inside the *noframes* tags is that whether the visitor is seeing frames or not, their "page" contains body tags and is thus a valid page.

Once we've entered this code, the environment will change to include the tabs shown in Figure 9-4. The additional tabs are provided so that in addition to viewing the code for the entire page, *Frames Page HTML*, we can look at the code for each individual frame by selecting the frame in the *Normal* view and click the *HTML* tag, and also see what the frameless browser would see by clicking the *No Frames* tag.

Figure 9-4   Additional Tabs to Handle Frames

You'll also notice that in the HTML listing, now viewable through the *Frames Page HTML* tab, there is some color-coding. Tag keywords are colored in red, and their parameters in blue. Often we'll forget an opening '<' or closing '>' or some other such mistake. If we're looking at what should be a tag, and it's not red, or some other color-coding discrepancy such as color being where it shouldn't be, it will be our first clue that the HTML is not being interpreted correctly.

However clicking the *Normal* or *Preview* tabs show us nothing, because in adding the *frameset* tags we have only defined the frames; we have not instantiated them yet. Let's move on to subdividing the top row into three columns.

We'll start by adding the definition of the columns after the existing *frameset* tag in our code:

```
<frameset frameborder="0" cols="375,*,*">
</frameset>
```

This definition is much like the last, except that here we're saying that the space is being divided into three columns, and that the two columns to the right of the first will equally divide whatever space is left.

Next, we'll instantiate each of the frames with *frame* tags.

```
<frame name="banner" scrolling="no" _
  noresize src frameborder="0" _
  target="contents" marginwidth="16" _
  marginheight="32">
<frame name="fp_ad" scrolling="no" noresize>
<frame name="np_ad" scrolling="no" noresize src>
```

The *frame* tag does not require a paired *</frame>*.

If we look at the first frame instantiation, we see that it's named *banner.* Giving it a name allows us to refer to the frame from another location, perhaps as the destination of some displayed information. Scrolling is turned off, which means that we don't have to worry about scroll bars appearing on the frame's boundaries. The *noresize* keyword means that we're not giving the visitor the capability of grabbing a frame border and changing the frame's dimensions. Why? Frankly, it's too easy for them to screw up the display. The *src* keyword, when followed by "=" and a file name, defines the file that should be opened to fill the frame. Since we haven't created that file yet, we'll leave *src* as a placeholder with no parameter. Why not leave the equal sign too? Because the key-words following the equal sign would be interpreted as being the target of the equal sign, messing up our statement and many of those that follow. The naming of a *target* frame here instructs the browser to take any hyperlink requests and display the resulting page in the *target* frame instead of this frame. The *marginheight* and *marginwidth* simply define a margin within the frame, the dimensions in pixels.

The two remaining frames use some of the keywords that we've already mentioned. The *fp_ad* frame will hold the for-profit static banner, and the *np_ad* frame the non-profit rotating banner.

With this being our first instantiation of frames, let's click on the *Preview* tab and see what we see—nothing. Well, we've defined three frames with no source pages and no borders and no scroll bars, so, yes, there's nothing to see. However, if we click the *Normal* tag (see Figure 9-5), we see the screen divided into the three columns, each offering buttons to define the frame's initial page (don't use the buttons). The reason the *entire* page is divided into what should be three columns at the *top* of a page, is because what should be the bottom row has not been instantiated yet.

To get the picture looking more like our intended layout we'll instantiate the second row. Remember, the second row is divided into two columns, and our code reflects that:

```
<frameset frameborder="0" cols="200,*">
</frameset>
```

Figure 9-5   New Frames Page

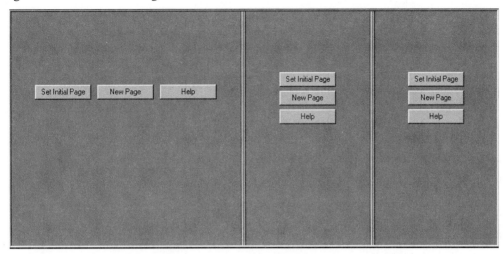

This code falls within our first *frameset*, coming directly after the definition of the first row. We see that we're dividing the second row into two columns, the first being 200 pixels in width, the second using whatever is left over. Next, let's add some code for the first column:

```
<frameset frameborder="0" _
   framespacing="0" rows="23,*">
</frameset>
```

This code subdivides the first column into two rows, one being 23 pixels high, and the other using what's left. Let's instantiate these rows:

```
<frame name="title" scrolling="no" _
   noresize frameborder="0" src _
   marginwidth="2" marginheight="1">
 <frame name="contents" noresize _
   frameborder="0" src marginheight="1"
   marginwidth="2">
```

Nothing earth-shattering here. The first row, named *title*, will hold the title bar that identifies the frame beneath, *contents*, as containing categories. Let's move now to the final lines of code, the right-hand column of the bottom row:

```
<frameset frameborder="0" rows="59,*">
</frameset>
```

This column will also have two rows, but the top row is a bit larger at 59 pixels. The following code instantiates the two rows:

```
<frame name="ad" scrolling="no" _
  noresize src frameborder="0">
  <frame name="main" noresize src _
  frameborder="0">
```

The first row is named *ad*, and will contain the main rotating ad banner. The second row is named *main*, and will be the main area of focus, containing either the utility pages when they are selected or the links applicable to a category.

If we now click on *Normal*, we'll see something that looks much more like our design (Figure 9-6).

Figure 9-6   The Home Page

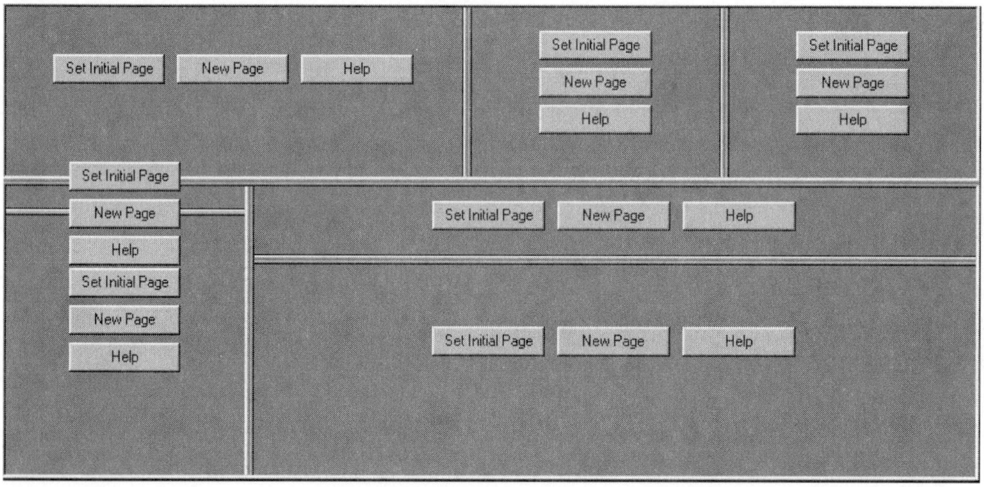

That's it. Let's take a look at the code before we move on to the next chapter.

```
<html>

<head>
<title>Home Page</title>
</head>

<frameset frameborder="0" rows="138,*">
  <frameset frameborder="0" cols="375,*,*">
    <frame name="banner" scrolling="no" noresize _
```

```
      src frameborder="0" target="contents" _
      marginwidth="16" marginheight="32">
     <frame name="fp_ad" scrolling="no" noresize>
     <frame name="np_ad" scrolling="no" noresize src>
    </frameset>
    <frameset frameborder="0" cols="200,*">
     <frameset frameborder="0" framespacing="0" _
     rows="23,*">
      <frame name="title" scrolling="no" noresize _
       frameborder="0" src marginwidth="2" _
       marginheight="1">
      <frame name="contents" noresize _
       frameborder="0" _
       src marginheight="1" marginwidth="2">
     </frameset>
     <frameset frameborder="0" rows="59,*">
      <frame name="ad" scrolling="no" noresize src _
       frameborder="0">
      <frame name="main" noresize src _
       frameborder="0">
     </frameset>
    </frameset>
    <noframes>
    <body>
    <p>This page uses frames, but your browser _
       doesn't support them.</p>
    </body>
    </noframes>
   </frameset>
   </html>
```

CHAPTER 10

The Utility Pages

I suppose you're wondering what in the world a utility page is. It's a page that provides certain value, but doesn't do all that much. We have a number of them that will be linked to from the main page:

- *Copyright* page
- *Ads* page
- *Web Rings* page
- *Awards* page

Each of these pages will be created in this chapter, but we'll start by creating a page that's *not* listed, because it's not a page in its own right.

10.1 Navigation Banner

Before we create any of the utility pages, we need to create a special page that will be included in all the pages above, and that's our navigation banner. This banner will look like the banner we'll create on the home page, but it needs to be different because on our home page we'll be taking advantage of the frames in the construction of our banner; the utility pages won't be using frames, so the navigation banner needs to be constructed somewhat differently.

The reason we need this element on our utility pages is that when the visitor has selected a utility page, we want to provide a means to jump to another utility page or return to the home page.

The first thing we need to do is create a new page in FrontPage. From the *File* menu in FrontPage Explorer, we'll select *New.* FrontPage will create a new page with a default

Figure 10-1   Creating a New Page in FrontPage

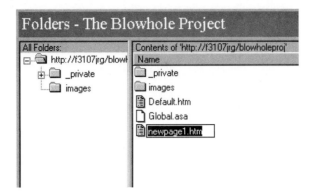

name in the file pane (Figure 10-1) and put the file name in edit mode in anticipation of our wanting to rename it. We'll name it *navbar2.htm.*

We'll double-click on the file name to invoke the FrontPage Editor. We now have a blank canvas with the three tabs we originally saw when we edited the home page. This time we can initially take advantage of some of FrontPage's functionality without hard-coding HTML.

We're going to insert a table onto the page. Normally we'd look for the menu command for this on the *Insert* menu, but you'll notice that FrontPage Editor has a *Table* menu, and one of its commands is *Insert Table* (Figure 10-2). We'll take it.

The next screen to appear is the dialog for *Insert Table* (Figure 10-3), where we'll set the characteristics we initially want for our table. We're going to change most of the default settings.

We want two rows and one column to begin with. The alignment can stay listed as *default.* The border size will stay as 0, since we don't actually want the table structure to show. The cell padding, the amount of space between the cell "walls" and its contents, will be 0. The same setting will be used for the cell spacing, the amount of space between cells. Figure 10-4 shows the values entered in the dialog.

When we click *OK*, we're back at the editor canvas within the *normal* view with the table cells represented as dotted lines.

We're going to begin by making changes to the cell properties of the top cell. If we right-click inside the top cell and select *Cell Properties* from the pop-up menu, we're given the cell properties dialog box shown in Figure 10-5.

We're going to have a number of graphics below the banner that will appear to be part of the banner image. To make sure this effect works, we need to align the image at the bottom of the cell so that it will provide a seamless transition to the other graphics. This is accomplished by setting the *Vertical Alignment* to *bottom.* We'll also set the *Horizontal Alignment* to *right.* We want the cell to be the same height as the image and no taller, so that there's no white space at its base; check the *Specify Height* box and set the

Figure 10-2   Inserting a Table

Figure 10-3   Default Table Settings

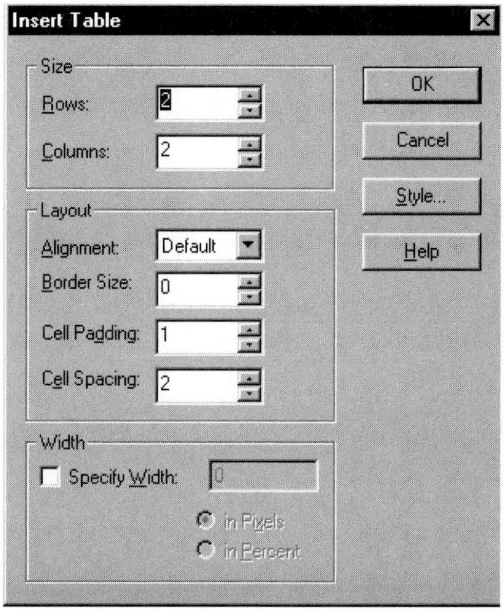

Figure 10-4   Insert Table Settings

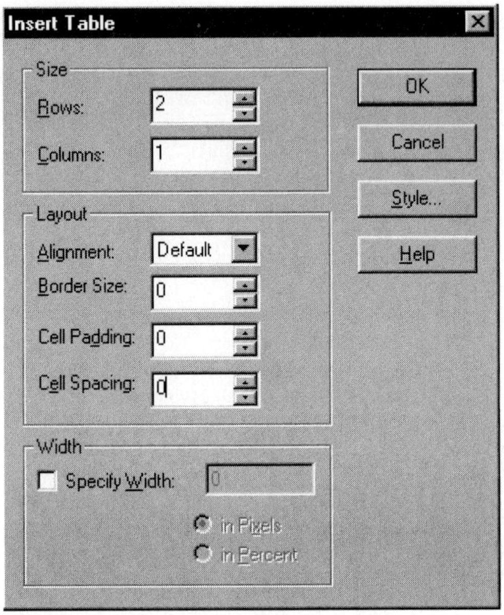

cell height to 85 pixels. When we click *OK*, we see that the height of the cell has changed (Figure 10-6).

Let's click in the bottom cell, then choose *Insert Cell* from the *Table* menu, and repeat the command selection four more times. The result is that we now have one cell on top and six on the bottom (Figure 10-6). We'll then drag the mouse across the six cells, bring up the properties menu, and set *Vertical Alignment* to *top* and the *Horizontal Alignment* to *center.*

Next, we will bring the properties box back up for the top cell and set the *Number of Columns Spanned* to 6 — this is so six cells can be placed below the cell we're working on (Figure 10-6).

We're ready to start populating our table. We'll click inside the top cell, and select *Image* from the *Insert* menu. This will bring up an *Image* dialog. No images will show because we haven't added any to our Web yet. We need to click on the image of the a magnifying glass hovering over a file folder, and navigate to where we put our *logo.jpg* file from Chapter 7. Double clicking on its file name, we'll have the image inserted into the table cell (Figure 10-7).

Just like we made some changes to the cell properties, we need to make some changes to the image properties. We do that by clicking on the image, and then right-clicking on the image and selecting *Properties* from the pop-up menu. We'll start on the *General* tab (Figure 10-8).

Figure 10-5   Cell Settings

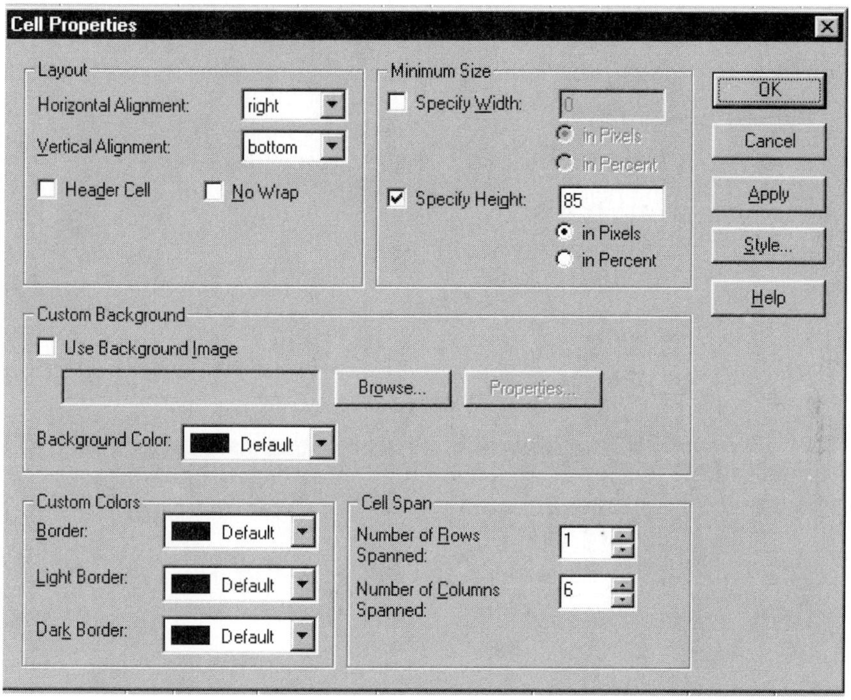

Cell Properties

Layout
Horizontal Alignment: right
Vertical Alignment: bottom
☐ Header Cell   ☐ No Wrap

Minimum Size
☐ Specify Width: 0
  ○ in Pixels
  ○ in Percent
☑ Specify Height: 85
  ● in Pixels
  ○ in Percent

OK
Cancel
Apply
Style...
Help

Custom Background
☐ Use Background Image
Browse...   Properties...
Background Color: ■ Default

Custom Colors
Border: ■ Default
Light Border: ■ Default
Dark Border: ■ Default

Cell Span
Number of Rows Spanned: 1
Number of Columns Spanned: 6

Figure 10-6   Spanning Table Cells

Figure 10-7   Table with Banner Link

Figure 10-8   Setting General Image Properties

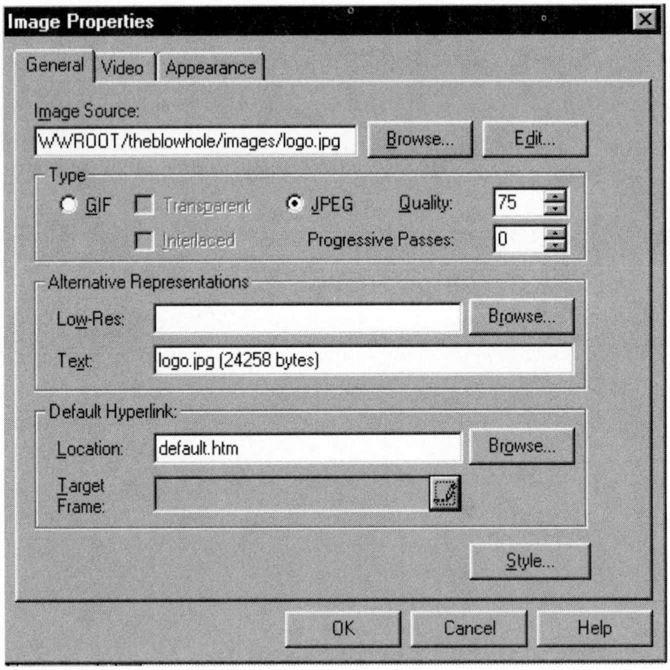

Right now the image source shows the image as a file instead of a Web location, but this should change once we save the components of this page to our Web. The *Alternative Representations* setting for *Text* is what will be shown on the Web page prior to the image being drawn, so the name and size of the image is fine. We can always change it to something else later. The banner will do double duty — it will be a ubiquitous reminder of whose Web site it is and a means for the visitor to return to the home page from anywhere on the Web site. The *Default Hyperlink* location is blank, and we want an entry there, because an entry in this field will convert the image from being simply an image to being an image hyperlink. We'll put *default.htm* in this field. Thus, when the image is clicked, the visitor will be returned to the home page. To make sure that we always end up loading the home page into a full browser page and not a frame, we'll click on the button to the right of the *Target Frame* field, which brings up the *Target Frame* dialog (Figure 10-10). From this dialog we'll select *Whole Page*, which in turn will put _top in the *Target Frame* field, indicating that when a page is loaded it will be loaded on top of whatever is showing in the browser.

We won't click *OK* just yet; instead, we'll move on to the *Appearance* tab (Figure 10-9). Here we can make changes to affect the way the image is displayed. The first change is to click the down-arrow next to *Border Thickness* so that the field changes from blank to 0; otherwise the image will have a border around it because we've made it a hyperlink. The other change we'll make is to check the *Specify Size* box. Doing this will cause the height and width of the image to be included in the HTML entry, which speeds painting of the page. Bear in mind that the next time the image properties for this image are shown, the check in this box will be cleared.

Figure 10-9   Setting Image Appearance Properties

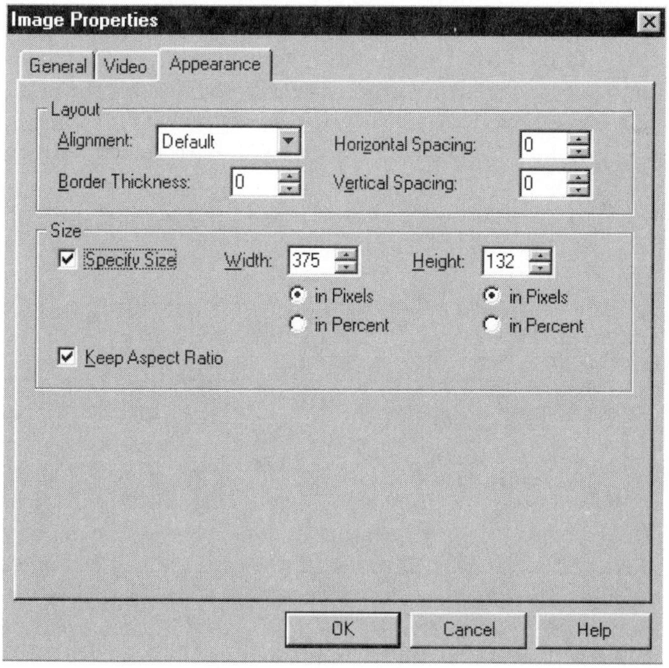

Figure 10-10   Defining the Target Frame

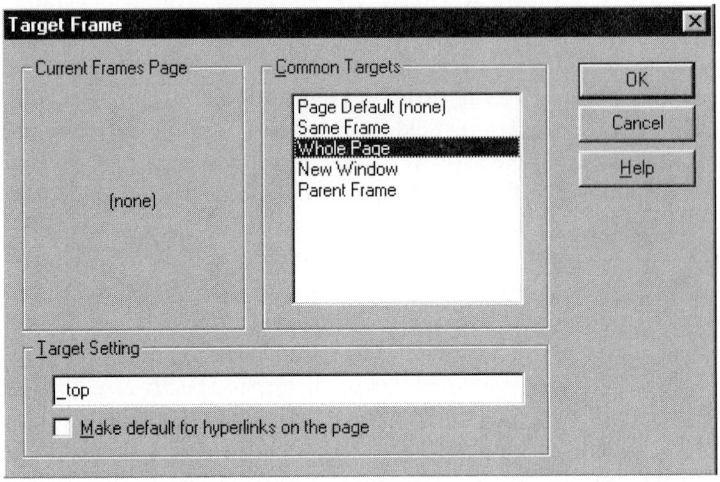

Okay, let's go back to our table. We've completed the first row. The second row will contain a series of prompts in the form of graphical images of words. We're using images for two reasons: the look will match the look of the banner, and since the only sure bet in the way of the fonts a browser will support are helvetica and Times Roman, it'll look much better.

We'll place the graphics in the cells first. Starting with the left-hand cell and working right, the graphics are:

- about.gif
- feedback.gif
- ad.gif
- awards.gif
- ring.gif
- copyrite.gif

We add each graphic to its respective cell by clicking on the cell by using the *Image* command of the *Insert* menu, clicking the magnifying glass over the file folder to the right of the *URL* text box, and navigating to the graphic. You'll notice when you click in each cell, that the cursor flashes from the middle of the cell. This is because we earlier set the horizontal alignment of each cell to *center*. The first few cells might appear overly large in width as each image is added, but they'll even themselves out.

Once we've placed the graphics, we need to edit the properties of each image and do the following with each:

- set the *Border Thickness* to 0
- enable *Specify Size*
- set the *Default Hyperlink Location* to the following, respectively (no, the pages don't exist yet, but it won't matter so long as we don't click the links)
  - about.htm
  - feedback.htm
  - ad.htm
  - awards.htm
  - rings.htm
  - copyrite.htm
- set the *Target Frame* to *_top*

We're done with the table. Just a few minor things to finish up. First, we'll click on the *HTML* tab and change the text between the TITLE tags to *Navbar2*. Then we'll select the *Save As* command from the *File* menu and change the title there to the same thing. Then we'll click on the diskette icon on the toolbar to save the page, at which point we'll receive a *Save Embedded Files* dialog (Figure 10-11). This is because we selected files through the file system to add as images, but haven't defined where they should be saved with regards to our page. The dialog defaults to the images being saved in the Web's root directory. We want to change the folder by clicking on the button, and then in the file window double-click on the *Images* folder. The folder for each image should now be *\images* instead of being blank, and we can click *OK*. That's our secondary navigation bar completed. Following is the *HTML* code that was generated by our activity.

Figure 10-11   Save Embedded Files Dialog

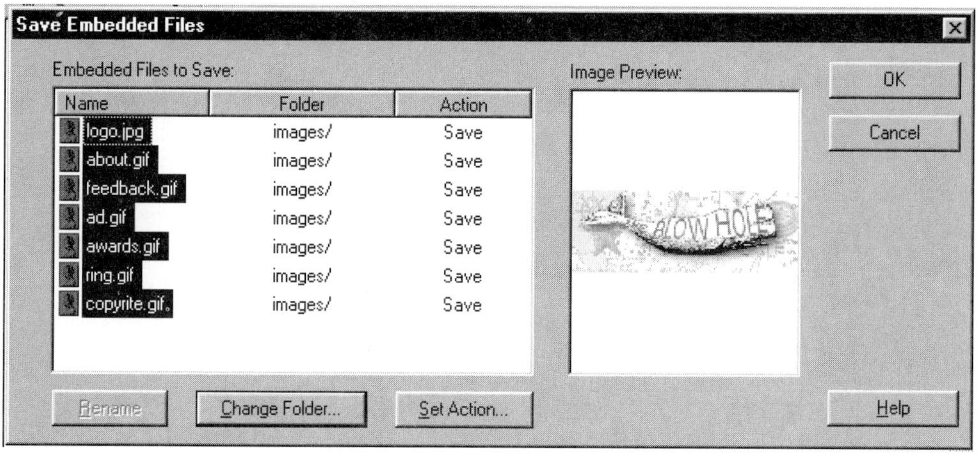

```html
<html>

<head>
<title>Navbar2</title>
</head>

<body>

<table border="0" cellpadding="0" cellspacing="0">
  <tr>
    <td valign="bottom" align="right" _
     height="85" colspan="6">
      <img src="images/logo.jpg" width="375" _
       height="132" alt="logo.jpg (24258 bytes)">
    </td>
  </tr>
  <tr>
    <td valign="top" align="center">
     <a href="about.htm" target="_top">
      <img src="images/about.gif" width="36" _
       height="15" alt="about.gif _
       (958 bytes)" border="0">
     </a>
    </td>
    <td valign="top" align="center">
     <a href="feedback.htm" target="_top">
      <img src="images/feedback.gif" width="56" _
       height="15" alt="feedback.gif _
       (1027 bytes)" border="0">
     </a>
    </td>
    <td valign="top" align="center">
     <a href="ad.htm" target="_top">
      <img src="images/ad.gif" width="60" _
       height="15" alt="ad.gif (1021 bytes)" _
       border="0">
     </a>
    </td>
    <td valign="top" align="center">
     <a href="awards.htm" target="_top">
      <img src="images/awards.gif" width="47" _
       height="15" alt="awards.gif (987 bytes)" _
       border="0">
     </a>
```

```
      </td>
      <td valign="top" align="center">
       <a href="rings.htm" target="_top">
        <img src="images/ring.gif" width="40" _
         height="15" alt="ring.gif _
         (968 bytes)" border="0">
       </a>
      </td>
      <td valign="top" align="center">
       <a href="copyrite.htm" target="_top">
        <img src="images/copyrite.gif" width="13" _
         height="16" alt="copyrite.gif _
         (898 bytes)" border="0">
       </a>
      </td>
    </tr>
  </table>
</body>
</html>
```

We could have entered this HTML directly, but as you see it was much easier to use the functionality of FrontPage to create the HTML for us. The navigation banner in *Normal* view is shown in Figure 10-12, and in *Preview* mode in Figure 10-13. With the navigation banner out of the way, we can start on our utility pages. The banner will be an element on each of those pages.

Figure 10-12   Navigation Banner - Normal View

Figure 10-13   Navigation Banner - Preview

Figure 10-14   Ad Page Layout

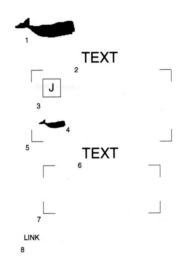

10.2 The Ad Page

The Ad page will be used to present and describe the various types of advertising available at the Web site. We've covered some of the techniques that will be used on this page, such as using a table to space elements as we did with our navigation banner, but we will be doing some new things too.

Let's take a look at the page design (Figure 10-14). The elements on the page are fairly straightforward.

- Some text
- A link
- Two tables
- An image
- The navigation banner
- A java applet

We'll start at the top of the page and work our way down. The first thing we want to do is create the page in FrontPage. We'll do that the same way we did for the navigation banner. This time we'll name the page *ad.htm.*

In order to place our navigation banner on the page, we'll choose the *FrontPage Component* command from the *Insert* menu (Figure 10-15). This will result in the presentation of the *Insert FrontPage Component* dialog (Figure 10-16) from which we'll select *Include Page.*

Figure 10-15   Ad Page Layout

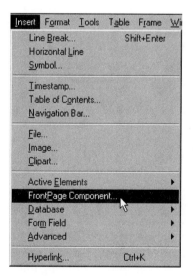

We then receive the *Include Page Component Properties* dialog (Figure 10-17), which asks us to identify the URL of the page to include. We'll type in *navbar2.htm* and click *OK.* This causes that page to be included in our current page, and since there's nothing else on the page, it will look exactly like the *navbar2.htm* page.

Figure 10-16   Including a Page

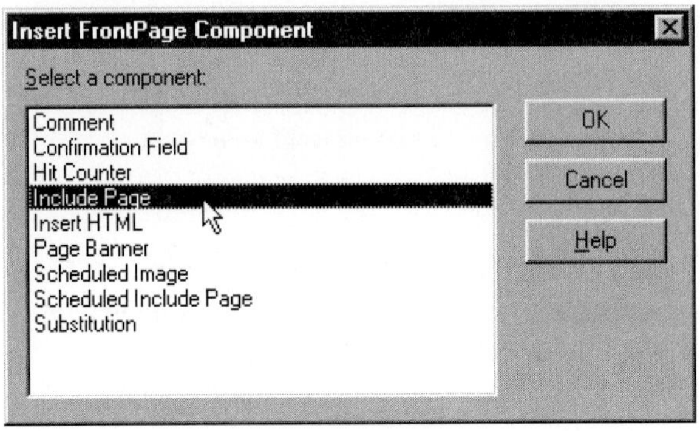

Figure 10-17   Include Page Component

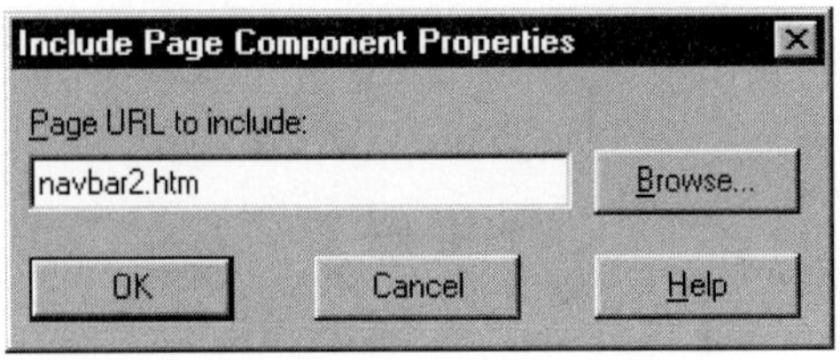

This Include Page facility, as well as many others, is managed on the Web site by FrontPage. Once the site is published, the server on which the Web site resides must support FrontPage extensions for the Include Page functionality to work. So, once we use this functionality, the site needs to be hosted on a server that supports FrontPage extensions. We could remove the component and simply copy the code from *navbar2.htm* and paste it in this page instead of linking it with the Include component. However, then if changes are made to *navbar2.htm*, they would also have to be made to this page because that code has been copied to our page instead of being linked. Think of the nightmare of copying the code to 20 pages instead of linking it.

Here is the HTML generated by our actions:

```
<!--Webbot bot="Include" U-Include="navbar2.htm" _
TAG="BODY" -->
```

Next up is the first block of text. We'll use the down-arrow key to move the cursor below the navigation banner and enter the following text.

```
Advertising

The Blowhole is a great place to advertise.
There is high exposure, and when people drill down to
a category of interest, the audience is motivated. For
example, someone seeing an ad for a sailboat manufac-
turer on a page listing links to sailboat manufactur-
ers is more likely to "click through" the ad than
someone interested in seashells seeing the same ad!

With any ad you place you can select up to three cat-
egories for it to appear under!

Not only does your ad appear on the category page you
select, but also on any category page with no pur-
chased ads.

There are three types of ads at The Blowhole. Each
provides the visitor an opportunity to click the ad to
be taken to a Web page for the advertiser. Don't have
a Web page? That's okay, we offer that service to go
with the ad. More on that later. Below is an example
of each type of ad.
```

Okay, the first thing we want to do is select the title, <u>Advertising</u>, and use the drop-down font list box and change the font to *Arial*. Then we'll place the cursor at the end of the word and hit the enter key to add a paragraph break, so that the changes we make only affect this line. Next, we'll click on the *Center* icon (Figure 10-18), the *Bold* icon (Figure 10-19), and the *Increase Font Size* icon, twice (Figure 10-20).

Figure 10-18   Centering

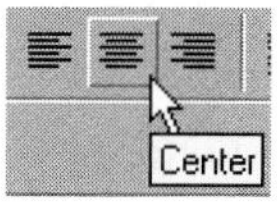

We'll move the cursor to the end of the sentence

```
The Blowhole is a great place to advertise.
```

Figure 10-19   Bold Font

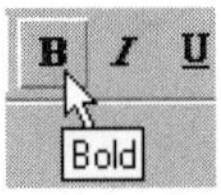

Figure 10-20   Increase Size

Here, and at the end of the next three paragraphs, we'll press the *delete* key so that the first word of the next paragraph moves to the current line, then we'll press *Enter* to create a paragraph break. We do it this way so that we only have a paragraph break and not line *and* paragraph breaks. Now, highlight the word 'great' and italicize it and make it bold.

We'll highlight the three paragraphs beginning

- There is high exposure . . .
- With any ad you place . . .
- Not only does your ad . . .

and click the bullet list icon (Figure 10-21) to create three bullets.

Figure 10-21   Bulleted List

The remaining paragraph needs no changes to be made to it, so we're finished with the initial block of text. Figure 10-22 shows what the text looks like after our changes. Following, generated by our actions, is the HTML that is behind our text block:

```
<p align="center">
<big><big><strong>
<font face="Arial"> Advertising
 </font></strong></big></big></p>
```

```
<p>The Blowhole is a <strong><em>great
</em></strong> place to advertise.

<ul>
   <li>There is high exposure, and when people drill
down to a category of interest, the audience is moti-
vated. For example, someone seeing an ad for a sailboat
manufacturer on a page listing links to sailboat manu-
facturers is more likely to &quot;click through &quot;
the ad than someone interested in seashells seeing the
same ad!</li>
   <li>With any ad you place you can select up to
three categories for it to appear under! </li>
   <li>Not only does your ad appear on the category
page you select, but also on any category page with no
purchased ads.</li>
   </ul>

   <p>There are three types of ads at The Blowhole.
Each provides the visitor an opportunity to click the
ad to be taken to a Web page for the advertiser. Don't
have a Web page? That's okay, we offer that service to
go with the ad. More on that later. Below is an example
of each type of ad.</p>
```

Figure 10-22   First Text Block

Advertising

The Blowhole is a **great** place to advertise.

- There is high exposure, and when people drill down to a category of interest, the audience is motivated. For example, someone seeing an ad for a sailboat manufacturer on a page listing links to sailboat manufacturers is more likely to "click through" the ad than someone interested in seashells seeing the same ad!
- With any ad you place you can select up to three categories for it to appear under!
- Not only does your ad appear on the category page you select, but also on any category page with no purchased ads

There are three types of ads at The Blowhole. Each provides the visitor an opportunity to click the ad to be taken to a web page for the advertiser. Don't have a web page? That's okay, we offer that service to go with the ad. More on that later. Below is an example of each type of ad.

Next up is our first table. We've done a table before, but this one will have different properties. We begin by invoking the *Insert Table* dialog. We'll set the table size to four rows and four columns. The table should be centered, with a border size of 1, cell padding of 1, and cell spacing of 4. Figure 10-23 shows what the table looks like at this point. Next, we want to select the first row in the table, either by dragging the mouse across it or by clicking in one of its cells and choosing the *Select Row* command from the *Table* menu, and bring up the row's properties (Figure 10-24) via the *Cell Properties* command. We'll check the boxes for *Header Cell* and *No Wrap*. The former will set the font for the cell to emphasize the text, and the latter will prevent the text from wrapping within the cell.

Figure 10-23   − New Table

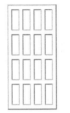

The first cell will remain blank. In the remaining three cells, we'll enter the following text:

- Size (pixels)
- Type
- Description

On the second row, we'll select the two center cells and set their horizontal alignment to *center.* We'll leave the first cell empty for now, it will later contain our Java applet. The remaining cells will contain the following text:

- 400x40
- .gif
- A rotating banner ad on the main (home) page with an audience of general marine interests. Does not necessarily show on every page hit.

In row 3 we'll set the horizontal alignment of the first cell to *center.* In this row, the two center cells will remain empty, but the outer cells will have the following text:

Figure 10-24   Row Properties

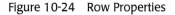

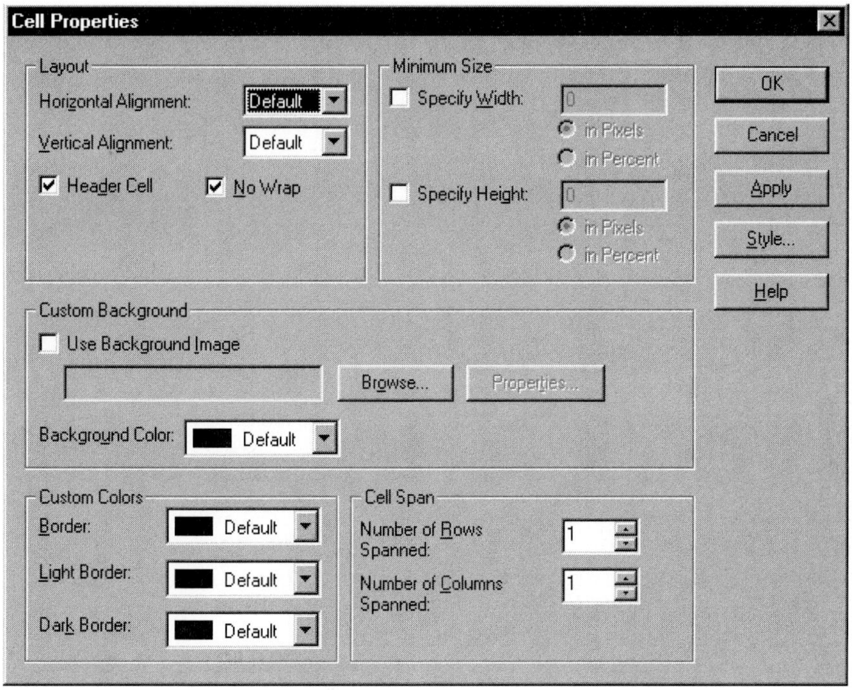

- Same as above [yes, that's the text]
- A more slowly cycling banner presented for specific categories. Each subsequent page represents a more specific category, and thus a more motivated reader. Does not necessarily show on every page hit.

On to the final row in this table. We'll set the horizontal alignment of the first three columns to *center*. The following text is for the three right-hand columns:

- 192x96
- .gif
- A static ad on every hit of the main page or every hit of specific category pages.

The first cell in this row will have an image in it. First we click in the cell, then we use the *Insert* menu and the *Image* command, and navigate to the file *blowholead.gif* and insert it. We'll then edit the image properties and set the border size to 1.

Here is the code for our table to this point:

```
<table border="1" cellspacing="4">
  <tr>
    <th nowrap> </th>
    <th nowrap>Size (pixels)</th>
    <th nowrap>Type</th>
    <th nowrap>Description</th>
  </tr>
  <tr>
    <td> </td>
    <td align="center">400x40</td>
    <td align="center">.GIF</td>
    <td>A rotating banner ad on the main _
        (home) page with an audience of _
        general marine interests. Does not _
        necessarily show on every page hit.</td>
  </tr>
  <tr>
    <td align="center">Same as above</td>
    <td> </td>
    <td> </td>
    <td>A more slowly cycling banner presented _
        for specific categories. Each _
        subsequent page represents a more _
        specific category, and thus a more _
        motivated reader. Does not necessarily _
        show on every page hit.
</td>
  </tr>
  <tr>
    <td align="center">
     <img src="file:///C:/WEBSHARE/WWWROOT/ _
    theblowhole/images/blowholead.gif" _
    width="192" height="96" alt="blowholead.gif _
    (3375 bytes)" border="1"></td>
    <td align="center">192x96</td>
    <td align="center">.GIF</td>
    <td>A static ad on every hit of the main _
        page or every hit of specific _
        category pages.</td>
  </tr>
</table>
</center></div>
```

Back to the first cell, and we'll add our applet. The code for the applet can be found at the Web site (see Appendix A). Then we need to bring up the FrontPage Explorer window, click on the root folder in the left pane, and use the *New* command in the *File* menu to add a new folder. We'll name the folder *java*.

We'll select the *Advanced* submenu from the *Insert* menu, and then select *Java Applet*. This will result in the *Java Applet Properties* dialog being shown. The first setting is the name of the Java class, which is *DynamicBillboard.class*. The *Applet Base URL* field is to identify the location of the code, which is *java/*.

We'll need to enter some applet parameters. We do this by clicking on the *Add* button and then specifying the parameter name and value in the *Set Attribute Value* dialog. Following in Table 10-1 is a list of the parameters.

Table 10-1   Java Applet Attributes

Parameter	Value
bgcolor	#FFFFFF
bill0	images/pduckb.gif,http://www.puddle-duck.com
bill1	images/yourad.gif,http://www.puddle-duck.com
billboards	2
delay	5000
transitions	2,RotateTransition,FadeTransition

The height needs to be *40*, and the width *400*. The alignment should be *center*. The *Java Applet Priorities* dialog is shown in Figure 10-25. When we click *OK* a place holder is inserted into the table cell.

Following is the HTML behind our Java applet:

```
<applet width="400" height="40" _
  code="DynamicBillboard.class" codebase="java/" _
  align="center">
    <param name="bgcolor" value="#FFFFFF">
    <param name="bill0" value= _
      "images/pduckb.gif, _
      http://www.puddleduck.com">
```

Figure 10-25   Java Applet Properties

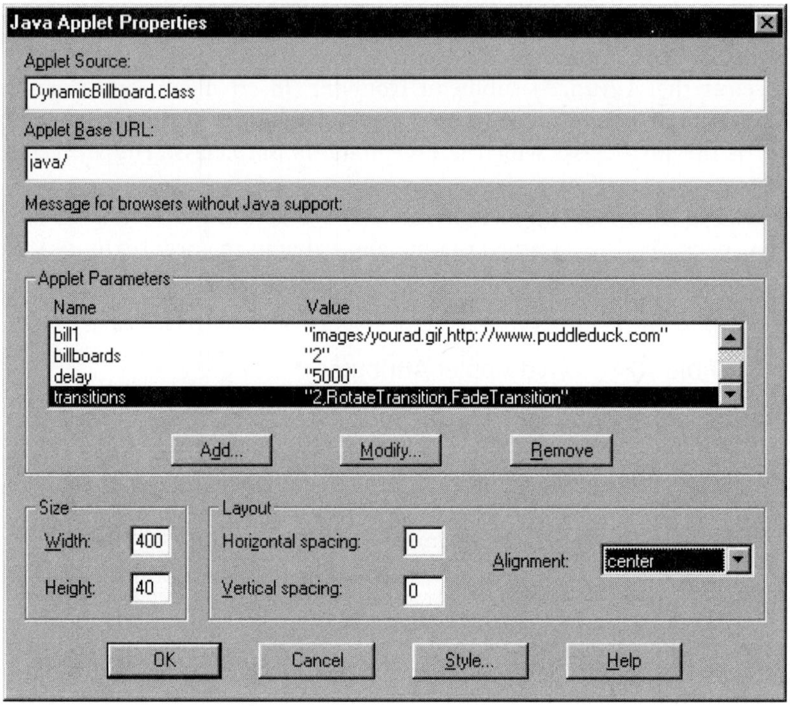

```
<param name="bill1" value= _
  "images/yourad.gif,http://www. _
  puddleduck.com">
<param name="billboards" value="2">
<param name="delay" value="5000">
<param name="transitions" value= _
  "2,RotateTransition,FadeTransition">
</applet>
```

The completed table is shown in Figure 10-26. Taking another look at it, one last adjustment we might want to make is to select the text cells in the right three columns and reduce the text size one click.

Beneath this table we have another text block. This block serves as an introduction on the advertising pricing and the pricing table that follows it. Following is the text for this text block:

Figure 10-26   Completed Table

	Size (pixels)	Type	Description
	400x40	.GIF	A rotating banner ad on t (home) page with an audi general marine interests.] necessarily show on ever hit.
Same as above			A more slowly cycling ba presented for specific cat Each subsequent page re more specific category, a more motivated reader. I necessarily show on ever hit.
	192x96	.GIF	A static ad on every hit o page or every hit of speci category pages.

AD PRICES
Ads are offered to non-profit conservation organizations at no charge.
* Special * Because we're a new site and don't have
volume yet, we can't guarantee a number of imprints
(showing of your ad). So we're offering the following
ads at 50% off the listed prices below for the first
year, and a guarantee of no more than the list price
below for the second year. Order the entire
year up front for additional savings!

Okay, touch-up time. We'll select the *AD PRICES* line, and choose *Heading 3* for its style. A paragraph break after it is needed. In the next paragraph, we'll italicize *non-profit* and *no charge*, and make *no charge* bold.

In the final paragraph we'll make ** Special ** and *50% off* bold, the latter a size larger too, and make both of them red by using the text color icon (Figure 10-27) and dialog (Figure 10-28). The text in its final form can be seen in Figure 10-29. Following is the HTML:

Figure 10-27   Text Color

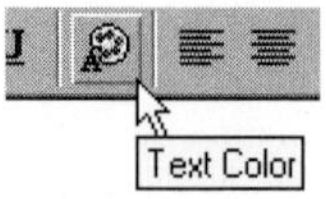

Figure 10-28   Select Text Color

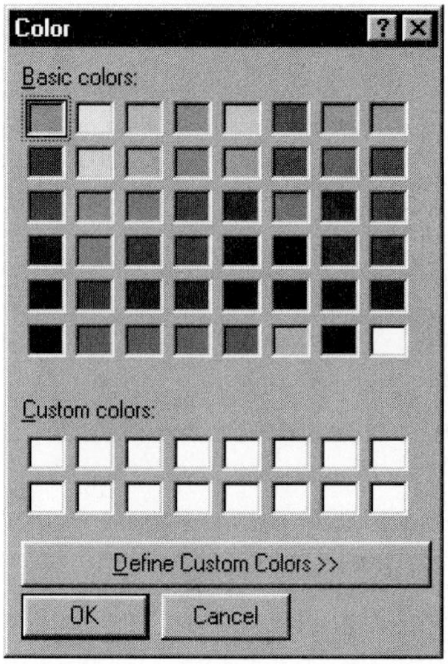

Figure 10-29   Ad Page Text

AD PRICES

Ads are offered to *non-profit* conservation organizations at ***no charge***.

* **Special** * Because we're a new site and don't have volume yet, we can't guarantee a number of imprints (showing of your ad). So we're offering the following ads at **50% off** the listed prices below for the first year, and a guarantee of no more than the list price below for the second year. Order the entire year up front for additional savings!

Finished Pricing Text Block

```
<p>
<font color="#ff0000">
<strong>* Special * </strong></font>
<font color="#000000">
Because we're a new site and don't have _
volume yet, we can't guarantee a number of _
 imprints (showing of your ad). So we're _
 offering the following ads at _
</font><strong><font color="#ff0000"><big> _
50% off</big></font></strong>
<font color="#000000">
the listed prices below for the first year, _
and a guarantee of no more than the list _
price below for the second year. Order the _
entire year up front for additional savings!
</font></p>
```

This brings us to our second table. The properties for this table are as follows — we'll use them to generate the table:

- Columns: 3
- Rows: 5
- Alignment: Center
- Border size: 1
- Cell Spacing: 4
- Cell Padding: 1

We'll select the first row and enable *No Wrap* and *Header Cell* in the properties. We also want to change the background color. We'll select *Custom* from the *Background Color* drop-down list, and set it to HSL 148, 240, 214, which is a deep baby blue.

The text for each cell in the header row is as follows:

- Ad Type
- Monthly
- Yearly

Each of the body cells in the table will have the text one size smaller than default. In the following bullets, | signifies a line break. Following is the text for each cell in the first body row:

- Main Page | Rotating
- $15
- $165

Here is the text for the second body row. The final cell in this row has no text, but it does have a background color, which is *Gray* from the drop-down list:

- Main Page | Static
- $15

The text for the third body row:

- Category Rotating | (Price covers 3 categories)
- $25
- $275

And the final body row's text:

- Category Static
- $50
- $100

The table in its final form can be seen in Figure 10-30. Following is the HTML code for it:

```
<div align="center"><center>

<table border="1" cellspacing="4">
  <tr>
    <th nowrap bgcolor="#C8D9FF">Ad Type</th>
    <th nowrap bgcolor="#C8D9FF">Monthly</th>
    <th nowrap bgcolor="#C8D9FF">Yearly</th>
  </tr>
  <tr>
    <td><small>Main Page<br>
    Rotating</small></td>
    <td align="right"><small>$15</small></td>
    <td align="right"><small>$165</small></td>
  </tr>
  <tr>
    <td><small>Main Page<br>
    Static</small></td>
    <td align="right"><small>$15</small></td>
```

```
      <td align="right" bgcolor="#808080">_
         </td>
    </tr>
    <tr>
      <td><small>Category Rotating</small><br>
      <small>(Price covers 3 categories)
      </small></td>
      <td align="right"><small>$25</small></td>
      <td align="right"><small>$275</small></td>
    </tr>
    <tr>
      <td><small>Category Static</small></td>
      <td align="right"><small>$50</small></td>
      <td align="right" bgcolor="#FFFFFF"> _
      <small>$500
        </small></td>
    </tr>
  </table>
  </center>
  </div>
```

Figure 10-30   Ad Table

Ad Type	Monthly	Yearly
Main Page Rotating	$15	$165
Main Page Static	$15	
Category Rotating (Price covers 3 categories)	$25	$275
Category Static	$50	$500

The final thing to do on this page is a final text block. Here is the text:

```
When your ad is clicked, the reader will be taken
to your Web page. If you need a banner ad designed, a
Web page designed, or a Web page hosted, you'll
receive a discount from Puddleduck Press.
```

The only formatting we want to apply to this text is to select the name Puddleduck Press and add a link by clicking the link icon (Figure 10-31). We'll set the URL to *http://www.puddleduck.com* and the *Target Frame* to *New Window*, so that we can send visitors to another site without losing them to our site. One interesting point is the appearance of the link. It will default to the standard link appearance: underlined blue text. Our site will have links that appear differently, but not until we create our CSS (Cascading Style Sheet).

Figure 10-31   Hyperlink

For now, we'll add a line directly to our HTML in the HEAD portion of this file to import a site style sheet, but it will only be a place-holder at this point. Here's the line:

```
<link rel="stylesheet" type="text/css" _
href="blowhole.css">
```

Figure 10-32   The Ad Page

Advertising

The Blowhole is a *great* place to advertise.

- There is high exposure, and when people drill down to a category of interest, the audience is motivated. For example, someone seeing an ad for a sailboat manufacturer on a page listing links to sailboat manufacturers is more likely to "click through" the ad than someone interested in seashells seeing the same ad!
- With any ad you place you can select up to three categories for it to appear under!!
- Not only does your ad appear on the category page you select, but also on any category page with no purchased ads

There are three types of ads at The Blowhole. Each provides the visitor an opportunity to click the ad to be taken to a web page for the advertiser. Don't have a web page? That's okay, we offer that service to go with the ad. More on that later. Below is an example of each type of ad.

	Size (pixels)	Type	Description
	400x40	GIF	A rotating banner ad on the main (home) page with an audience of general marine interests. Does not necessarily show on every page hit.
Same as above			A more slowly cycling banner presented for specific categories. Each subsequent page represents a more specific category, and thus a more motivated reader. Does not necessarily show on every page hit.
	192x96	GIF	A static ad on every hit of the main page or every hit of specific category pages.

AD PRICES

Ads are offered to *non-profit* conservation organizations at *no charge*.

* Special * Because we're a new site and don't have volume yet, we can't guarantee a number of imprints (showing of your ad). So we're offering the following ads at **50%** off the listed prices below for the first year, and a guarantee of no more than the list price below for the second year. Order the entire year up front for additional savings!

Ad Type	Monthly	Yearly
Main Page Rotating	$15	$165
Main Page Static	$15	
Category Rotating (Price covers 3 categories)	$25	$275

The last thing we need to do is change the title of this page to *Ad Information* and save it. Figure 10-32 shows the completed *Ad Page*. Following is the complete code of our page:

```
<html>

<head>
<title>Ad Information</title>
<link rel="stylesheet" type="text/css" _
 href="blowhole.css">
</head>

<body>
<!--Webbot bot="Include" U-Include="navbar2.htm" _
 TAG="BODY" -->

<p align="center"><big><big><strong> _
<font face="Arial">Advertising</font></strong> _
</big>
</big></p>

<p>The Blowhole is a <strong><em>great</em> _
</strong> place to advertise.
<ul>
   <li>There is high exposure, and when people _
      drill down to a category of interest, _
      the audience is motivated. For example, _
      someone seeing an ad for a sailboat _
      manufacturer on a page listing links _
      to sailboat manufacturers is more likely _
      to &quot;click through&quot;the ad than _
      someone interested in seashells seeing _
      the same ad!</li>
   <li>With any ad you place you can select _
      up to three categories for it to appear _
      under!! </li>
   <li>Not only does your ad appear on the _
      category page you select, but also on _
      any category page with no purchased ads</li>
</ul>

<p>There are three types of ads at The _
      Blowhole. Each provides the visitor an _
      opportunity to click the ad to be taken to _
```

```
        a Web page for the advertiser. Don't have a _
        Web page? That's okay, we offer that _
        service to go with the ad. More on that _
        later. Below is an example of each type _
        of ad.</p>
<div align="center"><center>

<table border="1" cellspacing="4">
  <tr>
    <th nowrap> </th>
    <th nowrap>Size (pixels)</th>
    <th nowrap>Type</th>
    <th nowrap>Description</th>
  </tr>
  <tr>
    <td>
    <applet width="400" height="40" code= _
"DynamicBillboard.class" codebase="java/ _
"align="center">
      <param name="bgcolor" value="#FFFFFF">
      <param name="bill0" value= _
"images/pduckb.gif,http://www.puddleduck.com">
      <param name="bill1" value= _
"images/yourad.gif,http://www.puddleduck.com">
      <param name="billboards" value="2">
      <param name="delay" value="5000">
      <param name="transitions" value= _
"2,RotateTransition,FadeTransition">
    </applet>
    </td>
    <td align="center"><small>400x40</small></td>
    <td align="center"><small>.GIF</small></td>
    <td><small>A rotating banner ad on the _
              main (home) page with an _
              audience of general marine _
              interests. Does not _
              necessarily show on _
            every page hit.</small> _
</td>
  </tr>
  <tr>
    <td align="center">Same as above</td>
    <td> </td>
    <td> </td>
```

```
      <td><small>A more slowly cycling banner _
                presented for specific _
                categories. Each subsequent _
                page represents a more _
                specific category, and thus a _
                more motivated reader. Does _
                not necessarily show on every _
                page hit. </small></td>
  </tr>
  <tr>
    <td align="center"><img src= _
"images/blowholead.gif" alt="blowholead.gif _
(3375 bytes)"
    border="1" WIDTH="192" HEIGHT="96"></td>
    <td align="center"><small>192x96</small></td>
    <td align="center"><small>.GIF</small></td>
    <td><small>A static ad on every hit of the _
                main page or every hit of _
                specific category pages.
                </small></td>
  </tr>
</table>
</center></div>

<h3>AD PRICES</h3>

<p>Ads are offered to <em>non-profit</em> _
conservation organizations at <em><strong>no _
charge </strong></em>. </p>

<p><font color="#ff0000"><strong> _
* Special * </strong></font>
<font color="#000000"> Because we're a new site _
and don't have volume yet, we can't guarantee _
a number of imprints (showing of your ad). So _
we're offering the following ads at _
</font><strong> <font color="#ff0000"> _
<big>50% off</big> </font>
</strong><font color="#000000">the listed _
 prices below for the first year, and a _
 guarantee of no more than the list price _
 below for the second year. Order the _
entire year up front for additional savings!
</font> </p> <div align="center"><center>
```

```html
<table border="1" cellspacing="4">
  <tr>
    <th nowrap bgcolor="#C8D9FF">Ad Type</th>
    <th nowrap bgcolor="#C8D9FF">Monthly</th>
    <th nowrap bgcolor="#C8D9FF">Yearly</th>
  </tr>
  <tr>
    <td><small>Main Page<br>
    Rotating</small></td>
    <td align="right"><small>$15</small></td>
    <td align="right"><small>$165</small></td>
  </tr>
  <tr>
    <td><small>Main Page<br>
    Static</small></td>
    <td align="right"><small>$15</small></td>
    <td align="right" bgcolor="#808080"> _
       </td>
  </tr>
  <tr>
    <td><small>Category Rotating</small><br>
    <small>(Price covers 3 categories) _
      </small></td>
    <td align="right"><small>$25</small></td>
    <td align="right"><small>$275</small></td>
  </tr>
  <tr>
    <td><small>Category Static</small></td>
    <td align="right"><small>$50</small></td>
    <td align="right" bgcolor="#FFFFFF">
<small>$500
</small></td>
  </tr>
</table></center></div>
<p>When your ad is clicked, the reader will _
be taken to your Web page. If you need a banner _
ad designed, a Web page designed, or a Web _
page hosted, you'll receive a discount from _
<a href= "http://www.puddleduck.com" _
target="_blank"> Puddleduck Press</a>.</p>
</body>
</html>
```

Let's move on to our next page.

10.3 The Copyright Page

Puddleduck Press have provided the HTML for the copyright page. We'll look at it as if we're developing it here, as it plays a role on our site since it already exists, however, we'll first present the page (Figure 10-33), then disassemble it.

Figure 10-33   The Copyright Page

Let's take a look at the *Head* portion of the page.

```
<html>
<head>
<title>Copyright info</title>
</head>
```

Okay, not much to talk about there. It's the standard fare for defining a Web page. The *Body* tag has parameters defined for link color. The links will be black as defined by the RGB color #000000 in the following:

```
<body bgcolor="#FFFFFF" link="#000000" _
   vlink="#000000" alink="#000000">
```

The body of the page is comprised of a table of three equal columns, as shown in the following table definition code:

```
<table border="0" cellpadding="3" _
   cellspacing="0" width="100%">
<td align="right" valign="top" width="33%"></td>
<td align="right" valign="top" width="33%"></td>
<td align="center" valign="top" width="33%"></td>
</table>
```

Easy going to this point. Now we just need to fill in each of the three columns. The first column serves to hold the site logo and an image link that facilitates sending email about the Web site to the site developers. Following is the code for the logo:

```
<img src="images/logo.jpg" width="240" _
    height="84" alt="logo.jpg (24258 bytes)">
```

The next element in this column is the image link and text for contacting the Webmaster. This information appears at the bottom of the column. There are two simple ways to position elements within HTML. We'll use the first method here, which is simply to place paragraphs between the two items. HTML doesn't like white space, so it's always a good idea when having an empty cell or paragraph to fill it with a place holder. In HTML, a valid place holder is , which stands for non-breaking space. The usage can be seen in the following code:

```
<p> </p>
<p> </p>
<p> </p>
<p> </p>
<p> </p>
```

And at the bottom of the cell we have an image link, which is an image reference within a hyperlink reference. The image isn't one that we created, but is available on the Web site (see Appendix A). Here's the code:

```
<p>
<a href="mailto:theblowhole@puddleduck.com">
<img src="images/mailmain.gif" _
    alt="mailmain.gif (9639 bytes)" _
    align="middle" border="0" WIDTH="65" _
    HEIGHT="35"></a>
Contact the Webmaster
```

This isn't a typical hyperlink in that it doesn't take the visitor to another page. You'll notice that the address in the *href* isn't a HTTP address, but a MAILTO address. Clicking this link, the image, will allow the site visitor to send an email message to that address.

The second column has some text, four different hyperlinks, and an image. The code for this isn't complicated:

```
<p>
<font size="3" face="Arial">
<strong>Copyright Information</strong>
</font></p>
<p><font size="2" face="Arial">
The pages and page elements on this site are _
all Copyright ©1998-1999 Puddleduck Press Inc. _
unless noted otherwise below. All Rights _
Reserved.
</font></p>
<p><font face="Arial">
<small>
We'd appreciate any
</small>
<font size="2" color="#000000">
<a href="mailto:TheBlowHole@puddleduck.com"> _
<strong>feedback</strong>
</a> you have<br>.
Feel free to drop by other
<font size="2" color="#000000"><strong>
<a href="http://www.puddleduck.com"> _
Puddleduck Press</a>
</strong> sites - click
<font size="2" color="#000000">
<a href="http://www.puddleduck.com/pdlinks.htm">
here</a> for a list.
</font></font></font></font>
<font size="2" face="Arial" color="#000000">
</p>
<p>
<a href="http://www.puddleduck.com/pduck.htm">
<img src="images/pdlogo.gif" alt="pduck2.gif _
  (1602 bytes)" border="0" align="middle" _
 width="86" height="110"></a></font>
```

The final column introduces the second method of positioning an element within a table: using another table. Yes, you can embed tables within tables. We'll have a table within our cell, as well as some text, an image and two image links. Here's the code:

```
<div align="center">
<center>
```

```
<!-- begin the embedded table -->
<table>
 <tr>
  <td width="50">
   <small>
   This site created by a member of
   </small>
  </td>
  <td>
   <img src="images/lo-025.gif" alt="lo-025.gif _
   (4162 bytes)" WIDTH="64" HEIGHT="90">
  </td>
 </tr>
</table>
<!-- end embedded table -->
</center>
</div>
<p align="center">
<a href="http://www.microsoft.com/frontpage">
<img src="images/FPCreated.gif" _
 alt="FPCreated.gif (9674 bytes)" border="0" _
 hspace="7" WIDTH="87" HEIGHT="41">
</a>
</p>
<p align="center">
<a href="http://www.microsoft.com/ie">
<img src="images/ie4get_animated.gif" _
 alt="ie4get_animated.gif (7090 bytes)" _
 border="0" WIDTH="88" HEIGHT="31">
</a>
```

That ends the *Copyright* page. We're ready to move on to the *Awards* page.

10.4 The Awards Page

The *Awards* page will be used to show the awards that The Blowhole presents to other Web sites, and to show any awards won. We have a design for the *Awards* page (Figure 10-34). It's a very straightforward page:

- the banner logo on top
- four sets of images and text, one for each award
- a link to the page for award nomination

Figure 10-34   The Awards Page Design

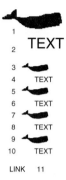

1
2   TEXT
3
4   TEXT
5
6   TEXT
7
8   TEXT
9
10   TEXT

LINK   11

All of the elements on this page are things we've already covered, so we'll move through them fairly quickly.

The first thing we'll do is create the page in FrontPage and name it *awards.htm*. Then we'll double click on the name to invoke the editor.

We need the banner at the top of the page, so we'll use the *Include* menu and the *FrontPage Component* command to include *navbar2.htm* in our page as we did when we created the *Ad* page.

Next we need to add each of the awards with the appropriate text below them. Following is the name of each image, and the text for each. Table 10-2 lays out the images and associated text.

We'll first add the image *se_award.gif*. We want it centered and the image to be aligned above its text. We'll specify the size, but won't bother changing the border setting since this won't be a link and the border won't show. The text needs to be indented on both sides. Following is the resulting code:

```
<p align="center">
<img src="images/se_award.jpg" width="199" _
 height="103" alt="se_award.jpg (9993 bytes)">
</p>

<blockquote>
  <blockquote>
    <blockquote>
      <blockquote>
        <blockquote>
```

Table 10-2   The Blowhole Awards

Award	File Name	Text
Spouting Excellence	se_award.gif	This is the highest award offered by The Blowhole. It is bestowed upon sites that reflect excellence in all the categories listed below.
Conservation Excellence	c_award.gif	Presented to sites representing organizations that provide selfless dedicated effort to conservation
Web Content Excellence	wc_award.gif	Presented to sites that do an outstanding service of providing information on a marine topic
Web Design Excellence	wd_award.gif	Presented to sites with a design that makes the Web surfing experience enjoyable and rewarding

```
        <p align="center">This is the highest _
award offered by The Blowhole. It is bestowed _
upon sites that reflect excellence in all the _
categories listed below.</p>
        </blockquote>
      </blockquote>
    </blockquote>
  </blockquote>
</blockquote>
```

This section of the page is shown in Figure 10-35. We can move on and add the remaining awards and text in Figure 10-36, Figure 10-37 and Figure 10-38.

Figure 10-35   The "Spouting Excellence" Award

This is the highest award offered by The Blowhole. It is bestowed upon sites that reflect excellence in all the categories listed below.

Figure 10-36   The "Conservation Excellence" Award

Presented to sites representing organizations
that provide selfless dedicated effort to
conservation

```
<p align="center">
<img src="images/c_award.jpg" width="197" _
height="101" alt="c_award.jpg (10287 bytes)">
</p>

<blockquote>
  <blockquote>
    <blockquote>
      <blockquote>
        <blockquote>
          <blockquote>
            <p align="center">
                Presented to sites representing _
                organizations that provide _
                selfless dedicated effort to _
                conservation
            </p>
          </blockquote>
        </blockquote>
      </blockquote>
    </blockquote>
  </blockquote>
</blockquote>
```

Figure 10-37   The "Web Design Excellence" Award

Presented to sites with a design that makes
the web surfing experience enjoyable and
rewarding

```
<p align="center">
<img src="images/wd_award.jpg"
width="197" height="101" alt="c_award.jpg _
(10287 bytes)">
</p>

<blockquote>
  <blockquote>
    <blockquote>
      <blockquote>
        <blockquote>
          <blockquote>
            <p align="center">Presented to sites_
              with a design that makes the Web _
              surfing experience enjoyable _
              and rewarding
          </p>
          </blockquote>
        </blockquote>
      </blockquote>
    </blockquote>
  </blockquote>
</blockquote>


<p align="center">
<img src="images/wc_award.jpg" width="194" _
 height="98" alt="wc_award.jpg (10166 bytes)">
</p>
```

Figure 10-38   The "Web Content Excellence" Award

Presented to sites that do an outstanding
service of providing information on a marine
topic

```
<blockquote>
  <blockquote>
    <blockquote>
      <blockquote>
        <blockquote>
          <blockquote>
            <p align="center">
                Presented to sites that do an _
                outstanding service of providing _
                information on a marine topic
            </p>
          </blockquote>
        </blockquote>
      </blockquote>
    </blockquote>
  </blockquote>
</blockquote>
```

The last thing to do on this page is create a link to the page that's used for nominating Web sites to receive these awards, *nominate.htm*. The final page is shown in Figure 10-39.

```
<p align="center">
<a href="nominate.htm">
Click here to nominate a Web site for one of
these awards
</a>
</p>
```

Figure 10-39   The "Awards" Page

That finishes the *Awards* page. We'll save it and, in so doing, add the graphics to our Web (make sure you change the folder to "images/"). Let's change the title in our HTML to *The Blowhole Awards Page*. Following is the code for the page:

```
<html>

<head>
<title>The Blowhole Awards Page</title>
</head>

<body>
<!--Webbot bot="Include" U-Include="navbar2.htm" _
  TAG="BODY" -->
```

```
<p align="center">
<img src="images/se_award.jpg" width="199" _
height="103" alt="se_award.jpg (9993 bytes)">
</p>

<blockquote>
  <blockquote>
    <blockquote>
      <blockquote>
        <blockquote>
          <p align="center">
          This is the highest award offered by _
          The Blowhole. It is bestowed upon _
          sites that reflect excellence in all _
          the categories listed below.
          </p>
        </blockquote>
      </blockquote>
    </blockquote>
  </blockquote>
</blockquote>

<p align="center">
<img src="images/c_award.jpg" width="197" _
height="101" alt="c_award.jpg (10287 bytes)">
</p>
<blockquote>
  <blockquote>
    <blockquote>
      <blockquote>
        <blockquote>
          <blockquote>
          <p align="center">
            Presented to sites representing _
            organizations that provide _
            selfless dedicated effort to _
            conservation
          </p>
          </blockquote>
        </blockquote>
      </blockquote>
    </blockquote>
  </blockquote>
</blockquote>
```

```
<p align="center">
<img src="images/wd_award.jpg" width="194" _
height="98" alt="wd_award.jpg (9835 bytes)">
</p>
<blockquote>
  <blockquote>
    <blockquote>
      <blockquote>
        <blockquote>
          <blockquote>
            <p align="center">
                Presented to sites with a design _
                that makes the Web surfing _
                experience enjoyable and _
                rewarding
            </p>
          </blockquote>
        </blockquote>
      </blockquote>
    </blockquote>
  </blockquote>
</blockquote>

<p align="center">
<img src="images/wc_award.jpg" width="194" _
height="98" alt="wc_award.jpg (10166 bytes)">
</p>
<blockquote>
  <blockquote>
    <blockquote>
      <blockquote>
        <blockquote>
          <blockquote>
            <p align="center">
                Presented to sites that do an _
                outstanding service of providing _
                information on a marine topic
            </p>
          </blockquote>
        </blockquote>
      </blockquote>
    </blockquote>
  </blockquote>
</blockquote>
```

```
</blockquote>

<p align="center">
<a href="nominate.htm">
Click here to nominate a Web site for one of _
these awards
</a>
</p>
</body>
</html>
```

The *Awards* page is an example of an extended vertical layout; the page is larger than can be viewed in its entirety on the screen, but the browser will automatically generate scroll bars so that the visitor can move the scroll bar, which in turn causes the page to scroll on the screen.

10.5 Rings Page

The *Rings* page provides the visitor access to the Web rings of which The Blowhole is a member. There is no distinct format for this page other than the navigation banner at the top, because the content is dependent on the ring code provided by each ring site. We'll give an example here, but keep in mind that it won't work for you if you run it. Ring code depends on the code being passed from the site to the ring including the site's member number. That aside, it's pretty cool code and worth taking a look at.

```
<!-- BEGIN AQUARIA WEB RING CODE -->
<font SIZE="-1">
        This
<a HREF="http://www.aquaworldnet.com" _
    target="_top">
        Aquaria Web Ring Site
</a> <br>
        is owned by
<a HREF="mailto:_yourname_">
        _yourname_
</a>.<br>
<a HREF="http://www.aquaworldnet.com" _
    target="_top">
<img SRC="images/rings/aquaria%20Web/awr.gif" _
 ALT="Aquaria Web Ring Home" BORDER="0" _
 WIDTH="208" HEIGHT="150">
</a><br>
</font> 
```

```
<a HREF="http://www.Webring.org/cgi-bin/ _
 Webring?ring=awmag;id=your_code;next">
  <img SRC="images/rings/aquaria%20Web/2awr.gif" _
   BORDER="0" ALT="Next" WIDTH="30" HEIGHT="20">
</a>
<a HREF="http://www.Webring.org/cgi-bin/ _
 Webring?ring=awmag;id=1;skip">
  <img SRC="images/rings/aquaria%20Web/3awr.gif" _
   BORDER="0" ALT="Skip Next" WIDTH="30" _
   HEIGHT="20">
</a>
<a HREF="http://www.Webring.org/cgi-bin/ _
 Webring?ring=awmag;id=1;prev">
  <img SRC="images/rings/aquaria%20Web/4awr.gif" _
   BORDER="0" ALT="Previous" WIDTH="30" _
   HEIGHT="20">
</a>
<a HREF="http://www.Webring.org/cgi-bin/ _
 Webring?ring=awmag&amp;id=1&amp;sprev">
  <img SRC="images/rings/aquaria%20Web/5awr.gif" _
   BORDER="0" ALT="Skip Previous" WIDTH="30" _
   HEIGHT="20">
</a>
<br>   
<a HREF="http://www.Webring.org/cgi-bin/ _
 Webring?home;ring=awmag">
  <img SRC="images/rings/aquaria%20Web/1awr.gif" _
   BORDER="0" ALT="Ring Info" WIDTH="30" _
   HEIGHT="20">
</a>
<a HREF="http://www.Webring.org/cgi-bin/ _
 Webring?ring=awmag;id=your_code;random">
  <img SRC="images/rings/aquaria%20Web/6awr.gif" _
BORDER="0" ALT="Random" WIDTH="30" HEIGHT="20">
</a>
<a HREF="http://www.Webring.org/cgi-bin/ _
Webring?ring=awmag;id=your_code;next5">
  <img SRC="images/rings/aquaria%20Web/7awr.gif" _
   BORDER="0" ALT="Next 5" WIDTH="30" HEIGHT="20">
</a>
<a HREF="http://www.Webring.org/cgi-bin/ _
 Webring?ring=awmag;id=your_code;list">
  <img SRC="images/rings/aquaria%20Web/8awr.gif" _
   BORDER="0" ALT="List Sites" WIDTH="30" _
```

```
      HEIGHT="20">
</a>
 <br>
<font SIZE="-2">
   The Aquaria Web Ring is managed by
   <a HREF="mailto:awrmaster@aquaworldnet.com">
     AWnet
   </a>
   <br> click
   <a HREF="http://www.aquaworldnet.com/ _
    joinawr.htm">here
   </a>
    for joining the AWnet Aquaria Web Ring
</font><br>
<!-- Replace _YourEmailAddress_ with your e-mail
address -->
   <!-- Replace_YourName_ with your own name -->
   <!-- Replace Your_Code with your IDcode -->
   <!-- END AQUARIA WEB RING CODE -->
```

The ring image is shown in Figure 10-40. This is representative of most rings. There is an image identifying the ring, with text informing you of who manages the ring. A link is provided for accessing the ring owner either by email or Web page, so that more information can be obtained or membership requested. There are a number of controls, and the method for providing these varies greatly in style, but the ultimate functionality is the same.

Figure 10-40   A Web Ring

Typically, there are controls for moving to:

- the next site in the ring
- the previous site in the ring
- the site after the next in the ring
- the site prior to the previous in the ring
- a site in the ring of random choosing
- ring information
- a list of all the sites in the ring

The idea of this page is to take advantage of the fact that a page can extend vertically indefinitely, so rings can be added one above the other. The page could become large
enough to require links to the ring entries, but this defeats the purpose of a ring, as it's
meant to provide easy access to subject matter without having to search for it.

There are a number of things we need to do when receiving the code. One is to
replace place holders like "yourname" with the name of our site. Also, change the place
holders such as "yourid" with our ring member ID number that will be given to us by the
owner of the ring.

Well, that's it for the utility pages. This was the easy stuff, straightforward HTML.
If you already knew HTML and found it boring, hang on, because in the next chapter we
plunge head-first into ASP coding.

Home Again

*E*arlier, we created the home page and its frame structure. Now, it's time to fill in each of those frames. There are seven of them, and each is different. Some will be quite a challenge, and five of the seven will involve programming. Here is a summary of what we'll accomplish in this chapter:

- *Contents* frame — a title bar with no real utility other than visual
- *Banner* frame — our ubiquitous navigational banner, with a twist
- *Fp_ad* frame — the frame to hold a static for-profit ad, which will be database driven by the current category and the date
- *Np_ad* frame — holds a rotating non-profit ad, database driven by the current category
- *Ad* frame — holds a rotating for-profit ad, database driven by the current category and the date
- *Categories* frame — this frame contains program driven image links for navigation, and database driven image links for both book recommendations and category lists
- *Links* frame — contains database-driven hyperlinks

The first thing to do is define the site's cascading style sheet, since it will be affecting the presentation of the text-based frames.

11.1 Cascading Style Sheet

The purpose of our CSS file will be to allow elements on different pages to be similarly formatted. We could do that by simply entering the same HTML on each page, but if we wanted to change one of the formats, we'd then have to make the change multiple times. With the style sheet we can have each page link to it, and thus changing a style in one place, the source file, will cause it to change on any page that uses it.

When you create styles for your site, you might be talented enough to decide on all the formatting factors the first time, but more likely it will be trial and error. The easiest way to do this is to keep the Notepad window with your CSS file in it up on the screen, tweak it, and click the *Refresh* button in your browser on a page that uses the styles. Of course, we don't have the pages at this point, but we will soon.

We'll use Notepad to create the CSS file. Let's create the skeleton, and then fill in the styles.

```
<STYLE>
<!--
-->
</STYLE>
```

That's all we need. This block identifies the contents as a style, and has a starting and ending comment line in which to embed the styles. They're embedded in comments in case the visitor is using a browser that doesn't understand styles — if they were not in comments, the browser would display them as text.

The first style we'll create is one to override the standard formatting of the H3 heading. Here we'd like white text on a brown background. The font should be *Arial*, a sans-serif typeface. The font size should be 24 pixels. Why pixels instead of points? I've found that the browsers present the font in a more predictable manner if defined in this way. The type should be bold, so that it stands out, and should be centered. Following is the coding for these attributes:

```
H3
{
        BACKGROUND-COLOR: brown;
        COLOR: white;
        FONT-FAMILY: arial;
        FONT-SIZE: 24px;
        FONT-WEIGHT: bold;
        TEXT-ALIGN: center
}
```

Notice that the final entry in the style has no ending semicolon. Okay, let's move on to the next. This one will override the H4 heading type. The only formatting we want to override here is the background color, which is white by default, but will be changed to *wheat*, a light golden-brown. The entry for this will be:

```
H4
{
     BACKGROUND-COLOR: wheat
}
```

That was simple. The final heading override will be for the H5 headings. Here we'll set the background color to powder blue, but leave the text as black. We'll use the Arial typeface again, bold, and set the size to 14 pixels. We'll center the text. We'll add two additional instructions to further fine-tune the presentation. We'll increase the spacing between each letter to 3 pixels, and the height of the text and its vertical white space to 4 points. Adding or removing white space, between lines, letters or words is an easy way to affect the presentation. Here is the code:

```
H5
{
     BACKGROUND-COLOR: powderblue;
     COLOR: black;
     FONT-FAMILY: arial;
     FONT-SIZE: 14px;
     FONT-WEIGHT: bold;
     LETTER-SPACING: 3px;
     LINE-HEIGHT: 4pt;
     TEXT-ALIGN: center
}
```

In most cases where we have links, they will be controlled by style class and ID (more on that in a moment). Where we have a link but don't use that control, I want to change the default presentation to something other than the blue underlined text. To do this, we need to override the settings for anchors, which are the "A" in "A HREF."

I'm going to specify the typeface as being Arial. The color will be maroon, and not be underlined. The font size will be set to 10 points. Here is the style:

```
A
{
     COLOR: maroon;
     FONT-FAMILY: arial;
     FONT-SIZE: 10px;
     TEXT-DECORATION: none
}
```

How do we handle overriding *some* links, but not all? We do it the way we would override *some* but not *all* of anything, with a class or ID. These are references back to a style that can be made within a specific occurrence of a tag, such as within a <FONT> tag.

One of the features of CSS is that elements belonging to other elements inherit the styles of those other elements, such as a paragraph inheriting the style associated with body text. When the styles conflict, the style more specific in scope wins. In the case of using an ID *and* a CLASS, ID wins.

We're going to create a class and ID for links. One will be used when the link is clickable. The other will be used when it is not. The latter will inherit all the attributes of the first style but will override the color so that it will be obvious to the visitor that something is different about it.

Up until now our styles have been named the same as the element they're overriding. When creating a class, the name must begin with a period in the definition, though the period is dropped when the style is referred to. We'll name our class clsLink. CSS won't know that it's to be used for links, it could be named anything. Let's set the color to be Navy Blue, and the typeface to 10-point Helvetica, another sans-serif typeface supported by Explorer and Navigator. We'll remove the underlining that normally accompanies a link. Lastly, we'll increase the white space between letters slightly by making it .8 points. Here is the code:

```
.clsLink
{
     COLOR: navy;
     FONT-FAMILY: helv;
     FONT-SIZE: 10px;
     TEXT-DECORATION: none;
     LETTER-SPACING: .8 pt
}
```

In the cases where we're presenting a list of links, but an item in the list will not be clickable (an explanation of this is forthcoming in the section for the Categories frame), we'll retain most of the attributes of *clsLink* with the exception of the font color. We'll make that color gray, which is the color most often used in the Windows environment to signify that a menu item is not available in the current context.

```
#idLtText
{
     COLOR: gray
}
```

This line of code provides us the opportunity for the override mentioned above. When the two styles above are invoked with

```
CLASS="clsLink" ID="idLtText"
```

the color in the class is overridden with the color in the ID. We could actually refer to the ID in any scenario and end up with the attributes of that context with gray text color, such as in:

```
<FONT ID="idLtText"> This is gray text
```

We'll also create an override for the links that will appear as a result of clicking on a category. They will look like the categories, but will be black and white and appear above a block of descriptive text with tight registration:

```
#idTightLink
{
    COLOR: black;
    MARGIN-BOTTOM: 0pt;
    PADDING-BOTTOM: 0;
}
```

For certain titles we'll want a different look. Something with maroon text and sans-serif typeface. We'll make it 10 pixels in height. Here's the code:

```
.clsTitle
{
    COLOR: maroon;
    FONT-FAMILY: helv;
    FONT-SIZE: 10px
}
```

Without interference, the body text of a page would be a black, serif font such as Times Roman, like you're looking at now. We'll make a few changes to the body text for our pages. First, we'll make certain that the characteristics that *should* be default *are* default. Then we'll set the paragraphs to indent as in normal writing, which is *not* typically what we see on a Web page.

```
.bodytext
{
    FONT-FAMILY: Times New Roman;
    FONT-SIZE: 10pt;
    TEXT-INDENT: 0.25in
}
```

The description that will accompany a link will be different in appearance than the above body text. We'll make it dark gray and sans-serif. We'll also make it 9 points in size. It will butt up against the link that it describes, but will be set off from the link that follows it. Like the body text, it will be indented at the start of each paragraph:

```
.clsDesc
{
        font-size:9pt;
        color:darkgray;
        font-family:helv;
        text-indent:32pt;
        margin-top:1pt;
        margin-bottom:2pt;
        padding-top:0
}
```

There will be some text used in conjunction with the category list navigation icons. This text will be white, sans-serif, 10 pixels in size, with leading (the white space between lines) of 11 pixels:

```
.clsNav
{
    COLOR: white;
    FONT-FAMILY: Arial;
    FONT-SIZE: 10px;
    LINE-HEIGHT: 11px
}
```

The final style we'll create is for the title bar that appears over the categories. It will be similar in appearance to the style we just created for the navigational icons but needs to be larger:

```
.clsBanner
{
    COLOR: white;
    FONT-FAMILY: Arial;
    FONT-SIZE: 14px;
}
```

There you go, we've created our site style sheet. Of course, we need some way for the Web page to make use of it. We'll save the file as *blowhole.css*. To use it, we'll put the following lines within the *head* section of each Web page:

```
<link rel="stylesheet" type="text/css" _
href="blowhole.css">
```

Let's take a quick look at the completed CSS file, and then move on to our first frame.

```
<style>
<!--
H3
{
     BACKGROUND-COLOR: brown;
     COLOR: white;
     FONT-FAMILY: arial;
     FONT-SIZE: 24px;
     FONT-WEIGHT: bold;
     TEXT-ALIGN: center
}

H4
{
     BACKGROUND-COLOR: wheat
}

H5
{
     BACKGROUND-COLOR: powderblue;
     COLOR: black;
     FONT-FAMILY: arial;
     FONT-SIZE: 14px;
     FONT-WEIGHT: bold;
     LETTER-SPACING: 3px;
     LINE-HEIGHT: 4pt;
     TEXT-ALIGN: center
}

A
{
     COLOR: maroon;
     FONT-FAMILY: arial;
     FONT-SIZE: 10px;
     TEXT-DECORATION: none
}

.clsLink
{
     COLOR: navy;
     FONT-FAMILY: helv;
```

```
    FONT-SIZE: 10px;
    TEXT-DECORATION: none;
    LETTER-SPACING: .8 pt
}

#idTightLink
{
    COLOR: black;
    MARGIN-BOTTOM: 0pt;
    PADDING-BOTTOM: 0;
}

#idGray
{
    COLOR: gray
}

.clsTitle
{
    COLOR: maroon;
    FONT-FAMILY: helv;
    FONT-SIZE: 10px
}

.bodytext
{
    FONT-FAMILY: Times New Roman;
    FONT-SIZE: 10pt;
    TEXT-INDENT: 0.25in
}

.clsNav
{
    COLOR: white;
    FONT-FAMILY: Arial;
    FONT-SIZE: 10px;
    TEXT-DECORATION: none;
    LINE-HEIGHT: 11px
}

.clsBanner
{
    COLOR: white;
    FONT-FAMILY: Arial;
```

```
      FONT-SIZE: 14px;
}
-->
</style>
```

11.2 The Title Bar

No reason why we shouldn't begin with the easiest frame on the page, the *title* frame. We'll create a new HTML file in FrontPage. This will give us the following skeletal code:

```
<html>
<head>
<title></title>
</head>
<body>
</body>
</html>
```

To this, we will add the line to our *head* section for linking our CSS file:

```
<link rel="stylesheet" type="text/css" _
 href="blowhole.css">
```

We want the background of the title bar to be colored, to stand out as a title *bar*. The problem is, if we simply give the text a background color, only the *text* will be colored. Why is this a problem? Because if the text is anything less than the width of the frame, the title bar will look as if it's extending only the width of the caption, not the width of the frame. So, how do we accomplish extending the color the width of the frame?

First, we'll insert a table from the *Table* menu. No, I'm not saying "when in doubt, create a table," but this is the first step in achieving our goal. We'll choose the following settings:

```
border="0"
cellpadding="1"
cellspacing="0"
```

Which takes us to the setting that will ensure that our color, when applied, will extend the width of the frame — the width:

```
width="100%"
```

This parameter ensures that the table width is the width of the window. In this case, since we are in a frame, it is the width of the frame. With that, we have thus added the following code:

```
<table border="0" cellpadding="1" cellspacing="0"_
  width="100%" id="Title">
    <tr>
      <td width="100%"></td>
    </tr>
</table>
```

We want to make two changes to the cell settings. The first change is regarding the alignment. We want the contents of this frame to rest atop the categories frame:

```
valign="bottom"
```

The other change we want to make will change the background color of the cell; this, combined with the width specification we made earlier, will provide the look we want, a gold-like color:

```
bgcolor="#ACA470"
```

The final thing we need to do is place the text in the table cell. We want the text to use the *clsBanner* style we created, but a class can not be assigned to a table cell, so we can't use *class=* as a parameter to the *<td>* tag. Luckily, HTML provides two tags for just such occurrences, *<div>* and *<span>*. The only difference between the two is that *<div>* causes a paragraph break. So, with that in mind, we'll add the following to our table cell:

```
<span class="clsBanner">Categories</span>
```

This concludes the *Title* frame. Following is the complete code for this frame:

```
<html>
<head>
<title></title>
<link rel="stylesheet" type="text/css" _
  href="blowhole.css">
</head>
<body>
<table border="0" cellpadding="1" _
  cellspacing="0" width="100%" id="Title">
    <tr>
      <td valign="bottom" bgcolor="#ACA470" _
        width="100%"><span class="clsBanner"> _
```

```
     Categories</span>
        </td>
     </tr>
  </table>
</body>
</html>
```

11.3 The Navigation Banner

You have that bored look on your face — that "oh, we've done this before" look. Put it away—we're going to do something very clever in this frame, something we haven't done yet. It just so happens that the graphic and links are the same, but there's much, much more to this frame than that.

We have to concede that the words that appear on the navigation banner don't necessarily offer much insight into the functionality they represent. What we're going to do is set up the navigation banner so that when the mouse is held over any of the navigation choices, a description of that choice will be presented.

The way we do this is by using graphics to overlap our banner — but there's a problem. With standard HTML, we can't have two images overlapping each other. The problem is that we need the descriptions to appear over the banner, because we don't want to waste valuable real estate by setting apart part of the screen for when a description needs to be displayed. How do we have the descriptions, in the form of images, appear over the banner, also an image?

The resolution to our problem is to forget about doing this at all, as it's very silly, and move on to something worthwhile. Kidding, kidding. The resolution actually is to not have the banner as an image — we'll display it as a background image, like we would a texture. Let's start by creating a new page in FrontPage, and then modify the page settings to identify the background as our *logo.jpg* file. At this point, our code looks as follows:

```
<html>
<head>
<title></title>
<body background="images/logo.jpg">
</body>
</html>
```

The next thing we need to do is create a table to sit at the bottom of the frame with the navigation links.

```
<div align="left">
<table border="0" cellpadding="0" cellspacing="0">
   <tr>
```

```
<td valign="top" align="center">
 <a HREF="about.htm" target="_top">
  <img src="images/about.gif" alt="about.gif _
  (1109 byte)" border="0" WIDTH="36" _
  HEIGHT="15">
 </a>
</td>
<td valign="top" align="center">
 <a HREF="feedback.htm" target="_top">
 <img src="images/feedback.gif" _
  alt="feedback.gif (1252 bytes)" _
  border="0" WIDTH="56" HEIGHT="15">
 </a>
</td>
<td valign="top" align="center">
 <a HREF="ad.htm" target="_top">
 <img src="images/ad.gif" alt="ad.gif _
  (1247 bytes)" border="0" WIDTH="60" _
  HEIGHT="15">
 </a>
</td>
<td valign="top" align="center">
 <a HREF="awards.htm" target="_top">
 <img src="images/awards.gif" _
  alt="awards.gif (1154 bytes)" _
   border="0" WIDTH="47" HEIGHT="15">
 </a>
</td>
<td valign="top" align="center">
 <a href="rings.htm" target="_top">
 <img src="images/ring.gif" alt="ring.gif _
  (979 bytes)" border="0" WIDTH="40" _
  HEIGHT="15">
 </a>
</td>
<td valign="top" align="center">
 <a href="copyrite.htm" target="_top">
 <img src="images/copyrite.gif" _
  alt="copyrite.gif (925 bytes)" _
  border="0" WIDTH="13" HEIGHT="16">
 </a>
</td>
  </tr>
 </table></div>
```

What we have in the preceding code is one row with a series of cells. Each cell contains a centered image, aligned at the top of the cell. Each of the images is a link leading to one of the utility pages.

There are two things we need to do to this table. We need to make certain that the rows of images we created are aligned in the proper place on our background image — the height of the row is less than the height of the frame, so it won't just fall into the right position.

We also need to make sure there is a specific amount of space reserved for the descriptions. Why? Because the way we're going to make the descriptions "appear" when the mouse is over an image link is to have a blank image that we'll replace on-the-fly with an image containing the description, until the mouse moves out of range. We'll take care of both requirements with one additional row in our table:

```
<tr>
   <td valign="bottom" align="right"      _
       colspan="6" height="85">
    <img src="images/_t.gif" name="helptext"    _
     alt="_t.gif (1062 bytes)" WIDTH="350"       _
     HEIGHT="66">
   </td>
</tr>
```

We've designed the cell to extend the width of the other six combined. Then, we introduce an image into the cell that is completely transparent. The image was created in Paint Shop Pro as a white rectangle, and when saved, the white was declared to be transparent. The idea is that when the mouse is held over an image link, we'll replace the transparent image with an image that has the description showing. Then, when the mouse moves away, we'll put the transparent image back. Figure 11-1 shows an example of one of these images.

Figure 11-1   Replacement Image with Description

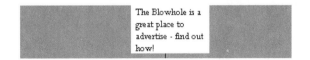

The next step in accomplishing this functionality is to attach code to the events triggered by the mouse being moved over the graphic and moved off the graphic. The events that are "fired" when this happens are *OnMouseOver* and *OnMouseOut*. Personally, I would have named them *OnMouseIsOver* and *OnMouseWasOver*, but no one asked me. *OnMouseOver* is fired whenever the visitor moves the mouse cursor over an element on the page — but nothing aside from the occasional change in the shape of the mouse cur-

sor happens unless you cause it to as a response to this event. *OnMouseOut* is fired when
the mouse cursor moves away from the element. The calls are placed as parameters
within the *<a href>* tag that is our hyperlink.

```
onMouseOver="show(1); return true;"
onMouseOut="hide(); return true;"
```

When the mouse moves over the element, our image link, we call a subroutine
named *show* and pass it the number of the element (we'll number each of them sequen-
tially). We'll see why in a little while. We'll ask that the call must return successfully for
the transfer of control to another page to occur, which normally accompanies a click on a
hyperlink.

When the mouse moves off the element, we call *hide*. No parameters will be passed
to this routine. We'll see why shortly. Here's the updated table code:

```
<div align="left">
<table border="0" cellpadding="0" cellspacing="0">
  <tr>
    <td valign="bottom" align="right"     _
        colspan="6" height="85">
     <img src="images/_t.gif" name="helptext"   _
      alt="_t.gif (1062 bytes)" WIDTH="350"   _
      HEIGHT="66">
    </td>
  </tr>
  <tr>
    <td valign="top" align="center">
     <a HREF="about.htm" target="_top"   _
       onMouseOver="show(1); return true;"   _
       onMouseOut="hide(); return true;">
      <img src="images/about.gif" alt="about.gif   _
      (1109 byte)" border="0" WIDTH="36"   _
      HEIGHT="15">
     </a>
    </td>
    <td valign="top" align="center">
     <a HREF="feedback.htm" target="_top"   _
       onMouseOver="show(2); return true;"   _
       onMouseOut="hide(); return true;">
      <img src="images/feedback.gif"   _
      alt="feedback.gif (1252 bytes)"   _
      border="0" WIDTH="56" HEIGHT="15">
     </a>
    </td>
```

```
        <td valign="top" align="center">
         <a HREF="ad.htm" target="_top" _
          onMouseOver="show(3); return true;" _
          onMouseOut="hide(); return true;"> _
         <img src="images/ad.gif" alt="ad.gif _
          (1247 bytes)" border="0" WIDTH="60" _
          HEIGHT="15">
         </a>
        </td>
        <td valign="top" align="center">
         <a HREF="awards.htm" target="_top" _
          onMouseOver="show(4); return true;" _
          onMouseOut="hide(); return true;">
         <img src="images/awards.gif" _
          alt="awards.gif (1154 bytes)" _
           border="0" WIDTH="47" HEIGHT="15">
         </a>
        </td>
        <td valign="top" align="center">
         <a href="rings.htm" target="_top" _
          onMouseOver="show(5); return true;" _
          onMouseOut="hide(); return true;">
         <img src="images/ring.gif" alt="ring.gif _
          (979 bytes)" border="0" WIDTH="40" _
          HEIGHT="15">
         </a>
        </td>
        <td valign="top" align="center">
         <a href="copyrite.htm" target="_top">
         <img src="images/copyrite.gif" _
          alt="copyrite.gif (925 bytes)" _
          border="0" WIDTH="13" HEIGHT="16">
         </a>
        </td>
      </tr>
  </table>
  </div>
```

Now, let's write the scripting code. The first thing we want to do is tell the browser what kind of script it should be expecting:

```
<script LANGUAGE="JavaScript">
```

This line appears in the *head* section before our script. Next, we'll put some code to set up the variables we need. We want this code to be executed as soon as the page is loaded, as opposed to being called later like a subroutine.

```
if (document.images) {
```

This line checks to make sure that the settings for the browser will allow images to be displayed — no sense doing all this if no one will see it.

```
var m_strShow1t=new Image()
m_strShow1t.src="images/about_t.gif"
var m_strShow2t=new Image()
m_strShow2t.src="images/feedback_t.gif"
var show3t=new Image()
m_strshow3t.src="images/ad_t.gif"
var m_strShow4t=new Image()
m_strShow4t.src="images/awards_t.gif"
var m_strShow5t=new Image()
m_strShow5t.src="images/ring_t.gif"
```

Each pair of statements above first creates a reference for a new image and then instantiates the image by assigning an image file to it. Each of these images, *1t* through *5t*, corresponds to the value we passed to the routine *show* earlier. The last thing we'll do here is account for that completely transparent image that's shown when the mouse isn't over one of our image links:

```
var m_strHidet=new Image()
m_strHidet.src="images/_t.gif"
}
```

Okay, now we need to write the routines *show* and *hide*. The idea behind *show* is for us to change the source image for the *<img>* in that row of our table. The first thing we need to do is declare the routine:

```
function show(iImgnum) {
}
```

We've declared the routine *show* as a function that will receive a parameter, which will be stored in *iImgnum*. Next we'll do something familiar:

```
if (document.images)  {
    }
```

Again, we don't want to perform this processing if the images can't be seen. If they can, we'll drop down to our processing:

```
document['helptext'].src = _
  eval("m_strShow"+iImgnum+"t.src");
```

The first thing we need to remember is that the *<img>* tag in which we display our transparent image has a name parameter:

```
<img src="images/_t.gif" name="helptext"
```

So, we refer to the element named "helptext" in our document, and set its source to a new image. The formula:

```
"m_strShow" + iImgnum + "t.src"
```

takes the word "show," appends to it the number that was passed to our routine, and appends "t.src" to that. Thus, when the routine is called with a parameter of 1, the resulting string is "m_strShow" + 1 + "t.src," or *m_strShow1t.src*. The final thing we do is to require the routine to evaluate this statement, to take the resulting string and have the file it represents loaded; otherwise, we change the textual value of the image source but don't end up with the file.

Now that we have it loaded, we need to worry about unloading it once the mouse cursor has moved away. For this we'll create the *hide* routine.

```
function hide(){
}
```

This routine doesn't need any parameters, since all we'll be doing is replacing whatever the current image is with our fully transparent image.

```
if(document.images) {
   document['helptext'].src=eval("m_strHidet.src");
   }
```

And that's it. Now, when the mouse cursor is held over any of the image links in the navigation banner except *Copyright*, a description of the destination Web page is given. When the mouse cursor is moved, the description "disappears."

Here's the code:

```
<html>
<head>
<title></title>
```

```
<script LANGUAGE="JavaScript">
if(document.images){
    var m_strShow1t=new Image()
    m_strShow1t.src="images/about_t.gif"
    var m_strShow2t=new Image()
    m_strShow2t.src="images/feedback_t.gif"
    var m_strShow3t=new Image()
    m_strShow3t.src="images/ad_t.gif"
    var m_strShow4t=new Image()
    m_strShow4t.src="images/awards_t.gif"
    var m_strShow5t=new Image()
    m_strShow5t.src="images/ring_t.gif"
    var strHidet=new Image()
    Hidet.src="images/_t.gif"
}

function show(iImgnum){
if(document.images) {
  document['helptext'].src = _
   eval("m_strShow"+iImgnum+"t.src");
  }
}

function hide(){
if(document.images) {
  document['helptext'].src=eval("m_strHidet.src");
  }
}

</script>

<body background="images/logo.jpg">
<div align="left">

<table border="0" cellpadding="0" cellspacing="0">
  <tr>
    <td valign="bottom" align="right" _
     colspan="6" height="85">
     <img src="images/_t.gif" name="helptext" _
      alt="_t.gif (1062 bytes)" WIDTH="350" _
      HEIGHT="66">
    </td>
  </tr>
  <tr>
```

```html
<td valign="top" align="center">
 <a HREF="about.htm" target="_top" _
  onMouseOver="show(1); return true;"
  onMouseOut="hide(); return true;">
 <img src="images/about.gif" _
  alt="about.gif (1109 byte)" _
   border="0" WIDTH="36" HEIGHT="15">
 </a>
</td>
<td valign="top" align="center">
 <a HREF="feedback.htm" target="_top" _
  onMouseOver="show(2); return true;" _
  onMouseOut="hide(); return true;">
  <img src="images/feedback.gif" _
    alt="feedback.gif (1252 bytes)" _
     border="0" WIDTH="56" HEIGHT="15">
 </a>
</td>
<td valign="top" align="center">
 <a HREF="ad.htm" target="_top" _
  onMouseOver="show(3); return true;" _
  onMouseOut="hide(); return true;">
   <img src="images/ad.gif" alt="ad.gif _
    (1247 bytes)" border="0" WIDTH="60" _
    HEIGHT="15">
 </a>
</td>
<td valign="top" align="center">
 <a HREF="awards.htm" target="_top" _
  onMouseOver="show(4); return true;" _
  onMouseOut="hide(); return true;">
   <img src="images/awards.gif" _
    alt="awards.gif (1154 bytes)" _
    border="0" WIDTH="47" HEIGHT="15">
 </a>
</td>
<td valign="top" align="center">
 <a href="rings.htm" target="_top" _
  onMouseOver="show(5); return true;" _
  onMouseOut="hide(); return true;">
  <img src="images/ring.gif" alt="ring.gif _
  (979 bytes)" border="0" WIDTH="40" _
  HEIGHT="15">
 </a>
```

```
        </td>
        <td valign="top" align="center">
         <a href="copyrite.htm" target="_top">
          <img src="images/copyrite.gif" _
           alt="copyrite.gif (925 bytes)" _
           border="0" WIDTH="13" HEIGHT="16">
         </a>
        </td>
      </tr>
    </table>
    </div>
    </body>
    </html>
```

11.4 ASP Files

We briefly discussed ASP technology in Chapter 2. Let's take a moment to discuss how the process actually works, as an understanding of that aids in the understanding of the architecture of the page.

HTML files are processed on the client by your browser. ASP files are processed on the server by the ASP engine. If there is output from the ASP file, it is provided to your browser. Nothing in the ASP file itself is viewable by the visitor, only what the file chooses to output.

When the file is opened, the execution is much like that of a piece of software, top to bottom except when altered by program statements. If HTML is encountered, it is transmitted to the client. HTML can be generated programmatically, too.

ASP files have two data streams. The input stream is via the REQUEST object, and makes values available via parameters passed in a hyperlink (HTTP method = GET) or embedded in the HTTP headers (HTTP method = POST). The output stream is via the RESPONSE object, which is used for transmitting generated HTML. Blocks of ASP script code are encase between <% and %> tags.

So, if the ASP file contains the following, the HTML display will be blank:

```
<HTML>
<HEAD>
<TITLE></TITLE>
</HEAD>
<BODY>
<% x = 2 %>
</BODY>
</HTML>
```

However, file that looked like this:

```
<HTML>
<HEAD>
<TITLE></TITLE>
</HEAD>
<BODY>
Click to see appointments for
<%
  response.write "<a href=""appts.htm"">date</a>"
%>
</BODY>
</HTML>
```

would result in output much like the following:

```
Click to see appointments for 2/1/99
```

You might be wondering why the line above had two quotes around *appts.htm*. This is very important. Reading this carefully will save you much debugging heartache. In a VBScript command, quotation marks delimit a string value, like:

```
x = "hello"
```

We want the VBScript routine to write out a string that not only is delimited by quotation marks, but *contains* quotation marks — because the HTML we are spitting out has a syntax that requires quotation marks in it.

If we were to have the following:

```
<% response.write "hello" %>
```

we'd end up with

```
hello
```

If we were to have:

```
<% response.write ""hello"" %>
```

we'd receive an error, because the ASP processor would look at the statement as three items as shown by the brackets:

```
<% response.write [""] [hello] [""] %>
```

Here, *hello* could be a variable, but it is invalid in the syntax because, in order to print multiple items with one *response.write* statement, there should be concatenation (&) symbols between the elements. To get the results we want, the statement needs to look like this:

```
<% response.write """hello""" %>
```

and we end up with HTML that says:

```
"hello"
```

because the first quotation mark is interpreted as delimiting the string which follows, and the pair following it are interpreted as being a literal quotation mark.

One other thing that's similar and very important: When generating output that will become HTML code and that code will contain script — so we're outputting strings that are source code that contains script — we will need the script to contain the <% and %> delimiters of ASP script. However, our write statements that output the code should never have those two characters together, even when embedded in a string, because both FrontPage and Visual Interdev interpret those characters as delimiting a script, and aren't "intelligent" enough to realize that they're part of an output string. Thus, that line, and most probably a cascading effect to much of the file, will become corrupted.

So, instead of this:

```
"<% if x > 1 then y = 2 %>"
```

we'll use the ampersand (&) concatenation character to fool the application:

```
"<" & "% if x > 1 then y = 2 %" & ">"
```

11.5 The Categories Frame

You don't realize just how complicated something can be until it comes time for you to explain it to someone else. The *Categories* frame is a complicated beast. There's a tremendous amount that will be going on in it. I'm going to provide a snapshot narrative of the flow, and then we can move on to coding it routine by routine.

When the page first loads, we'll do some initialization of our data elements. The next thing we're going to do is paint the categories. In order to paint them, we need to retrieve them from the database. To do that, we need to know which to retrieve. If this is our first time through the program (we tell this by no parameters being passed), or if the parent category number is 0, we'll grab the initial list. Otherwise, we're going to first get the information for the parent category, because we'll display the parent category as a link to allow the visitor to navigate to the previous level of categories. Complicated. Okay, an example.

If the initial list of categories were:

- Countries
- States
- Cities

we'd print that list in the absence of any parameters to the contrary. Let's say we've now clicked on *States*. The code in the link is going to request the same page, but this time with a parameter of the parent being equal to the ID for *States*. Now, when we eventually print our list of categories, it will be a level lower that looks like this:

- States
  - Alabama
  - Alaska
  - Arizona, etc.

In clicking *States* in the above list, the visitor would return to the list in which it was a member—the next level up. Once we've decided whether we need that, again, based on whether there's a *parent* parameter, we're ready to go get the categories. We also want to check to see if the visitor has requested us to *find* categories containing a specific string. If so, we'll use the string to select our categories instead of a parent number.

We retrieve all the categories that have a parent category number equal to the parent category (the passed parameter, or 0 in its absence). Once we have that dataset available, we have some decisions to make.

If we go back and look at the design layout for this frame, we'll note that there are directional icons. If we have displayed a list of categories from a dataset of more records than will fit on the screen at one time, the visitor can move forward or backward in that list. We need to be able to determine whether the user has requested this forward or backward movement as opposed to an upward (previous level, as discussed earlier) or downward (next level of categories) movement. If they have, then we will have shown the remarkable foresight of passing as a parameter not only the direction of travel the visitor wants to take, but with what record our list started last time, so we know where to begin this time.

Now it's time for a double-take of sorts. We're going to hit the database again, not once, but twice. There are tremendous benefits to the design of our database, but a drawback or two as well. Design can often be a two-edged sword. We need to know whether each of the categories we'll display has any categories the claim it as a parent. If so, the current category will be presented with "..." appended to it, to denote that clicking it will provide a subsequent list of categories. We also want to check to see if each of the categories has links and/or a book recommendation.

If the category has any "stuff" associated with it, subsequent categories, links or a book, we'll paint this category as a link. Otherwise, we'll just paint it as a word. And that's it for the categories themselves, but there's more to this frame.

Navigation. That's the name of the game. If there weren't navigation, you'd never have a visitor to your site. If there weren't navigation on your site, the visitor would never see anything but the first page. If we don't provide navigation, the first page of categories is all the visitor will ever see, which would make the site less meaningful, and certainly not make the advertisers for those other categories happy.

Our navigation will be in the form of an icon to go "home" — back to the initial list of categories — as well as arrows to request forward and backward movement within the category list. We're going to paint them, but with some qualification. If we're already home, there's no need to activate the icon for going home, so we won't. We'll know if we're home by the fact that our categories have no parents. If we're at the beginning of the list of categories at the current level, we won't activate the arrow that requests we move backward through the list. If we're at the end of the list at the current level, we won't bother activating the arrow that requests the forward navigation.

The next thing we'll paint is the *Find* dialogue, which consists of an icon, a text box and the graphic of the word *Find* that we created in Chapter 7, which will act as an image link. Should the link be clicked, we call this page again but pass a parameter that says we want to find the categories that contain the string in the text box, which in turn affects our retrieval of categories as mentioned earlier.

The last thing we'll do in this frame is to evaluate where we stand on a book recommendation. If we have a recommendation *and* an image of the book cover, we'll present that graphic as an image link. If we don't have a graphic, but we do have a recommendation, we'll offer the visitor the opportunity to purchase a recommended book. If we have neither, but the category is flagged as having a name that is meaningful in searching for a book (such as "anemone" as opposed to "invertebrate"), we'll offer the visitor the ability to search for a book on the category.

If all that weren't enough, we have another job to do during all this. We'll need to tell the other non-static frames, the frame for links, non-profit ad, for-profit static ad and for-profit rotating ad—what the current category is, so that they can repaint themselves in the context of the current category. The *Links* page will display links reflecting the current category, as will the ads shown.

So, that's it. Now that you understand the flow, all we have to do is code. Hang on, this is going to be a blast.

Initialization

The first thing we need to do is overcome a current problem with ASP and ADO. Our *global.asa* file contains code that should be executed when a session begins, a session being the initial connection of a visitor to our site. That code reads as follows:

```
Sub Session_OnStart
'--Project Data Connection
Session("DataConn_ConnectionString") _
  = "DSN=TheBlowholeDSN"
Session("DataConn_ConnectionTimeout") = 15
```

```
Session("DataConn_CommandTimeout") = 30
Session("DataConn_RuntimeUserName") = "admin"
Session("DataConn_RuntimePassword") = ""
End Sub
```

ASP is supposed to cause those session variables — variables that retain their scope until either the visitor leaves or times out — to be initialized when the session begins. However, my experience is that it doesn't work. There are numerous technical help reports on the Microsoft support network that attempt to document and resolve the reasons why, with a valid *global.asa* in place, error messages are received stating that the *Data Source Name* doesn't exist. One could spend hours, days absorbing these and taking the action they recommend. I have — to no avail. I find that the suggested causes can be summarized as:

- global.asa isn't located in the Web's root directory
- the Web directory does not have *execute* access
- one of the two zillion supporting pieces of middleware is the wrong version

and after spending hours eliminating each of the possibilities, I still can't get it to work most of the time. So, I've stopped trying. The first thing I do is create a routine that sets the session variables that are supposed to be set in *global.asa*. When we create a new *ASP* file in Visual Interdev, we end up with a typical skeleton:

```
<%@ Language=VBScript %>
<HTML>
<HEAD>
<META NAME="GENERATOR" Content= _
  "Microsoft Visual Studio 6.0">
```

Let's add a routine in the *Head* section to provide the initialization of our database variables.

```
<% sub global_asa()
'This routine is here because the _
 global.asa functionality
' doesnt work as advertised - remove _
   this routine and the
' call to it when it does
 Session("DataConn_ConnectionString") = _
   "DSN=TheBlowholeDSN"
 Session("DataConn_ConnectionTimeout") = 15
 Session("DataConn_CommandTimeout") = 30
 Session("DataConn_RuntimeUserName") = "admin"
```

```
    Session("DataConn_RuntimePassword") = ""
end sub %>
```

Okay, now we need code that will invoke that routine added to the file. So, in the *body* section we'll add the following:

```
<% call global_asa() %>
```

Next, we'll set aside the storage for some database-related objects.

```
set DataConn = _
 Server.CreateObject("ADODB.Connection")
set SQLQuery = Server.CreateObject("ADODB.Command")
set SQLQuery2 = _
 Server.CreateObject("ADODB.Command")
set SQLQuery3 = _
 Server.CreateObject("ADODB.Command")
set RecordSet1 = _
 Server.CreateObject("ADODB.Recordset")
set RecordSet2 = _
 Server.CreateObject("ADODB.Recordset")
set RecordSet3 = _
 Server.CreateObject("ADODB.Recordset")
```

These objects are used in our ADO (ActiveX Data Object) calls to the MS Access database that we'll be making. The lines above are a prescribed format for ADO. The *SQLQuery* variables will be used to hold the SQL *select* string that queries the database, such as:

```
select * from categories
```

The *RecordSet* objects will hold record sets, which are the collection of database records returned from a SQL query. Now we'll define some other variables that we need:

```
dim m_iParent          'id number of parent
dim m_iRet             'holds call return values
dim m_flgBack          'flag, true if not first level
dim m_strIndent        'indentation string for _
                        formatting
'*********************
'The following variables are for use in the routine
'   ConditionalWrite
dim m_strBackT         'string to use if m_flgBack _
                        is true
```

```
dim m_strBackF          'string to use if m_flgBack _
                         is false

dim m_strInitT          'string to use if m_flgInit _
                         is true
dim m_strInitF          'string to use if m_flgInit _
                         is false

'* * * * * * * * * * * * * * * * * *

dim m_iStartPos         'first category in record _
                         set when not on page 1
dim m_iEndPos           'final category in record _
                         set when not on page 1
dim m_iRecCnt           'number of records in _
                         record set
dim m_flgNext           'true if there are more _
                         records for current _
                         level than will fit _
                         on current display page
dim m_flgPrev           'true if there are _
                         preceding records for _
                         current level not _
                         showing on current _
                         display page
dim m_strPrevCat        'name of last category _
                         clicked
dim m_iPageSize         'how many categories to _
                         display at once
dim m_straCatInfo()     'additional info about _
                         display categories
dim m_flgBookSearch     'Should a book search be _
                         offered for this category?
dim m_strISBN           'ISBN of recommended book
dim m_flgImage          'Is there an image of a _
                         book cover?
```

That's it for the definitions. It's not really too long a list considering what some mainstream applications look like, pages and pages of data definitions. Anyway, let's initialize some of this stuff. First, let's open our database.

```
'
' Open the database
'
Set DataConn = _
```

```
     Server.CreateObject("ADODB.Connection")
DataConn.Open Session("DataConn_ConnectionString")
```

The following lines state that we'll do our SQL access using a query based on a text statement.

```
SQLQuery.CommandType = 1
SQLQuery2.CommandType = SQLQuery.CommandType
SQLQuery3.CommandType = SQLQuery.CommandType
```

The next three lines connect the connection method (the instantiating of the ODBC connection we defined in our MS Interdev project) to each of the three dataset objects.

```
Set SQLQuery.ActiveConnection = DataConn
Set SQLQuery2.ActiveConnection = DataConn
set SQLQuery3.ActiveConnection = DataConn

m_iPageSize = 6          'set the category page size
```

The line above determines how many categories we'll display at one time. I've tried it with different values, and you're free to too, but I found a half-dozen to look the best.

```
'
' The following array will contain information
'   about each category. It was defined earlier.
'   This instantiates it as a 4-dimension array.
'   Dimension 1 - category number
'   Dimension 2 - category name
'   Dimension 3 - levels below this category?
'   Dimension 4 - links/book associated with this?
redim m_straCatInfo(m_iPageSize,4)
'
' We'll set the environment for the initial
'   loading of this page, and change that later
'   if needed based on any parameters passed
m_flgBack = FALSE
m_flgInit = TRUE
m_strIndent = ""
m_liStartRec = 0
m_iParent = 0
m_flgBookSearch = FALSE
m_flgImage = FALSE
'
' The following lines will create application
```

```
'   variables, the values of which are retained
'   in state between browser connections by
'   the parameters we pass
Application("Direction") = ""
Application("Start")=""
Application("GP")="0"    'grandparent category
```

The next thing we want to do is start processing. Going back to the narrative, we see that we want to check to see if we are in receipt of parameters in our input stream, as these parameters will inform us of where we left off with the site visitor and where we need to go next. First, we'll add a line calling this routine:

```
call CheckCategoryRequestLevel _
  (m_iParent,m_flgBack,m_strIndent, m_flgInit,_
   m_iReturnTo, m_strPrevCat, _
   m_flgImage, m_flgBookSearch, m_strISBN, _
   RecordSet1, SQLQuery)
```

We need to create some boundary for the actual routine:

```
<%
sub CheckCategoryRequestLevel _
(l_iParent,l_flgBack,l_strIndent, l_flgInit,_
 l_iReturnTo, l_strPrevCat, RS1, SQ1)
'------------------------------------
'Categories below main level requested?
'------------------------------------
end sub
%>
```

and now we can add some logic to it. This routine checks on the settings of parameters passed by an earlier instance of our Web page. Therefore, we only need to do something if there are parameters, so let's set up the block of code to check.

```
if len(Request.QueryString)>0 then
```

You might recall our earlier discussion on the input stream. If we pass parameters to an ASP file using the HREF in a link, those parameters are contained in the *Request* object, in the *QueryString*. The object always exists, so to check whether there are actually parameters we can check its length. No length, no parameters.

Und zo (my German scientist impression), once we know that there *are* parameters, how do we get our hands on them? We create another routine. Let's put the invoking line in our present routine, as part of the "true" body of the *if* statement (if statements work like *if* blah *then* do if blah is true *else* do if blah is false):

```
    call ParseQueryString(Request.QueryString)
```

and now, the routine:

```
<%
Sub ParseQueryString(l_strObj)
'
' This routine moves through the parameters
'   passed to us and creates an application variable
'   for each
'
  for each item in l_strObj
      Application(item)= l_strObj(item)
  next
end sub
%>
```

The comments in this routine pretty much explain what it does. So, we can move back to the body of our *if* statement. *Parent* should be one of the parameters that are passed to invocations of our page subsequent to the first. As we discussed earlier, if we got here by clicking a category, we'll list that category first as a place to click to move back up a level, and the categories a level down from it will be indented beneath it. We thus need to check if a parent value was passed (the parent being the category that was clicked). Now that all parameters have been converted into application variables, can't we just check to see if the variable exists? Well, no. The reason is that just referring to the application variable results in its creation if it was not there before. So, we need to check its value to be greater than zero.

```
    l_iParent = Application("parent")
    if l_iParent > 0 then
```

If we're not at the first level of categories (as determined by there being a *parent* value), then a route back to the initial list of categories will be needed. When it comes time for that, we'll be checking a flag to see if we should provide that route:

```
    l_flgBack = TRUE
```

Once we print the name of the category that will take us back up a level, we will indent the categories subordinate to it so the visitor can see the relationship. Indentation is not really viable in HTML on a line level — it can be done at the paragraph level, but we're not treating each category as a separate paragraph — so we'll achieve the indentation by using non-breaking spaces (remember, we can just use spaces because HTML removes soft white space).

```
'
' set indent so category links will be indented
'   below return path link
      l_strIndent = "     _
          "  'indentation for subcategories
```

If we are in the position of providing a link to move up one level, then when we actually get to painting the links we'll want to know that. We'll be using the *m_flgInit* at that point. If we're not at the initial list of categories, which we're not if *m_flgInit* is false, then we'll paint that link. So we need to set it to false.

```
'
' set flag to false so we'll get the return _
    path link later
'

      l_flgInit = FALSE
```

The last thing we need to do in processing this logic for a return path link is to get the information for *it* that we will need to put in its hyperlink information. That is, once we paint it, if the visitor clicks it, the hyperlink will call the same page again, but will pass this category's parent information. We don't have that information right now, because the category we'll use for the return path is the current category's parent. What we need is, in effect, the current category's *grand*parent. Confusing, I know. Here's an example.

We have been presented with *United States* and *Canada*. We clicked on *United States*, and will now have a list of states. We have the category number for *United States*, because we will include it in the hyperlink for each of the states, categories, as the parent category for that child category. However, when we paint the list of states, they will be indented under a hyperlink that says *United States*. Clicking on this top-level category will take the visitor back to the list containing *United States* and *Canada* — a return path to the previous level.

- United States (clicking this takes me to next level *up* the chain)
  - Alabama (clicking this takes me to next level *down* the chain)
  - Alaska (same with this one)

To do that, the link behind that category name needs to have the category number of *its* parent as the parameter for that link's destination. So we need to look up what that information is.

```
'
' construct sql query to gather information
' about what is now the parent category
'
```

```
        SQ1.CommandText = _
          "SELECT strCategory_db, liCatNo_db, _
           liParentCatNo_db, strISBN_db, _
           ynImage_db, ynOfferSearch_db_
           FROM Categories WHERE _
           (liCatNo_db = " & l_iParent & ")"
```

We need to construct a routine to open the record set:

```
    <%
    sub OpenRecordSet(rsobj,commandstr,parm1,parm2)
        rsobj.Open commandstr, , parm1, parm2
    end sub
    %>
```

and then we'll invoke that routine and continue on:

```
    '
    ' get the record set
        call OpenRecordSet(RS1, SQ1,0,1)
    '
    ' hold the data for use later
    '
        l_iReturnTo = _
         RS1.Fields("liParentCatNo_db")
        l_strPrevCat= _
         RS1.Fields("strCategory_db")
        l_flgBookSearch = _
         RS1.Fields("ynOfferSearch_db")
        l_flgImage = _
         RS1.Fields("ynImage_db")
        l_strISBN = RecordSet1.Fields("strISBN_db")
```

You might have noticed that in our SQL statement we asked for a few fields that we haven't used. We'll be using them later — no sense hitting the database again. That's it for this routine, so we need to close our *if* statements.

```
        end if
    end if
    RS1.Close
```

This gives us routines as follows:

```
<%
Sub ParseQueryString(l_strObj)
'
' This routine moves through the parameters
'  passed to us and creates an application variable
'  for each
'
 for each item in l_strObj
     Application(item) = l_strObj(item)
 next
end sub
%>


<%
sub OpenRecordSet(rsobj,commandstr,parm1,parm2)
    rsobj.Open commandstr, , parm1, parm2
end sub
%>



<%
sub CheckCategoryRequestLevel _
(l_iParent,l_flgBack,l_strIndent, l_flgInit,_
 l_iReturnTo, l_strPrevCat, DBQueryObj _
 l_flgImage, l_flgBookSearch, l_strISBN)
'-------------------------------------
'Categories below main level requested?
'-------------------------------------
if len(Request.QueryString)>0 then
   call ParseQueryString(Request.QueryString)
   l_iParent=Application("parent")
   if l_iParent > 0 then
      l_flgBack = TRUE
'
' set indent so category links will be indented
'  below return path link
'
      l_strIndent="     " _
      'indentation for subcategories
'
' set flag to false so we'll get the return
' path link later
'
      l_flgInit = FALSE
```

```
'
' construct sql query to gather information
' about what is now the parent category
'
      DBQueryObj.CommandText = _
       "SELECT strCategory_db, liCatNo_db,_
        liParentCatNo_db, strISBN_db, _
        ynImage_db, ynOfferSearch_db _
        FROM Categories _
        WHERE (liCatNo_db = " & l_iParent & ")"
'
' get the record set
      call OpenRecordSet _
       (RecordSet, DBQueryObj, 0, 1)
'
' hold the data for use later
'
      l_iReturnTo = _
       RecordSet1.Fields("liParentCatNo_db")
      l_strPrevCat= _
       RecordSet1.Fields("strCategory_db")
    end if
end if
end sub
%>
```

The *Call OpenRecordSet* line calls a subroutine that creates our dataset. Here is the code for that subroutine:

```
<%
sub OpenRecordSet(rsobj,commandstr,parm1,parm2)
    rsobj.Open commandstr, , parm1, parm2
end sub
%>
```

We're ready to move on to the next block of code, a routine that obtains the dataset containing the categories having the current category as a parent. We're going to create a routine that handles this activity, thus separating the code out from the main body of code, which improves readability. For this routine to be executed, we'll need to call it from our main body of code. Let's insert it now.

```
call CheckCategoryRequestLevel _
  (m_iParent,m_flgBack,m_strIndent, m_flgInit, _
```

```
        m_iReturnTo, m_strPrevCat, SQLQuery)

    call GetCategories(RecordSet2, _
            SQLQuery2, m_iParent, m_flgInit)

    %>
```

We've passed the items necessary to obtain the database records we'll be using later. Technically, since these data items were created in the main body of code, they could be accessed in any routine without being passed as parameters, but that's a lousy coding practice and opens the code up to breaking at a later date or being very hard to debug. Let's frame a routine.

```
    <%
    sub GetCategories(RS2, SQ2, l_iParent, l_flgInit)
    '--------------
    'Get Categories
    '--------------
    end sub
    %>
```

Next, we're going to call a function to provide some information to us. The categories we retrieve will normally be based on the current parent category number, which is the category number of the last category clicked, or 0 if we're at the beginning of the list. However, there is an instance where the parent category does *not* drive our retrieval, and that's when the visitor has used the *Find* dialog. In that case, we'll be retrieving categories based on the search string. First, let's invoke the function from our current routine.

```
    if len(Application("find")) > 1 then
        l_strSearch = fnBuildFindQuery()
```

We need an *else* here, but we'll put this *if* statement on hold until we build the function.

```
    <%
    function fnBuildFindQuery()
    '--------------
    'Build a select statement based on a Find string
    '--------------
     l_strTemp = ""
     for l_iCtr = 1 to len(Application("find"))
         if mid(Application("find"),l_iCtr,1) <> _
            """" then
            l_strTemp = _
```

```
        l_strTemp & mid(Application("find") _
        ,l_iCtr,1)
    end if
  next
  fnBuildFindQuery = l_strTemp
 end function
 %>
```

The lines in the *for* statement above check for quotation marks within the string. Some people would tend to put "moose" as the search string instead of just *moose*, and since we won't find occurrences of quotation marks in the database, we'll remove those characters from the search string. By setting the function name equal to the string at the end, we're returning that string to the calling line of code. We now need to return to that code, in our interrupted *if* statement, and continue.

```
    l_strSearch = fnBuildFindQuery()

    SQ2.CommandText = _
      "SELECT strCategory_db, liCatNo_db, _
        liParentCatNo_db, strISBN_db, _
        ynOfferSearch_db _
      FROM Categories _
      WHERE strCategory_db LIKE '%" &_
      l_strSearch & _
      "%' ORDER BY strCategory_db;"
    l_flgInit = TRUE
  else
```

What we've done here is to say that if we *are* working with a visitor's *Find*, we're going to base the category retrieval on a search of all category names, *strCategory_db*, and that the value to search for is contained in *l_strSearch*. The unusual part of the statement equates to:

```
WHERE strCategory_db LIKE %x%
```

This is syntax expected by ADO. It took me quite awhile to figure out why "x" didn't work. This parameter will look for any occurrence of the string *x* in the category name. *l_flgInit* is set to *true* because our list of categories will most likely have no common parent information, so we won't provide a path back up through the tree.

We received the string back from our function call. Now, we need to construct a query statement to follow our *else* statement in the event that the category retrieval is being based on the parent category number and *not* a visitor *Find* request.

```
SQ2.CommandText = _
 "SELECT strCategory_db, liCatNo_db, _
   liParentCatNo_db, strISBN_db, ynOfferSearch_db _
  FROM Categories _
  WHERE (liParentCatNo_db = " & l_iParent & " _
   OR liParentCatNo2_db = " & l_iParent & ") _
  ORDER BY strCategory_db"
```

Here we have created the query based on the parent category number passed to us when the subroutine was invoked. At this point we need to end the if statement, and then open the dataset for which this query was constructed.

```
end if
Call OpenRecordSet(RS2, SQ2, 3, 1)
Application("find") = ""
```

The last line in our subroutine sets the application variable named *find* to null. The reason we do this is that the variable will otherwise retain its value for the duration of the application. That means, if the visitor had requested a find with the search string "shark," and we didn't clear the variable as we have done above, the next iteration of this page would pass through the code and result in the *find* being done again, because the *find* variable has a value. So we clear it here to avoid a remnant, but if the visitor supplies another *find* string in the dialog, that value will be present when we check for it next time around.

Here's our completed subroutine:

```
<%
sub GetCategories(RS2, SQ2, l_iParent, l_flgInit)
'--------------
'Get Categories
'--------------
if len(Application("find")) > 1 then
    l_strSearch = fnBuildFindQuery()
    SQ2.CommandText = _
     "SELECT strCategory_db, liCatNo_db, _
       liParentCatNo_db, strISBN_db, _
       ynOfferSearch_db _
      FROM Categories _
      WHERE strCategory_db LIKE '%" &_
      l_strSearch & _
      "%' ORDER BY strCategory_db;"
    l_flgInit = TRUE
else
    SQ2.CommandText = _
```

```
    "SELECT strCategory_db, liCatNo_db, _
     liParentCatNo_db, strISBN_db, ynOfferSearch_db _
       FROM Categories _
       WHERE (liParentCatNo_db = " & l_iParent & " _
        OR liParentCatNo2_db = " & l_iParent & ") _
       ORDER BY strCategory_db"
  end if
  Call OpenRecordSet(RS2, SQ2, 3, 1)
  Application("find") = ""
  %>
```

This ends our subroutine for retrieving the categories. At this point, we've used our query string to create a record set, and we're ready to start looking at the content and doing some things with it in preparation for painting the screen.

First, we'll invoke a new routine for processing the category information:

```
call ProcessCategories(m_iStartPos, m_iEndPos, _
     m_flgPrev, m_flgNext, m_iPageSize, _
     m_liStartRec, m_iRecCnt, m_straCatInfo, _
     RecordSet2, RecordSet3, SQLQuery3, _
     m_flgInit, m_iParent, m_strPrevCat)
```

and then begin creating the routine:

```
  <%
  sub ProcessCategories(l_iStartPos, l_iEndPos,_
     l_flgPrev, l_flgNext, l_iPageSize, _
     l_liStartRec, l_iRecCnt, l_straCatInfo, _
     RS2, RS3, SQ3, l_flgInit, l_iParent, _
     l_strPrevCat)
  end sub
  %>
```

We need to calculate what the starting position is for our list. We might have a record set of 50 categories, but we're only going to display six at a time. We need to determine where in the record set to start displaying from. In the absence of any parameters to the contrary, we'll start at the beginning. Let's call a function to decide this for us:

```
    l_iStartPos = fnDetermineStartPos(l_iPageSize)
```

and then create the function:

```
    <%
    function fnDetermineStartPos(l_iPageSize)
```

```
' Determine from where in our list we'll start
'   displaying categories
  select case Application("Direction")
    case "P": l_iStartPos = Application("Start")_
              - (l_iPageSize - 1)
              if l_iStartPos < 0 then l_iStartPos = 0
```

With these initial lines of code we're looking at whether the visitor has had a previous instance of this page up, and from that instance clicked the icon for moving backwards through the category list. If so, when this instance of the page was requested the passed parameters will have included "Direction=P." In addition, there will have been a parameter of "Start=n," where *n* is the position in the record set of the starting record the last time around. We'll want to start displaying from a page before that record, or the beginning of the list if there aren't a page full (six) of records prior. So, if the list we were looking at when we clicked the icon for previous page were:

- Colorado
- Connecticut
- Delaware
- Florida
- Georgia
- Hawaii

the list now will be:

- Alabama
- Alaska
- Arizona
- Arkansas
- California
- Colorado

So far in our *if* statement we've accounted for the *previous* page icon having been clicked, but we still need to account for the *next* page icon having been clicked:

```
  else
    case "N": l_iStartPos = Application("Start") _
              + l_iPageSize - 1
```

The above lines account for the visitor having clicked on the icon for moving forward through the list of categories, the *next* page icon. There is one final possibility, and that is that neither icon was clicked, at which case we're at the beginning of our list:

```
    case else:l_iStartPos = 0
end select
fnDetermineStartPos = l_iStartPos
```

Now that we've determined the starting position, we need to determine the ending position. If there are no records, then our ending position is fairly simple; otherwise, we'll base it on the starting position. First, let's determine how many records there are, and then we'll determine our ending position.

```
l_iStartPos = fnDetermineStartPos(l_iPageSize)


l_iRecCnt = fnDetermineRecordCnt(RS2)
l_iEndPos = fnDetermineEndPos(l_iRecCnt, _
 l_iStartPos, l_iPageSize)
```

And now we can create the functions *fnDetermineRecordCnt* and *fnDetermineEndPos*.

```
<%
function fnDetermineRecordCnt(recset)
 if not recset.EOF then
    l_iRecCnt = recset.RecordCount
 else
    l_iRecCnt = 0
 end if
 fnDetermineRecordCnt = l_iRecCnt
end function
%>
```

In this function we've looked at the record set containing the list of categories, and if we're positioned at its end-of-file, it's empty and we know that there are no records. Otherwise we'll go by the number of records in the dataset.

```
<%
function fnDetermineEndPos(l_iRecCnt, _
  l_iStartPos, l_iPageSize)
 if l_iStartPos + l_iPageSize <= l_iRecCnt then
    l_iEndPos = l_iStartPos + l_iPageSize - 1
 else
    l_iEndPos = l_iRecCnt
 end if
 fnDetermineEndPos = l_iEndPos
end function
%>
```

Now that we know what records we'll be working with, let's get the information we need about them into an array.

```
call Move2StartPos(l_iStartPos, RS2)
```

This gets us to the routine — now we need the routine to get to.

```
<%
sub Move2StartPos(l_iStartPos, recset)
 if l_iStartPos > 0 then recset.Move l_iStartPos
end sub
%>
```

When we start processing the dataset, we will be doing a sequential read, so we need to set the starting point. Now we'll start loading the category array.

```
for i = 1 to l_iPageSize
    if not RS2.EOF then
        l_straCatInfo(i,1) = _
          RS2.Fields("liCatNo_db")
        l_straCatInfo(i,2) = _
          RS2.Fields("strCategory_db")
```

There are two dimensions of the array that still need to be loaded. We'll depend on functions to determine their value.

```
straCatInfo(i,3) = _
  fnCheckForMoreCatLevels(RS2, RS3, SQ3)
straCatInfo(1,4) = _
  fnCheckForLinksNBooks(RS2, RS3, SQ3)
```

And here are the functions we've called.

```
<%
sub CloseRecordSet(rs)
 rs.close
end sub
%>
<%
function fnCheckForMoreCatLevels(RS2, RS3, SQ3)
'
'Check for more category levels below current level
'
 SQ3.CommandText = _
```

```
   "SELECT liCatNo_db FROM Categories _
    WHERE (liParentCatNo_db = " & _
     RS2.Fields("liCatNo_db") & " _
    OR liParentCatNo2_db = " & _
     RS2.Fields("liCatNo_db") & ")"
  call OpenRecordSet(RS3, SQ3, 3, 1)
  if RS3.RecordCount > 0 then
     l_ret = true
  else
     l_ret = false
  end if
  RecordSet3.Close
  fnCheckForMoreCatLevels = l_ret
end function
%>
<%
function fnCheckForLinksNBooks(RS2, RS3, SQ3)
'
'Check if any links exist for category
' or a book recommendation
'
  SQ3.CommandText = _
   "SELECT liCatNo_db FROM LinkCat _
    WHERE (liCatNo_db = " & _
     RS2.Fields("liCatNo_db") & ")"
  call OpenRecordSet(RS3, SQ3, 3, 1)
  if RS3.RecordCount > 0 or _
     RS2.Fields("strISBN_db") > "" then
     l_ret = true
  else
     l_ret = false
  end if
  fnCheckForLinksNBooks = l_ret
end function
%>
```

Now that we've loaded the array, we need to continue looping through the record set. If there were no records in the record set, make an entry in the array signifying that.

```
        straCatInfo(1,4) = _
          fnCheckForLinksNBooks(RS2, RS3, SQ3)
     l_liStartRec = l_iStartPos
     RS2.MoveNext
     RS3.Close
```

```
        else
            l_straCatInfo(i,1) = -1
        end if
    next
```

Earlier, I mentioned that if we ended up here by way of a category being clicked, we would print the category name and then the category list indented under it. We'll follow the lines above with a call to the routine that handles this processing:

```
call WriteClickedCategory _
        (l_flgInit, l_iParent, l_strPrevCat)
```

Here's the function:

```
<%
sub WriteClickedCategory _
        (l_flgInit, l_iParent, l_strPrevCat)
    call PaintInit(l_iParent)
    if l_flgInit = FALSE then _
        Response.Write "<a href=""categories.asp _
        ?parent=" & Application("GP") & _
        """ class=""clsTitle""> _
        <font=""clsTitle"">..." & l_strPrevCat _
        & "</a><br></font>"
end sub
%>
```

This routine first calls *PaintInit*, a routine we'll be defining next. Then, if this is not the first time our page has been displayed this session and it is not being displayed due to a *find* request, then a category was clicked to get us here. That category was passed as a parameter, and its name captured in *m_strPrevCat*, which was passed to our routine as *l_strPrevCat*. We'll display it and make it a link. We want to define the link so that clicking it will call this page and request the link category's parent. Since this category is the parent of our current context, *its* parent is the *grand*parent of our current context, and thus that category number is being held in the application variable *GP*.

The *PaintInit* routine begins the generation of the HTML code that makes up the body of the page we'll pass to the visitor. Up until now, almost everything we've seen is code that will be processed by the ASP engine, but not passed to the visitor. Let's create the routine's frame, then fill it in.

```
<%
sub PaintInit(l_iKey)
end sub
%>
```

Next, we want to check to see if we've been passed a non-zero key. The key is the number of the category that was clicked to get us here. One of the results of the click is that any links that apply to this category will be displayed in the *links* frame. How, though, do we cause that to happen in a different frame? The secret is some JavaScript.

We already have the information that the links frame and the other frames need when our page first loads, because the contents of those frames will be based on the category we already clicked. So, we can affect the contents of those frames as soon as our page allows us. The easiest place to do that is in the *body* tag, which supports an *onload* event. This event "fires" as soon as the page is loaded. If we tell the *onload* event to call a JavaScript function, we can code the function to reset the pages loaded into the other frames:

```
sub PaintInit(l_iKey)

Response.Write "<script>" & chr(13)
Response.Write "<!--" & chr(13)
Response.Write "function fnFrameLoad()" & chr(13)
Response.Write "{" & chr(13)
if l_iKey > 0 then
  Response.Write _
    "parent.main.location=""links.asp?p=" _
    & l_iKey & """;" & chr(13)
else
  Response.Write _
    "parent.main.location=""testd.htm"";" & chr(13)
end if
Response.Write "}" & chr(13)
Response.Write "-->" & chr(13)
Response.Write "</script>" & chr(13)
Response.Write "<body onload=""fnFrameLoad()"">" _
  & chr(13)
Response.Write "<table border='0' cellpadding='1' _
  cellspacing='2' width='100%' _
  id='tabContent'>" & chr(13)
Response.Write "<TR><TD>" & chr(13)

end sub
```

That's all we needed to do to process the categories. Now we need to write them. We have some rules to follow when writing the categories. They are:

- If the category has subsequent levels, it will be a hyperlink, and the category name will be appended with "...".
- If the category has links associated with it, it will be a hyperlink.

- It the visitor's browser is Internet Explorer, we'll include a *mouseover* script that will cause the appearance of the category name to change while the visitor's mouse cursor hovers over it.
- We'll use the styles we create for both links and non-links.

We'll go back to the main body of our page, where we haven't been for quite a while, and call this new routine.

```
call ProcessCategories(m_iStartPos, m_iEndPos,
m_flgPrev, m_flgNext, _
    m_iPageSize, m_liStartRec, m_iRecCnt,
m_straCatInfo, RecordSet2, _
    RecordSet3, SQLQuery3, m_flgInit, m_iParent,
m_strPrevCat)

    call WriteCategories(m_iStartPos, m_iEndPos, _
    m_iParent, m_straCatInfo(), m_strIndent)
```

Here's the routine that prints the categories:

```
<%
sub WriteCategories(l_iStartPos, l_iEndPos, _
    l_iParent, l_straCatInfo, l_strIndent)
  for i = l_iStartPos to l_iEndPos
      l_iMoreCatLevels = l_straCatInfo _
      (i - l_iStartPos + 1,3)
      l_iLinksExist = l_straCatInfo _
      (i - l_iStartPos + 1,4)
      if (l_iMoreCatLevels) or (l_iLinksExist) then
         Response.Write "<font class=""clsLink"">" _
         & chr(13)
         Response.Write "<a name=""a" & i _
         & """ class=""clsLink"" href= _
         ""categories.asp?gp= " & l_iParent & _
         "&parent=" & l_straCatInfo(i - _
         l_iStartPos + 1,1) & chr(13)
```

The *response.write* line above is where we create the hyperlink. The class we refer to is the one we created for links in our cascading style sheet. The HREF in the link calls our page again. The parameters being passed might be somewhat confusing. If the link is clicked, we will be processing the child of this link when we process the parameters. Therefore, the parent of the current category will be the grandparent at that point; hence we pass *l_iParent* as the grandparent, and the category number stored in the first dimension of *l_straCatInfo* as the parent.

```
if bc.browser = "IE" then Response.Write _
   """ onMouseOver=""MouseOn(); return true; _
   "" onMouseOut=""MouseOff(); return true;" _
   & chr(13)
```

We've checked above to see if the browser is Internet Explorer. The reason is that at the time of this writing Netscape Communicator doesn't support the hover events in the same manner. We call JavaScript routines to handle the hover events. We'll send the code for those events later.

```
Response.Write """>" & l_strIndent & _
   l_straCatInfo(i - l_iStartPos + 1,2) & _
   chr(13)
```

These lines close the HREF we began earlier. Depending on the visitor's browser, that HREF might now contain hover calls. We're displaying the contents of *l_strIndent* first. If we have displayed a previously clicked category at the top of our list, then this variable contains a number of non-breaking space characters that, when displayed, effect an indent. We then display the category name.

```
if (l_iMoreCatLevels) then _
   Response.Write "..."
```

We've checked to see if there are categories that claim this one as a parent. If so, then clicking this category will result in their being displayed, and thus we want "..." appended to the name so that the visitor knows there are more categories *below* it.

```
Response.write "</a>"
if i <> l_iEndPos then _
   Response.Write "<BR>"
Response.Write "</font>"
else
```

We've closed the hyperlink with the *</a>* tag. If this is not the last category in the list, we'll put a hard line-feed after it. That ends the branch of logic we take if this category is to be displayed as a hyperlink. Now we have to address the other situation, the category that has neither links nor children, and thus is not displayed as a hyperlink.

```
Response.Write chr(13) & _
   "<font id=""idNoLink"" class=""clsLink""> _
   " & chr(13)
Response.Write l_strIndent & _
   l_straCatInfo(i - l_iStartPos + 1,2) _
   & chr(13)
```

```
      if i <> l_iEndPos then Response.Write  _
      "<BR>"
      Response.Write "</font>" & chr(13)
   end if
```

That ends the *if* statement. We now loop back for the next category, and when we finish the list we end the table.

```
   next
call PaintNavigationHint(m_flgNext,m_flgPrev)
response.write "</td></tr>" & chr(13)
Response.Write "</td></tr>" & chr(13)
Response.Write "</table>" & chr(13)
end sub
%>
```

It just occurred to me that you might be wondering why these lines end with "& chr(13)." It's so the next line of HTML begins on a new line.

In the preceding block of code we called the routine *PaintNavigationHint*, which will indicate to the visitor that the use of the navigation icons (we'll process them later) might be in order.

```
<%
sub PaintNavigationHint(l_flgNext,l_flgPrev)
   if (l_flgNext) or (l_flgPrev) then
      Response.Write "<br><hr width=""10%" & _
         """ align=""left"">"
      Response.Write "<FONT CLASS=""clsLink"" _
         ID=""idNoLink"" color=""maroon"">"
      Response.Write "(more - use arrow button) _
         </font>"
   end if
end sub
%>
```

Okay, time to move on to the next section in our *Categories* frame, the navigation bar. Let's call and create a new routine for this.

```
   call WriteCategories(m_iStartPos, m_iEndPos,
m_iParent, _
   m_straCatInfo, m_strIndent)

   call CreateCatNavBar(m_flgBack, m_flgPrev, _
   m_flgNext, m_iParent, m_liStartRec)
```

and the code for the routine:

```
CreateCatNavBar(l_flgBack,l_flgPrev,l_flgNext, _
  l_iParent, l_liStartRec)
 Response.Write "<TABLE  bgcolor=""#ACA470"" _
  width=""100" & "%"" cellspacing=""0"" _
  cellpadding=""0"" border=""0"">" & chr(13)
 Response.Write "<TR><TD align=""center"" _
  valign=""middle"">" & chr(13)
```

With those lines we've created the table to hold the navigation icons and associated text.

```
call ProcessNavHome(l_flgBack)
```

We're calling a routine, which we need to create, to handle the processing of the icon that sends the visitor back to the initial category list.

```
<%
sub ProcessNavHome(l_flgBack)
 Response.Write "<SPAN class=""clsNav""> _
  Top of<br>List</span></td><td align=""center"" _
  valign=""middle"">" & chr(13)
 if l_flgBack = TRUE then
    Response.Write "<" & "!--Webbot bot= _
     ""ImageMap""  rectangle="" (0,0) (14, 12) _
     categories.asp"" src=""images/home.gif"" _
     alt=""Top level of category list"" _
     border=""0"" startspan --> _
     <MAP NAME=""FrontPageMap1""> _
     <AREA SHAPE=""RECT"" COORDS=""0, 0, 14, _
     12"" HREF=""categories.asp""></MAP> _
     <a href=""_vti_bin/shtml.dll/categories. _
     asp/map""><img ismap usemap= _
     ""#FrontPageMap1""  border=""0""  _
     height=""15"" alt=""beginning of _
     categories"" src=""images/home.gif"" _
     width=""18""></a><!--Webbot bot ImageMap"" _
     endspan i-checksum 16062"" -->" & chr(13)
  else
     Response.Write "<img src=""images/home_off _
     .gif"" height=""15"" width=""18"">" & chr(13)
  end if
end sub
%>
```

It's a small routine with a very big write statement! If there is a backward path to our categories, if we're not at the start of the list as determined by *m_flgBack*, the first statement produces an image map — an image that is clickable. The easiest way to produce this code is to create a blank page in FrontPage, insert the image, use the image map tool bar (Figure 11-2) to create a rectangular click region, save the page (this is very important: FrontPage creates the HTML string when the page is saved) and then copy the HTML.

Figure 11-2   Image Map Tool Bar in FrontPage

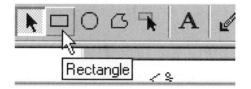

If *m_flgBack* is *false*, then we display the *home_off* icon, which is the *home* icon in gray and don't make it an image link, because the visitor is already home. With that icon out of the way we want to move on to the icon for *prev* and *next* page.

We have our starting and ending position, so we want to determine whether our starting and ending positions, with respect to our category list, warrant either the icon for *previous* page or *next* page to be made active. For example, if our ending position will be the end of the category records, then there's not another page to display, so the *next* page icon will be disabled. So, we need to add a couple invocation lines after our call to *fnDetermineEndPos* in our *ProcessCategories* routine:

```
l_iEndPos = fnDetermineEndPos(l_iRecCnt,
l_iStartPos, l_iPageSize)

l_flgPrev = fnEvaluatePrev(l_iStartPos)
l_flgNext = fnEvaluateNext(l_iStartPos, _
  l_iRecCnt, l_iPageSize)
```

and now we need to create each of the functions that we've referenced above:

```
<%
function fnEvaluatePrev(l_iStartPos)
    if iStartPos > 0 then
       fnEvaluatePrev = TRUE
    else
       fnEvaluatePrev = FALSE
    end if
end function
```

```
%>

<%
function fnEvaluateNext(l_iStartPos, _
                        l_iRecCnt, l_iPageSize)
  if iStartPos + iPageSize <= iRecCnt then
     fnEvaluateNext = TRUE
  else
     fnEvaluateNext = FALSE
  end if
end function
%>
```

These routines will have set the flags *m_flgPrev* and *m_flgNext*. With that information, we're ready to process this part of our navigation from within *CreateCatNavBar*.

```
call ProcessNavHome(l_flgBack)

call ProcessPrevNext(l_flgPrev, l_flgNext _
 , l_iParent, l_liStartRec)
```

and the routine to go with it — be prepared for some more *long* write statements:

```
<%
sub ProcessPrevNext(l_flgPrev, l_flgNext, _
  l_iParent, l_liStartRec)
 Response.Write "</td>" & chr(13)
 Response.Write "<td align=""center"" _
  valign=""middle""><DIV class=""clsNav"">Prev _
  <br>page</div>" & chr(13)
 Response.Write "</td>" & chr(13)
 Response.Write "<td align=""center"" _
  valign=""middle"">" & chr(13)
 if l_flgNext = true then
    if l_flgPrev = false then
       Response.Write "<" & "!--Webbot _
        bot=""ImageMap"" rectangle="" (13,0) _
        (25, 15) categories.asp?direction= _
        N&parent=" & l_iParent & "&start=" & _
        l_liStartRec & """ src=""images/ _
        r_u.gif"" alt=""Next"" border=""0"" _
        startspan  --> _
        <MAP NAME=""FrontPageMap2""> _
        <AREA SHAPE=""RECT"" COORDS=""13, 0, _
```

```
                25, 15"" HREF=""categories.asp? _
                direction=N&parent=" & l_iParent &  _
                "&start=" & l_liStartRec & """></MAP> _
                <a href=""_vti_bin/shtml.dll/categories _
                .asp/map""><img ismap usemap= _
                ""#FrontPageMap2"" border=""0"" _
                height=""15"" alt=""Next page of _
                categories"" src=""images/r_u.gif"" _
                width=""25""></a><!--Webbot bot _
                ImageMap"" endspan -->" & chr(13)
            else
                response.write "<" & "!--Webbot bot= _
                 ""ImageMap"" rectangle="" (0,0) (11, 15) _
                categories.asp?direction=P&parent=" & _
                l_iParent & "&start=" & l_liStartRec _
                & """ rectangle="" (13,0) (25, 15) _
                categories.asp?direction=N&parent=" & _
                l_iParent & "&start=" & l_liStartRec _
                & """ src=""images/lr_u.gif""  _
                alt=""Prev/Next""  _
                border=""0"" startspan --><MAP NAME= _
                ""FrontPageMap2""><AREA SHAPE=""RECT"" _
                COORDS=""0, 0, 11, 15"" HREF= _
                ""categories.asp?direction=P&parent=" & _
                l_iParent & "&start=" & l_liStartRec & _
                """> <AREA SHAPE=""RECT"" COORDS=""13, 0, _
                25, 15"" HREF=""categories.asp? _
                direction=N&parent=" & l_iParent & _
                "&start=" & l_liStartRec & """></MAP> _
                <a href=""_vti_bin/shtml.dll/categories _
                .asp/map""><img ismap usemap="" _
                #FrontPageMap2"" border=""0""  _
                height=""15"" alt=""Prev/Next page _
                of categories"" src=""images/lr_u.gif"" _
                width=""25""></a><!--Webbot bot _
                ImageMap"" endspan -->" & chr(13)
        end if
    else
        if l_flgPrev = true then
            response.write "<" & "!--Webbot bot= _
            ""ImageMap"" rectangle="" (0,0) _
            (11, 15) categories.asp?direction= _
            P&parent=" & l_iParent & "&start=" & _
            l_liStartRec & """ src=""images/l_u.gif _
```

```
                "" alt="""Next"" border="""0"" startspan --> _
                <MAP NAME="""FrontPageMap2""> _
                <AREA SHAPE="""RECT"" COORDS="""0, 0, _
                11, 15"" HREF="""categories.asp? _
                direction=P&parent=" & l_iParent & _
                "&start=" & l_liStartRec & """></MAP> _
                <a href=""_vti_bin/shtml.dll/categories _
                .asp/map""><img ismap usemap="" _
                #FrontPageMap2 "" border="""0"" _
                height="""15"" alt="""Previous page of _
                categories"" src="""images/l_u.gif"" _
                width="""25""></a><!--Webbot bot _
                ImageMap"" endspan -->" & chr(13)
          else
                Response.Write "<" & "img src="""images/ _
                lr_o.gif"" height="""15"" width="""25""> _
                & chr(13)
          end if
       end if
       Response.Write "</td><td align="""center"" _
        valign="""middle""><DIV class="""clsNav""> _
        Next<br>page</div>" & chr(13)
      end sub
   %>
```

Okay, *huge* write statements. Here's what we're doing. If there is a backward path through our categories, *m_flgPrev* is *true* and we'll take this graphic of a two-headed arrow and set the left-hand side up as a clickable region. If there is a forward path, *m_flgNext* is *true* and we'll do the same for the right-hand side.

The next thing in our frame is the *find* dialog. Let's set it up.

```
   call CreateCatNavBar(m_flgBack, m_flgPrev,
m_flgNext, m_iParent, _
     m_liStartRec)

   call PaintSearch()
```

We don't need to pass any parameters to this routine, as its content is not driven by the state of our page.

```
   <%
   sub PaintSearch()
    Response.Write "<table align="""center"">" & chr(13)
    Response.Write "<form name="""fSearch"" _
```

```
            action="""categories.asp"">" & chr(13)
    Response.Write "<img src=""images/mglass.gif"" _
        alt= ""search for a category"">" & chr(13)
    Response.Write "<input name=""find"" size=""12"" _
        type=""text"">" & chr(13)
    Response.Write "<input type=""image"" _
     src=""images/find.gif"" border=""0""><br>" _
     & chr(13)
    Response.Write "</form>" & chr(13)
    Response.Write "</table>" & chr(13)
    end sub
    %>
```

Next is the logic for the book recommendation. The invoking line:

```
call DecideOnAmazon(m_strISBN, m_flgImage, _
    m_flgBookSearch, m_strPrevCat)
```

and the routine:

```
<%
sub DecideOnAmazon(l_strISBN, l_flgImage, _
    l_flgBookSearch, l_strPrevCat)
  if (l_flgImage) or (l_flgBookSearch) or _
      l_strISBN > "" then
      Response.Write "<HR WIDTH=""50%"">" & chr(13)
      if l_strISBN > "" then
          if l_flgImage = TRUE then
              Response.Write "<table><tr><td>" & chr(13)
              Response.Write "<font id=""idNoLink"" _
              class=""clsLink"">Click to buy this book _
              </font><br>" & chr(13)
              Response.Write "<a target=""_blank"" _
                href=""http://www.amazon.com/exec/ _
                obidos/ASIN/" & l_strISBN & _
                "/theblowhole""><img _
                src=""images/book/" & l_strISBN _
                & ".gif"" border=""0""></a>" & chr(13)
              Response.Write "</td></tr></table>"
          else
              Response.Write "<CENTER><SMALL>Click the _
              books for our<br><a target=""_blank"" _
              href=""http://www.amazon.com/exec/ _
              obidos/ASIN/" & l_strISBN & _
```

```
                "/theblowhole"""><img src= _
                ""images/bk22.gif"" border=""0""> _
                </a><br>recommendation on this topic _
                from<br>" & chr(13)
                Response.Write "<img src= _
                  ""images/90X29-w-logo.gif""></small> _
                </center>" & chr(13)
            end if
        else
            if l_flgBookSearch = TRUE then
                Response.Write "<CENTER>"
                Response.Write "<FORM METHOD=""get"" _
                  ACTION=""http://www.amazon.com/exec/ _
                  obidos/external-search"" id=""form1"" _
                  name=""form1"" target=""_blank"">" _
                  & chr(13)
                Response.Write "<SMALL>Click for books" _
                  & chr(13)
                 Response.Write "<INPUT type=""hidden"" _
                 name=""mode"" value=""books"">" & _
                 chr(13)
                Response.Write "<INPUT type=""hidden"" _
                  name=""keyword"" value=""" & _
                  l_strPrevCat & """>" & chr(13)
                Response.Write "<INPUT TYPE=""hidden"" _
                  NAME=""tag"" VALUE=""theblowhole"">" _
                  & chr(13)
                Response.Write "<CENTER> _
                  <INPUT TYPE=""image"" BORDER=""0"" _
                  SRC=""images/90X29-w-logo.gif"" _
                  NAME=""Search""></center>" & chr(13)
                Response.Write "on <B><i>" & _
                  l_strPrevCat & "</i></b></small> _
                  </center>" & chr(13)
                Response.Write "</FORM>" & chr(13)
            end if
        end if
    end if
end sub
%>
```

Earlier, we discussed the hover routines. Let's go back to the start of our page and generate that code. We'll put these lines at the beginning of our *Head* section.

```
<% Set bc = Server.CreateObject("MSWC.BrowserType")
  if bc.browser = "IE" then
    Response.Write "<script language= _
     ""JavaScript"">" & chr(13)
    Response.Write "<!--" & chr(13)
    Response.Write "function MouseOn() {" _
     & chr(13)
    Response.Write "window.event.srcElement _
     .style.color=""#ACA470"";" & chr(13)
    Response.Write "}" & chr(13)
    Response.Write "function MouseOff() {" _
     & chr(13)
    Response.Write "window.event.srcElement _
     .style.color=""navy"";" & chr(13)
    Response.Write "}" & chr(13)
    Response.Write "-->" & chr(13)
    Response.Write "</script>" & chr(13)
  end if
%>
```

The last, yes *last* thing we need to put in *categories.asp* is the line that links in our cascading style sheet. This will go right after the *<head>* tag:

```
<link rel="stylesheet" type="text/css" _
 href="blowhole.css">
```

Whew. I promise that this was the longest of our pages. Below is the complete code for the *Categories* page.

```
<%@ Language=VBScript %>
<HTML>
<HEAD>
<link rel="stylesheet" type="text/css" _
 href="blowhole.css">
<TITLE></title>
<% Set bc = Server.CreateObject("MSWC.BrowserType")
  if bc.browser = "IE" then
    Response.Write "<script language= _
     ""JavaScript"">" & chr(13)
    Response.Write "<!--" & chr(13)
    Response.Write "function MouseOn() {" _
```

```
        & chr(13)
     Response.Write "window.event.srcElement. _
       style.color=""#ACA470"";" & chr(13)
     Response.Write "}" & chr(13)
     Response.Write "function MouseOff() {" _
       & chr(13)
     Response.Write "window.event.srcElement. _
       style.color=""navy"";" & chr(13)
     Response.Write "}" & chr(13)
     Response.Write "-->" & chr(13)
     Response.Write "</script>" & chr(13)
 end if
%>
<%
sub global_asa()
'This routine is here because the global.asa _
   functionality
' doesnt work as advertised - remove this _
 routine and the
' call to it when it does
 Session("DataConn_ConnectionString") = _
   "DSN=TheBlowholeDSN"
 Session("DataConn_ConnectionTimeout") = 15
 Session("DataConn_CommandTimeout") = 30
 Session("DataConn_RuntimeUserName") = "admin"
 Session("DataConn_RuntimePassword") = ""
end sub
%>
<%
Sub ParseQueryString(l_strObj)
 '
 ' This routine moves through the parameters
 '  passed to us and creates a application variable
 '  for each
 '
  for each item in l_strObj
      Application(item)=l_strObj(item)
  next
end sub
%>
<%
sub OpenRecordSet(rsobj,commandstr,parm1,parm2)
  'Response.Write commandstr.commandtext & "<br>" _
   & parm1 & "<br>" & parm2 & chr(13)
```

```
        rsobj.Open commandstr, , parm1, parm2
end sub
%>
<%
function fnBuildFindQuery()
'--------------
'Build a select statement based on a Find string
'--------------
 l_strTemp = ""
 for l_iCtr = 1 to len(Application("find"))
    if mid(Application("find"),l_iCtr,1) <> """" _
      then
         l_strTemp = _
         l_tmpstr & mid(Application("find")_
         ,l_iCtr,1)
      end if
 next
 fnBuildFindQuery = l_strTemp
end function
%>
<%
sub GetCategories(RS2, SQ2, l_iParent, l_flgInit)
'--------------
'Get Categories
'--------------
 if len(Application("find")) > 1 then
    l_strSearch = fnBuildFindQuery()
    SQ2.CommandText = "SELECT strCategory_db, _
     liCatNo_db, liParentCatNo_db, strISBN_db, _
     ynOfferSearch_db FROM Categories WHERE _
     strCategory_db LIKE '%" & l_strSearch & _
     "%' ORDER BY strCategory_db;"
    l_flgInit = TRUE
 else
    SQ2.CommandText = "SELECT strCategory_db, _
     liCatNo_db, liParentCatNo_db, strISBN_db, _
     ynOfferSearch_db FROM Categories WHERE _
     (liParentCatNo_db = " & l_iParent & " OR _
     liParentCatNo2_db = " & l_iParent & ") ORDER _
     BY strCategory_db"
 end if
 Call OpenRecordSet(RS2, SQ2, 3, 1)
 Application("find") = ""
end sub
```

```
%>
<%
sub CheckCategoryRequestLevel(l_iParent, _
 l_flgBack, l_strIndent, l_flgInit, l_iReturnTo, _
 l_strPrevCat, l_flgImage, l_flgBookSearch, _
 l_strISBN, RS1, SQ1)
'-------------------------------------
'Categories below main level requested?
'-------------------------------------
if len(Request.QueryString) > 0 then
    call ParseQueryString(Request.QueryString)
    l_iParent=Application("parent")
    if l_iParent > 0 then
        l_flgBack = TRUE
'
' set indent so category links will be indented
'  below return path link
'
        l_strIndent = "     _
          " 'indentation for subcategories
'
' set flag to false so we'll get the return _
 path link later
'
        l_flgInit = FALSE
'
' construct sql query to gather information
' about what is now the parent category
'
        SQ1.CommandText = "SELECT strCategory_db, _
         liCatNo_db, liParentCatNo_db, strISBN_db, _
         ynImage_db, ynOfferSearch_db _
         FROM Categories WHERE (liCatNo_db = " _
         & l_iParent & ")"
'
' get the record set
'
        call OpenRecordSet(RS1, SQ1,0,1)
'
' hold the data for use later
'
        l_iReturnTo = RS1.Fields("liParentCatNo_db")
        l_strPrevCat = RS1.Fields _
         ("strCategory_db")
```

```
       l_flgBookSearch = _
        RS1.Fields("ynOfferSearch_db")
       l_flgImage = RS1.Fields("ynImage_db")
       l_strISBN = RS1.Fields("strISBN_db")
       RS1.Close
    end if
 end if
 end sub
 %>
 <%
 function fnDetermineStartPos(l_iPageSize)
 '
 ' Determine from where in our list we'll start
 '   displaying categories
 '
  select case Application("Direction")
    case "P": l_iStartPos = Application("Start") _
     - (l_iPageSize - 1)
            if l_iStartPos < 0 then l_iStartPos = 0
    case "N": l_iStartPos = Application("Start") _
     + l_iPageSize - 1
    case else:l_iStartPos = 0
  end select
  fnDetermineStartPos = l_iStartPos
 end function
 %>
 <%
 function fnDetermineRecordCnt(recset)
  if not recset.EOF then
    l_iRecCnt = recset.RecordCount
  else
    l_iRecCnt = 0
  end if
  fnDetermineRecordCnt = l_iRecCnt
 end function
 %>
 <%
 function fnDetermineEndPos(l_iRecCnt, l_iStartPos _
 , l_iPageSize)
  if l_iStartPos + l_iPageSize <= l_iRecCnt then
    l_iEndPos = l_iStartPos + l_iPageSize - 1
  else
    l_iEndPos = l_iRecCnt
  end if
```

```
   fnDetermineEndPos = l_iEndPos
end function
%>
<%
function fnEvaluatePrev(l_iStartPos)
   if l_iStartPos > 0 then
      fnEvaluatePrev = TRUE
   else
      fnEvaluatePrev = FALSE
   end if
end function
%>
<%
function fnEvaluateNext(l_iStartPos, l_iRecCnt, _
 l_iPageSize)
 if l_iStartPos + l_iPageSize <= l_iRecCnt then
    fnEvaluateNext = TRUE
 else
    fnEvaluateNext = FALSE
 end if
end function
%>
<%
sub Move2StartPos(l_iStartPos, recset)
 if l_iStartPos > 0 then recset.Move l_iStartPos
end sub
%>
<%
sub CloseRecordSet(rs)
 rs.close
end sub
%>
<%
function fnCheckForMoreCatLevels(RS2, RS3, SQ3)
 '
 'Check for more category levels below current level
 '
 SQ3.CommandText = "SELECT liCatNo_db _
  FROM Categories WHERE (liParentCatNo_db = " _
  & RS2.Fields("liCatNo_db") & " OR _
  liParentCatNo2_db = " & RS2.Fields("liCatNo_db") _
  & ")"
 call OpenRecordSet(RS3, SQ3, 3, 1)
 if RS3.RecordCount > 0 then
```

```
      l_ret = true
   else
      l_ret = false
   end if
   RS3.Close
   fnCheckForMoreCatLevels = l_ret
end function
%>
<%
function fnCheckForLinksNBooks(RS2, RS3, SQ3)
'
'Check if any links exist for category
' or a book recommendation
'
   SQ3.CommandText = "SELECT liCatNo_db _
    FROM LinkCat WHERE (liCatNo_db = " & _
    RS2.Fields("liCatNo_db") & ")"
   call OpenRecordSet(RS3, SQ3, 3, 1)
   if RS3.RecordCount > 0 or RS2.Fields _
    ("strISBN_db") > "" then
      l_ret = true
   else
      l_ret = false
   end if
   fnCheckForLinksNBooks = l_ret
end function
%>
<%
sub PaintInit(l_iKey)
 Response.Write "<script>" & chr(13)
 Response.Write "<!--" & chr(13)
 Response.Write "function fnFrameLoad()" & chr(13)
 Response.Write "{" & chr(13)
 if l_iKey > 0 then
   Response.Write "parent.main.location= _
    ""links.asp?p=" & l_iKey & """;" & chr(13)
 else
   Response.Write "parent.main.location= _
    ""testd.htm"";" & chr(13)
 end if
 Response.Write "}" & chr(13)
 Response.Write "-->" & chr(13)
 Response.Write "</script>" & chr(13)
 Response.Write "<body onload=""fnFrameLoad()"" _
```

```
     >" & chr(13)
   Response.Write "<table border='0' _
    cellpadding='1' cellspacing='2' width='100%' _
    id='tabContent'>" & chr(13)
   Response.Write "<TR><TD>" & chr(13)
  end sub
  %>
  <%
  sub WriteClickedCategory(l_flgInit, l_iParent, _
   l_strPrevCat)
   call PaintInit(l_iParent)
   if l_flgInit = FALSE then Response.Write  _
    "<a href=""categories.asp?parent=" &  _
    Application("GP") & """ class=""clsTitle""> _
    <font=""clsTitle"">..." & l_strPrevCat &   _
    "</a><br></font>"
  end sub
  %>
  <%
  sub ProcessCategories(l_iStartPos, l_iEndPos, _
   l_flgPrev, l_flgNext, l_iPageSize, l_liStartRec, _
   l_iRecCnt, l_straCatInfo, RS2, RS3, SQ3, _
   l_flgInit, l_iParent, l_strPrevCat)
   l_iStartPos = fnDetermineStartPos(l_iPageSize)
   l_iRecCnt = fnDetermineRecordCnt(RS2)
   l_iEndPos = fnDetermineEndPos(l_iRecCnt, _
    l_iStartPos, l_iPageSize)
   l_flgPrev = fnEvaluatePrev(l_iStartPos)
   l_flgNext = fnEvaluateNext(l_iStartPos,   _
    l_iRecCnt, l_iPageSize)
   call Move2StartPos(l_iStartPos, RS2)
   for i = 1 to l_iPageSize
      if not RS2.EOF then
         l_straCatInfo(i,1) = RS2.Fields("liCatNo_db")
         l_straCatInfo(i,2) = _
          RS2.Fields("strCategory_db")
         l_straCatInfo(i,3) = _
          fnCheckForMoreCatLevels(RS2, RS3, SQ3)
         l_straCatInfo(1,4) = _
          fnCheckForLinksNBooks(RS2, RS3, SQ3)
         l_liStartRec = l_iStartPos
     RS2.MoveNext
         RS3.Close
   else
```

```
    l_straCatInfo(i,1) = -1
 end if
 next
 call WriteClickedCategory(l_flgInit, l_iParent, _
  l_strPrevCat)
end sub
%>
<%
sub PaintNavigationHint(l_flgNext,l_flgPrev)
    if (l_flgNext) or (l_flgPrev) then
        Response.Write "<br><hr width=""10%" & _
        """ align=""left"">"
        Response.Write "<FONT CLASS=""clsLink"" _
        ID=""idNoLink"" color=""maroon"">"
        Response.Write "(more - use arrow button) _
        </font>"
    end if
end sub
%>
<%
sub WriteCategories(l_iStartPos, l_iEndPos, _
  l_iParent, l_straCatInfo(), l_strIndent)
 for i = l_iStartPos to l_iEndPos
        l_iMoreCatLevels = l_straCatInfo _
        (i - l_iStartPos + 1,3)
        l_iLinksExist = l_straCatInfo _
        (i - l_iStartPos + 1,4)
        if (l_iMoreCatLevels) or (l_iLinksExist) then
            Response.Write "<font class=""clsLink"">" _
            & chr(13)
          Response.Write "<a name=""a" & i & _
          """ class=""clsLink"" href= _
          ""categories.asp?gp=" & l_iParent & _
          "&parent=" & l_straCatInfo_
          (i - l_iStartPos + 1,1) & chr(13)
          if bc.browser = "IE" then Response.Write _
          """ onMouseOver=""MouseOn(); return true; _
          "" onMouseOut=""MouseOff(); return true;" _
          & chr(13)
         Response.Write """>" & l_strIndent & _
         l_straCatInfo(i - l_iStartPos + 1,2) & _
         chr(13)
        if (l_iMoreCatLevels) then Response.Write "..."
         Response.write "</a>"
```

```
         if i <> l_iEndPos then Response.Write _
          "<BR>"  ' dont want a br after the _
          last entry
         Response.Write "</font>"
      else
         Response.Write chr(13) & "<font id= _
          ""idNoLink"" class=""clsLink"">" _
          & chr(13)
         Response.Write l_strIndent & _
          l_straCatInfo(i - l_iStartPos + 1,2) _
          & chr(13)
         if i <> l_iEndPos then Response.Write _
          "<BR>" ' dont want a br after the _
          last entry
         Response.Write "</font>" & chr(13)
      end if
   next
   call PaintNavigationHint(m_flgNext,m_flgPrev)
   Response.Write "</td></tr>" & chr(13)
   Response.Write "</td></tr>" & chr(13)
   Response.Write "</table>" & chr(13)
end sub
%>
<%
sub ProcessNavHome(l_flgBack)
 Response.Write "<SPAN class=""clsNav""> _
 Top of<br>List</span></td><td align=""center"" _
 valign=""middle"">" & chr(13)
 if l_flgBack = TRUE then
    Response.Write "<" & "!--Webbot bot= _
     ""ImageMap"" rectangle="" (0,0) (14, 12) _
     categories.asp"" src=""images/home.gif"" _
     alt=""Top level of category list"" border= _
     ""0"" startspan -->>MAP NAME= _
     ""FrontPageMap1""><AREA SHAPE=""RECT"" _
     COORDS=""0, 0, 14, 12"" HREF= _
     ""categories.asp""></MAP><a href= _
     ""_vti_bin/shtml.dll/categories.asp/map""> _
     <img ismap usemap=""#FrontPageMap1"" _
     border=""0"" height=""15"" alt= _
     ""beginning of categories"" src= _
     ""images/home.gif"" width=""18""></a> _
     <!--Webbot bot ImageMap"" endspan  _
     i-checksum 16062"" -->" & chr(13)
```

```
    else
        Response.Write "<img src= _
         """images/home_off.gif"" height=""15"" _
         width=""18"">" & chr(13)
    end if
end sub
%>
<%
sub ProcessPrevNext(l_flgPrev, l_flgNext, _
   l_iParent, l_liStartRec)
 Response.Write "</td>" & chr(13)
 Response.Write "<td align=""center"" valign= _
   ""middle""><DIV class=""clsNav"">Prev<br> _
   page</div>" & chr(13)
 Response.Write "</td>" & chr(13)
 Response.Write "<td align=""center""   _
   valign=""middle"">" & chr(13)
 if l_flgNext = true then
     if l_flgPrev = false then
         response.write "<" & "!--Webbot bot= _
           ""ImageMap"" rectangle="" (13,0) _
           (25, 15)  categories.asp?direction=N _
           &parent=" & l_iParent & "&start=" _
           & l_liStartRec & """ src= _
           ""images/r_u.gif"" alt=""Next""  _
           border=""0"" startspan --> _
           <MAP NAME=""FrontPageMap2""> _
           <AREA SHAPE=""RECT"" COORDS= _
           ""13, 0, 25, 15"" HREF=""categories.asp _
           ?direction=N&parent=" & l_iParent _
           & "&start=" & l_liStartRec & """"></MAP> _
           <a href=""_vti_bin/shtml.dll/ _
           categories.asp/map""> _
           <img ismap usemap=""#FrontPageMap2"" _
           border=""0"" height=""15"" alt= _
           ""Next page of categories"" src= _
           ""images/r_u.gif"" width=""25""></a> _
            <!--Webbot bot ImageMap"" endspan -->" _
           & chr(13)
     else
         response.write "<" & "!--Webbot bot= _
           ""ImageMap"" rectangle="" (0,0) _
           (11, 15)  categories.asp?direction= _
           P&parent=" & l_iParent & "&start=" _
```

```
            & l_liStartRec & """ rectangle=""  _
            (13,0) (25, 15)  categories.asp? _
            direction=N&parent=" & l_iParent &  _
            "&start=" & l_liStartRec & _
            """ src="""images/lr_u.gif"" alt= _
            ""Prev/Next"" border=""0""    _
            startspan -->"& <MAP NAME= _
            ""FrontPageMap2"">< AREA SHAPE= _
            ""RECT"" COORDS=""0, 0, 11, 15""  HREF= _
            ""categories.asp?direction=P&parent=" _
            & l_iParent & "&start=" & l_liStartRec _
            & """><AREA SHAPE=""RECT"" COORDS= _
            ""13, 0, 25, 15"" HREF= _
            ""categories.asp?direction=N&parent=" _
            & l_iParent & "&start=" & l_liStartRec _
            & """></MAP><a href=""_vti_bin/ _
            shtml.dll/categories.asp/map""> _
            <img ismap usemap=""#FrontPageMap2"" _
            border=""0"" height=""15""   _
            alt=""Prev/Next page of categories"" _
            src=""images/lr_u.gif"" width=""25""> _
            </a><!--Webbot bot ImageMap""    _
            endspan -->" & chr(13)
    end if
    else
        if l_flgPrev = true then
        response.write "<" & "!--Webbot bot= _
            ""ImageMap"" rectangle="" (0,0)   _
            (11, 15)  categories.asp?direction=P _
            &parent=" & l_iParent & "&start="  _
            & l_liStartRec & """ src= _
            ""images/l_u.gif"" alt=""Next""   _
            border=""0"" startspan --><MAP _
            NAME=""FrontPageMap2"">< AREA SHAPE= _
            ""RECT"" COORDS=""0, 0, 11, 15""   _
            HREF=""categories.asp?direction=P _
            &parent=" & l_iParent & "&start="  _
            & l_liStartRec & """></MAP><a href= _
            ""_vti_bin/shtml.dll/categories _
            .asp/map""><img ismap usemap= _
            ""#FrontPageMap2"" border=""0""  _
            height=""15"" alt=""Previous page of _
            categories"" src=""images/l_u.gif"" _
            width=""25""></a><!--Webbot bot _
```

```
            ImageMap"" endspan -->" & chr(13)
        else
            Response.Write "<" & "img src= _
            ""images/lr_o.gif"" height=""15"" _
            width=""25"">" & chr(13)
        end if
    end if
    Response.Write "</td><td align=""center"" _
     valign=""middle""><DIV class=""clsNav""> _
     Next<br>page</div>" & chr(13)
end sub
%>
<%
sub CreateCatNavBar(l_flgBack,l_flgPrev,l_flgNext _
, l_iParent, l_liStartRec)
    Response.Write "<TABLE  bgcolor=""#ACA470"" _
     width=""100" & "%"" cellspacing=""0"" _
     cellpadding=""0"" border=""0"">" & chr(13)
    Response.Write "<TR><TD align=""center"" _
     valign=""middle"">" & chr(13)
    call ProcessNavHome(l_flgBack)
    call ProcessPrevNext(l_flgPrev, l_flgNext, _
     l_iParent, l_liStartRec)
    Response.Write "</td></tr>" & chr(13)
    Response.Write "</table>" & chr(13)
end sub
%>
<%
sub PaintSearch()
    Response.Write "<table align=""center"">" & chr(13)
    Response.Write "<form name=""fSearch"" _
     action=""categories.asp"">" & chr(13)
    Response.Write "<img src=""images/mglass.gif"" _
     alt=""search for a category"">" & chr(13)
    Response.Write "<input name=""find"" _
     size=""12"" type=""text"">" & chr(13)
    Response.Write "<input type=""image"" _
     src=""images/find.gif"" border=""0""><br>" _
     & chr(13)
    Response.Write "</form>" & chr(13)
    Response.Write "</table>" & chr(13)
end sub
%>
<%
```

```
sub DecideOnAmazon(l_strISBN, l_flgImage, _
l_flgBookSearch, l_strPrevCat)
  if (l_flgImage) or (l_flgBookSearch) then
      Response.Write "<HR WIDTH=""50%"">" & chr(13)
      if l_strISBN > "" then
          if l_flgImage = TRUE then
              Response.Write "<table><tr><td>" & chr(13)
              Response.Write "<font id=""idNoLink"" _
                class=""clsLink"">Click to buy this _
                book</font><br>" & chr(13)
              Response.Write "<a target=""_blank"" _
                href=""http://www.amazon.com/exec/ _
                obidos/ASIN/" & l_strISBN & _
                "/theblowhole""><img src= _
                ""images/book/" & l_strISBN & ".gif"" _
                border=""0""></a>" & chr(13)
              Response.Write "</td></tr></table>"
          else
              Response.Write "<CENTER><SMALL>Click _
                the books for our<br><a target= _
                ""_blank"" href=""http: _
                //www.amazon.com/exec/obidos/ASIN/" _
                & l_strISBN & "/theblowhole""> _
                <img src=""images/bk22.gif"" _
                 border=""0""></a><br>recommendation _
                on this topic from<br>" & chr(13)
              Response.Write "<img src= _
                ""images/90X29-w-logo.gif""> _
                </small></center>" & chr(13)
          end if
      else
          if l_flgBookSearch = TRUE then
              Response.Write "<CENTER>"
              Response.Write "<FORM METHOD=""get"" _
                ACTION=""http://www.amazon.com/ _
                exec/obidos/external-search"" _
                id=""form1"" name=""form1"" _
                target=""_blank"">" & chr(13)
              Response.Write "<SMALL>Click for books" _
                & chr(13)
              Response.Write "<INPUT type=""hidden"" _
                name=""mode"" value=""books"">" & chr(13)
              Response.Write "<INPUT type=""hidden"" _
                name=""keyword"" value="" & _
```

```
                    l_strPrevCat & """>" & chr(13)
                  Response.Write "<INPUT TYPE="""hidden"" _
                   NAME=""tag"" VALUE=""theblowhole"">" _
                   & chr(13)
                  Response.Write "<CENTER> _
                   <INPUT TYPE="""image"" BORDER="""0"" _
                    SRC=""images/90X29-w-logo.gif"" _
                    NAME=""Search"">""</center>" & chr(13)
                  Response.Write "on <B><i>" & _
                   l_strPrevCat & "</i></b></small> _
                   </center>" & chr(13)
                  Response.Write "</FORM>" & chr(13)
              end if
          end if
      end if
  end sub
%>
</HEAD>
<BODY>
<% call global_asa() %>
<%
set DataConn = Server.CreateObject _
 ("ADODB.Connection")
set SQLQuery = Server.CreateObject("ADODB.Command")
set SQLQuery2 = Server.CreateObject _
 ("ADODB.Command")
set SQLQuery3 = Server.CreateObject _
 ("ADODB.Command")
set RecordSet1 = Server.CreateObject _
 ("ADODB.Recordset")
set RecordSet2 = Server.CreateObject _
 ("ADODB.Recordset")
set RecordSet3 = Server.CreateObject _
 ("ADODB.Recordset")

dim m_iParent             'id number of parent
dim m_iRet                'holds call return values
dim m_flgBack             'flag, true if not _
 first level
dim m_flgInit             'flag, true if start _
 of session
dim m_strIndent           'indentation string _
 for formatting
```

```
'********************
'The following variables are for use in the routine
'  ConditionalWrite
dim m_strBackT          'string to use if m_flgBack  _
  is true
dim m_strBackF          'string to use if m_flgBack  _
  is false
dim m_strInitT          'string to use if m_flgInit  _
  is true
dim m_strInitF          'string to use if m_flgInit  _
  is false
'********************
dim m_iStartPos         'first category in record    _
  set when not on page 1
dim m_iEndPos           'final category in record    _
  set when not on page 1
dim m_iRecCnt           'number of records in        _
  record set
dim m_flgNext           'true if there are more      _
  records for current level than will fit on   _
  current display page
dim m_flgPrev           'true if there are           _
preceding records for current level not showing   _
on current display page

dim m_strPrevCat        'name of last category clicked
dim m_iPageSize         'how many categories to      _
  display at once
dim m_straCatInfo()     'additional info about       _
  display categories

dim m_flgBookSearch     'Should a book search be     _
  offered for this category?
dim m_strISBN           'ISBN of recommended book
dim m_flgImage          'Is there an image of a      _
  book cover?

'
'  Open the database
'
Set DataConn = Server.CreateObject _
  ("ADODB.Connection")
DataConn.Open Session("DataConn_ConnectionString")
```

```
SQLQuery.CommandType = 1
SQLQuery2.CommandType = SQLQuery.CommandType
SQLQuery3.CommandType = SQLQuery.CommandType
Set SQLQuery.ActiveConnection = DataConn
Set SQLQuery2.ActiveConnection = DataConn
set SQLQuery3.ActiveConnection = DataConn

m_iPageSize = 6          'set the category page size
'
' The following array will contain information
'  about each category. It was defined earlier.
'  This instantiates it as a 4-dimension array.
'  Dimension 1 - category number
'  Dimension 2 - category name
'  Dimension 3 - levels below this category?
'  Dimension 4 - links/book associated with this?
redim m_straCatInfo(m_iPageSize,4)

' We'll set the environment for the initial
'  loading of this page, and change that later
'  if needed based on any parameters passed
m_flgBack = FALSE
m_flgInit = TRUE
m_strIndent = ""
m_liStartRec = 0
m_iParent = 0
m_flgBookSearch = FALSE
m_flgImage = FALSE
'
' The following lines will create application
'  variables, the values of which are retained
'  in state between browser connections by the
'  same user during a session
Application("Direction") = ""
Application("Start")=""
Application("GP")="0"    'grandparent category

call CheckCategoryRequestLevel _
  (m_iParent,m_flgBack,m_strIndent, m_flgInit, _
   m_iReturnTo, m_strPrevCat, m_flgImage, _
   m_flgBookSearch, m_strISBN, RecordSet1, SQLQuery)
call GetCategories(RecordSet2, SQLQuery2, _
  m_iParent, m_flgInit)
call ProcessCategories(m_iStartPos, m_iEndPos, _
```

```
    m_flgPrev, m_flgNext, m_iPageSize, m_liStartRec, _
    m_iRecCnt, m_straCatInfo, RecordSet2, RecordSet3, _
    SQLQuery3, m_flgInit, m_iParent, m_strPrevCat)
call WriteCategories(m_iStartPos, m_iEndPos, _
    m_iParent, m_straCatInfo, m_strIndent)
call CreateCatNavBar(m_flgBack, m_flgPrev, _
    m_flgNext, m_iParent, m_liStartRec)
call PaintSearch()
call DecideOnAmazon(m_strISBN, m_flgImage, _
    m_flgBookSearch, m_strPrevCat)
%>
<P> </P>

</BODY>
</HTML>
```

11.6 The For-Profit Rotating Ad

This first banner is the one that rotates. The banner is provided by a Java applet that is a "freeware" application — Dynamic Billboard. The code for this applet is available at the Web site (see Appendix A) and is listed in Appendix B. The applet comes with classes to provide various forms of transitions between each ad.

The ads are graphic files that will all be kept in the same directory for ease of organization, not because the applet requires it. The way we determine what ads we have, and which of those should be presented, is via an Active Server page that pulls the information from our database. So, lets create a new ASP file, *adframe.asp*, and get to work.

```
<%@ Language=VBScript %>
<html>
<head>
<title>For Profit Rotating Banner</title>
</head>
<body>
</body>
</html>
```

The first thing we'll do is borrow some routines from our *Categories* frame, and then declare some variables.

```
<%
sub OpenRecordSet(rsobj,commandstr,parm1,parm2)
  'Response.Write commandstr.commandtext & "<br>" _
   & parm1 & "<br>" & parm2 & chr(13)
```

```
      rsobj.Open commandstr, , parm1, parm2
   end sub
   %>
   <%
   sub global_asa()
   'This routine is here because the _
    global.asa functionality
   ' doesnt work as advertised - remove _
      this routine and the
   ' call to it when it does
    Session("DataConn_ConnectionString") = _
      "DSN=TheBlowholeDSN"
    Session("DataConn_ConnectionTimeout") = 15
    Session("DataConn_CommandTimeout") = 30
    Session("DataConn_RuntimeUserName") = "admin"
    Session("DataConn_RuntimePassword") = ""
   end sub
   %>

   <%
   call global_asa()
   set DataConn = Server.CreateObject _
    ("ADODB.Connection")
   set SQLQuery = Server.CreateObject("ADODB.Command")
   set RecordSet = Server.CreateObject _
    ("ADODB.Recordset")

   dim m_strAdPath    'path to append ad name to
   dim m_iCatNo       'category for selecting ads
```

Then we'll do some initialization:

```
   m_strAdPath = "images/ads/"
```

If we're not on the initial list of categories, our category frame will need to call this frame and pass a category number. We need to take care of that. So let's add some lines to that code:

```
   if l_iKey > 0 then
      Response.Write "parent.main.loca-
tion=""links.asp?p=" _
        & l_iKey & """;" & chr(13)
      Response.Write _
       "parent.ad.location=""adframe.asp?cat=" _
```

```
    & l_iKey & """;" & chr(13)
  else
    Response.Write "parent.main.loca-
tion=""testd.htm"";" & chr(13)
    Response.Write _
      "parent.ad.location=""adframe.asp?cat=0"";" _
      & chr(13)
  end if
```

So, when we begin execution we'll be expecting a parameter passed as *cat*. We'll be retrieving the ads that apply to this category.

```
m_iCatNo = Request.QueryString("cat")
```

With that done, it's time to prepare to retrieve our record set. We'll be selecting only those records that we'll use and driving the creation of our Java Applet directly from the record set.

```
'
'Prepare to open record set
'
DataConn.Open Session("DataConn_ConnectionString")
SQLQuery.CommandType = 1
Set SQLQuery.ActiveConnection = DataConn
SQLQuery.CommandText = "SELECT AdCat.liCatNo_db, _
  Ads.strImage_db, Ads.strURL_db _
  FROM AdCat INNER JOIN Ads _
   ON AdCat.liAdNo_db = Ads.liAdNo_db _
  WHERE ((((AdCat.liCatNo_db)=" & m_iCatNo & ") AND _
   (Ads.strAdType_db)="FR") AND _
   ((Ads.dtExpiration_db)>=Now())));"
```

And now we'll open the record set:

```
call OpenRecordSet(RecordSet,SQLQuery,3,1)
```

Let's check the record set. If it's empty, we'll grab all ads that haven't expired, since the policy of the site is that if there are no paid ads for a given category, all paid ads will be used.

```
if RecordSet.RecordCount = 0 then
   RecordSet.Close
   SQLQuery.CommandText = _
     "SELECT AdCat.liCatNo_db, _
```

```
      Ads.strImage_db, Ads.strURL_db _
      FROM AdCat INNER JOIN Ads _
      ON AdCat.liAdNo_db = Ads.liAdNo_db _
      WHERE ((((AdCat.liCatNo_db)=0) AND _
        (Ads.strAdType_db)=""FR"") AND _
        ((Ads.dtExpiration_db)>=Now())));"
    call OpenRecordSet(RecordSet,SQLQuery,3,1)
  end if
```

The next thing we'll do is declare the Java Applet and process the record set.

```
%>
<center>
<APPLET align=center code=DynamicBillboard.class _
  codeBase=java/ height=40 width=400>
<PARAM NAME="delay" VALUE="5000">
<PARAM NAME="target" value="_blank">
<PARAM NAME="bgcolor" VALUE="#FFFFFF">
<PARAM NAME="transitions" VALUE="4, _
  RotateTransition,FadeTransition, _
  TearTransition,RotateTransition">
<PARAM NAME="billboards" VALUE= _
  "<%=RecordSet.RecordCount%>">
```

We've processed what we can directly; now we need to use some script to generate the rest of the Java Applet entry. Oh, you may have noticed that we did use some script above. It's embedded in the final line, and will be evaluated by the script engine even though it appears within a string.

```
<%
For i = 1 to RecordSet.RecordCount
  Response.Write "<PARAM NAME=""bill" & _
    i & """"
  Response.Write " VALUE=""" & m_strAdPath _
    & RecordSet.Fields("strImage_db") & ".gif," _
    & RecordSet.Fields("strURL_db") & """>" _
    & chr(13)
  RecordSet.MoveNext
Next
%>
```

And now that we've listed the ads, we can end the applet, close the record set, and we're done.

```
</APPLET>
</center>
<%RecordSet.Close%>
```

So, in summary, what we've done is to accept a category number from our *categories* frame—for example, 123 for the category of *Fishing*. We then retrieve every ad record from our database that has an entry in the bridge table with *liCatNo_db=123*. The other requirements for the records to be selected are that they are of the type For-Profit Rotating (*strAdType_db="FR")*, and the expiration date is today or later.

With the records we retrieve, we generate the appropriate parameter lines for the Java Applet. Following is the complete code for the page:

```
<%@ Language=VBScript %>
<HTML>
<HEAD>
<META NAME="GENERATOR" Content="Microsoft _
  Visual Studio 6.0">
<title>For Profit Rotating Banner</title>
<%
sub OpenRecordSet(rsobj,commandstr,parm1,parm2)
      rsobj.Open commandstr, , parm1, parm2
end sub
%>
<%
sub global_asa()
'This routine is here because the global.asa _
  functionality
' doesnt work as advertised - remove this    _
  routine and the
' call to it when it does
  Session("DataConn_ConnectionString") = _
    "DSN=TheBlowholeDSN"
  Session("DataConn_ConnectionTimeout") = 15
  Session("DataConn_CommandTimeout") = 30
  Session("DataConn_RuntimeUserName") = "admin"
  Session("DataConn_RuntimePassword") = ""
end sub
%>
</HEAD>
<BODY>
<%
call global_asa()
set DataConn = Server.CreateObject _
  ("ADODB.Connection")
```

```
set SQLQuery = Server.CreateObject("ADODB.Command")
set RecordSet = Server.CreateObject _
  ("ADODB.Recordset")
dim m_strAdPath    'path to append ad name to
dim m_iCatNo       'category for selecting ads

m_strAdPath = "images/ads/"
m_iCatNo = Request.QueryString("cat")

'
'Prepare to open record set
'
set DataConn = Server.CreateObject _
  ("ADODB.Connection")
DataConn.Open Session("DataConn_ConnectionString")
SQLQuery.CommandType = 1
Set SQLQuery.ActiveConnection = DataConn
SQLQuery.CommandText = "SELECT AdCat.liCatNo_db, _
  Ads.strImage_db, Ads.strURL_db _
  FROM AdCat INNER JOIN Ads _
    ON AdCat.liAdNo_db = Ads.liAdNo_db _
  WHERE (((AdCat.liCatNo_db)=" & m_iCatNo & ") _
    AND ((Ads.strAdType_db)='FR') _
    AND ((Ads.dtExpiration_db)>=Now()));"
call OpenRecordSet(RecordSet,SQLQuery,3,1)
if RecordSet.EOF then
  RecordSet.Close
  SQLQuery.CommandText = _
    "SELECT AdCat.liCatNo_db, Ads.strImage_db, _
      Ads.strURL_db FROM AdCat _
      INNER JOIN Ads ON AdCat.liAdNo_db = _
        Ads.liAdNo_db _
      WHERE ((((AdCat.liCatNo_db)=0) _
        AND (Ads.strAdType_db)='FR') _
        AND ((Ads.dtExpiration_db)>=Now()));"
  call OpenRecordSet(RecordSet,SQLQuery,3,1)
end if
%>
<center>
<APPLET align=center code=DynamicBillboard.class _
 codeBase=java/ height=40 width=400>
<PARAM NAME="delay" VALUE="5000">
<PARAM NAME="bgcolor" VALUE="#FFFFFF">
<PARAM NAME="target" value="_blank">
```

```
<PARAM NAME="transitions" VALUE="4, _
 RotateTransition,FadeTransition, _
 TearTransition,RotateTransition">
<PARAM NAME="billboards" VALUE= _
 "<%=RecordSet.RecordCount%>">
<%
For i = 0 to RecordSet.RecordCount - 1
  Response.Write "<PARAM NAME=""bill" & i _
    & """"
    Response.Write " VALUE=""" & m_strAdPath _
    & RecordSet.Fields("strImage_db") & ".gif," _
    & RecordSet.Fields("strURL_db") & """>" _
    & chr(13)
    RecordSet.MoveNext
Next
%>
</APPLET>
<%RecordSet.Close%>
</center>
</BODY>
</HTML>
```

That completes our For-Profit Rotating Banner. We're now ready to move on to the next ad, our For-Profit Static Ad.

11.7 For-Profit Static Ad

This banner is static. There should only be one available paid ad per category, since that ad will always be present on the page. Therefore, the banner does not require an applet to be displayed — it can be treated as a normal image.

The ads are graphic files that will all be kept in the same directory as those for the rotating banner. We determine what ads should be presented in an Active Server page that pulls the information from our database. We'll first create this ASP file, *fp_ad.asp*.

```
<%@ Language=VBScript %>
<html>
<head>
<title>For Profit Static Banner</title>
</head>
<body>
</body>
</html>
```

Next, we'll borrow some routines from our *Ad* frame, and then declare some variables.

```
<%
sub OpenRecordSet(rsobj,commandstr,parm1,parm2)
  'Response.Write commandstr.commandtext & "<br>" _
    & parm1 & "<br>" & parm2 & chr(13)
      rsobj.Open commandstr, , parm1, parm2
end sub
%>
<%
sub global_asa()
'This routine is here because the _
 global.asa functionality
' doesnt work as advertised - remove _
    this routine and the
' call to it when it does
 Session("DataConn_ConnectionString") = _
  "DSN=TheBlowholeDSN"
 Session("DataConn_ConnectionTimeout") = 15
 Session("DataConn_CommandTimeout") = 30
 Session("DataConn_RuntimeUserName") = "admin"
 Session("DataConn_RuntimePassword") = ""
end sub
%>

<%
call global_asa()
set DataConn = Server.CreateObject _
 ("ADODB.Connection")
set SQLQuery = Server.CreateObject("ADODB.Command")
set RecordSet = Server.CreateObject _
 ("ADODB.Recordset")

dim m_strAdPath    'path to append ad name to
dim m_iCatNo       'category for selecting ads
```

Then we'll do some initialization:

```
m_strAdPath = "images/ads/"
```

Our category frame will need to call this frame and pass a category number. We need to take care of that. So let's add some lines to that code:

```
Response.Write "parent.ad.loca-
```

```
tion=""adframe.asp?cat=" _
        & l_iKey & """;" & chr(13)
      Response.Write "parent.fp_ad.location= _
        ""fp_ad.asp?cat=" & l_iKey & """;" & chr(13)
    else
      Response.Write "parent.ad.loca-
tion=""adframe.asp?cat=0"";" _
        & chr(13)
      Response.Write "parent.fp_ad.location= _
        ""fp_ad.asp?cat=0"";" & chr(13)
    end if
```

So, when we begin execution we'll be expecting a parameter passed as *cat*. We'll be retrieving the ads that apply to this category.

```
m_iCatNo = Request.QueryString("cat")
```

With that done, it's time to prepare to retrieve our record set. We'll be selecting only those records that we'll use and driving the creation of our Java Applet directly from the record set.

```
'
'Prepare to open record set
'
DataConn.Open Session("DataConn_ConnectionString")
SQLQuery.CommandType = 1
Set SQLQuery.ActiveConnection = DataConn
SQLQuery.CommandText = "SELECT AdCat.liCatNo_db, _
  Ads.strImage_db, Ads.strURL_db _
  FROM AdCat INNER JOIN Ads _
  ON AdCat.liAdNo_db = Ads.liAdNo_db _
  WHERE ((((AdCat.liCatNo_db)=" & m_iCatNo & ") AND _
  (Ads.strAdType_db)='FS') AND _
  ((Ads.dtExpiration_db)>=Now())));"
```

And now we'll open the record set:

```
call OpenRecordSet(RecordSet,SQLQuery,3,1)
```

Let's check the record set. If it's empty, we'll use a random ad.

```
if RecordSet.RecordCount = 0 then
   RecordSet.Close
   SQLQuery.CommandText = _
```

```
        "SELECT AdCat.liCatNo_db, _
         Ads.strImage_db, Ads.strURL_db _
         FROM AdCat INNER JOIN Ads _
         ON AdCat.liAdNo_db = Ads.liAdNo_db _
         WHERE (((Ads.strAdType_db)='FS') AND _
           ((Ads.dtExpiration_db)>=Now())) ;"
      call OpenRecordSet(RecordSet,SQLQuery,3,1)
      Randomize
      l_iStart = int((RecordSet.Recordcount) * Rnd)
      RecordSet.Move l_iStart
   end if
%>
```

The next thing we'll do is place the ad.

```
<center>
<a href=<%=strURL_db%>>
<img align=center height=96 width=192 border=0 _
   target="_blank" src=<%=m_strAdPath _
     & RecordSet.Fields("strImage_db")%>.gif>
</a>
</center>
<%RecordSet.Close%>
```

So, in summary, what we've done is to accept a category number from our *categories* frame. We then retrieve the ad record from our database that has an entry in the bridge table with a matching category number. The other requirements for the records to be selected are that they are of the type For-Profit Static (*strAdType_db="FS"*) and the expiration date is today or later.

With the record we retrieve, we post the image. Following is the complete code for the page:

```
<%@ Language=VBScript %>
<HTML>
<HEAD>
<title>For Profit Static Banner</title>
<META NAME="GENERATOR" Content= _
   "Microsoft Visual Studio 6.0">
<%
sub OpenRecordSet(rsobj,commandstr,parm1,parm2)
     rsobj.Open commandstr, , parm1, parm2
end sub
%>
<%
```

```
sub global_asa()
'This routine is here because the global.asa _
 functionality
' doesnt work as advertised - remove this  _
  routine and the
' call to it when it does
 Session("DataConn_ConnectionString") = _
  "DSN=TheBlowholeDSN"
 Session("DataConn_ConnectionTimeout") = 15
 Session("DataConn_CommandTimeout") = 30
 Session("DataConn_RuntimeUserName") = "admin"
 Session("DataConn_RuntimePassword") = ""
end sub
%>
</HEAD>
<BODY>
<%
call global_asa()
set DataConn = Server.CreateObject _
  ("ADODB.Connection")
set SQLQuery = Server.CreateObject _
  ("ADODB.Command")
set RecordSet = Server.CreateObject _
  ("ADODB.Recordset")
dim m_strAdPath    'path to append ad name to
dim m_iCatNo       'category for selecting ads
m_strAdPath = "images/ads/"
m_iCatNo = Request.QueryString("cat")
'
'Prepare to open record set
'
DataConn.Open Session("DataConn_ConnectionString")
SQLQuery.CommandType = 1
Set SQLQuery.ActiveConnection = DataConn
SQLQuery.CommandText = _
  "SELECT AdCat.liCatNo_db, Ads.strImage_db, _
    Ads.strURL_db _
   FROM AdCat INNER JOIN Ads _
   ON AdCat.liAdNo_db = Ads.liAdNo_db _
   WHERE (((( AdCat.liCatNo_db)=" & m_iCatNo & ") _
   AND (Ads.strAdType_db)='FS') _
   AND ((Ads.dtExpiration_db)>=Now())));"
call OpenRecordSet(RecordSet,SQLQuery,3,1)
if RecordSet.RecordCount = 0 then
```

```
      RecordSet.Close
      SQLQuery.CommandText = _
        "SELECT AdCat.liCatNo_db, Ads.strImage_db, _
          Ads.strURL_db _
          FROM AdCat INNER JOIN Ads _
           ON AdCat.liAdNo_db = Ads.liAdNo_db _
           WHERE ((((AdCat.liCatNo_db)=0) _
            AND (Ads.strAdType_db)='FS') _
            AND ((Ads.dtExpiration_db)>=Now())));"
      call OpenRecordSet(RecordSet,SQLQuery,3,1)
  end if
%>
<center>
<a href=<%=strURL_db%>>
<img align=center height=96 width=192 border=0 _
src= "<%=m_strAdPath & Recorddet.Fields _
  ("strImage_db")%>.gif" target="_blank">
</a>
</center>
<%RecordSet.Close%>
</BODY>
</HTML>
```

This finishes our static for-profit ad. We can now move on to our last banner, the
rotating banner for non-profit ads.

11.8 The Non-Profit Rotating Ad

This last banner is the rotating banner for non-profit ads. The banner works almost
exactly the same as the *for*-profit rotating banner, aside from the size, the transition style,
and the ad type. Lets create a new ASP file, *np_ad.asp*, and get to work.

```
<%@ Language=VBScript %>
<html>
<head>
<title>Non Profit Rotating Banner</title>
</head>
<body>
</body>
</html>
```

We'll borrow some routines from our *For-Profit Rotating Banner* frame, and then
declare some variables.

```
<%
sub OpenRecordSet(rsobj,commandstr,parm1,parm2)
  'Response.Write commandstr.commandtext & "<br>" _
   & parm1 & "<br>" & parm2 & chr(13)
     rsobj.Open commandstr, , parm1, parm2
end sub
%>
<%
sub global_asa()
'This routine is here because the _
 global.asa functionality
' doesnt work as advertised - remove _
   this routine and the
' call to it when it does
 Session("DataConn_ConnectionString") = _
  "DSN=TheBlowholeDSN"
 Session("DataConn_ConnectionTimeout") = 15
 Session("DataConn_CommandTimeout") = 30
 Session("DataConn_RuntimeUserName") = "admin"
 Session("DataConn_RuntimePassword") = ""
end sub
%>

<%
call global_asa()
set DataConn = Server.CreateObject _
 ("ADODB.Connection")
set SQLQuery = Server.CreateObject("ADODB.Command")
set RecordSet = Server.CreateObject _
 ("ADODB.Recordset")

dim m_strAdPath    'path to append ad name to
dim m_iCatNo       'category for selecting ads
```

Then we'll do some initialization:

```
m_strAdPath = "images/ads/"
```

If we're not on the initial list of categories, our category frame will need to call this frame and pass a category number. We need to take care of that. Let's add some lines to that code:

```
Response.Write "parent.fp_ad.location= _
   ""fp_ad.asp?cat=" & l_iKey & """;" & chr(13)
```

```
Response.Write _
  "parent.np_ad.location=""np_ad.asp?cat=" _
& l_iKey & """;" & chr(13)
else
  Response.Write "parent.fp_ad.location= _
    ""fp_ad.asp?cat=0"";" & chr(13)
  Response.Write _
  "parent.np_ad.location=""np_ad.asp?cat=0"";" _
  & chr(13)
end if
```

So, when we begin execution we'll be expecting a parameter passed as *cat*. We'll be
retrieving the ads that apply to this category.

```
m_iCatNo = Request.QueryString("cat")
```

With that done, it's time to prepare to retrieve our record set and drive the creation
of our Java Applet. The difference between this retrieval and that for the *for*-profit ads is
that there is no expiration date on non-profit ads.

```
'
'Prepare to open record set
'
DataConn.Open Session("DataConn_ConnectionString")
SQLQuery.CommandType = 1
Set SQLQuery.ActiveConnection = DataConn
SQLQuery.CommandText = "SELECT AdCat.liCatNo_db, _
 Ads.strImage_db, Ads.strURL_db _
 FROM AdCat INNER JOIN Ads _
  ON AdCat.liAdNo_db = Ads.liAdNo_db _
 WHERE ((((AdCat.liCatNo_db)=" & m_iCatNo & ") AND _
  (Ads.strAdType_db)='NP');"
```

And now we'll open the record set:

```
call OpenRecordSet(RecordSet,SQLQuery,3,1)
```

Let's check the record set. If it's empty, we'll grab all non-profit ads that haven't
expired, since the policy of the site is that if there are no non-profit ads for a given category, all non-profit ads will be used.

```
if RecordSet.RecordCount = 0 then
   RecordSet.Close
   SQLQuery.CommandText = _
```

```
     "SELECT AdCat.liCatNo_db, _
      Ads.strImage_db, Ads.strURL_db _
      FROM AdCat INNER JOIN Ads _
      ON AdCat.liAdNo_db = Ads.liAdNo_db _
      WHERE ((((AdCat.liCatNo_db)=0) AND _
       (Ads.strAdType_db)='NP');"
   call OpenRecordSet(RecordSet,SQLQuery,3,1)
end if
```

The next thing we'll do is declare the Java Applet and process the record set.

```
%>
<center>
<APPLET align=center code=DynamicBillboard.class _
   codeBase=java/ height=96 width=192>
<PARAM NAME="delay" VALUE="500">
<PARAM NAME="target" value="_blank">
<PARAM NAME="bgcolor" VALUE="#FFFFFF">
<PARAM NAME="transitions" value= "2, _
   ColumnTransition,ColumnTransition">
<PARAM NAME="billboards" VALUE= _
   "<%=RecordSet.RecordCount%>">
```

We've processed what we can directly and now we need to use some script to generate the rest of the Java Applet entry.

```
<%
For i = 1 to RecordSet.RecordCount
   Response.Write "<PARAM NAME=""bill" & _
      i & """"
   Response.Write " VALUE=""" & m_strAdPath _
      & RecordSet.Fields("strImage_db") & ".gif," _
      & RecordSet.Fields("strURL_db") & """>" _
      & chr(13)
   RecordSet.MoveNext
Next
%>
```

And now that we've listed the ads, we can end the applet, close the record set, and we're done.

```
</APPLET>
</center>
<%RecordSet.Close%>
```

In summary, we've accepted a category number from our *categories* frame. We then retrieve every ad record from our database that has an entry in the bridge table with the same category number. The other requirements for the records to be selected are that they are of the type Non-Profit Rotating *(strAdType_db="NP")*.

With the records we retrieve, we generate the appropriate parameter lines for the Java Applet. Following is the complete code for the page:

```
<%@ Language=VBScript %>
<html>
<head>
<title>Non Profit Rotating Banner</title>

<%
sub OpenRecordSet(rsobj,commandstr,parm1,parm2)
 'Response.Write commandstr.commandtext & "<br>" _
  & parm1 & "<br>" & parm2 & chr(13)
    rsobj.Open commandstr, , parm1, parm2
end sub
%>
<%
sub global_asa()
'This routine is here because the _
 global.asa functionality
' doesnt work as advertised - remove _
   this routine and the
' call to it when it does
 Session("DataConn_ConnectionString") = _
  "DSN=TheBlowholeDSN"
 Session("DataConn_ConnectionTimeout") = 15
 Session("DataConn_CommandTimeout") = 30
 Session("DataConn_RuntimeUserName") = "admin"
 Session("DataConn_RuntimePassword") = ""
end sub
%>

</head>
<body>
<%
call global_asa()
set DataConn = Server.CreateObject _
 ("ADODB.Connection")
set SQLQuery = Server.CreateObject("ADODB.Command")
set RecordSet = Server.CreateObject _
 ("ADODB.Recordset")
```

```
dim m_strAdPath     'path to append ad name to
dim m_iCatNo        'category for selecting ads

m_strAdPath = "images/ads/"

'
'Prepare to open record set
'
DataConn.Open Session("DataConn_ConnectionString")
SQLQuery.CommandType = 1
Set SQLQuery.ActiveConnection = DataConn
SQLQuery.CommandText = "SELECT AdCat.liCatNo_db, _
 Ads.strImage_db, Ads.strURL_db _
 FROM AdCat INNER JOIN Ads _
  ON AdCat.liAdNo_db = Ads.liAdNo_db _
  WHERE ((((AdCat.liCatNo_db)=" & m_iCatNo & ") AND _
   (Ads.strAdType_db)='NP');"

call OpenRecordSet(RecordSet,SQLQuery,3,1)

if RecordSet.RecordCount = 0 then
   RecordSet.Close
   SQLQuery.CommandText = _
     "SELECT AdCat.liCatNo_db, _
      Ads.strImage_db, Ads.strURL_db _
      FROM AdCat INNER JOIN Ads _
      ON AdCat.liAdNo_db = Ads.liAdNo_db _
      WHERE ((((AdCat.liCatNo_db)=0) AND _
       (Ads.strAdType_db)='NP');"
   call OpenRecordSet(RecordSet,SQLQuery,3,1)
end if



%>
<center>
<APPLET align=center code=DynamicBillboard.class _
  codeBase=java/ height=40 width=400>
<PARAM NAME="delay" VALUE="500">
<PARAM NAME="bgcolor" VALUE="#FFFFFF">
<PARAM NAME="target" value="_blank">
<PARAM NAME="transitions"" value= ""2, _
  ColumnTransition,ColumnTransition"">" & chr(13)
<PARAM NAME="billboards" VALUE= _
  "<%=RecordSet.RecordCount%>">
```

```
<%
For i = 0 to RecordSet.RecordCount - 1
  Response.Write "<PARAM NAME=""bill" & _
    i & """"
  Response.Write " VALUE=""" & m_strAdPath _
    & RecordSet.Fields("strImage_db") & ".gif," _
    & RecordSet.Fields("strURL_db") & """>" _
    & chr(13)
  RecordSet.MoveNext
Next
%>


</APPLET>
</center>
<%RecordSet.Close%>

</body>
</html>
```

That completes our Non-Profit Rotating Banner. We're now ready to move on to the final frame — the Links frame.

11.9 The Links Frame

When a visitor clicks on a category, a search is done on the database to see if that category has any recommended links. If so, the links will be presented, with the link name given the functionality of a hyperlink and a description, if present on the database, displayed beneath it.

As usual, we'll begin by creating a new ASP file: *links.asp.*

```
<%@ LANGUAGE="VBSCRIPT" %>

<html>
<head>
<link rel="stylesheet" type="text/css" _
  href="blowhole.css">
<title>The Blowhole Links</title>
</head>
<body>
</body>
</html>
```

We'll create a *global_asa* routine like in the other ASP files and invoke it.

```
<%
sub global_asa()
'This routine is here because the global.asa _
 functionality
' doesnt work as advertised - remove this _
  routine and the
' call to it when it does
 Session("DataConn_ConnectionString") = _
    "DSN=TheBlowholeDSN"
 Session("DataConn_ConnectionTimeout") = 15
 Session("DataConn_CommandTimeout") = 30
 Session("DataConn_RuntimeUserName") = "admin"
 Session("DataConn_RuntimePassword") = ""
end sub
%>


<%
call global_asa()
```

Then we'll do some data declarations and initialization:

```
dim m_liLinkno
dim m_tfLinks
Set DataConn = _
 Server.CreateObject("ADODB.Connection")
DataConn.ConnectionTimeout = _
 Session("DataConn_ConnectionTimeout")
DataConn.CommandTimeout = _
 Session("DataConn_CommandTimeout")
DataConn.Open Session("DataConn_ConnectionString")
Set RecordSet = _
 Server.CreateObject("ADODB.Recordset")
Set SQLQuery = _
   Server.CreateObject("ADODB.Command")
SQLQuery.CommandType = 1
Set SQLQuery.ActiveConnection = DataConn
```

We're going to receive a parameter containing the category number to which the links need to apply. Let's put that into a variable.

```
m_liKey = Request.QueryString("p")
m_tfLinks = FALSE
```

Now we'll create a query statement and create a record set from the database.

```
SQLQuery.CommandText = _
  "SELECT Links.liLinkNo, Links.strLinkTitle, _
     Links.strSiteDesc, Links.strURL _
   FROM LinkCat INNER JOIN Links _
     ON LinkCat.liLinkNo = Links.liLinkNo _
   WHERE (liCatNo_db = " & m_liKey & ") _
   ORDER BY Links.strLinkTitle;"
RecordSet.Open SQLQuery, , 3, 1
```

At this point, if we have records, we'll start the formatting. The first thing we want to do is create a small form to contain a graphic of a broken chain link. If the visitor clicks one of our links and that link turns out to be broken, the visitor can then click the broken link icon to report the broken link to The Blowhole Webmaster.

```
if RecordSet.RecordCount > 0 then
    m_tfLinks = TRUE
    Response.Write "<FORM Method=""POST"" _
      Action=""blink.asp"" Target=""_blank"">" _
      & chr(13)
    Response.Write "<SMALL>Click" & chr(13)
    Response.Write "<INPUT type=""image"" _
      src=""images/broklink.gif"" border=""0"">" _
      & chr(13)
    Response.Write "if the link you choose is _
      broken</small><br><br>" & chr(13)
    Response.Write "</form>" & chr(13)
```

Next, we want to loop through the record set and display the links and, if present, their descriptions.

```
'
' Loop through list of links
'
    Do while not RecordSet.EOF
'
' Write link
'
        Response.Write "<a href= _
          ""redirect.asp?url=http://" _
          & RecordSet.Fields("strURL") _
          & "&title=" _
          & RecordSet.Fields ("strLinkTitle") _
```

```
        & """ target=""_blank"" _
        class=""clsLink"">" _
        & RecordSet.Fields("strLinkTitle") _
        & "</a><br>"
```

In the HREF above we set it up so that if the link is clicked the visitor is taken to *redirect.asp*. Why? Why aren't we taking them to the URL of the site we're linking? Because if they go right to that URL, we haven't captured any information about which link they clicked. If we don't know which link they clicked, then there's no way for them to report that the link is broken without typing the information in to a form. Most visitors won't be zealous enough to want to do that. If we, however, go to an ASP file on our site, and pass that file the ultimate URL as a parameter, we can capture that information before passing the visitor on to the link destination.

```
'
' Write link description, if any
'
        if len(RecordSet.Fields("strSiteDesc")) _
          >=1 then
          response.write "<div class=""clsDesc"">" _
          & fNoBlanks(RecordSet.Fields _
          ("strSiteDesc")) & _
          "</div>"
        end if
        RecordSet.MoveNext
    Loop
```

You might have noticed the function call to *fnNoBlanks()* embedded in the preceding lines. Remember that we're passing the description as a parameter in a HREF. If we have a description such as "My Wonderful Site," HTTP will complain about the spaces in the string. We need to remove the spaces and replace them with their ASCII code equivalent. Let's craft the routine:

```
<%
function fnNoBlanks(l_strSource)
'
' This routine changes blanks in a string to %20
'   to keep HTTP happy
'
```

We've been passed *l_strSource* by the calling routine:

```
dim l_strDest
dim l_strByte
```

The first variable will hold the string that we build from the parameter passed to us, and the second, the character we're currently testing from the string.

```
l_strDest = ""
if len(l_strSource) > 0 then
    for i = 1 to len(l_strSource)
        l_strByte =  mid(l_strSource,i,1)
```

We've started a loop. The value of *i* will increase during the execution of the loop from 1 to the number of characters in the passed string. In the final line above, we're taking one character from the passed string, the character that begins at the relative position in the string equal to *i*.

```
if strByte = chr(32) then
    l_strDest = l_strDest & "%20"
```

If the character we're testing is a space, then we move the string %20, the ASCII code for space, to the destination string—

```
else
    l_strDest = l_strDest & strByte
end if
```

—otherwise we move the character we've tested to the result string.

```
    next
  end if
  fnNoBlanks = l_strDest
end function
%>
```

We then return the resulting string. Okay, we've linked through all the records in our record, nothing left to do but close it all out.

```
    RecordSet.Close
end if
%>
```

Here then is the code for *links.asp*:

```
<%@ LANGUAGE="VBSCRIPT" %>

<html>
<head>
```

```
<link rel="stylesheet" type="text/css" _
  href="blowhole.css">
<title>The Blowhole Links</title>
<%
function fnNoBlanks(l_strSource)
'
' This routine changes blanks in a string to %20
'  to keep HTTP happy
'
 dim l_strDest
 dim l_strByte
 l_strDest = ""
 if len(l_strSource) > 0 then
    for i = 1 to len(l_strSource)
        l_strByte =  mid(l_strSource,i,1)
        if l_strByte = chr(32) then
           l_strDest = l_strDest & "%20"
        else
           l_strDest = l_strDest & l_strByte
        end if
    next
 end if
 fnNoBlanks = l_strDest
end function
%>
</head>
<body>
<%
sub global_asa()
'This routine is here because the global.asa _
  functionality
' doesnt work as advertised - remove this _
  routine and the
' call to it when it does
 Session("DataConn_ConnectionString") = _
   "DSN=TheBlowholeDSN"
 Session("DataConn_ConnectionTimeout") = 15
 Session("DataConn_CommandTimeout") = 30
 Session("DataConn_RuntimeUserName") = "admin"
 Session("DataConn_RuntimePassword") = ""
end sub
%>
```

```
<%
call global_asa()
 dim m_liLinkno
 dim m_tfLinks
 Set DataConn = Server.CreateObject _
  ("ADODB.Connection")
 DataConn.ConnectionTimeout = _
  Session("DataConn_ConnectionTimeout")
 DataConn.CommandTimeout = _
  Session("DataConn_CommandTimeout")
 DataConn.Open Session("DataConn_ConnectionString")
 Set RecordSet = _
  Server.CreateObject("ADODB.Recordset")
 Set SQLQuery = _
  Server.CreateObject("ADODB.Command")
 SQLQuery.CommandType = 1
 Set SQLQuery.ActiveConnection = DataConn
 m_liKey = Request.QueryString("p")
 m_tfLinks = FALSE
 SQLQuery.CommandText = _
  "SELECT Links.liLinkNo_db, _
   Links.strLinkTitle_db, Links.strSiteDesc_db,_
   Links.strURL_db FROM LinkCat INNER JOIN Links _
   ON LinkCat.liLinkNo_db = Links.liLinkNo_db _
   WHERE (liCatNo_db = " & m_liKey & ") _
   ORDER BY Links.strLinkTitle_db;"
 RecordSet.Open SQLQuery, , 3, 1
 if RecordSet.RecordCount > 0 then
    m_tfLinks = TRUE
    Response.Write "<FORM Method=""POST"" _
    Action=""blink.asp"" Target=""_blank"">" _
    & chr(13)
    Response.Write "<SMALL>Click" & chr(13)
    Response.Write "<INPUT type=""image"" _
    src=""images/broklink.gif"" border=""0"">" _
    & chr(13)
    Response.Write "if the link you choose is _
      broken</small><br><br>" & chr(13)
    Response.Write "</form>" & chr(13)
'
' Loop through list of links
'
    Do while not RecordSet.EOF
'
```

```
' Write link
'

     Response.Write "<a href= _
""redirect.asp?url=http://" & _
RecordSet.Fields("strURL_db") & "&title=" _
& fnNoBlanks(RecordSet.Fields _
   ("strLinkTitle_db")) & """ _
target=""_blank"" class=""clsLink"" _
id=""idTightLink"">" & RecordSet.Fields _
("strLinkTitle_db") & "</a><br>"
'
' Write link description, if any
'
     if len(RecordSet.Fields("strSiteDesc_db")) _
     >= 1 then
        Response.Write "<div class=""clsDesc"">" _
     & RecordSet.Fields("strSiteDesc_db") & _
     "</div>"
     end if
     RecordSet.MoveNext
   Loop
   RecordSet.Close
end if
%>
</body>
</html>
```

This final page has left us with three additional Web pages to create. They are:

- blink.asp — a page that processes the visitor's report of a broken link
- redirect.asp — a page that receives and records information regarding the link that has been clicked by the visitor
- testd.htm — the default page of text that appears in the links frame before any categories are chosen

We'll save *blink.asp* for the next chapter, in which we assemble the feedback suite of pages. Let's get the straightforward *testd.htm* out of the way, and then we can tackle *redirect.asp*.

11.10 The Greeting

The greeting page is simply a text page that appears in the *links* frame when the visitor first arrives at the site. So, let's create *testd.htm* and add the following text. We can do it using a text editor, Visual Interdev or FrontPage's "wysiwyg" editor, but the final result should be as follows:

```
<html>
<head>
</head>

<body>
<big>
<p align="center">
Thank you for visiting The Blowhole, <u>the</u> _
  Internet portal for all matters marine,</big> _
  <big>from aquarium suppliers to yachts.</big> </p>

<p align="center"><big>
<u>Please</u> submit feedback (without feedback _
we can't improve).
Add your site's link, sign up as an advertiser _
(non-profit sites can advertise free) or _
nominate a site for an award. </big></p>

<p align="center"><big>
All profit from The Blowhole goes to non-profit _
conservation societies.</big></p>
</body>
</html>
```

11.11 The Redirect Page

The purpose of the redirect page is to make it possible for the Web site to record what link is clicked by a visitor. This is to be a transparent operation. We receive the information as a parameter in the input stream.

How, though, do we retain that information? The same way we have maintained any state information — by putting it in a session variable. Once we've done that, we send the visitor on his way, and he doesn't even know his travel was rerouted.

So, let's get to it. We'll need another ASP file. We'll call it *redirect.asp*. The skeleton looks like what you've now seen many times before.

```
<%@ LANGUAGE="VBSCRIPT" %>

<html>
<head>
<title>Link Redirection</title>
```

```
</head>
<body>
</body>
</html>
```

This page is very small. There are a number of things we need to do, but they happen quickly. So let's break it down one line at a time.

```
<%
Session("LastLink") = _
   Request.QueryString("url")
```

This line creates (or edits, if it already exists) a session variable, named *LastLink*, and sets it equal to the parameter passed to us that contains the destination URL of the link that was clicked — the place the visitor wants to go.

```
Session("LinkDesc") = _
   Request.QueryString("title")
```

Here we're working with another session variable, this time holding the name of the link the visitor clicked. We want the name because if the link is reported to be broken, the resulting email will contain the name of the link and the URL, to make identification easier.

```
Response.Clear
```

This is a key line. This command clears the response buffer, the buffer that would contain whatever we will send to the visitor to see. We haven't produced any HTML that would be visible, but we *have* done some things. We need the buffer to be cleared and considered clean in order for the next command to work.

```
Response.Redirect Request.QueryString("url")
%>
```

This line tells the server to redirect the page the visitor is looking at (which right now is blank with a spinning icon) to the URL that was passed to us — the address of the page the visitor requested, keeping what we've done completely transparent.

Now that we've captured the information in session variables, should the visitor end up needing to report the link as broken, we can pass the information on.

Here's the complete code for the page:

```
<%@ LANGUAGE="VBSCRIPT" %>

<html>
```

```
<head>
<title>Link Redirection</title>
</head>
<body>
<%
'
'store requested URL
'
Session("LastLink") = Request.QueryString("url")
'
'store name of site
'
Session("LinkDesc") = Request.QueryString("title")
'
'clear response buffer
'
Response.Clear
'
'send visitor on their way
'
Response.Redirect Request.QueryString("url")
%>
</body>
</html>
```

This just about finishes our chapter, but there are a couple things I'd like to do to wrap-up. The first is to discuss the SQL used in the chapter. You might think that I'm a real SQL guru, and that those large complex statements are beyond your ability to compose. However, I'm going to let the secret out. There's a way to generate the SQL even if you don't know the first thing about it.

11.12 Creating an SQL Query

We'll create an SQL statement now. The first thing we want to do is open our database in MS Access. Then we'll click on the *Query* tab, click on the *New* button, and ask for the design view (Figure 11-3).

Figure 11-3   New Query

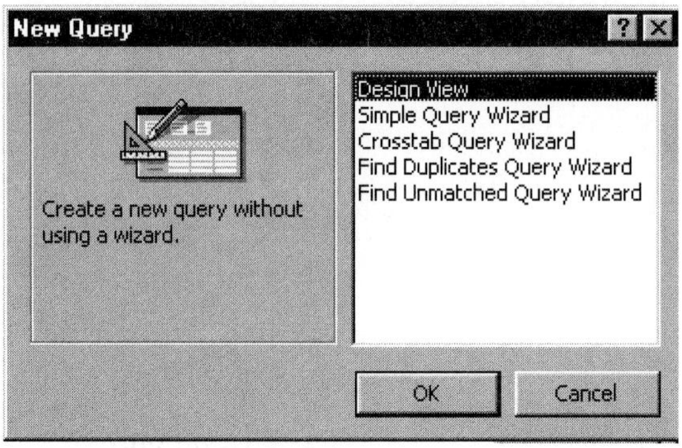

We'll click *OK*, and will then be asked to select a table or tables to use in our query (Figure 11-4). Let's create a query like we did for our links page. We'll select the LinkCat table, and then the Links table. Click *Add* after each selection. Then we'll click *Close*.

We'll now be presented with the query design view. The two tables we selected are shown at the top. You'll notice that Access has automatically established a connection between the two tables (Figure 11-5). It has anticipated our need to relate one table to another, and since the two tables had an index in common, Access used that index to form the relationship. We'll be taking advantage of that in forming our query. What we want to do is access the *LinkCat* table through the use of the clicked category, stored in *m_liCatNo*, being equal to the key *liCatNo_db*.

Figure 11-4   Table Selection Dialog

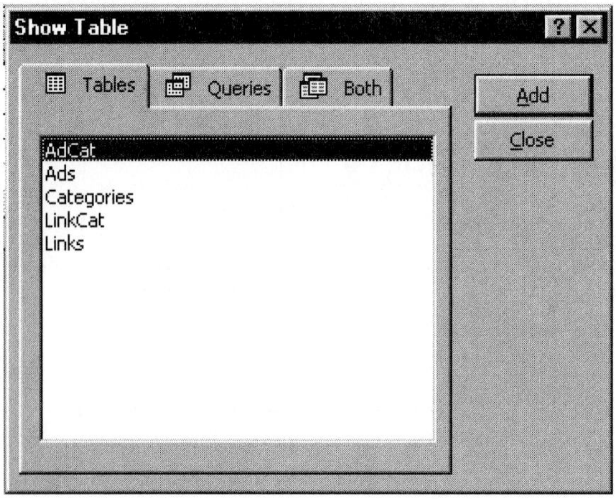

Figure 11-5   Table Relationship

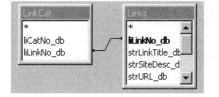

The area below the tables in the design view is for identifying what fields will be used in the query. Sometimes fields are used for retrieval only (we want to retrieve based on the value of the data item, but don't need to retrieve it). The decision on each field is made based on whether the *Show* check box is marked.

We need to select the fields for our query. Selecting a field is accomplished either by double-clicking the field name in the table box, by dragging the field name down to an open column in the grid and dropping it in the *Field* cell, or by clicking on the *Field* cell and selecting the field name from the drop-down list box that appears. We'll start by selecting *liCatNo_db*. We'll put an entry in the *Criteria* cell, *[m_liCatNo]*. Access doesn't know what that variable, is, but that's okay because we won't be executing the query—we just want to set it up. Putting the brackets around it identifies it as a parameter; otherwise Access would think we want the actual index value to be the string "m_liCatNo." We're not interested in the link number, and since the relationship is established, that index will be used to link one table to the other without our adding the field to the grid. The additional fields we want are the link name, the description and the URL. We'll select each of those fields as well. The completed grid is shown in Figure 11-6.

Figure 11-6   Completed Query Grid

Field:	liCatNo_db	strLinkTitle_db	strSiteDesc_db	strURL_db
Table:	LinkCat	Links	Links	Links
Sort:				
Show:	☐	☑	☑	☑
Criteria:	[m_liCatNo]			
or:				

Okay, so what does all of this have to do about an SQL statement? Here's the magic. Click on the *View* menu, and then on *SQL*, and voilá, a full SQL statement (Figure 11-7) ready to be copied and pasted into a variable definition.

The only alteration needed is around the parameter, so that we would go from:

```
=[m_liCatNo]));
```

with a syntax fitting for an Access query, but not ASP script, to:

```
=" & m_liCatNo & "));"
```

Figure 11-7   SQL Query

```
SELECT Links.strLinkTitle_db, Links.strSiteDesc_db, Links.strURL_db
FROM LinkCat INNER JOIN Links ON LinkCat.liLinkNo_db = Links.liLinkNo_db
WHERE (((LinkCat.liCatNo_db)=[m_liCatNo]));
```

That takes care of the SQL query. There's only one thing left for this chapter, and that's a look at the page we've worked so hard to compile. We'll be doing the testing of this and the other pages later, but for now, let's take a peek (Figure 11-8). Oh, one thing first, I *have* cheated a bit. Well, maybe "cheated" is a bit harsh — "jumped the gun" might be more appropriate. We're not going to be covering the actual data that goes into the database, but I've added some to make the page look right, and to enable the testing we'll do later. Just didn't want you to think that database-driven pages will magically work despite an empty database. That's it for the frames of the main page.

11.13 What's it All About?

We've been waiting for the main page to be viewable so that we can create the *About* page. The page was to have two sections, one describing the company, and the other describing the use of the main page. Instead, we're going to process a Change Order that will result in separating the functionality into two pages. The first, which describes the company and site, will be created here. We'll save the other for Chapter 13.

There really aren't any design considerations for this page, other than whether we need a Canadian version, *Aboot*. There is no special coding needed either, since this page will be all text.

We'll create a new page in FrontPage, which will give us the framework below.

```
<html>
<head>
<title>About The Blowhole</title>
</head>
<body>
</body>
</html>
```

Figure 11-8   The Blowhole Home Page

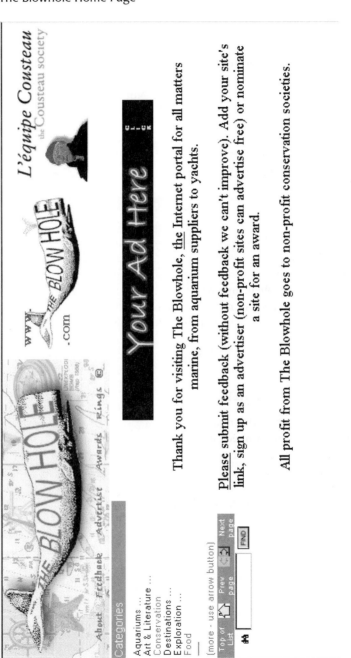

To that framework we need to add the following to the *head* section, so that we get our navigation banner.

```
<!--Webbot bot="Include" U-Include="navbar2.htm" _
TAG="BODY"-->
```

Let's add a background image to this page. Nothing fancy, just something textured enough to add some subliminal interest to black text on a white page. We'll use the *Page Properties* command off the *File* menu, and select the graphic *texture.jpg* for our background image. We'll also select it to be treated as a watermark (Figure 11-9).

Figure 11-9   Page Properties

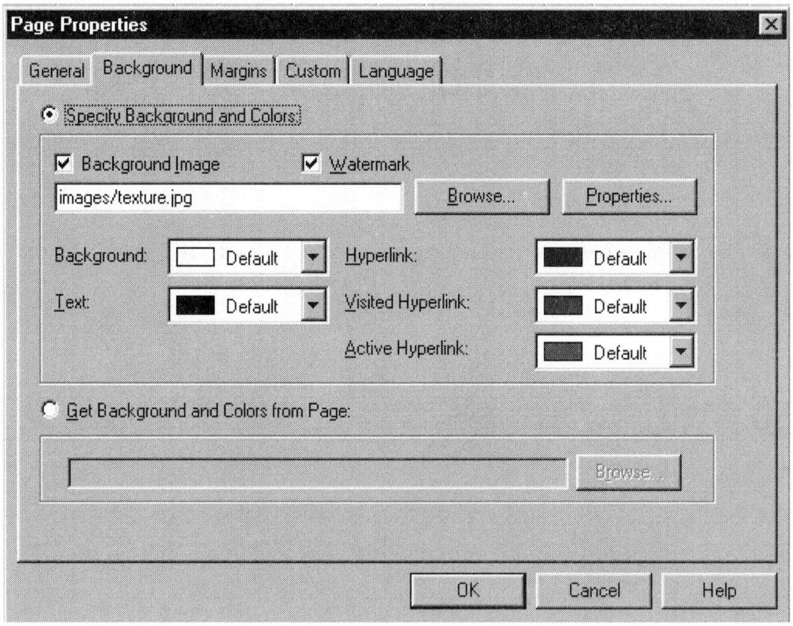

For browsers in which that is supported, the text will move when the page is scrolled, but the backround will remain stationary.

Between the body tags we'll put the text for our page.

```
About The Blowhole
The Blowhole started as a family project. My son
decided that he wants to become a marine biologist, and
I enjoy sailing and having a salt-water aquarium, so
there ya go, a mix destined for a marine-topic Web por-
tal.
```

Since we're not in it for the money, and since as a
family we're very environmentally concerned, we decided
that we'd offer site advertising as a service to the
site visitors, promote conservationist causes, and
donate our profits to those causes.

The content for the site - the categories and links
- come from exhaustive searching and reviewing. Any
assistance in the form of recommendations are always
welcome!!

We'll make some cosmetic changes to the text to liven it up a bit for reading, and
we're done. The complete page code follows, and the page is shown in Figure 11-10.

```
<html>
<head>
<title>About The Blowhole</title>
<meta name="GENERATOR" _
 content="Microsoft FrontPage 3.0">
</head>
<body background="images/texture.jpg" _
 bgproperties="fixed">
<!--Webbot bot="Include" U-Include="navbar2.htm" _
 TAG="BODY" -->
<p align="center">
 <font face="Arial" color="#8080FF">
 <strong><big><big><big>
 About The Blowhole
 </big></big></strong></big>
 </font>
</p>
<p>
 <big>
 The Blowhole started as a family project. My son, _
 11, decided that he wants to become a marine _
 biologist, and I enjoy sailing and having a _
 salt-water aquarium, so there ya go, a mix _
 destined  for a marine-topic Web portal.
 </big>
</p>
<p>
 <big>
 Since we're not in it for the money, and since _
 as a family we're very environmentally concerned, _
 we decided that we'd offer site advertising as _
```

```
 a service to the site visitors, promote    _
 conservationist causes, and donate our profits _
 to those causes.
 </big>
</p>
<p>
 <big>
 The content for the site - the categories and   _
 links - come from exhaustive searching and    _
 reviewing. Any assistance in the form of      _
 recommendations are always welcome!!
 </big>
</p>
</body>
</html>
```

Our next challenge is to develop the suite of feedback changes, which will have us doing new and adventurous programming. See you in Chapter 12 — I'll leave the lights on.

Figure 11-10   Page Properties

About The Blowhole

The Blowhole started as a family project. My son, 11, decided that he wants to become a marine biologist, and I enjoy sailing and having a salt-water aquarium, so there ya go, a mix destined for a marine-topic web portal.

Since we're not in it for the money, and since as a family we're very environmentally concerned, we decided that we'd offer site advertising as a service to the site visitors, promote conservationist causes, and donate our profits to those causes.

The content for the site - the categories and links - come from exhaustive searching and reviewing. Any assistance in the form of recommendations are always welcome!!

CHAPTER 12

Feedback

*C*over your ears — feedback can be a killer. If you put the microphone too close to the — huh? Oh, not *that* kind of feedback. We're going to be developing a number of pages in this chapter to address customer feedback about the site:

- Feedback frame page
- Feedback main frame
- Feedback contents frame
- Feedback preprocessor
- Feedback postprocessor
- Broken Link report page
- Award nomination page

These pages as a group provide the visitor with the ability to send comments and suggestions on various topics back to the Webmaster. The success of a site depends on it not becoming static (unless it provides static information that will always be of value). Feedback as a means of ensuring that its dynamic nature translates to value is indispensable.

The aim is to make providing feedback an easy experience for the visitor, or they won't take the time to do it. Making the process easy includes some of the following considerations:

- Ask for only non-essential information
- Where there are likely lists of responses, provide them to be chosen from

- If using a form, try to arrange it so that the user isn't constantly having to switch from mouse to keyboard and back.

12.1 The Feedback Page

The Feedback page, *feedback.htm*, is a frames page containing two frames, the information area (*fbinit.htm*) and the contents (*fbmenu.htm*). Let's create these.

We'll create this page using MS FrontPage. From the *Tools* menu in FrontPage Explorer, we'll select *Show FrontPage Editor*. Once the FrontPage Editor has loaded, we'll select the *New* command from the *File* menu. We'll then click on the *Frames* tab of the *New* dialog presented to us, to create a 'frames' page.

The *New Frames* dialog offers a number of popular frame formats. We're going to be selecting the *Contents* format. As you can see from the thumbnail of that format in Figure 12-1, the contents frame is on the left, and the information area is on the right. We could alternatively select a format that has the contents on top and the information on the bottom.

Figure 12-1   New Frames Dialogue

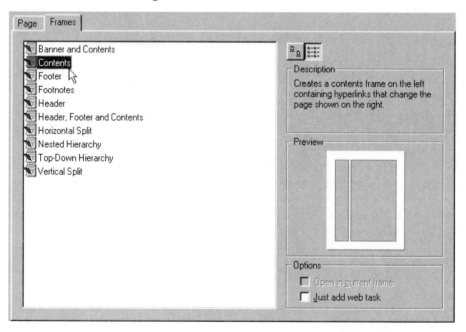

The reason the frames are aligned that way is simple, though not obvious. Web pages expand and contract to fit screen resolution, and they do so from the right and from the bottom. Therefore, since we never know what will be showing on the right and bottom of the page, it's best to put the static contents information on the 'fixed' side.

Once we've selected the frame format, we'll receive a new page with the frame division we requested (Figure 12-2). What we're looking at is the frames page, which we'll later save as *feedback.htm*.

Figure 12-2   Frames Page

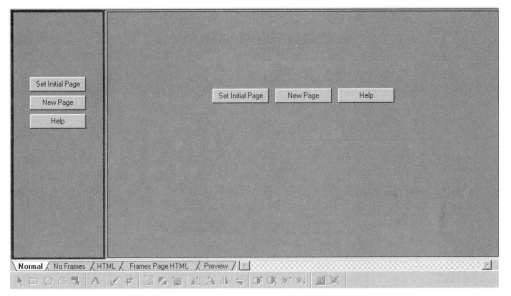

A number of tabs are shown at the bottom of the screen:

- Normal — the design view of the frames page
- No Frames — this view shows what visitors will see if their browsers don't support frames (a small subset of users these days). A non-frames version of the page can be designed here.
- HTML — shows the source code for the whichever of the frames is selected (the frame with a blue border around it)
- Frames Page HTML — the source code for the frames page
- Preview — a view of the page as it would be seen in a browser (except that currently the preview pane doesn't support ASP)

We'll start by working on the contents frame. Let's begin by clicking on *New Page*. If we had already created a page that we wanted to use here, we'd use *Set Initial Page*. Clicking on *New Page* brings up one, and we're ready either to enter page content directly, or to enter HTML by clicking on that instead.

We're going to choose to enter content directly. The first thing on our page will be the navigation banner. To do this, we'll select the *FrontPage Component* command from the *Insert* menu. When we receive the dialog , we'll select *Include Page* (Figure 12-3).

Figure 12-3   Including a Page

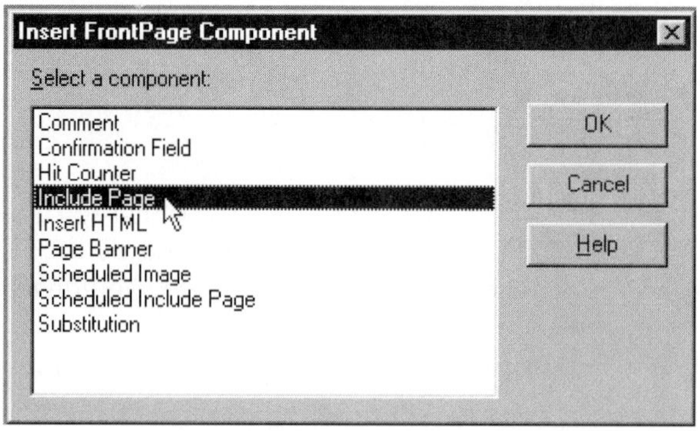

Figure 12-4   Selecting the Page to Include

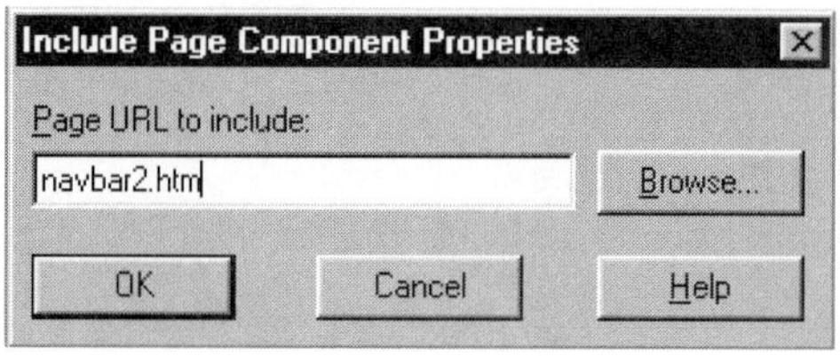

When we click *OK* we get the *Include Page Components Properties* dialog (Figure 12-4). This allows us to name a page, or if we don't know the name, we can choose *Browse* and go look for it. We'll enter *navbar2.htm* and click *OK*.

FrontPage then loads the page we named into memory, puts a FrontPage "Webbot" command into the HTML (a command encased in comments that only a FrontPage server would execute), and displays the contents of the page within our frame. At the moment, our frame is too small to display the entire navigation bar, but we can grab the frame divider (Figure 12-5) and move it to the right until the entire navigation banner is visible.

Figure 12-5   Included Page

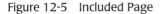

[Set Initial Page]   [New Page]   [Help]

When I look at the size of the frame that will be needed for the banner, I think we ought to put it in the other frame. This frame is meant to be the menu, and the other frame is meant to hold the information. The menu frame shouldn't be taking up all the real estate, but would if it held the navigation banner. So we'll click on the navigation banner and cut it. You'll notice that the mouse cursor is a cartoon robot, and that's because the navigation banner is included as a Webbot; it's components are not part of the page. It can't be edited from this page. Anyway, we cut it, and now we'll choose *New Page* on the right-hand frame, then we'll paste. Then we'll change the left-hand frame back to about its initial size. Let's type in some text:

```
Feedback Types
General Comments
New Category
Category comments
New link
Award Nomination
```

We'll then select the first line, *Feedback Selector.* Click on the icon to increase the font size. We'll then highlight all of the text, select *Arial* from the drop-down list box of fonts, and click on the icon for centered text. If the text tools aren't showing, select *Format Toolbar* from the *View* menu.

Let's reduce or increase the size of the frame so that the margin on both sides of the text is equal. Then we'll right-click on the frame and select *Frame Properties.* We want to deselect the *Resizable in Browser* check box. This will prevent the visitor from changing the frame size, but if needed we can still change it in our development environment. We'll also change the frame's name from *contents* to *fmContents.*

We'll then right-click and select *Page Properties.* From the dialog we'll select the *Background* tab, click the arrow on the *Background* color drop-down list box, and select *Custom* from the end of the list. We'll click on a blue, and then slide the right-hand arrow up until we have a nice shade of baby blue similar to the blue on the chart in our naviga-

Figure 12-6   Creating an Email Hyperlink

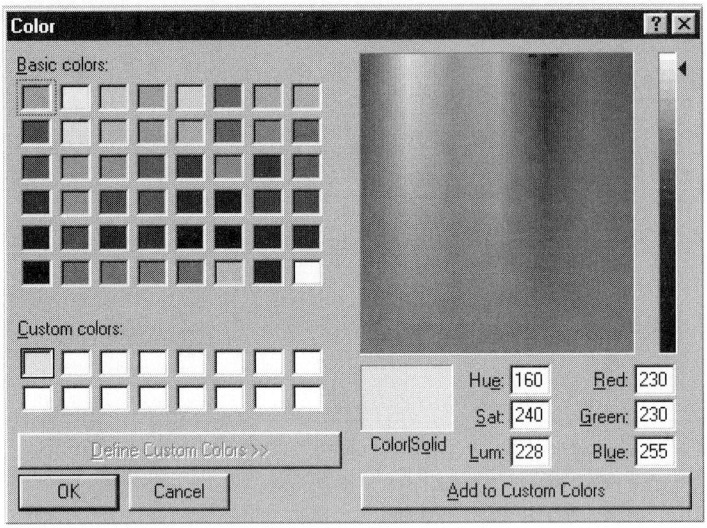

tion banner (Figure 12-6). We then click on *Add to Custom Colors*, highlight the new custom color by clicking on it, and click *OK*.

Next, we'll click on the *General* tab. Here we want to change the title to *The Blowhole Feedback Menu*. We then click *OK*, and you'll see that the background color of the frame is now that same light shade of blue. We'll leave this *contents* frame alone for a moment and turn our attention to the *fmMain* frame.

We'll click in the main frame, and the text cursor appears below the navigation banner. Let's edit its frame properties, deselect the *Resizable in Browser* box, and change the name of the frame to *fmMain*. We'll press *Enter* to add another paragraph, and enter some text.

```
    We appreciate your taking the time to provide us
with feedback. Please choose the type of feedback you
want to provide.

    Click here if you'd rather just send an email mes-
sage.
```

Right now the text wouldn't exactly grab one's attention. Let's select it all, increase the font size a click, and make it bold. Next, select the words "Click here" and click the Hyperlink icon — a blue globe with a chain link below it. This will bring up the *Create Hyperlink* dialog box. We want to create a mail link, so that when the user clicks on the link she can send an email message (assuming she is on a client with mail capability), so

click on the envelope icon. This brings up the *Create Email Hyperlink* dialog (Figure 12-7).
We'll enter

```
info@theblowhole.com
```

and click *OK*. You'll see that the URL text box now has a *mailto:* entered in it instead of a *HTTP:* URL (Figure 12-8).

Figure 12-7   The Mail Link URL

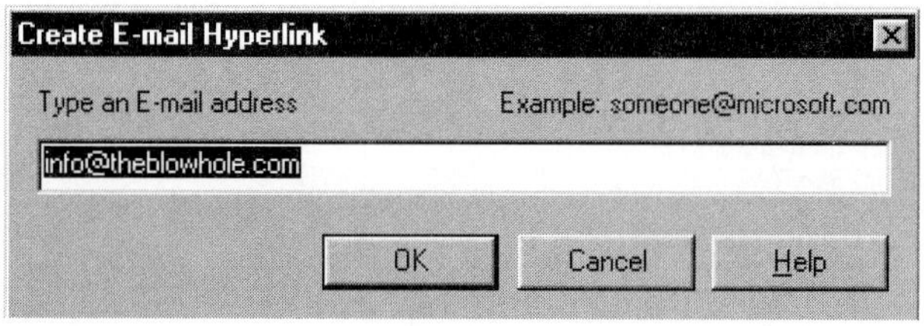

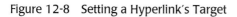

Figure 12-8   Setting a Hyperlink's Target

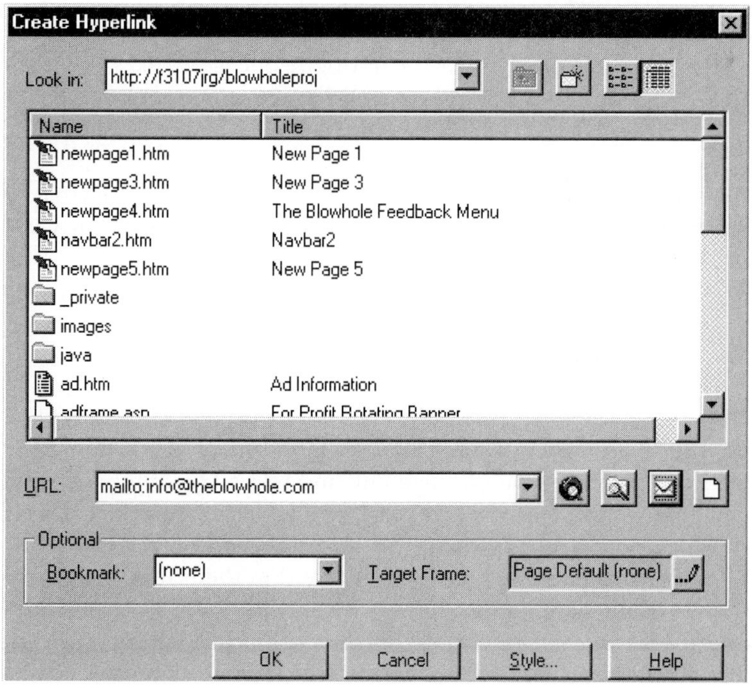

There are some manual adjustments we want to make to the frame page. We don't want a border between the frames; want them to be seamless, so we'll click on the *Frames Page HTML* and add the following line to each of the *<frame>* tags:

```
frameborder="0"
```

We're almost done with the frames page now. We need to take each of the menu choices and make them into hyperlinks. Each of the links, when clicked, will cause a feedback dialog to be presented in the main frame. The visitor will then use the dialog to enter their comments or suggestions.

We'll go back to our detailed design to get the information we need to set up the links, as shown in Table 12-1.

Table 12-1   Preprocessor Parameters

Functionality	HREF	Get Parms	Target Frame
General Comments	fbPrepro.asp	feedbackcode=general	fmMain
New Category	fbPrepro.asp	feedbackcode=newcategory	fmMain
Category Comments	fbPrepro.asp	feedbackcode=category	fmMain
New Link	fbPrepro.asp	feedbackcode=newlink	fmMain
Award Nomination	nominate.htm		fmMain

We'll use the information in the HREF, GET PARMS and TARGET FRAME columns to develop the hyperlinks. We'll highlight the first item, *General Comments*, and click the hyperlink icon. We'll backspace over the *http://* since the page we'll be linking to is local and won't need to be fully qualified. Then we'll enter the following line:

```
fbPrepro.asp?feedbackcode=  _
general
```

and click *OK*. The result is that our menu line is now displayed as a link. We need to edit the link properties. Right-click on our new link and select *Hyperlink Properties* from the pop-up menu. What we want to change is the handling of the hyperlink, the way in which the resulting Web page is displayed on the screen. Specifically, by default, clicking a hyperlink causes the destination page to be displayed in the frame in which the link was located. We don't want that to happen here. We want the destination page to be displayed in the larger main frame. So, we'll click on the little pencil next to the grayed *Target Frame* text box. This results in the *Target Frame* dialog being displayed. On the left of the screen is an illustration of the page's frame layout. We'll click on the right-hand frame, which causes its name to appear in the *Target Setting* text box (Figure 12-9), and then click *OK*. For other possible settings, see the sidebar *Destination Frames*. We'll also check the box to make this setting the default for the page, so we won't have to perform this same operation for the remaining links.

Let's create the remaining links in our menu. The link entries, in order respective to the menu items in the frame, are as follows:

```
fbPrepro.asp?feedbackcode= _
  newcategory
fbPrepro.asp?feedbackcode= _
  category
fbPrepro.asp?feedbackcode= _
  newlink
nominate.htm
```

Destination Frames

There are a number of possible destination frames that can be named within the definition of a hyperlink.

They are as follows:

_self

Overwrites the calling frame

_top

Overwrites all frames with a new page

_blank

Creates a new page

_parent

Displays in the page from which the current page was created

It's time to save the pages — remember that we have three of them working here. If we click on the *save* icon, or select *Save* from the *File* menu, we're presented with a succession of dialogs. Each dialog graphically depicts the frame to be saved, and ultimately, the frame page itself. We'll name the file for the left-hand *fmContents* frame *fbMenu.htm*. The right-hand *fmMain* frame will be saved as *fbInit*. The frames page itself, depicted by a border around the entire page, will be saved as *feedback.htm*. Following is the code for the frames page:

```
<html>
<head>
<title>The Blowhole Feedback</title>
<meta name="GENERATOR" content= _
  "Microsoft FrontPage 3.0">
</head>
<frameset cols="214,*">
  <frame name="fmContents" target="fmMain" _
    src="fbMenu.htm" scrolling="auto" noresize _
    frameborder="0">
  <frame name="fmMain" src="fbInit.htm" noresize _
    frameborder="0" scrolling="auto">
  <noframes>
  <body>
  <p>This page uses frames, but your browser _
    doesn't support them.</p>
```

```
   </body>
   </noframes>
 </frameset>
 </html>
```

Figure 12-9 Setting Target Frame

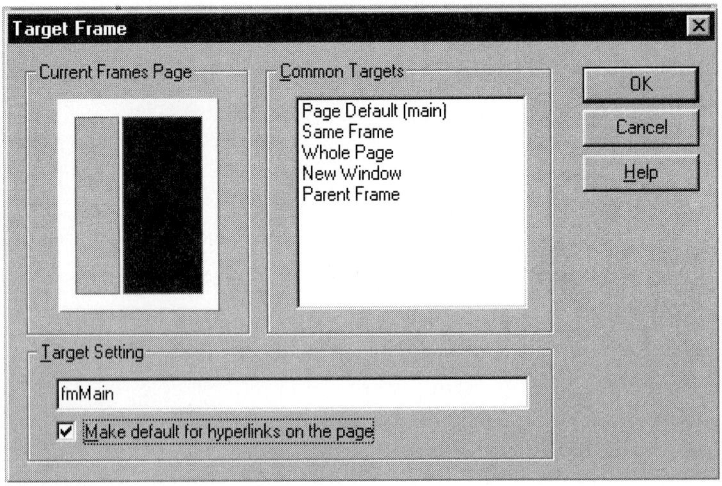

The code for the *fmMenu* frame:

```
<html>
<head>
<meta name="GENERATOR" content= _
  "Microsoft FrontPage 3.0">
<meta name="Microsoft Border" content="none">
<base target="fmMain">
<title>The Blowhole Feedback Menu</title>
</head>
<body bgcolor="#E6E6FF">
<p align="center">
 <big>
 <font face="Arial"> Feedback Types </font>
 </big>
</p>
<p align="center">
 <font face="Arial">
 <a href="fbPrepro.asp?feedbackcode=general"> _
   General Comments</a>
```

```
 </font>
</p>
<p align="center">
 <font face="Arial">
 <a href="fbPrepro.asp?feedbackcode= _
  newcategory">NewCategory</a>
 </font></p>
<p align="center">
 <font face="Arial">
 <a href="fbPrepro.asp?feedbackcode= category"> _
  CategoryComments</a>
 </font>
</p>
<p align="center">
 <font face="Arial">
 <a href="fbPrepro.asp?feedbackcode=newlink"> _
   New link</a>
 </font>
</p>
<p align="center">
 <font face="Arial">
 <a href="nominate.htm">Award Nomination</a>
 </font>
</p>
</body>
</html>
```

And the code for the *fmMain* frame:

```
<html>
<head>
<meta name="GENERATOR" content= _
  "Microsoft FrontPage 3.0">
<title>The Blowhole Feedback Init</title>
<meta name="Microsoft Border" content="none">
</head>
<body>
<!--Webbot bot="Include" U-Include= _
  "navbar2.htm" TAG="BODY" -->
<p>
  
</p>
<p>
 <strong>
```

```
<big>We appreciate your taking the time to _
   provide us with feedback. Please
   choose the type of feedback you want to _
   provide.
</big>
</strong>
</p>
<p>
 <strong>
 <big>
 <a href="mailto:info@theblowhole.com"> _
  Click here</a> if you'd rather just _
  send an email message.
 </big>
 </strong>
</p>
</body>
</html>
```

Figure 12-10   The Feedback Page

The last thing involving this page is to take a look at it. It is shown in Figure 12-10. Remember that the lines on the left will be invoking other pages in our Feedback "suite," as indicated in the hyperlink HREFs we created for each line.

Four of the hyperlinks call the same ASP, *fbPrePro.asp*. This will be the next application we work on. Before we work on it, though, we need to discuss file inclusion. We used inclusion with the navigation banner on this page. Inclusion isn't just for graphical items, though. We can also include chunks of code. Why would we want to do that? Well, consider the subroutines we created in the *categories.asp* page. What if we had several pages that wanted to use the same subroutines? Sure, we could copy them to each page—but then whenever a line of code needed to be changed, we'd be making the change in several places. Instead, we can put the subroutines in their own file, and include that file in the pages that use the routines. Putting the routines into a library means segregating the nongeneric code from the generic. For example, in the *Categories* page, where we check for a book cover as part of the processing, we'll want to extract that logic from the routine that will go in the library, because the *Categories* page is the only one that cares about a book cover. A subroutine library takes intense planning at the front end. We didn't have the luxury of that time. Creating if after the fact will be more work than if it had been done originally.

12.2 Subroutine Library

The idea of a subroutine library is to populate it with routines that will be used in more than one place. That can mean massaging the code of some routines to make them more generic, so that they *can* apply in more than one scenario.

I've saved you the groundwork of deciding what routines make sense to put in the library. A list is given below. If the routine had to be changed to accommodate its being in the library, the code change will be described.

- Mouse On/Mouse Off routine (unnamed)
- global_asa
- OpenRecordSet
- fnBuildFindQuery
- CheckCategoryRequestLevel
- fnCheckForLinksNBooks
- fnDetermineStartPos
- fnDetermineRecordCnt
- fnDetermineEndPos
- fnEvaluatePrev
- fnEvaluateNext
- Move2StartPos
- CloseRecordSet
- fnCheckForMoreCatLevels
- WriteClickedCategory
- ProcessCategories
- WriteCheckBox
- WriteCategories

- ProcessNavHome
- ProcessPrevNext
- CreateCatNavBar
- ParseQueryString
- GetCategories
- PaintNavigationHint

The only routine that had substantial changes made was *WriteCategories*. It now checks a flag to see if a check box is needed; if so, WriteCheckBox is called. Also, another flag is used to determine whether category names should be formatted as links in the absence of child categories, since the feedback program won't be showing links. This will allow navigating through the category tree only to find one to select; thus, categories that lead to no further categories don't need to be clickable.

Following are the flags that were added to *categories.asp*:

- m_tfCatOnly — TRUE if categories will be clickable only if there are children
- Application("Progname") — will hold the name of the Web page. The Web page name had been hardcode into the statements that generate the code for the category hyperlinks, but now those routines can be used by more than one Web page, so this variable will be inserted
- Application("NeedCheckBox") = TRUE if the category name is to be selectable (feedback pages)
- Application("NeedNavHint") = TRUE if the navigation hint about the page scrolling for category names needs to be displayed

So, how do we create the subroutine library? It's a simple text file. We'll just cut the routines out of our page and paste them into the file. We don't need any header tags like <head> or <body>, because we'll be inserting this file into a Web page that already has those tags. We'll save the file as *sublib.inc*, with the *.inc* standing for "include," because it will be included in our Web page file.

Once we have the file created, how do we get it into our Web page? We do it through the use of a directive, like this:

```
<!-- #Include file="sublib.inc"-->
```

We can put the directive anywhere we want in our Web page, but the best place will be either the first line after the <title> tag in the *head* section, or the last line in that section.

Following is the contents of our subroutine library:

```
<% Set bc = Server.CreateObject("MSWC.BrowserType")
   if bc.browser = "IE" then
```

```
      Response.Write "<script language= _
        ""JavaScript"">" & chr(13)
      Response.Write "<!--" & chr(13)
      Response.Write "function MouseOn() {" _
        & chr(13)
      Response.Write "window.event. _
        srcElement.style.color=""#ACA470"";" _
        & chr(13)
      Response.Write "}" & chr(13)
      Response.Write "function MouseOff() {" _
        & chr(13)
      Response.Write "window.event. _
        srcElement.style.color=""navy"";" & chr(13)
      Response.Write "}" & chr(13)
      Response.Write "-->" & chr(13)
      Response.Write "</script>" & chr(13)
  end if
%>
<%
sub global_asa()
'This routine is here because the global.asa _
  functionality
' doesnt work as advertised - remove this _
    routine and the
' call to it when it does
  Session("DataConn_ConnectionString") = _
    "DSN=TheBlowholeDSN"
  Session("DataConn_ConnectionTimeout") = 15
  Session("DataConn_CommandTimeout") = 30
  Session("DataConn_RuntimeUserName") = "admin"
  Session("DataConn_RuntimePassword") = ""
end sub
%>
<%
sub OpenRecordSet(rsobj,commandstr,parm1,parm2)
      rsobj.Open commandstr, , parm1, parm2
end sub
%>
<%
function fnBuildFindQuery()
'--------------
'Build a select statement based on a Find string
'--------------
  l_strTemp = ""
```

```
 for l_iCtr = 1 to len(Session("find"))
     if mid(Session("find"),l_iCtr,1) <> """" then
         l_strTemp = l_strTemp & _
          mid(Session("find"),l_iCtr,1)
     end if
 next
 fnBuildFindQuery = l_strTemp
end function
%>
<%
sub CheckCategoryRequestLevel _
 (l_iParent,l_flgBack,l_strIndent, l_flgInit, _
  l_iReturnTo, l_strPrevCat, l_flgImage, _
  l_flgBookSearch, l_strISBN, RS1, SQ1)
    if l_iParent > 0 then
        l_flgBack = TRUE
'
' set indent so category links will be indented
'  below return path link
'
        l_strIndent = "     "
'
' set flag to false so we'll get the return _
  path link later
'
        l_flgInit = FALSE
'
' construct sql query to gather information
' about what is now the parent category
'
        SQ1.CommandText = "SELECT strCategory_db, _
         liCatNo_db, liParentCatNo_db, strISBN_db, _
         ynImage_db, ynOfferSearch_db _
        FROM Categories WHERE (liCatNo_db = _
        " & l_iParent & ")"
'
' get the record set
'
        call OpenRecordSet(RS1, SQ1, 0, 1)
'
' hold the data for use later
'
        l_iReturnTo = RS1.Fields("liParentCatNo_db")
        l_strPrevCat = RS1.Fields("strCategory_db")
```

```
            l_flgBookSearch = _
             RS1.Fields("ynOfferSearch_db")
            l_flgImage = RS1.Fields("ynImage_db")
            l_strISBN = RS1.Fields("strISBN_db")
            RS1.Close
        end if
end sub
%>
<%
function fnCheckForLinksNBooks(RS2, RS3, SQ3)
 SQ3.CommandText = "SELECT liCatNo_db _
  FROM LinkCat WHERE (liCatNo_db = " & _
  RS2.Fields("liCatNo_db") & ")"
 call OpenRecordSet(RS3, SQ3, 3, 1)
 if RS3.RecordCount > 0 or _
  RS2.Fields("strISBN_db") > "" or _
  RS2.Fields("ynOfferSearch_db") = TRUE then
     fnCheckForLinksNBooks = TRUE
 else
     fnCheckForLinksNBooks = FALSE
 end if
end function
%>
<%
function fnDetermineStartPos(l_iPageSize)
'
' Determine from where in our list we'll start
'  displaying categories
'
 select case Application("Direction")
    case "P": l_iStartPos = Application _
     ("Start") - (l_iPageSize - 1)
             if l_iStartPos < 0 then l_iStartPos = 0
    case "N": l_iStartPos = Application _
     ("Start") + l_iPageSize - 1
    case else:l_iStartPos = 0
 end select
 fnDetermineStartPos = l_iStartPos
end function
%>
<%
function fnDetermineRecordCnt(recset)
 if not recset.EOF then
    l_iRecCnt = recset.RecordCount
```

```
else
    l_iRecCnt = 0
 end if
 fnDetermineRecordCnt = l_iRecCnt
end function
%>
<%
function fnDetermineEndPos(l_iRecCnt, _
 l_iStartPos, l_iPageSize)
 if l_iStartPos + l_iPageSize <= l_iRecCnt then
    l_iEndPos = l_iStartPos + l_iPageSize - 1
 else
    l_iEndPos = l_iRecCnt
 end if
 fnDetermineEndPos = l_iEndPos
end function
%>
<%
function fnEvaluatePrev(l_iStartPos)
   if l_iStartPos > 0 then
      fnEvaluatePrev = TRUE
   else
      fnEvaluatePrev = FALSE
   end if
end function
%>
<%
function fnEvaluateNext(l_iStartPos, l_iRecCnt, _
 l_iPageSize)
 if l_iStartPos + l_iPageSize <= l_iRecCnt then
    fnEvaluateNext = TRUE
 else
    fnEvaluateNext = FALSE
 end if
end function
%>
<%
sub Move2StartPos(l_iStartPos, recset)
 if l_iStartPos > 0 then recset.Move l_iStartPos
end sub
%>
<%
sub CloseRecordSet(rs)
 rs.close
```

```
end sub
%>
<%
function fnCheckForMoreCatLevels(RS2, RS3, SQ3)
 '
 'Check for more category levels below current level
 '
 SQ3.CommandText = "SELECT liCatNo_db _
  FROM Categories WHERE (liParentCatNo_db = " _
  & RS2.Fields("liCatNo_db") & " OR _
  liParentCatNo2_db = " & RS2.Fields("liCatNo_db") _
  & ")"
 call OpenRecordSet(RS3, SQ3, 3, 1)
 if RS3.RecordCount > 0 then
    l_ret = true
 else
    l_ret = false
 end if
 RS3.Close
 fnCheckForMoreCatLevels = l_ret
end function
%>
<%
sub WriteClickedCategory(l_flgInit, l_iParent, _
 l_strPrevCat)
 call PaintInit(l_iParent)
 if l_flgInit = FALSE then Response.Write _
  "<a href="""" & Application("Progname") & _
  "?Parent=" & Application("GP") & """ _
  class=""""clsTitle""""><font=""""clsTitle"""">..." & _
  l_strPrevCat & "</a><br></font>"
end sub
%>
<%
sub ProcessCategories(l_iStartPos, l_iEndPos, _
 l_flgPrev, l_flgNext, l_iPageSize, _
 l_liStartRec, l_iRecCnt, l_straCatInfo(), RS2, _
 RS3, SQ3, l_flgInit, l_iParent, l_strPrevCat)
 l_iStartPos = fnDetermineStartPos(l_iPageSize)
 l_iRecCnt = fnDetermineRecordCnt(RS2)
 l_iEndPos = fnDetermineEndPos(l_iRecCnt, _
  l_iStartPos, l_iPageSize)
 l_flgPrev = fnEvaluatePrev(l_iStartPos)
 l_flgNext = fnEvaluateNext(l_iStartPos, _
```

```
    l_iRecCnt, l_iPageSize)
call Move2StartPos(l_iStartPos, RS2)
for i = 1 to l_iPageSize
    if not RS2.EOF then
        l_straCatInfo(i,1) = _
         RS2.Fields("liCatNo_db")
        l_straCatInfo(i,2) = _
         RS2.Fields("strCategory_db")
        l_straCatInfo(i,3) = _
         fnCheckForMoreCatLevels(RS2, RS3, SQ3)
        l_straCatInfo(i,4) = _
         fnCheckForLinksNBooks(RS2, RS3, SQ3)
        l_liStartRec = l_iStartPos
        RS2.MoveNext
        RS3.Close
    else
        l_straCatInfo(i,1) = -1
    end if
next
call WriteClickedCategory(l_flgInit, _
 l_iParent, l_strPrevCat)
end sub
%>
<%
sub WriteCheckBox(category)
    Response.Write "<input type=""radio"" _
    name=""cat"" value=""" & _
    Application("Parent") & "/" & category _
    & """>"
end sub
%>
<%
sub WriteCategories(l_iStartPos, l_iEndPos, _
 l_iParent, l_straCatInfo(), l_strIndent, _
 l_tfCatOnly)
 for i = l_iStartPos to l_iEndPos
    l_iMoreCatLevels = l_straCatInfo _
     (i - l_iStartPos + 1,3)
    l_iLinksExist = l_straCatInfo _
     (i - l_iStartPos + 1,4)
    if (l_iMoreCatLevels) or (l_iLinksExist _
     = TRUE and l_tfCatOnly = FALSE) then
        Response.Write "<font class=""clsLink"">" _
        & chr(13)
```

```
            if Application("NeedCheckBox") = TRUE then
               call WriteCheckBox (l_straCatInfo _
               (i - l_iStartPos + 1,2))
            end if
            Response.Write "<a name=""a" & i & """ _
             class=""clsLink"" href=""" & _
             Application("Progname") & "?gp=" & _
             l_iParent & "&Parent=" & l_straCatInfo _
             (i - l_iStartPos + 1,1) & chr(13)
            if bc.browser = "IE" then Response.Write   _
             """ onMouseOver=""MouseOn(); return true; _
             "" onMouseOut=""MouseOff(); return true;" _
           & chr(13)
            Response.Write """>" & l_strIndent & _
             l_straCatInfo(i - l_iStartPos + 1,2) & _
             chr(13)
            if (l_iMoreCatLevels) then _
             Response.Write "..."
            Response.write "</a>"
            if i <> l_iEndPos then Response.Write "<BR>"
            Response.Write "</font>"
         else
            Response.Write chr(13) & "<font id= _
             ""idNoLink"" class=""clsLink"">" & chr(13)
            if Application("NeedCheckBox") = TRUE then
               call WriteCheckBox (l_straCatInfo _
               (i - l_iStartPos + 1, 2))
            end if
            Response.Write l_strIndent & _
             l_straCatInfo(i - l_iStartPos + 1, 2) _
             & chr(13)
            if i <> l_iEndPos then Response.Write "<BR>"
            Response.Write "</font>" & chr(13)
         end if
      next
 if Application("NeedNavHint") = TRUE then _
   call PaintNavigationHint(m_flgNext,m_flgPrev)
 Response.Write "</td></tr>" & chr(13)
 Response.Write "</td></tr>" & chr(13)
 Response.Write "</table>" & chr(13)
 end sub
 %>
 <%
 sub ProcessNavHome(l_flgBack)
```

```
Response.Write "<SPAN class=""clsNav"">_
 Top of<br>List</span></td><td align= _
 ""center"" valign=""middle"">" & chr(13)
if l_flgBack = TRUE then
    Response.Write "<" & "!--Webbot _
    bot=""ImageMap"" rectangle="" (0,0) (14, 12) _
    " & Application("Progname") & """ src= _
    ""images/home.gif"" alt=""Top level of _
    category list"" border=""0"" startspan --> _
 <MAP NAME=""FrontPageMap1""><AREA SHAPE= _
 ""RECT"" COORDS=""0, 0, 14, 12"" HREF=""" & _
 Application("Progname") & """></MAP> _
 <a href=""_vti_bin/shtml.dll/" & _
 Application("Progname") & "/map""><img _
 ismap usemap=""#FrontPageMap1"" border=""0"" _
 height=""15"" alt=""beginning of _
 categories"" src=""images/home.gif"" _
 width=""18""></a><" & "!--Webbot bot _
 ImageMap"" endspan i-checksum 16062"" --" & ">" _
 & chr(13)
else
    Response.Write "<img src=""images/home_off. _
    gif"" height=""15"" width=""18"">" & _
    chr(13)
end if
end sub
%>
<%
sub ProcessPrevNext(l_flgPrev, l_flgNext, _
 l_iParent, l_liStartRec)
 Response.Write "</td>" & chr(13)
 Response.Write "<td align=""center"" valign= _
 ""middle""><DIV class=""clsNav"">Prev<br> _
 page</div>" & chr(13)
 Response.Write "</td>" & chr(13)
 Response.Write "<td align=""center"" valign= _
 ""middle"">" & chr(13)
 if l_flgNext = true then
     if l_flgPrev = false then
         Response.Write "<" & "!--Webbot _
         bot=""ImageMap"" rectangle="" _
         (13,0) (25, 15) "
         Response.Write Application("Progname") _
         & "?direction=N&Parent=" & l_iParent _
```

```
            & "&start=" & l_liStartRec & """ _
            src=""images/r_u.gif"" alt=""Next"" _
            border=""0"" startspan --> _
            <MAP NAME=""FrontPageMap2""> _
            <AREA SHAPE=""RECT"" COORDS=""13, 0, _
             25, 15"" HREF="""
        Response.Write Application("Progname") _
            & "?direction=N&Parent=" & l_iParent _
             & "&start=" & l_liStartRec & """></MAP> _
            <a href=""_vti_bin/shtml.dll/" & _
            Application("Progname") & "/map""> _
            <img ismap usemap=""#FrontPageMap2"" _
            border=""0"" height=""15"" alt= _
            ""Next page of categories"" src= _
            ""images/r_u.gif"" width=""25""></a> _
            <!--Webbot bot ImageMap"" endspan -->" _
            & chr(13)
    else
        Response.Write "<" & "!--Webbot _
            bot=""ImageMap"" rectangle="" (0,0) _
            (11, 15)  " & Application("Progname") _
            & "?direction=P&Parent=" & l_iParent _
            & "&start=" & l_liStartRec & """ _
            rectangle="" (13,0) (25, 15)  " & _
            Application("Progname") & _
            "?direction=N&Parent=" & l_iParent _
            & "&start=" & l_liStartRec & """ _
            src=""images/lr_u.gif"" alt= _
            ""Prev/Next"" border=""0"" _
            startspan --><MAP NAME= _
            ""FrontPageMap2""><AREA SHAPE= _
            ""RECT"" COORDS=""0, 0, 11, 15"" _
            HREF=""" & Application("Progname") & _
            "?direction=P&Parent=" & l_iParent & _
            "&start=" & l_liStartRec & """> _
            <AREA SHAPE=""RECT"" COORDS=""13, 0, _
            25, 15"" HREF=""" & Application _
            ("Progname") & "?direction=N&Parent=" _
            & l_iParent & "&start=" & l_liStartRec _
            & """></MAP><a href= _
            ""_vti_bin/shtml.dll/" & _
            Application("Progname") & "/map""> _
            <img ismap usemap=""#FrontPageMap2"" _
            border=""0"" height=""15"" alt= _
```

```
            ""Prev/Next page of categories"" _
            src=""images/lr_u.gif"" width=""25"">  _
            </a><!--Webbot bot ImageMap"" _
            endspan -->" & chr(13)
     end if
     else
         if l_flgPrev = true then
             Response.Write "<" & "!--Webbot bot= _
             ""ImageMap"" rectangle="" (0,0) (11, 15) "
             Response.Write Application("Progname")
             Response.Write "?direction=P&Parent=" _
              & l_iParent & "&start=" & l_liStartRec & _
             """ src=""images/l_u.gif"" alt= _
             ""Next"" border=""0"" startspan --> _
             <MAP NAME=""FrontPageMap2"">  _
             <AREA SHAPE=""RECT"" COORDS=""0, 0, _
             11, 15"" HREF="""
             Response.Write Application("Progname") _
              & "?direction=P&Parent=" & l_iParent _
              & "&start=" & l_liStartRec & """"></MAP> _
             <a href=""_vti_bin/shtml.dll/"
             Response.Write Application("Progname") _
              & "/map""><img ismap usemap= _
             ""#FrontPageMap2"" border=""0"" _
             height=""15"" alt=""Previous page of _
             categories"" src=""images/l_u.gif"" _
             width=""25""></a><!--Webbot bot _
             ImageMap"" endspan -->" & chr(13)
         else
             Response.Write "<" & "img src= _
             ""images/lr_o.gif"" height=""15"" _
             width=""25"">" & chr(13)
         end if
      end if
    Response.Write "</td><td align=""center"" _
     valign=""middle""><DIV class=""clsNav""> _
     Next<br>page</div>" & chr(13)
   end sub
   %>
   <%
   sub CreateCatNavBar(l_flgBack,l_flgPrev, _
    l_flgNext, l_iParent, l_iStartRec)
    Response.Write "<TABLE  bgcolor=""#ACA470"" _
     width=""100" & "%"" cellspacing=""0"" _
```

```
    cellpadding=""0"" border=""0"">" & chr(13)
  Response.Write "<TR><TD align=""center"" _
   valign=""middle"">" & chr(13)
  call ProcessNavHome(l_flgBack)
  call ProcessPrevNext(l_flgPrev, l_flgNext, _
   l_iParent, l_iStartRec)
  Response.Write "</td></tr>" & chr(13)
  Response.Write "</table>" & chr(13)
end sub
%>
<%
Sub ParseQueryString(l_strObj)
 for each item in l_strObj
     Application(lcase(item))= l_strObj(item)
 next
end sub
%>
<%
sub GetCategories(RS2, SQ2, l_iParent, _
  l_flgInit)
 if len(Application("find")) > 1 then
    l_strSearch = fnBuildFindQuery()
    SQ2.CommandText = "SELECT strCategory_db, _
     liCatNo_db, liParentCatNo_db, strISBN_db, _
     ynOfferSearch_db FROM Categories   _
    WHERE strCategory_db LIKE '%" & l_strSearch _
     & "%' ORDER BY strCategory_db;"
    l_flgInit = TRUE
 else
    SQ2.CommandText = "SELECT strCategory_db, _
     liCatNo_db, liParentCatNo_db, strISBN_db, _
     ynOfferSearch_db FROM Categories _
    WHERE (liParentCatNo_db = " & l_iParent & _
     " OR liParentCatNo2_db = " & l_iParent & ") _
    ORDER BY strCategory_db"
 end if
 Call OpenRecordSet(RS2, SQ2, 3, 1)
 Application("find") = ""
end sub
%>
<%
sub PaintNavigationHint(l_flgNext,l_flgPrev)
   if (l_flgNext) or (l_flgPrev) then
      Response.Write "<br><hr width=""10%" & _
```

```
      """ align=""left"">"
   Response.Write "<FONT CLASS=""clsLink""  _
      ID=""idNoLink"" color=""maroon"">"
   Response.Write "(more - use arrow button)  _
      </font>"
   end if
end sub
%>
```

12.3 Feedback Preprocessor

The purpose of the preprocessor is to display a variety of forms based on the type of feedback, forms through which the visitor will provide feedback. In HTML, forms are merely a collection of tags like anything else on the Web page, so we can easily control the layout of the form programmatically to suit our needs.

In terms of lines of code, the majority of the preprocessor will be the lines of the subroutine library. We'll cover the remaining lines.

Let's begin by creating a new ASP file. We'll name it *fbprepro.asp*.

```
<html>
<head>
<title></title>
</head>
<body>
<!--Webbot bot="Include" U-Include="navbar2.htm"  _
 TAG="BODY" startspan --><strong>[navbar2.htm]  _
 </strong><!--Webbot bot="Include" endspan  _
 i-checksum="3991" -->
</body>
</html>
```

Next, we want to add the lines that will bring our Cascading Style Sheet and sub-routine library into the page:

```
<link REL="stylesheet" HREF="blowhole.css"  _
 TYPE="text/css">
<!-- #Include file="sublib.inc"-->
```

Next, we drop down into the body and declare some variables, some of them already familiar:

```
<%
 dim m_tfCategories
```

```
dim m_tfInstructionsCategory
dim m_tfInstructionsParent
dim m_tfInstructionsLinkParent
dim m_tfName
```

The next set of declarations are for flags that will be used to determine what fields should be present in the feedback form.

```
dim m_tfEmail
dim m_tfNewCategory
dim m_tfNewLink
dim m_tfURL
dim m_tfDescription
dim m_tfComment
dim m_tfContact
```

When our page starts executing, we'll want to determine if any parameters have been passed to us. We do that by checking the input stream to see if it contains anything. If it does, we'll call the routine in our subroutine library that assigns the parameters to Application variables.

```
if len(Request.QueryString) > 0 then
    call ParseQueryString(Request.QueryString)
```

One of our parameters may have been the now familiar *parent*. If it is present, it will be assigned to one of our variables; if not, the variable will receive 0.

```
    m_iParent = Application("Parent")
end if
```

Some of the feedback forms will have a text introduction above them. Whether one is used, and if so, what its content is, will be decided in a routine. Let's invoke it:

```
call WriteIntro()
```

and create the routine:

```
<%
sub WriteIntro()
end sub
%>
```

We could determine what we want to do with a nested *if* statement, but they can get really ugly. When checking a variable against a list of known values, the better way to go is a *case* statement. The cases we'll be handling are, in order, category comments, new category recommendations and a new link request. General comments won't have an introduction.

```
select case Application("feedbackcode")
    case "category":
        Response.Write "<p class=""bodytext""> _
        We're always looking to better _
        organize our categories. If you think _
        that one of our categories needs to be _
        moved, removed or renamed, please let _
        us know. </p>"
        Response.Write "<p class=""bodytext""> _
        Simply navigate to the appropriate _
        category, click the circle next to it, _
        complete the form and click on _
        'Submit'.</p>"
    case "newcategory":
        Response.Write "<p class=""bodytext""> _
        We're always looking to add new _
        categories.</p>"
        Response.Write "<p class=""bodytext""> _
        Simply navigate to the category that _
        would be the parent of the new one, _
        click the circle next to it, complete _
        the form and click on 'Submit'.</p>"
    case "newlink":
        Response.Write "<p class=""bodytext""> _
        We're always looking to add new links. _
        </p>"
        Response.Write "<p class=""bodytext""> _
        Simply navigate to the category that _
        would be the parent of the link, click _
        the circle next to it, complete the form _
        and click on 'Submit'.</p>"
end select
```

Now that we've printed the introduction, it's time to decide what fields need to be on our feedback form. So, we'll invoke the routine:

```
call DetermineWhichFieldsToUse( _
    m_tfCategories, _
    m_tfInstructionsCategory, _
    m_tfInstructionsParent, _
```

```
    m_tfInstructionsLinkParent, _
    m_tfName, _
    m_tfEmail, _
    m_tfNewCategory, _
    m_tfNewLink, _
    m_tfURL, _
    m_tfDescription, _
    m_tfComment, _
    m_tfContact)
```

and put the routine together. This routine will use a case statement, like the one we just finished. We'll be using the case statement to set flags, which will be used later when compiling the actual feedback form.

```
<%
sub DetermineWhichFieldsToUse( _
    l_tfCategories, _
    l_tfInstructionsCategory, _
    l_tfInstructionsParent, _
    l_tfInstructionsLinkParent, _
    l_tfName, _
    l_tfEmail, _
    l_tfNewCategory, _
    l_tfNewLink, _
    l_tfURL, _
    l_tfDescription, _
    l_tfComment, _
    l_tfContact)
  select case Application("feedbackcode")
    case "category":
        l_tfCategories = true
        l_tfInstructionsCategory = true
        l_tfInstructionsParent = false
        l_tfInstructionsLinkParent = false
        l_tfName = true
        l_tfEmail = true
        l_tfNewCategory = false
        l_tfNewLink = false
        l_tfURL = false
        l_tfDescription = false
        l_tfComment = true
        l_tfContact = true
    case "general":
```

```
                l_tfCategories = false
                l_tfInstructionsCategory = false
                l_tfInstructionsParent = false
                l_tfInstructionsLinkParent = false
                l_tfName = true
                l_tfEmail = true
                l_tfNewCategory = false
                l_tfNewLink = false
                l_tfURL = false
                l_tfDescription = false
                l_tfComment = true
                l_tfContact = true
        case "newcategory":
                l_tfCategories = true
                l_tfInstructionsCategory = false
                l_tfInstructionsParent = true
                l_tfInstructionsLinkParent = false
                l_tfName = true
                l_tfEmail = true
                l_tfNewCategory = true
                l_tfNewLink = false
                l_tfURL = false
                l_tfDescription = false
                l_tfComment = true
                l_tfContact = true
        case "newlink":
                l_tfCategories = true
                l_tfInstructionsCategory = false
                l_tfInstructionsParent = false
                l_tfInstructionsLinkParent = true
                l_tfName = true
                l_tfEmail = true
                l_tfNewCategory = false
                l_tfNewLink = true
                l_tfURL = true
                l_tfDescription = true
                l_tfComment = true
                l_tfContact = true
    end select
end sub
%>
```

Now that we have the form components identified (those items marked *true*), it's time to create the form. First we'll invoke a new routine:

```
call WriteIntro()

call CreateForm()
```

This routine creates the form structure.

```
<%
sub CreateForm()
'
'Create form
'Set form for validation
'
Response.Write chr(13)
Response.Write "<FORM method=""POST"" _
```

This is the tag that defines a form. We'll be using the *POST* method instead of *GET*, because it will pass the form information on to our postprocessor transparent to the site visitor, instead of passing it in the URL like *GET* does.

```
onsubmit= _
""return Validate(this)"" _
```

This line will trap the *onsubmit* event, the event that's "fired" when the visitor clicks the submit button. It will call *Validate* to check the form and make sure that the information needed to process the form has been provided by the visitor. If not, a message will be displayed requesting the information. The key to the success of this is twofold: the *return* keyword, which determines whether the form being should be submitted based on the return sent from the call to *Validate* (if it fails, the result when information is missing, then no submit) and the *Validate* routine itself. We'll be constructing the code for that routine shortly. By the way, "validate this" is not an exclamation hurled at a parking lot attendant by an irate New Yorker—well, it is, but not in this context—*this* is a reserved word, a variable that refers to the object using it, in this case the form we're passing to the *Validate* routine.

```
name=""Form1"" _
action=""fbPostpro.asp"">" & chr(13)
```

Here we're stating that the form data should be sent to *fbPostpro.asp*, the postprocessor.

```
Response.Write "<INPUT type=""hidden"" _
 name=""feedbackcode"" value=""" _
 & Application("feedbackcode") & """>" & chr(13)
end sub
%>
```

When our *post*processor begins execution, it will need to know which form it's processing. We'll let it know via a hidden field on the form. A hidden field is not visible to the visitor, and can contain whatever data you want to put in it, either for passing on to the form handler or for use by other fields on the form. The contents of the field is the feedback code we are storing in our application variable.

Up next is form content. If we are processing feedback on an existing category or a request for a new category or link, the visitor will be asked to identify the category by selecting it from a list. There are many ways in which we could present that list, but since we already have logic on the *Categories* page to handle just such a presentation, we'll reuse it here (for you programmers out there an actual example of code reuse!). We'll call routines in our subroutine library for much of the logic, but some will be fresh. When categories *do* need to be displayed (they don't for general feedback), we'll perform that processing before painting the form, since we'll be painting the categories on the left-hand side. Let's set up the initial invocation:

```
call CreateForm()

  if m_tfCategories = true then
     call PaintCat()
  end if
```

We check to see if our flag is *true*. The flag is set based on the type of feedback. If it is true, we call a routine *PaintCat*. Let's set up that routine. We'll begin with a call to our *global_asa* routine, which is in the subroutine library, and then some declarations.

```
<%
sub PaintCat()
call global_asa()
Set DataConn = Server.CreateObject _
  ("ADODB.Connection")
Set SQLQuery = Server.CreateObject("ADODB.Command")
set SQLQuery2 = Server.CreateObject _
  ("ADODB.Command")
set SQLQuery3 = Server.CreateObject _
  ("ADODB.Command")
Set RecordSet1 = Server.CreateObject _
  ("ADODB.Recordset")
Set RecordSet2 = Server.CreateObject _
  ("ADODB.Recordset")
Set RecordSet3 = Server.CreateObject _
  ("ADODB.Recordset")
Set DataConn = Server.CreateObject _
  ("ADODB.Connection")
DataConn.Open Session("DataConn_ConnectionString")
```

```
SQLQuery.CommandType = 1
SQLQuery2.CommandType = SQLQuery.CommandType
SQLQuery3.CommandType = SQLQuery.CommandType
Set SQLQuery.ActiveConnection = DataConn
Set SQLQuery2.ActiveConnection = DataConn
set SQLQuery3.ActiveConnection = DataConn

dim m_iRet, m_flgBack, m_flgInit, m_iReturnTo, _
 m_strIndent
dim m_iStartPos, m_iEndPos, m_iRecCnt, m_iCurrRec, _
 m_flgNext, m_flgPrev
dim m_strPrevCat
dim m_iPageSize
dim m_straCatInfo()
dim m_tfCatOnly  'true if we only want categories _
 to be clickable if there are children
```

So far the logic looks much the same as it did for the categories processing. We are going to make the page size somewhat larger, because the layout will support additional categories.

```
m_iPageSize = 10
'
' The following array will contain information
'   about each category. It was defined earlier.
'   This instantiates it as a 4-dimension array.
'   Dimension 1 - category number
'   Dimension 2 - category name
'   Dimension 3 - levels below this category?
'   Dimension 4 - links/book associated with this?
redim m_straCatInfo(m_iPageSize,4)

' We'll set the environment for the initial
'   loading of this page, and change that later
'   if needed based on any parameters passed
m_flgBack=false
m_flgInit=true
m_strIndent=""
m_liStartRec=0
m_iParent = 0
m_tfCatOnly = TRUE
```

We've set this to *true* because we are only presenting categories, not links. So if a category has no child categories, there is no reason to make it clickable — it doesn't lead anywhere.

```
'
' The following lines will create application
'  variables
'
Application("Direction") = ""
Application("Start") = ""
Application("GP") = "0"
Application("Progname") = "fbPrePro.asp"
Application("NeedCheckBox") = TRUE
Application("NeedNavHint") = FALSE
```

The last three Application variables are new, as we mentioned earlier. The value of *progname* will be used when generating hyperlinks that iterate this page, such as the logic when clicking categories. We do need the categories to be selectable, hence the second setting, and in this context we will not be displaying our navigation "hint."

Let's start by creating the table for our categories to reside in.

```
<%
sub PaintInit(l_iParent)
'
'Create table to hold categories and feedback form
'
   Response.Write "<table border='1' cellpadding= _
   '1' cellspacing='2' width='100%' id= _
   'tabContent'>" & chr(13)
   Response.Write "<tr>" & chr(13)
   Response.Write "<td width=""25%"" _
    valign=""top"" align=""left"" bgcolor= _
    ""#FFFFFF"">" & chr(13)
   Response.Write "<TABLE  bgcolor=""#FFC2C2"" _
    width=""100" & "%"" cellspacing=""0"" _
    cellpadding=""0"" border=""0"">" & chr(13)
   Response.Write "<TR><TD valign=""middle"">" _
    & chr(13)
end sub
%>
```

and now move on to further processing:

```
call PaintInit(m_iParent)
call CheckCategoryRequestLevel _
(m_iParent,m_flgBack,m_strIndent,m_flgInit, _
 m_iReturnTo,m_strPrevCat,m_flgImage, _
 m_flgBookSearch, m_strISBN, RecordSet1, SQLQuery)
call GetCategories(RecordSet2, SQLQuery2, _
 m_iParent, m_flgInit)
call ProcessCategories(m_iStartPos, m_iEndPos, _
 m_flgPrev, m_flgNext, m_iPageSize, _
 m_liStartRec, m_iRecCnt, m_straCatInfo, _
 RecordSet2, RecordSet3, SQLQuery3, m_flgInit, _
 m_iParent, m_strPrevCat)
call WriteCategories(m_iStartPos, m_iEndPos, _
 m_iParent, m_straCatInfo, m_strIndent, _
 m_tfCatOnly)
call CreateCatNavBar(m_flgBack, m_flgPrev, _
 m_flgNext, m_iParent, m_liStartRec)
```

All of the preceding calls are to routines we've already seen, routines that have been added to our subroutine library. We have one last thing to do with our categories:

```
'
'Create group for radio buttons (there will be one
radio button for each category)
'
Response.Write chr(13) & "<INPUT TYPE=""hidden"" _
 NAME=""VTI-GROUP"" VALUE=""0""><!--Webbot bot _
 SaveResults"" endspan -->"
end sub
%>
```

The preceding *input* line takes the controls we'll use to have the visitor select the category and defines them as a group. That way, if one is selected and another is clicked, the latter becomes selected and the former, unselected. That's it for the category processing; now back to the rest of the form. It's time for the meat—the controls that make the form a form. A call:

```
if m_tfCategories = true then
    call PaintCat()
 end if
```

```
call WriteInfoPartOfForm(m_tfName, m_tfEmail, _
m_tfNewCategory, m_tfNewLink, m_tfURL, _
m_tfDescription, m_tfComment, m_tfContact)
```

and the processing:

```
<%
sub WriteInfoPartOfForm(l_tfName, l_tfEmail, _
l_tfNewCategory, l_tfNewLink, l_tfURL, _
l_tfDescription, l_tfComment, l_tfContact)
 Response.write  "<td><table border=""0"" _
 width=""330"">" & chr(13)
```

To this point we've set up a table. We'll now take note of all the components that have been flagged as needing to be on the form and generate the appropriate HTML code.

```
if l_tfName = true then
   Response.Write  "<tr>" & chr(13)
   Response.Write  "  <td width=""100""> _
    <small>Name:</small></td>" & chr(13)
   Response.Write  "<" & "!--Webbot bot= _
    ""Validation"" startspan S-Display-Name _
    =""Name"" B-Value-Required=""TRUE"" --> _
    <" & "!--Webbot bot=""Validation""  _
    endspan -->" & chr(13)
   Response.Write  "  <td width=""224""> _
    <input type=""text"" name=""name"" size= _
    ""20"" tabindex=""1""></td>" & chr(13)
   Response.Write  "</tr>" & chr(13)
end if
```

In the preceding block of code we defined a cell in the table to contain the field label, in this case *name*; we set up an event call for validation of the field and label the field as being required; and we have defined the actual input field, a text box. This field only appears on the form if the flag *l_tfName* is *true*. We'll now do the same with the remaining potential fields.

```
if l_tfEmail = true then
  Response.Write  "<tr>" & chr(13)
  Response.Write  "  <td width=""100""> _
   <small>Email:</small></td>" & chr(13)
  Response.Write  "<" & "!--Webbot bot= _
   ""Validation"" startspan S-Display-Name= _
```

```
      ""Email"" B-Value-Required=""TRUE""  _
      I-Minimum-Length 7"" --><" & "!--Webbot _
      bot=""Validation"" endspan -->" & chr(13)
      Response.Write  "  <td width=""224"">  _
      <input type=""text"" name=""email"" size= _
      ""20"" tabindex=""2""></td>" & chr(13)
      Response.Write  "</tr>" & chr(13)
   end if
   if l_tfNewCategory = true then
      Response.Write  "<tr>" & chr(13)
      Response.Write  "  <td width=""100"">  _
      <small>New Category:</small></td>" & chr(13)
      Response.Write  "<" & "!--Webbot bot= _
      ""Validation"" startspan S-Display-Name= _
      ""NewCategory"" B-Value-Required TRUE""  _
      I-Minimum-Length 2"" --><" & "!--Webbot _
      bot=""Validation"" endspan -->" & chr(13)
      Response.Write  "  <td width=""224"">  _
      <input type=""text"" name=""newcategory"" _
      size=""20"" tabindex=""3""></td>" & chr(13)
      Response.Write  "</tr>" & chr(13)
   end if
   if l_tfNewLink = true then
      Response.Write  "<tr>" & chr(13)
      Response.Write  "  <td width=""100"">  _
      <small>New Link:</small></td>" & chr(13)
      Response.Write  "<" & "!--Webbot bot= _
      ""Validation"" startspan S-Display-Name= _
      ""NewLink"" B-Value-Required=""TRUE"" _
      I-Minimum-Length 2"" --><" & "!--Webbot bot= _
      ""Validation"" endspan -->" & chr(13)
      Response.Write  "  <td width=""224"">  _
      <input type=""text"" name=""newlink"" _
      size=""20"" tabindex=""4""></td>" & chr(13)
      Response.Write  "</tr>" & chr(13)
   end if
   if l_tfURL = true then
      Response.Write  "<tr>" & chr(13)
      Response.Write  "  <td width=""100"">  _
      <small>URL:</small></td>" & chr(13)
      Response.Write  "<" & "!--Webbot bot= _
      ""Validation"" startspan S-Display-Name= _
      ""URL"" B-Value-Required=""TRUE""  _
      I-Minimum-Length 2"" --><" & "!--Webbot bot= _
```

```
      ""Validation"" endspan -->" & chr(13)
    Response.Write  "  <td width=""224""> _
     <input type=""text"" name=""url""  _
     size=""40"" tabindex=""5""></td>" & chr(13)
    Response.Write  "</tr>" & chr(13)
  end if
  if l_tfDescription = true then
    Response.Write  "<tr>" & chr(13)
    Response.Write  "  <td width=""100""> _
     <small> Description:</small></td>" & chr(13)
    Response.Write  "<" & "!--Webbot bot= _
     ""Validation"" startspan S-Display-Name= _
     ""Description"" B-Value-Required= _
     ""FALSE"" --><" & "!--Webbot bot= _
     ""Validation"" endspan -->" & chr(13)
    Response.Write  "  <td width=""224""> _
     <textarea rows=""4"" name=""description"" _
     cols=""40"" tabindex=""6""></textarea> _
     </td>" & chr(13)
    Response.Write  "</tr>" & chr(13)
  end if
  if l_tfComment = true then
    Response.Write  "<tr>" & chr(13)
    Response.Write  "  <td width=""100""> _
     <small>Comment:</small></td>" & chr(13)
    Response.Write  "<" & "!--Webbot bot= _
     ""Validation"" startspan S-Display-Name= _
     ""Comment"" B-Value-Required=""TRUE""  _
     I-Minimum-Length=""1"" --><" & _
     "!--Webbot bot=""Validation"" endspan -->" _
     & chr(13)
    Response.Write  "  <td width=""224""> _
     <textarea rows=""4"" name=""comment""  _
     cols=""40"" tabindex=""7""></textarea> _
     </td>" & chr(13)
    Response.Write  "</tr>" & chr(13)
  end if
  if l_tfContact = true then
    Response.Write  "<tr>" & chr(13)
    Response.Write  "  <td width=""100""> _
     <small>Please contact me:</small></td>" _
     & chr(13)
    Response.Write  "  <td width=""224""> _
     <input type=""checkbox"" name= _
```

```
    ""contactme"" value=""ON"" tabindex= _
    ""8""></td>" & chr(13)
  Response.Write  "</tr>" & chr(13)
  end if
  Response.Write  "</table>" & chr(13)
end sub
%>
```

The typical validation checks made in the preceding routine include required fields—fields that we want to be filled in—and minimum length.

Once we've generated the HTML for the form elements, we need to complete the form. We'll invoke another routine:

```
call WriteInfoPartOfForm(m_tfName, m_tfEmail, _
  m_tfNewCategory, m_tfNewLink, m_tfURL, _
  m_tfDescription, m_tfComment, m_tfContact)

call FinishForm()
```

and the routine:

```
<%
sub FinishForm()
 Response.Write  "<p><input type=""submit"" _
  value=""Submit"" name=""Submit""   _
  tabindex=""99""></p>" & chr(13)
 Response.Write  "</form>" & chr(13)
 Response.Write "</td></tr></table>"
end sub
%>
```

Here we've defined a submit button, and we end the form and the table in which the form resides. Not too much to it. Finally, we need to write the routine that performs the validation of the form. This routine is somewhat confusing because it's VBScript generating JavaScript encased in an HTML wrapper. The reason we're using JavaScript is that we want the validation to occur on the visitor's computer, and we don't know if their browser will support VBScript.

```
call FinishForm()

call WriteValidation()

<%
sub WriteValidation()
```

```
Response.Write "<script Language=""JavaScript"">" _
& chr(13)
Response.write "function Validate(theForm)" _
& chr(13)
Response.write "{" & chr(13)
if m_tfCategories = true then
    Response.Write "  var radioSelected = false;" _
       & chr(13)
    Response.Write "  for (i = 0; _
     i < theForm.cat.length;  i++)" & chr(13)
    Response.Write "  {" & chr(13)
    Response.Write "    if (theForm.cat[i] _
      .checked)" & chr(13)
    Response.Write "        radioSelected = _
     true;" & chr(13)
    Response.Write "  }" & chr(13)
    Response.Write "  if (!radioSelected)" _
       & chr(13)
    Response.Write "  {" & chr(13)
    Response.Write "    alert(""Please select _
     one of the categories."");" & chr(13)
    Response.Write "    return (false);" & chr(13)
    Response.Write "  }" & chr(13)
end if
Response.write "  if (theForm.name.value == _
 """")"   & chr(13)
Response.write "  {" & chr(13)
Response.write "    alert(""Please enter a name"")_
 ;" & chr(13)
Response.write "    theForm.name.focus();" & chr(13)
Response.write "    return (false);" & chr(13)
Response.write "  }" & chr(13)
Response.write "  if (theForm.email.value _
 == """")" & chr(13)
Response.write "  {" & chr(13)
Response.write "    alert(""Please enter your _
 email address."");" & chr(13)
Response.write "    theForm.email.focus();" _
   & chr(13)
Response.write "    return (false);" & chr(13)
Response.write "  }" & chr(13)
Response.write "  return (true);" & chr(13)
Response.write "  if (theForm.comment.value _
 == """")" & chr(13)
```

```
Response.write "  {" & chr(13)
Response.write "    alert(""Please enter your _
 comment.""); " & chr(13)
Response.write "    theForm.comment.focus(); " _
 & chr(13)
Response.write "    return (false); " & chr(13)
Response.write "  }" & chr(13)
Response.write "  return (true); " & chr(13)
Response.write "}" & chr(13)
Response.write "--></script>" & chr(13)
end sub
%>
```

That ends the preprocessor. The next step is for the postprocessor to process the data that gets passed from the preprocessor's form. Let's take a look at the final preprocessor code, and then move on.

```
<html>
<head>
<title>The Blowhole Feedback PreProcessor</title>
<link REL="stylesheet" HREF="blowhole.css" _
 TYPE="text/css">
<!-- #Include file="sublib.inc"-->
<%
sub WriteIntro()
 select case Application("feedbackcode")
    case "category":
        Response.Write "<p class=""bodytext""> _
        We're always looking to better _
        organize our categories. If you think _
        that one of our categories needs to be _
        moved, removed or renamed, please let _
        us know. </p>"
        Response.Write "<p class=""bodytext""> _
        Simply navigate to the appropriate _
        category, click the circle next to it, _
        complete the form and click on _
        'Submit'.</p>"
    case "newcategory":
        Response.Write "<p class=""bodytext""> _
        We're always looking to add new _
        categories.</p>"
        Response.Write "<p class=""bodytext""> _
        Simply navigate to the category that _
```

```
                    would be the parent of the new one, _
                    click the circle next to it, complete _
                    the form and click on 'Submit'.</p>"
             case "newlink":
                Response.Write "<p class=""bodytext""> _
                    We're always looking to add new links. _
                    </p>"
                Response.Write "<p class=""bodytext""> _
                    Simply navigate to the category that _
                    would be the parent of the link, click _
                     the circle next to it, complete the form _
                    and click on 'Submit'.</p>"
        end select
     end sub
     %>
     <%
     sub DetermineWhichFieldsToUse( _
         l_tfCategories, _
         l_tfInstructionsCategory, _
         l_tfInstructionsParent, _
         l_tfInstructionsLinkParent, _
         l_tfName, _
         l_tfEmail, _
         l_tfNewCategory, _
         l_tfNewLink, _
         l_tfURL, _
         l_tfDescription, _
         l_tfComment, _
         l_tfContact)
       select case Application("feedbackcode")
          case "category":
                l_tfCategories = true
                l_tfInstructionsCategory = true
                l_tfInstructionsParent = false
                l_tfInstructionsLinkParent = false
                l_tfName = true
                l_tfEmail = true
                l_tfNewCategory = false
                l_tfNewLink = false
                l_tfURL = false
                l_tfDescription = false
                l_tfComment = true
                l_tfContact = true
          case "general":
```

```
            l_tfCategories = false
            l_tfInstructionsCategory = false
            l_tfInstructionsParent = false
            l_tfInstructionsLinkParent = false
            l_tfName = true
            l_tfEmail = true
            l_tfNewCategory = false
            l_tfNewLink = false
            l_tfURL = false
            l_tfDescription = false
            l_tfComment = true
            l_tfContact = true
        case "newcategory":
            l_tfCategories = true
            l_tfInstructionsCategory = false
            l_tfInstructionsParent = true
            l_tfInstructionsLinkParent = false
            l_tfName = true
            l_tfEmail = true
            l_tfNewCategory = true
            l_tfNewLink = false
            l_tfURL = false
            l_tfDescription = false
            l_tfComment = true
            l_tfContact = true
        case "newlink":
            l_tfCategories = true
            l_tfInstructionsCategory = false
            l_tfInstructionsParent = false
            l_tfInstructionsLinkParent = true
            l_tfName = true
            l_tfEmail = true
            l_tfNewCategory = false
            l_tfNewLink = true
            l_tfURL = true
            l_tfDescription = true
            l_tfComment = true
            l_tfContact = true
    end select
end sub
%>
<%
sub CreateForm()
    '
```

```
'Create form
'Set form for validation
'
Response.Write chr(13)
Response.Write "<FORM method=""POST"" _
 onsubmit= _
 ""return Validate(this)"" _
 name=""Form1"" _
 action=""fbPostpro.asp"">" & chr(13)
Response.Write "<INPUT type=""hidden"" _
 name=""feedbackcode"" value=""" _
 & Application("feedbackcode") & """>" & chr(13)
end sub
%>
<%
sub PaintCat()
call global_asa()
Set DataConn = Server.CreateObject _
 ("ADODB.Connection")
Set SQLQuery = Server.CreateObject("ADODB.Command")
set SQLQuery2 = Server.CreateObject _
 ("ADODB.Command")
set SQLQuery3 = Server.CreateObject _
 ("ADODB.Command")
Set RecordSet1 = Server.CreateObject _
 ("ADODB.Recordset")
Set RecordSet2 = Server.CreateObject _
 ("ADODB.Recordset")
Set RecordSet3 = Server.CreateObject _
 ("ADODB.Recordset")
Set DataConn = Server.CreateObject _
 ("ADODB.Connection")
DataConn.Open Session("DataConn_ConnectionString")

SQLQuery.CommandType = 1
SQLQuery2.CommandType = SQLQuery.CommandType
SQLQuery3.CommandType = SQLQuery.CommandType
Set SQLQuery.ActiveConnection = DataConn
Set SQLQuery2.ActiveConnection = DataConn
set SQLQuery3.ActiveConnection = DataConn
dim m_iRet, m_flgBack, m_flgInit, m_iReturnTo, _
 m_strIndent
dim m_iStartPos, m_iEndPos, m_iRecCnt, m_iCurrRec, _
 m_flgNext, m_flgPrev
```

```
dim m_strPrevCat
dim m_iPageSize
dim m_straCatInfo()
dim m_tfCatOnly   'true if we only want categories _
 to be clickable if there are children
m_iPageSize = 10
'
' The following array will contain information
'  about each category. It was defined earlier.
'  This instantiates it as a 4-dimension array.
'  Dimension 1 - category number
'  Dimension 2 - category name
'  Dimension 3 - levels below this category?
'  Dimension 4 - links/book associated with this?
redim m_straCatInfo(m_iPageSize,4)

' We'll set the environment for the initial
'  loading of this page, and change that later
'  if needed based on any parameters passed
m_flgBack=false
m_flgInit=true
m_strIndent=""
m_liStartRec=0
m_iParent = 0
m_tfCatOnly = TRUE

'
' The following lines will create application
'  variables
'
Application("Direction") = ""
Application("Start") = ""
Application("GP") = "0"
Application("Progname") = "fbPrePro.asp"
Application("NeedCheckBox") = TRUE
Application("NeedNavHint") = FALSE
call PaintInit(m_iParent)
call CheckCategoryRequestLevel _
(m_iParent,m_flgBack,m_strIndent,m_flgInit, _
 m_iReturnTo,m_strPrevCat,m_flgImage, _
 m_flgBookSearch, m_strISBN, RecordSet1, SQLQuery)
call GetCategories(RecordSet2, SQLQuery2, _
 m_iParent, m_flgInit)
call ProcessCategories(m_iStartPos, m_iEndPos, _
```

```
   m_flgPrev, m_flgNext, m_iPageSize,    _
   m_liStartRec, m_iRecCnt, m_straCatInfo, _
   RecordSet2, RecordSet3, SQLQuery3, m_flgInit, _
   m_iParent, m_strPrevCat)
 call WriteCategories(m_iStartPos, m_iEndPos, _
   m_iParent, m_straCatInfo, m_strIndent, _
   m_tfCatOnly)
 call CreateCatNavBar(m_flgBack, m_flgPrev, _
   m_flgNext, m_iParent, m_liStartRec)
 '
 'Create group for radio buttons (there will be one
radio button for each category)
   '
 Response.Write chr(13) & "<INPUT TYPE=""hidden"" _
   NAME=""VTI-GROUP"" VALUE=""0""><!--Webbot bot _
   SaveResults"" endspan -->"
 end sub
%>
<%
 sub PaintInit(l_iParent)
   '
 'Create table to hold categories and feedback form
   '
   Response.Write "<table border='1' cellpadding= _
   '1' cellspacing='2' width='100%' id= _
   'tabContent'>" & chr(13)
   Response.Write "<tr>" & chr(13)
   Response.Write "<td width=""25%"" _
    valign=""top"" align=""left"" bgcolor= _
    ""#FFFFFF"">" & chr(13)
   Response.Write "<TABLE  bgcolor=""#FFC2C2"" _
    width=""100" & "%"" cellspacing=""0"" _
    cellpadding=""0"" border=""0"">" & chr(13)
   Response.Write "<TR><TD valign=""middle"">" _
    & chr(13)
 end sub
%>
<%
 sub WriteInfoPartOfForm(l_tfName, l_tfEmail, _
  l_tfNewCategory, l_tfNewLink, l_tfURL, _
  l_tfDescription, l_tfComment, l_tfContact)
   Response.write  "<td><table border=""0"" _
   width=""330"">" & chr(13)
   if l_tfName = true then
```

```
     Response.Write  "<tr>" & chr(13)
     Response.Write  "  <td width="""100"""> _
      <small>Name:</small></td>" & chr(13)
     Response.Write  "<" & "!--Webbot bot= _
      ""Validation"" startspan S-Display-Name _
      ="""Name"" B-Value-Required="""TRUE"" --> _
      <" & "!--Webbot bot="""Validation"" _
      endspan -->" & chr(13)
     Response.Write  "  <td width="""224"""> _
      <input type="""text"" name="""name"" size= _
      ""20"" tabindex="""1"""></td>" & chr(13)
     Response.Write  "</tr>" & chr(13)
  end if
  if l_tfEmail = true then
     Response.Write  "<tr>" & chr(13)
     Response.Write  "  <td width="""100"""> _
      <small>Email:</small></td>" & chr(13)
     Response.Write  "<" & "!--Webbot bot= _
      ""Validation"" startspan S-Display-Name= _
      ""Email"" B-Value-Required="""TRUE"" _
      I-Minimum-Length 7"" --><" & "!--Webbot _
      bot="""Validation"" endspan -->" & chr(13)
     Response.Write  "  <td width="""224"""> _
      <input type="""text"" name="""email"" size= _
      ""20"" tabindex="""2"""></td>" & chr(13)
     Response.Write  "</tr>" & chr(13)
  end if
  if l_tfNewCategory = true then
     Response.Write  "<tr>" & chr(13)
     Response.Write  "  <td width="""100"""> _
      <small>New Category:</small></td>" & chr(13)
     Response.Write  "<" & "!--Webbot bot= _
      ""Validation"" startspan S-Display-Name= _
      ""NewCategory"" B-Value-Required TRUE"" _
      I-Minimum-Length 2"" --><" & "!--Webbot _
      bot="""Validation"" endspan -->" & chr(13)
     Response.Write  "  <td width="""224"""> _
      <input type="""text"" name="""newcategory"" _
      size="""20"" tabindex="""3"""></td>" & chr(13)
     Response.Write  "</tr>" & chr(13)
  end if
  if l_tfNewLink = true then
     Response.Write  "<tr>" & chr(13)
     Response.Write  "  <td width="""100"""> _
```

```
      <small>New Link:</small></td>" & chr(13)
    Response.Write  "<" & "!--Webbot bot= _
    ""Validation"" startspan S-Display-Name= _
    ""NewLink"" B-Value-Required=""TRUE"" _
    I-Minimum-Length 2"" --><" & "!--Webbot bot= _
    ""Validation"" endspan -->" & chr(13)
    Response.Write  "  <td width=""224""> _
    <input type=""text"" name=""newlink"" _
    size=""20"" tabindex=""4""></td>" & chr(13)
    Response.Write  "</tr>" & chr(13)
  end if
  if l_tfURL = true then
    Response.Write  "<tr>" & chr(13)
    Response.Write  "  <td width=""100""> _
    <small>URL:</small></td>" & chr(13)
    Response.Write  "<" & "!--Webbot bot= _
    ""Validation"" startspan S-Display-Name= _
    ""URL"" B-Value-Required=""TRUE"" _
    I-Minimum-Length 2"" --><" & "!--Webbot bot= _
    ""Validation"" endspan -->" & chr(13)
    Response.Write  "  <td width=""224""> _
    <input type=""text"" name=""url"" _
    size=""40"" tabindex=""5""></td>" & chr(13)
    Response.Write  "</tr>" & chr(13)
  end if
  if l_tfDescription = true then
    Response.Write  "<tr>" & chr(13)
    Response.Write  "  <td width=""100""> _
    <small> Description:</small></td>" & chr(13)
    Response.Write  "<" & "!--Webbot bot= _
    ""Validation"" startspan S-Display-Name= _
    ""Description"" B-Value-Required= _
    ""FALSE"" --><" & "!--Webbot bot= _
    ""Validation"" endspan -->" & chr(13)
    Response.Write  "  <td width=""224""> _
    <textarea rows=""4"" name=""description"" _
    cols=""40"" tabindex=""6""></textarea> _
    </td>" & chr(13)
    Response.Write  "</tr>" & chr(13)
  end if
  if l_tfComment = true then
    Response.Write  "<tr>" & chr(13)
    Response.Write  "  <td width=""100""> _
    <small>Comment:</small></td>" & chr(13)
```

```
      Response.Write  "<" & "!--Webbot bot= _
      ""Validation"" startspan S-Display-Name= _
      ""Comment"" B-Value-Required=""TRUE""  _
      I-Minimum-Length=""1"" --><" & _
      "!--Webbot bot=""Validation"" endspan -->" _
      & chr(13)
      Response.Write  "  <td width=""224"">  _
      <textarea rows=""4"" name=""comment""  _
      cols=""40"" tabindex=""7""></textarea> _
      </td>" & chr(13)
      Response.Write  "</tr>" & chr(13)
    end if
    if l_tfContact = true then
      Response.Write  "<tr>" & chr(13)
      Response.Write  "  <td width=""100"">  _
      <small>Please contact me:</small></td>" _
      & chr(13)
      Response.Write  "  <td width=""224"">  _
      <input type=""checkbox"" name= _
      ""contactme"" value=""ON"" tabindex= _
      ""8""></td>" & chr(13)
      Response.Write  "</tr>" & chr(13)
    end if
    Response.Write  "</table>" & chr(13)
end sub
%>
<%
sub FinishForm()
  Response.Write  "<p><input type=""submit"" _
  value=""Submit"" name=""Submit""   _
  tabindex=""99""></p>" & chr(13)
  Response.Write  "</form>" & chr(13)
  Response.Write "</td></tr></table>"
end sub
%>
<%
sub WriteValidation()
Response.Write "<script Language=""JavaScript"">" _
  & chr(13)
Response.write "function Validate(theForm)" _
  & chr(13)
Response.write "{" & chr(13)
if m_tfCategories = true then
    Response.Write "  var radioSelected = false;" _
```

```
            & chr(13)
      Response.Write " for (i = 0; _
       i < theForm.cat.length;  i++)" & chr(13)
      Response.Write " {" & chr(13)
      Response.Write "    if (theForm.cat[i] _
       .checked)" & chr(13)
      Response.Write "         radioSelected = _
       true;" & chr(13)
      Response.Write "  }" & chr(13)
      Response.Write "  if (!radioSelected)" _
        & chr(13)
      Response.Write "  {" & chr(13)
      Response.Write "    alert(""Please select _
       one of the categories."");" & chr(13)
      Response.Write "    return (false);" & chr(13)
      Response.Write "  }" & chr(13)
end if
Response.write "  if (theForm.name.value == _
 """")"  & chr(13)
Response.write "  {" & chr(13)
Response.write "    alert(""Please enter a name"")_
 ;" & chr(13)
Response.write "    theForm.name.focus();" & chr(13)
Response.write "    return (false);" & chr(13)
Response.write "  }" & chr(13)
Response.write "  if (theForm.email.value _
 == """")" & chr(13)
Response.write "  {" & chr(13)
Response.write "    alert(""Please enter your _
 email address."");" & chr(13)
Response.write "    theForm.email.focus();" _
 & chr(13)
Response.write "    return (false);" & chr(13)
Response.write "  }" & chr(13)
Response.write "  return (true);" & chr(13)
Response.write "  if (theForm.comment.value _
 == """")" & chr(13)
Response.write "  {" & chr(13)
Response.write "    alert(""Please enter your _
 comment."");" & chr(13)
Response.write "    theForm.comment.focus();" _
 & chr(13)
Response.write "    return (false);" & chr(13)
Response.write "  }" & chr(13)
```

```
Response.write "  return (true);" & chr(13)
Response.write "}" & chr(13)
Response.write "--></script>" & chr(13)
end sub
%>
</head>
<body>
<!--Webbot bot="Include" U-Include="navbar2.htm" _
 TAG="BODY" startspan --><strong>[navbar2.htm] _
 </strong><!--Webbot bot="Include" endspan _
 i-checksum="3991" -->

<%
 dim m_tfCategories
 dim m_tfInstructionsCategory
 dim m_tfInstructionsParent
 dim m_tfInstructionsLinkParent
 dim m_tfName
 dim m_tfEmail
 dim m_tfNewCategory
 dim m_tfNewLink
 dim m_tfURL
 dim m_tfDescription
 dim m_tfComment
 dim m_tfContact
 if len(Request.QueryString) > 0 then
    call ParseQueryString(Request.QueryString)
    m_iParent = Application("Parent")
 end if
 call WriteIntro()
 call DetermineWhichFieldsToUse( _
    m_tfCategories, _
    m_tfInstructionsCategory, _
    m_tfInstructionsParent, _
    m_tfInstructionsLinkParent, _
    m_tfName, _
    m_tfEmail, _
    m_tfNewCategory, _
    m_tfNewLink, _
    m_tfURL, _
    m_tfDescription, _
    m_tfComment, _
    m_tfContact)
 call CreateForm()
```

```
if m_tfCategories = true then
   call PaintCat()
end if
call WriteInfoPartOfForm(m_tfName, m_tfEmail, _
 m_tfNewCategory, m_tfNewLink, m_tfURL, _
 m_tfDescription, m_tfComment, m_tfContact)

call FinishForm()
call WriteValidation()
</body>
</html>
```

The images from the four preprocessor forms are shown in Figure 12-11 through Figure 12-14. The list of categories are there because the data was added to the database.

Figure 12-11   General Feedback Form

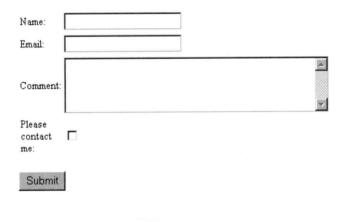

Figure 12-12 Category Feedback Form

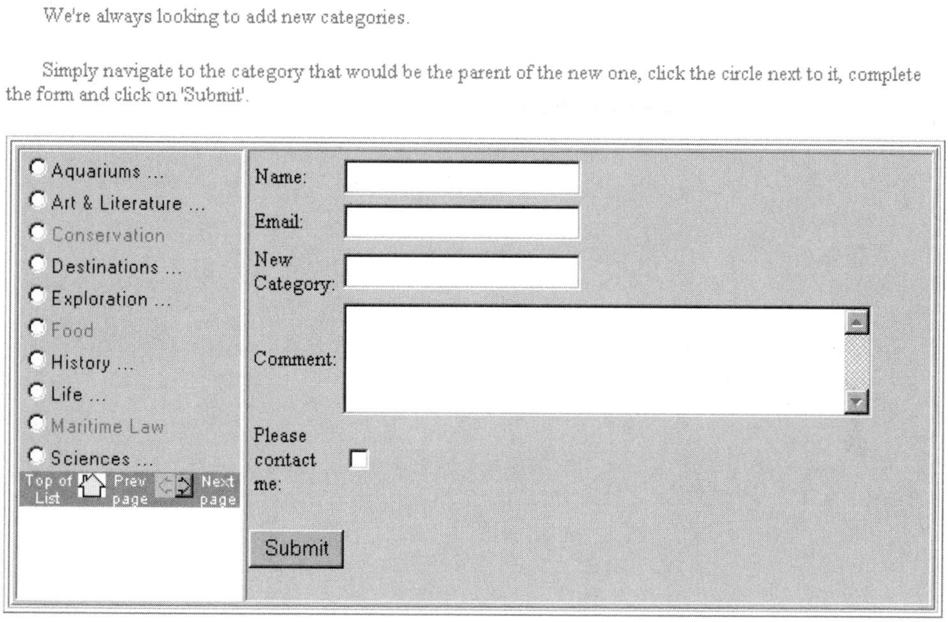
We're always looking to add new categories.
Simply navigate to the category that would be the parent of the new one, click the circle next to it, complete the form and click on 'Submit'.
Aquariums ...
Art & Literature ...
Conservation
Destinations ...
Exploration ...
Food
History ...
Life ...
Maritime Law
Sciences ...
Top of List
Prev page
Next page
Name:
Email:
New Category:
Comment:
Please contact me:
Submit

Figure 12-13 New Category Form

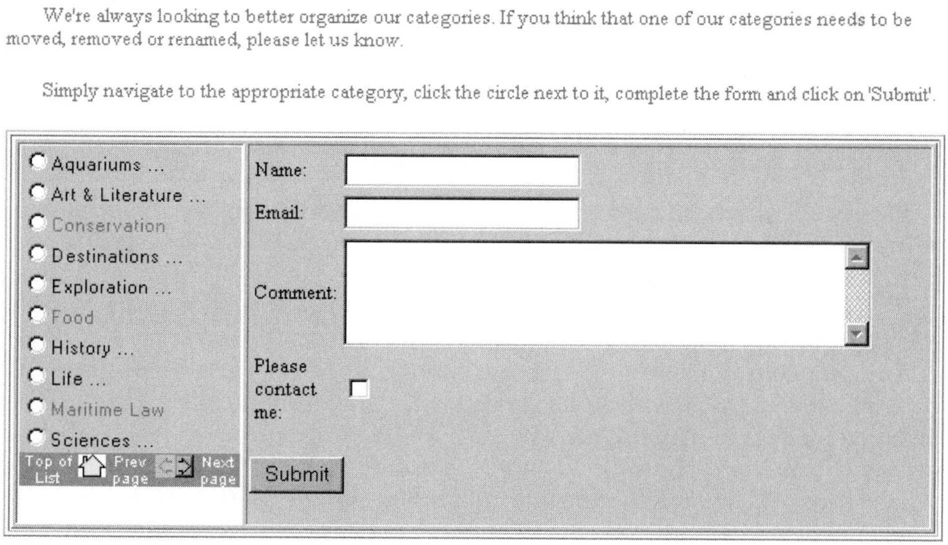
We're always looking to better organize our categories. If you think that one of our categories needs to be moved, removed or renamed, please let us know.
Simply navigate to the appropriate category, click the circle next to it, complete the form and click on 'Submit'.
Aquariums ...
Art & Literature ...
Conservation
Destinations ...
Exploration ...
Food
History ...
Life ...
Maritime Law
Sciences ...
Top of List
Prev page
Next page
Name:
Email:
Comment:
Please contact me:
Submit

Figure 12-14   New Link Form

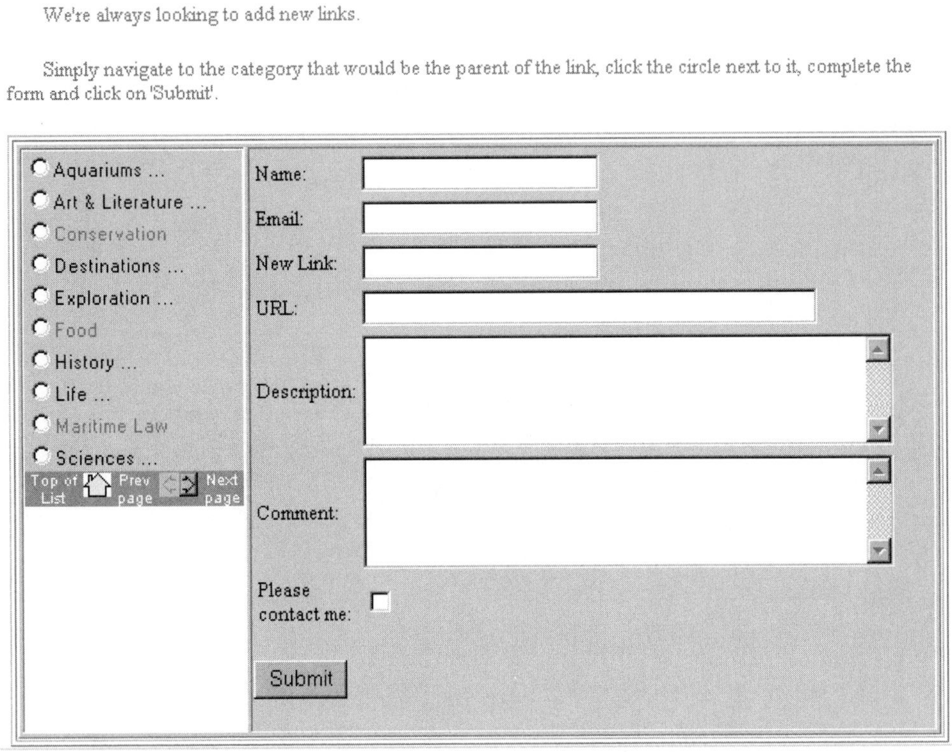

We're always looking to add new links.

Simply navigate to the category that would be the parent of the link, click the circle next to it, complete the form and click on 'Submit'.

12.4 Postprocessor

Once we've processed the form data, we're ready to do something with it. When we have more time, we can process the data directly into our database. On our first release though, we want to keep things as uncomplicated as possible. To that end, we'll take the data passed from the preprocessor, format it, and then send it in an email. We'll also thank the visitor for taking the time to provide the feedback.

The data coming into the postprocessor won't all be from the preprocessor. We'll also be taking data from *blink.asp* for broken links, and from *nominate.htm* for award nominations. It doesn't matter what Web page we accept data from so long as that page knows how to interface with us — knows what data to send.

Let's begin like we have been, by creating a new ASP file — *fbPostPro.asp*.

```
<%@ Language=VBScript %>
<html>
```

```
<head>
<title>Thank You</title>
<link REL="stylesheet" HREF="blowhole.css" _
 TYPE="text/css">
<!-- #Include file="sublib.inc"-->
</head>
<body>
<!--Webbot bot="Include" U-Include= _
 "navbar2.htm" TAG="BODY"-->
<p>
</body>
</html>
```

We threw in a paragraph break after the navigation banner, just to add a little more white space between it and the text the visitor reads. The first thing we want to do is clean up our old Application variables and pick up whatever parameter were sent to us.

```
<%
Application("name")=""
Application("email")=""
Application("newcategory")=""
Application("newlink")=""
Application("url")=""
Application("description")=""
Application("comment")=""
Application("contact")=""
Application("link")=""
%>

<%
'
'This section handles the sending of an email _
 message
' containing the feedback information.
'
call ParseQueryString(Request.Form)
```

Remember that we send the data from the preprocessor to here using the POST method. That means when we want to access that data, we use the *Request.Form* object instead of the *Request.QueryString*.

```
'
'We'll create a session variable for each item
' passed from the feedback form
```

```
strCRLF = chr(13) & chr(10)
```

This variable is set to contain the ASCII codes that form a new line. In the old days of teletypes, one code—a line-feed—was sent to them to cause the carriage to move up a line — the print to move down a line — and another, a carriage-return, to cause the carriage to move all the way to the right — the printing to begin at the left once more. When sending emails, printing reports, etc., a new paragraph is obtained by sending a carriage-return, ASCII code 13, followed by a line-feed, ASCII code 10.

The method of sending an email programmatically from a Web page depends on the service put in place by the Web hoster. It's not a standard technology. Although the mail *transport* typically is SMTP, the user service that allows the message to be sent varies as much as the software used by the recipients to obtain their email messages. The Blowhole's host uses *JMail*, a Java service. Although the general steps necessary for forming and sending a message should be similar for you, there most certainly will be differences.

We begin by creating a mail object:

```
Set JMail = Server.CreateObject("JMail.SMTPMail")
```

We then identify the name of the mail server that will perform the mail handling for us:

```
JMail.ServerAddress = "jmail.theblowhole.com:67"
JMail.AddHeader "Originating-IP", _
  Request.ServerVariables("REMOTE_ADDR")
```

Okay, with that stuff out of the way, it's time to build the email message itself. The first thing we'll do is identify who the message is from:

```
Jmail.Sender = fnSetEmailFROM()

<%
function fnSetEmailFROM()
  if len(Application("Name")) >= 5 then
     fnSetEmailFROM = Application("Email")
  else
     fnSetEmailFROM = "feedback@theblowhole.com"
  end if
end function
%>
```

What we've done is check whether the visitor has supplied an email address. If so, we'll identify him as the sender, since he is the one providing the feedback; otherwise we'll identify the site as the sender. The reason we check the *Name* variable for a length >= 5 is that the smallest email address one can have is of the form x@x.x — five characters. Now we'll identify who the message is to:

```
JMail.AddRecipient "info@theblowhole.com"
```

Next up is the subject. This will be dependent on the type of feedback.

```
JMail.Subject = fnSetEmailSUBJECT()

<%
function fnSetEmailSUBJECT()
 select case Application("feedbackcode")
    case "general": l_iFeedbackType = _
     "General Feedback"
    case "category": l_iFeedbackType = _
     "Category Feedback"
    case "newcategory": l_iFeedbackType = _
     "New Category Request"
    case "newlink": l_iFeedbackType = _
     "New Link Request"
    case "award": l_iFeedbackType = _
     "Award Nomination"
    case "brokenlink": l_iFeedbackType = _
     "Broken Link"
    case else: l_iFeedbackType = _
     "Unknown Feedback Type"
 end select
 fnSetEmailSUBJECT = _
   "The Blowhole " & l_iFeedbackType
end function
%>
```

You might not know this, but email can have a priority assigned to it. If you don't specify one, your mail is sent with normal priority, but most email systems treat urgent mail differently, and actually process it first. We're going to determine the priority based on the type of feedback.

```
JMail.Priority = fnSetEmailPRIORITY

<%
function SetEmailPRIORITY()
' 1 - highest priority (Urgent)
' 3 - normal
' 5 - lowest
 if Application("FeedbackCode") = "brokenlink" _
```

```
      then
         SetEmailPRIORITY = 1
      else
         SetEmailPRIORITY = 3
      end if
   end function
   %>
```

Now let's create the body of the message:

```
   call CreateMessageBody()
```

```
<%
Sub CreateMessageBody()
   dim l_strTemp
   JMail.Body = "The following feedback was _
   received from The Blowhole Site"
   JMail.AppendText strCRLF
   JMail.AppendText strCRLF
   for each item in Request.Form
       l_strTemp = Request.Form(item)
       if item = "description" then l_strTemp = _
        fnBlanks(Request.Form(item))
       if (ValidateParm(item)) then
          JMail.AppendText item & ": "
          JMail.AppendText Request.Form(item)
          JMail.AppendText chr(13) & chr(10)
       end if
   next
end sub
%>
```

We need to create the function *fnBlanks* referred to in this function. When we passed the description of the link site as a parameter, we removed the blanks in it (since HTTP truncates following a blank) and replaced them with the string "%20." We now need to put the blanks back before we send the string out in an email message.

```
<%
function fnBlanks(l_strSource)
'
' This routine changes %20 in a string to blanks
'   to keep HTTP happy
'
   dim l_strDest
```

```
dim l_strByte
l_strDest = ""
if len(l_strSource) > 0 then
    for i = 1 to len(l_strSource) - 2
        l_strBytes =  mid(l_strSource,i,3)
        if l_strBytes = "%20" then
            l_strDest = l_strDest & " "
            i = i + 2
        else
          l_strDest = l_strDest & left(l_strBytes,1)
        end if
    next
 if i < len(l_strSource) then l_strDest = _
  l_strDest  & right(l_strSource, 2)
 end if
 fnBlanks = l_strDest
end function
%>
```

The call to *ValidateParm* results in a TRUE or FALSE value based on whether it's a known item that we want put in the email message — there can be some residual information passed in form processing that we choose to ignore. Let's create the function to check.

```
<%
Function ValidateParm(l_strItem)
 select case l_strItem
    case "name": iRet = true
    case "email": iRet = true
    case "newcategory": iRet = true
    case "cat": iRet = true
    case "newlink": iRet = true
    case "url": iRet = true
    case "description": iRet = true
    case "comment": iRet = true
    case "contact": iRet = true
    case else: iRet = false
 end select
 ValidateParm = iRet

end function
%>and now we'll send the message
```

and now we'll send the message

```
    JMail.Execute
%>
```

Okay, we've sent the email message, but we still have something to do, because the users are sitting there looking at a blank browser window right now. Let's say something to them.

```
<p align="center"><big><big> _
 Thank you for taking the time to provide us with _
 your feedback</big></big></p>
```

That's it. That wasn't too bad, was it? Let's take a look at the entire page of code, and then move on to handling broken links.

```
<%@ Language=VBScript %>
<html>
<head>
<title>Thank You</title>
<link REL="stylesheet" HREF="blowhole.css" _
 TYPE="text/css">
<!-- #Include file="sublib.inc"-->
<%
function fnSetEmailFROM()
 if len(Application("Name"))>= 5 then
    fnSetEmailFROM = Application("Email")
 else
    fnSetEmailFROM = "feedback@theblowhole.com"
 end if
end function
%>
<%
<%
function fnSetEmailSUBJECT()
 select case Application("feedbackcode")
    case "general": l_iFeedbackType = _
     "General Feedback"
    case "category": l_iFeedbackType = _
     "Category Feedback"
    case "newcategory": l_iFeedbackType = _
     "New Category Request"
    case "newlink": l_iFeedbackType = _
     "New Link Request"
```

```
      case "award": l_iFeedbackType = _
        "Award Nomination"
      case "brokenlink": l_iFeedbackType = _
        "Broken Link"
      case else: l_iFeedbackType = _
        "Unknown Feedback Type"
  end select
  fnSetEmailSUBJECT = _
    "The Blowhole " & l_iFeedbackType
end function
%>
<%
function SetEmailPRIORITY()
' 1 - highest priority (Urgent)
' 3 - normal
' 5 - lowest
  if Application("FeedbackCode") = "brokenlink" _
    then
      SetEmailPRIORITY = 1
  else
      SetEmailPRIORITY = 3
  end if
end function
%>
<%
function fnBlanks(l_strSource)
'
' This routine changes %20 in a string to blanks
'  to keep HTTP happy
'
  dim l_strDest
  dim l_strByte
  l_strDest = ""
  if len(l_strSource) > 0 then
      for i = 1 to len(l_strSource) - 2
          l_strBytes =  mid(l_strSource,i,3)
          if l_strBytes = "%20" then
              l_strDest = l_strDest & " "
              i = i + 2
          else
            l_strDest = l_strDest & left(l_strBytes,1)
          end if
      next
  if i < len(l_strSource) then l_strDest = _
```

```
        l_strDest & right(l_strSource, 2)
    end if
    fnBlanks = l_strDest
end function
%>
<%
Sub CreateMessageBody()
    dim l_strTemp
    JMail.Body = "The following feedback was _
     received from The Blowhole Site"
    JMail.AppendText strCRLF
    JMail.AppendText strCRLF
    for each item in Request.Form
        l_strTemp = Request.Form(item)
        if item = "description" then l_strTemp = _
         fnBlanks(Request.Form(item))
         JMail.AppendText item & ": "
         JMail.AppendText Request.Form(item)
         JMail.AppendText chr(13) & chr(10)
    next
end sub
%>
</head>
<body>
<!--Webbot bot="Include" U-Include= _
  "navbar2.htm" TAG="BODY"-->
<p>

<%
Application("name")=""
Application("email")=""
Application("newcategory")=""
Application("newlink")=""
Application("url")=""
Application("description")=""
Application("comment")=""
Application("contact")=""
Application("link")=""
%>
<%
'
'This section handles the sending of an email _
  message
' containing the feedback information.
```

```
'
'
'We'll create a session variable for each item
' passed from the feedback form
'

call ParseQueryString(Request.Form)
strCRLF = chr(13) & chr(10)
Set JMail = Server.CreateObject("JMail.SMTPMail")
JMail.ServerAddress = "mail.theblowhole.com:25"
JMail.AddHeader "Originating-IP", _
  Request.ServerVariables("REMOTE_ADDR")
Jmail.Sender = fnSetEmailFROM()
JMail.AddRecipient "info@theblowhole.com"
JMail.Subject = fnSetEmailSUBJECT()
JMail.Priority = fnSetEmailPRIORITY
call CreateMessageBody()
JMail.Execute
%>
<p align="center">
<big>
<big>
Thank you for taking the time to provide us _
  with your feedback
</big>
</big>
</p>
</body>
</html>
```

12.5 Broken Links

Gosh but people hate broken links. Don't you? You finally find the link you want, click on it, and receive the dreaded 404 error. We can't easily stop that from happening, because five minutes after we verify that one of a thousand links is still valid, the site owner can change the link's location and the link is then broken. When we have broken links, we want the visitor to let us know.

Earlier, we designed *redirect.asp* to create two Session variables for us, one to hold the link URL and the other to hold the link description. If the visitor clicks on the broken link icon, *blink.asp* will be launched. We'll access the two Session variables, and let the visitor review the information and decide whether it should be submitted to our Webmaster. Let's create the skeleton for *blink.asp*.

```
<html>
<head>
<title>The Blowhole Broken Link Report</title>
</head>
<body>
</body>
</html>
```

In this case we won't include the navigation bar, because when the visitor clicks on the broken link icon, a new window is opened. If she decides not to submit the broken link report, she can simply close the window.

Let's put in the routine to keep the blanks out of our link description:

```
function fnNoBlanks(l_strSource)
'
' This routine changes blanks in a string to %20
'   to keep HTTP happy
'
 dim l_strDest
 dim l_strByte
 l_strDest = ""
 if len(l_strSource) > 0 then
    for i = 1 to len(l_strSource)
        l_strByte =  mid(l_strSource,i,1)
        if l_strByte = chr(32) then
           l_strDest = l_strDest & "%20"
        else
           l_strDest = l_strDest & l_strByte
        end if
    next
 end if
 fnNoBlanks = l_strDest
end function
%>
```

We'll be doing something a little different on this page, and that is using in-line script in our HTML instead of generating the HTML. The only reason for this is that the quantity of HTML is greater than that of script.

```
<p>
<font size=4>
You have requested that the following _
 link be reported as broken:
</font>
```

```
</p>
<p>
 <font face=Arial>Name:
  <font color="red">
   <% = Session("LinkDesc")%>
  </font>
  <br>
  URL:
  <font color="red">
   <% = Session("LastLink")%>
  </font>
 </font>
</p>
<p>
If this is correct, click the
<strong>Report</strong>
 button, otherwise just close this window.
</p>
```

You can see in the preceding lines that we can throw a line of script, called a "snippet" or "scriptlet," just about anywhere in our code so long as we put the server script designators (<% and %>) around it.

We've now presented the information to the visitor; let's provide a form to use. You're thinking, "Hey, I thought we created *redirect.asp* to store this information because we didn't want to ask the visitor to fill in a form." Yes — and hold that thought. Here's the form:

```
<form Method="post" Action="fbPostpro.asp">
<input Type="hidden" Name="feedbackcode" _
 Value="brokenlink">
<input Type="hidden" Name="link" _
 Value = <% =fnNoBlanks(Session("LastLink"))%>>
<input Type="hidden" Name="description" _
 Value = <% =fnNoBlanks(Session("LinkDesc"))%>>
<input Type="submit" Value="Report">
</form>
```

If you look closely at the form you'll see that the only user control on the form is the *submit* button. The rest of the information is stuff we'll need for processing, which is contained in hidden fields that the visitor won't have to interact with. Here then is the completed page:

```
<html>
<head>
```

```
<title>The Blowhole Broken Link Report</title>
function fnNoBlanks(l_strSource)
'
' This routine changes blanks in a string to %20
'  to keep HTTP happy
'
 dim l_strDest
 dim l_strByte
 l_strDest = ""
 if len(l_strSource) > 0 then
    for i = 1 to len(l_strSource)
        l_strByte =  mid(l_strSource,i,1)
        if l_strByte = chr(32) then
           l_strDest = l_strDest & "%20"
        else
           l_strDest = l_strDest & l_strByte
        end if
    next
 end if
 fnNoBlanks = l_strDest
end function
%>
</head>
<body>
<p>
<font size=4>
You have requested that the following _
 link be reported as broken:
</font>
</p>
<p>
 <font face=Arial>Name:
  <font color="red">
   <% = Session("LinkDesc")%>
  </font>
  <br>
  URL:
  <font color="red">
   <% = Session("LastLink")%>
  </font>
 </font>
</p>
<p>
If this is correct, click the
```

```
<strong>Report</strong>
 button, otherwise just close this window.
</p>
<form Method="post" Action="fbPostpro.asp">
<input Type="hidden" Name="feedbackcode" _
 Value="brokenlink">
<input Type="hidden" Name="link" _
 Value = <% =fnNoBlanks(Session("LastLink"))%>>
<input Type="hidden" Name="description" _
 Value = <% =fnNoBlanks(Session("LinkDesc"))%>>
<input Type="submit" Value="Report">
</form>
</body>
</html>
```

We need to add a line to our postprocessor so that it won't "throw away" the information coming from our form:

```
case "contact": iRet = true

case "link": iRet = true

case else: iRet = false
```

and we're done.

12.6 Award Nomination

Back when we designed the Web site, I was under the impression that the award nomination page would be sufficiently different from the other types of feedback. As it sometimes turns out in software development, my assumptions were flawed. Since we presented the award graphics on the *Awards* page, we don't need to show them again. So the selection can be simplified and will fit nicely into a form. Therefore, we can simply add a few lines here and there to *fbPrePro.asp* and *fpPostPro.asp*, and we're done. The first thing we'll do is add an entry to the *WriteIntro* routine, which writes some introductory text based on the feedback code.

```
case "nomination":
   Response.Write "<p class=""bodytext""> _
    The Blowhole wants to award merit in _
    marine topic Web sites to help promote _
    those sites, and to encourage site _
    excellence.</p>"
```

```
Response.Write "<p class=""bodytext"">  _
Please select the award you feel _
applies and provide the other _
information.</p>"
```

Next, we'll add the field selections to *DetermineWhichFieldsToUse.*

```
case "nomination":
    l_tfCategories = false
    l_tfInstructionsCategory = false
    l_tfInstructionsParent = false
    l_tfInstructionsLinkParent = false
    l_tfName = true
    l_tfEmail = true
    l_tfNewCategory = false
    l_tfNewLink = false
    l_tfURL = true
    l_tfDescription = true
    l_tfComment = true
    l_tfContact = false
    l_tfAwards = true
```

The last assignment statement is based on a new form field, so we'll have to add a line setting this variable to *false* to the other feedback types in this routine as well as to the routine declaration, the line that calls the routine, and the list of variable declarations.

We'll move now to *WriteInfoPartOfForm*, which generates the HTML for each form field, and add the HTML for the award selection control.

```
if l_tfAwards = true then
    Response.Write  "<tr>" & chr(13)
    Response.Write  "  <td witdh=""100""> _
    <small>Award:</small></td>" & chr(13)
    Response.Write  "<" & "!--Webbot bot= _
    ""Validation"" startspan S-Display-Name= _
    ""Award"" B-Value-Required=""TRUE"" --> _
    <" & "!--Webbot bot=""Validation""  _
    endspan -->" & chr(13)
    Response.Write  "  <td width=""224""> _
    <select name=""award"" size=""20""  _
    tabindex=""10"">" & chr(13)
    Response.Write  "  <option value= _
    Spouting>Spouting Excellence</option>" _
    & chr(13)
    Response.Write  "  <option value= _
    Conservation>Conservation Excellence _
```

```
      </option>" & chr(13)
      Response.Write  "  <option value=Design> _
      Web Design Excellence</option>" & chr(13)
      Response.Write  "  <option value= _
      Content> Web Content Excellence _
      </option>" & chr(13)
      Response.Write "  </select></td></tr>"  _
      & chr(13)
```

The next place we need to make a change is in the routine *Write Validation* that generates the JavaScript for the form validation.

```
if l_tfAwards = true then
   Response.Write "  if (theForm.award.value  _
   == """")"  & chr(13)
   Response.Write "  {" & chr(13)
   Response.Write "    alert(""Please select  _
   an award"");" & chr(13)
   Response.Write "    theForm.award.focus();"  _
   & chr(13)
   Response.Write "    return (false);" & chr(13)
   Response.Write "  }" & chr(13)
end if
```

That's all the change we need to make for *fbPrePro.asp*. Let's make two changes to the postprocessor. We need to change the *ValidateParm* function to recognize our new feedback type:

```
      case "award": iRet = true
```

and we also need to add the initialization of the corresponding Application variable to the list:

```
Application("award")=""
```

Well, that's it. Our feedback suite is now complete. Figure 12-15 shows our Awards Nomination feedback form. With that done, we're ready to move on to the *Help* page. See you in Chapter 13.

Figure 12-15   Award Nomination Form

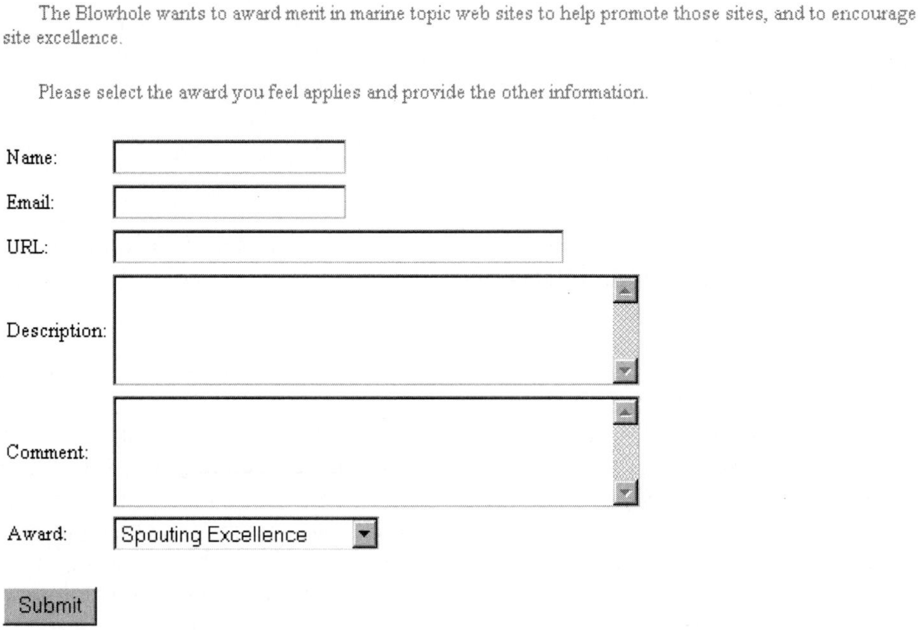

The Blowhole wants to award merit in marine topic web sites to help promote those sites, and to encourage site excellence.

Please select the award you feel applies and provide the other information.

Name:

Email:

URL:

Description:

Comment:

Award: Spouting Excellence

Submit

Help!

We've created what I'd view as an intuitive design for our site. But no matter how many studies you do before you design the user interface, it will end up catering to either the majority or the lowest common denominator, and that leaves room for the thoroughly confused.

With the *Help* page we hope to be able to steer the confused through using the site. What we're going to do is create a two-framed page. One frame will contain an image of the main page. When the visitor's mouse is moved over a functional area of the "main page," the other frame will display information about the use of that functional area.

We'll begin by creating the skeleton for this page in FrontPage, using the frames dialog that we used for the *Feedback* page. We're going to choose a different layout this time. From the *FrontPage Editor* we'll select the *New* command from the *File* menu, and then select *Frames*. This time we're going to select a *Header* template. As you can see in the Preview Pane in Figure 13-1, this template gives us a layout of one frame atop another, with the larger one on the bottom.

Since Web pages grow downwards, the top frame will remain constant in size, and the bottom frame grows to accommodate the content. Let's click *OK*, and FrontPage will put us into the Normal view of our new frames page. The top frame, *header*, will contain the text we use for explanations. We'll get to that later. We'll start working with the bottom frame, *main*. This frame will contain the image of our main page — flash — we need an image of the main page.

Let's fire up Paint Shop Pro. From the *Capture* menu we'll select *Setup*. This gives us the Capture Setup dialog (see Figure 13-2). We want to capture our browser window, so we'll select *Window*. You can choose whatever "hot key" you want to initiate the screen capture; I typically use the F11 key, since I seldom use it for anything else. I also typically keep the capture configuration set for multiple captures, so that Paint Shop Pro doesn't pop up when I've done my capture. With our settings in place, we can click on

Capture Now. Next, we need to launch our browser and bring up the main page of our development site. We want the entire page to show, so we might need to go into the *View* menu of our browser and start freeing up real estate by shutting off toolbars until the entire page is viewable. When we can see all of it, we'll click the "hot key" we selected earlier, and then bring up the Paint Shop Pro (PSP) window to find an image of our page. Crop the image so that only the Web page is showing and no browser stuff.

Figure 13-1   New Frames Dialogue

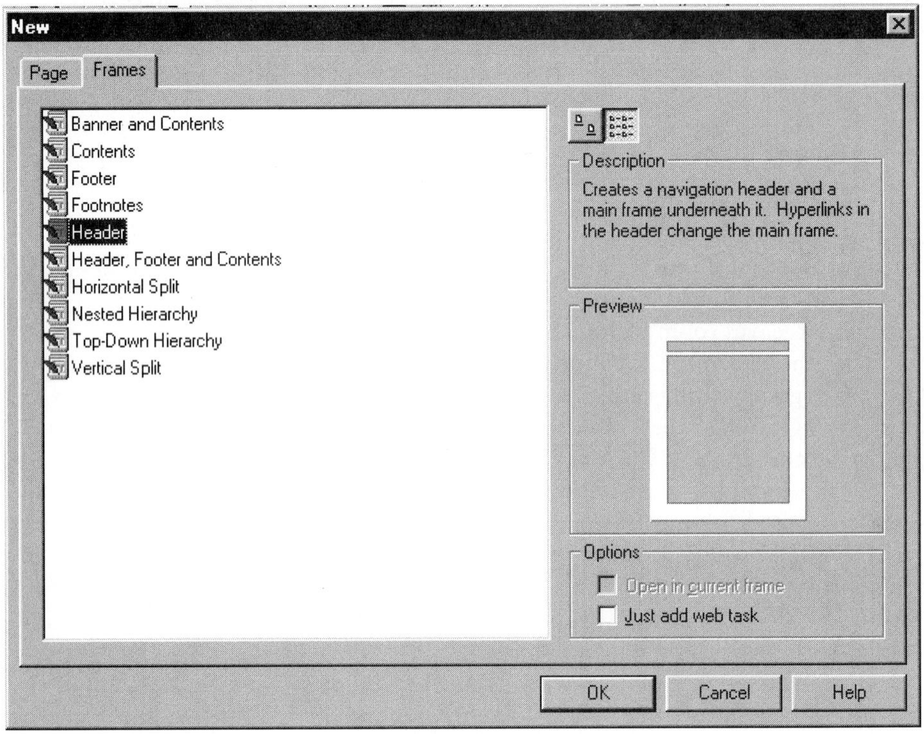

It would be nice if the entire image would fit in the browser window when the user selects help. Since we have no control over the client system, the one virtually foolproof way to get it to fit is to make sure it's no more than 600 pixels wide, since this dimension fits in almost every monitor being used. Most support 640, but we need to leave room for the browser's window borders and so forth.

Let's select the *Resize* command from the *Image* menu. We'll want to select the *Pixel Size* option, and put 600 in as the width. As long as the box next to *Maintain Aspect Ration of* is checked, *PSP* will automatically provide the size for the height. The only other setting we need to make is for the *Resize Type*. The best setting for this type of graphic is *Bicubic Resample*. The settings are shown in Figure 13-3. Click *OK* and it will be resized. It may look a bit odd wen the resizing has completed. Look up at the title bar of the window next to the file name (which is probably Image1 at this point). Does it show "1:2"?

Figure 13-2 — Preparing for a Screen Capture

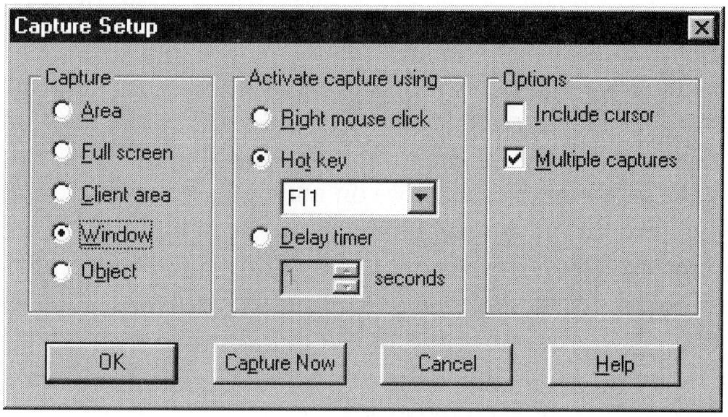

Capture Setup

Capture
- Area
- Full screen
- Client area
- Window
- Object

Activate capture using
- Right mouse click
- Hot key
  - F11
- Delay timer
  - seconds

Options
- Include cursor
- Multiple captures

OK   Capture Now   Cancel   Help

Figure 13-3 — Resizing an Image

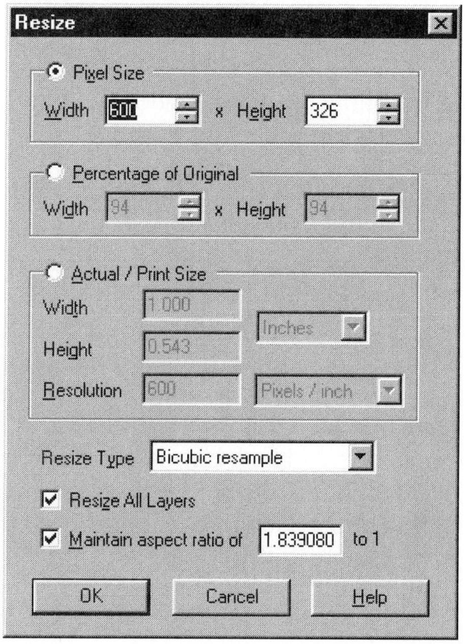

Resize

Pixel Size
- Width 600 x Height 326

Percentage of Original
- Width 94 x Height 94

Actual / Print Size
- Width 1.000
- Height 0.543
- Resolution 600   Inches   Pixels / inch

Resize Type   Bicubic resample

Resize All Layers

Maintain aspect ratio of 1.839080 to 1

OK   Cancel   Help

Once a resize operation has been performed, PSP sometimes zooms out on the graphic, showing it at 50% (1:2) view or less. If that's happened, just click on the *View* menu and select *1:1* and it will look much better.

We're ready to save the image. Save it as a .gif file, and name it *screencap*. Now we'll close *PSP* and go back to *FrontPage Editor*. In the bottom 'pane' of our frames page, let's click on *New Page* to get a blank page. Then, we'll select the *Image* command from the *Insert* menu, and insert our *screencap.gif*.

With our image in place, let's click on it. Doing so causes the *image toolbar* to appear at the bottom of the screen (see Figure 13-4). The rectangle, circle and polygon on the left of the toolbar are used for drawing on an image, and the drawn shape becomes a clickable region. Drawing multiple shapes on an image makes it an image map, and that's what we're going to do to our image. One thing to keep in mind about drawing the clickable regions is that each time you draw one, a dialog box will appear to prompt you for the hyperlink information, the location you want to go to when the region you just drew is clicked. We don't have that information yet. So why are we drawing the regions now? Because seeing them on the image will help us to gather the hyperlink information, and then we can go back and edit each hyperlink.

Figure 13-4   FrontPage's Image Toolbar

We'll start at the top left of the image, and work our way around the image drawing rectangular regions on every element with which the visitor might interact this were the real Web page. Every time we draw an image, a dialog box will appear. We'll cancel out of the dialog box, and then select the rectangular tool again. We can use the circular tool to draw a region around the copyright symbol. Figure 13-5 shows the completed effort.

We'll take this image and create a separate Web page that contains the help text. Each item in this page will be a separate paragraph, and each paragraph will be "bookmarked." We'll do this because we can specify that the Web page be displayed in our upper frame *starting at a specific bookmark*! Thus, we can jump around to different sections in the same file; this allows us to accomplish what we need, with only one file holding the help text. Let's create that file.

We'll click on *New Page* to get a blank canvas. At the moment there isn't much canvas space to work with. Let's drag the divider between the two frames downward until the line bisects the navigation banner. Now, we're going to switch to the HTML view for a moment. Here's what FrontPage provided for us:

Figure 13-5   Creating Hot-Spots

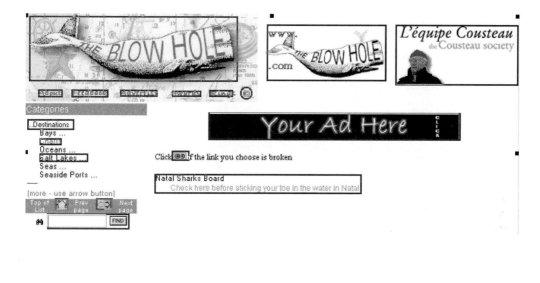

```
<html>
<head>
<title>The Blowhole Help Header</title>
<meta name="GENERATOR" content= _
 "Microsoft FrontPage 3.0">
<base target="main">
</head>
<body>
<h2>test</h2>
</body>
</html>
```

We'll change the title to *The Blowhole Help Information*. The *base target* tag specifies that any hyperlink clicked on the page will default to sending the resulting content to the main frame. This is normal functionality for the frame layout that we've selected, but not what we want. We want just the opposite, for clicks on the image regions in the *main* frame to cause a change to the *head* frame. Let's cut this line, paste it in the same place in the lower frame, and change the "main" to "head."

We're going to create a couple styles in our *head* frame, one for each heading section, the other for the body text. If we ever decide to use the styles in more than one page, we'll add them to our Cascading Style Sheet.

```
<style>
<!--
H2          {color: olive; font-family: arial; _
             font-size: 14pt; letter-spacing: 2px}
.clsHelp {margin-left: 1.5in; font-size: 9px}
-->
</style>
```

It's worth noting that when we start entering text and assigning these styles to it, certain style attributes such as *font-family* and *color* won't appear in the *Normal* view of the FrontPage Editor, but this will in the *Preview* view. Following is the text we need to enter (text shown in italics will have the *H2* format assigned to it, the rest will have *clsHelp*):

```
The Logo
Clicking on the sperm whale logo will return you to
the main page from all other pages.
     About
Clicking here brings you to the page that describes
The Blowhole
     Feedback
Clicking here brings you to a page from which you
can provide general feedback, feedback on an existing
category, recommendations for new categories or links,
or nominate a site to receive one of our rewards.
     Advertise
Clicking here brings you to a page that describes
the advertising opportunities and prices at The Blow-
hole.
     Awards
Clicking here brings you to a page that describes
the awards that The Blowhole presents, and shows those
that we've won.
     Rings
Clicking here brings you to a page that gives you
access to a number of Web rings, banners that when
clicked will take you to other sites of a singular
topic.
     Copyright
Clicking here brings you to a page that defines the
copyright on site elements.
     Commercial Billboard
```

This is a billboard for commercial advertising that is available for monthly rental.

Non-Profit Rotating Billboard

This is a rotating billboard on which non-profit organizations receive free advertising.

Commercial Rotating Billboard

This is a rotating billboard on which commercial organizations can purchase advertising space

Broken Link

Click here if you try a link and it turns out to be broken. The information will be sent to us and we'll investigate it.

Links

We are constantly searching for good links that apply to the categories we list. Whenever you click on a category that has links associated with it, they will appear here. Click on them to open a window to the site they describe.

Parent Category

When you click on a category, it moves to the top of the list, and its children are then indented below it, much like clicking on a directory in a directory tree. Clicking on this parent category (preceded by ...) will return you to the list you found it in when you clicked it.

Childless Categories

If a category has no information to drill down to, no child categories and no links, then it is listed but can not be clicked.

Child Categories

If a child category has links associated with it, it is clickable. If it has children itself, its name is appended with "..."

Top of List (Home)

When the home icon is colored, it is clickable, and clicking it will rewind the category list to the beginning.

Previous Page

When the arrow pointing to the left is colored, the current list of categories is not the first page of this level (the parent shown has more children than are showing). Clicking will list the previous page.

Next Page

When the arrow pointing to the right is colored, the

```
current list of categories is not the final page of
this level (the parent shown has more children than are
showing). Clicking will list the next page.
     Find
     If you don't want to navigate the categories, you
can enter a keyword in this box and click 'find' and
all categories containing that word will be presented.
```

That's all the text. What we need to do now is select each of the headings, choose *Bookmark* from the *Edit* menu, and add a bookmark name, typically a word from the highlighted text. The bookmark dialog can be seen in Figure 13-6.

Now we need to go back to *helpmain.htm* and add the links to the hot spots we drew on the image. We'll click on the image to make the hot spots show, and then click on one of them, such as the one over the logo. Then we'll select *Hyperlink* from the *Edit* menu. We'll enter *helphead.htm* as the URL (remove the HTTP://). The destination frame will show *head* as the default. In the bookmark area, if we drop down the list box you'll see that the bookmarks we defined on that page are now listed, so we can simply select the bookmark that goes with the block of text we want this hyperlink to lead to (see Figure 13-7).

Once all hyperlinks are defined, we'll want to go to the HTML view and paste "head" at the end of each hyperlink. Following is the code for the frames page, the *head* frame and the *main* frame.

```
<html>
<head>
<title>The Blowhole Help</title>
<meta name="GENERATOR" content= _
  "Microsoft FrontPage 3.0">
</head>
<frameset rows="136,*">
  <frame name="head" noresize src= _
    "helphead.htm" target="main">
  <frame name="main" src="helpmain.htm" _
    target="head">
  <noframes>
  <body>
  <p>This page uses frames, but your browser _
      doesn't support them.</p>
  </body>
  </noframes>
</frameset>
</html>
```

Figure 13-6   Adding a Bookmark

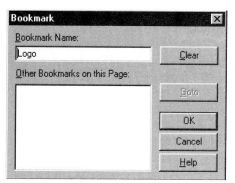

Figure 13-7   Selecting a Hyperlinked Bookmark

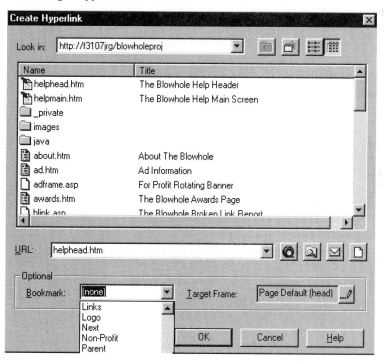

```
<html>
<head>
<title>The Blowhole Help Header</title>
<meta name="GENERATOR" content= _
 "Microsoft FrontPage 3.0">
<style>
<!--
H2         {color: olive; font-family: arial; _
           font-size: 14pt; letter-spacing: 2px}
.clsHelp {margin-left: 1.5in; font-size: 16px}
-->
</style>
<base target="main">
</head>
<body>
Click items on the image below for a description.
<h2><a name="Logo">The Logo</a></h2>
<p class="clsHelp">Clicking on the sperm whale _
 logo will return you to the main page from all _
 other pages.</p>
<h2><a name="About">About</a></h2>
<p class="clsHelp">Clicking here brings you to _
 the page that describes The Blowhole</p>
<h2><a name="Feedback">Feedback</a></h2>
<p class="clsHelp">Clicking here brings you to _
 a page from which you can provide general _
 feedback, feedback on an existing category, _
 recommendations for new categories or links, _
 or nominate a site to receive one of our  _
 rewards.</p>
<h2><a name="Advertise">Advertise</a></h2>
<p class="clsHelp">Clicking here brings you to _
 a page that describes the advertising _
 opportunities and prices at The Blowhole.</p>
<h2><a name="Awards">Awards</a></h2>
<p class="clsHelp">Clicking here brings you to _
a page that describes the awards that The
Blowhole presents, and shows those that we've _
won.</p>
<h2><a name="Rings">Rings</a></h2>
<p class="clsHelp">Clicking here brings you to _
 a page that gives you access to a number of _
 Web rings, banners that when clicked will take _
 you to other sites of a singular topic.</p>
```

```
<h2><a name="Copyright">Copyright</a></h2>
<p class="clsHelp">Clicking here brings you to _
 a page that defines the copyright on site _
 elements.</p>
<h2><a name="Commercial">Commercial Billboard _
 </a></h2>
<p class="clsHelp">This is a billboard for _
 commercial advertising that is available for _
 monthly rental.</p>
<h2><a name="Non-Profit">Non-Profit Rotating _
 Billboard</a></h2>
<p class="clsHelp">This is a rotating billboard _
 on which non-profit organizations receive
 free advertising.</p>
<h2>Commercial <a name="Rotating">Rotating _
 Billboard</a></h2>
<p class="clsHelp">This is a rotating billboard _
 on which commercial organizations can purchase _
 advertising space</p>
<h2><a name="Broken">Broken Link</a></h2>
<p class="clsHelp">Click here if you try a link _
 and it turns out to be broken. The information _
 will be sent to us and we'll investigate it.</p>
<h2><a name="Links">Links</a></h2>
<p class="clsHelp">We are constantly searching _
 for good links that apply to the categories _
 we list. Whenever you click on a category that _
 has links associated with it, they will appear _
 here. Click on them to open a window to the _
 site they describe.</p>
<h2><a name="Parent">Parent Category</a></h2>
<p class="clsHelp">When you click on a category, _
 it moves to the top of the list, and its _
 children are then indented below it, much like _
 clicking on a directory in a directory tree. _
 Clicking on this parent category (preceded _
 by ...) will return you to the list you found _
 it in when you clicked it.</p>
<h2><a name="Childless">Childless Categories</a>
</h2>
<p class="clsHelp">If a category has no _
 information to drill down to, no child _
 categories and no links, then it is listed but _
 can not be clicked.</p>
```

```
<h2><a name="Child">Child Categories</a></h2>
<p class="clsHelp">If a child category has _
 links associated with it, it is clickable. If _
 it has children itself, its name is appended  _
 with "..."</p>
<h2><a name="Top">Top of List (Home)</a></h2>
<p class="clsHelp">When the home icon is colored, _
 it is clickable, and clicking it will rewind _
 the category list to the beginning.</p>
<h2><a name="Previous">Previous Page</a></h2>
<p class="clsHelp">When the arrow pointing to _
 the left is colored, the current list of _
 categories is not the first page of this level _
 (the parent shown has more children than are _
 showing). Clicking will list the previous page.</p>
<h2><a name="Next">Next Page</a></h2>
<p class="clsHelp">When the arrow pointing to _
 the right is colored, the current list of _
 categories is not the final page of this level _
 (the parent shown has more children than are _
 showing). Clicking will list the next page.</p>
<h2><a name="Find">Find</a></h2>
<p class="clsHelp">If you don&#146;t want to _
 navigate the categories, you can enter a keyword _
 in this box and click 'find' and all _
 categories containing that word will be _
 presented.</p>
</body>
</html>

<html>
<head>
<title>The Blowhole Help Main Screen</title>
<meta name="GENERATOR" content= _
 "Microsoft FrontPage 3.0">
<base target="head">
<meta name="Microsoft Border" content="none">
</head>
<body>
<p>
<!--Webbot bot="ImageMap" rectangle= _
 "(96,222) (107, 230)  helphead.htm#Next#head" _
 rectangle="(24,232) (131, 252)   _
 helphead.htm#Find#head"
```

```
rectangle="(86,219) (96, 234)    _
helphead.htm#Previous#head"
rectangle="(154,187) (421, 212)    _
helphead.htm#Links#head"
rectangle="(38,216) (56, 231)    _
helphead.htm#Top#head"
rectangle="(209,114) (535, 149)  _
helphead.htm#Rotating#head"
rectangle="(179,160) (202, 173) )  _
helphead.htm#Broken#head"
rectangle="(15,173) (78, 184)    _
helphead.htm#Child#head"
rectangle="(20,145) (49, 154)    _
helphead.htm#Childless#head"
rectangle="(4,123) (65, 137)  _
helphead.htm#Parent#head"
circle="(269,93) 8  helphead.htm#  _
Copyright#head"
rectangle="(225,89) (256, 98)    _
helphead.htm#Rings#head"
rectangle="(178,89) (216, 97)    _
helphead.htm#Awards#head"
rectangle="(114,89) (163, 98)   _
helphead.htm#Advertise#head"
rectangle="(54,88) (102, 98)    _
helphead.htm#Feedback#head"
rectangle="(17,88) (49, 98)    _
helphead.htm#About#head"
rectangle="(446,10) (599, 86)    _
helphead.htm#Non-Profit#head"
rectangle="(290,9) (444, 80)  _
helphead.htm#Commercial#head"
rectangle="(6,3) (284, 85)  _
helphead.htm#Logo#head"  _
src="images/screencap.gif"  _
alt="screencap.gif (54721 bytes)"  _
border="0" width="600" height="326"  -->
</p>
</body>
</html>
```

The only thing left to do here is decide how visitors will access the *Help* page. Right now we have no link that would get them here. Let's find a nice piece of clipart and add it to the *Categories* title bar. Here is what the code for that table row will now look like:

```
<td valign="middle" bgcolor="#ACA470" _
 width="*">
<span class="clsBanner">Categories</span>
</td>
<td align="right" bgcolor="#ACA470" _
 valign="middle">
 <a href="help.htm" target="_blank">
 <img src="images/qmark.jpg" alt= _
   "Click for help" WIDTH="21" HEIGHT="21" _
   border="0"></a>
 </td>
```

We changed the first cell, which had been the only cell, by specifying that the width will be * — indicating that its width will be whatever is left over in the row after the other cell is positioned.

The second cell contains our graphic; it is a link that will take the visitor to *help.htm*; and will provide the text, "Click for help," when a mouse cursor hovers over it.

And that's it for the coding! We should have a fully functional Web site at this point. It's time to go and test that theory. I'll meet you in the next chapter — drive carefully.

CHAPTER 14

This is Only a Test!

". . . And Away We Go!"
- Jackie Gleason

*I*t's time to get this puppy working. Let's first decide what we're going to be testing, and then go to it.

14.1 Test Plan

How to we go about testing Web pages? If we had a large amount of functionality and code to test, I would suggest using the remote testing capability of Visual InterDev. However, I'd like to get us through the testing without sending you off to read a large volume on how to master that part of VI. Certainly once mastered, it's a very powerful capability, allowing you to place break points, interrogate variable contents, etc. But getting it working when you're not using a separate server is not trivial, and neither is its use. So instead, we'll simply test the functionality. The fact is, all of the code works at this point. I'm certainly not going to take you through all the bug fixing that went on to get to this point, as it would add another 500 pages to the book. We'll be testing just to cover all the functionality so you'll have a visual reference of what we've been trying to accomplish.

Still, if you were to test ASP code and wanted to verify that that a particular branch of code was being touched, or check on the contents of a variable, it's a simple measure to insert a statement such as:

```
Response.Write "myvar= " & myvar & "<br>"
```

I start these statements in column one and the rest of my code in column two. That way when it comes time to remove them, they're easy to find.

Using the data from our design, and from those items that have been added via change order, let's put together a list of the items that need to be tested.

[ ] 1. Main page loads without errors
[ ] 2. *banner* frame loads banner
[ ] 3. Hover functionality over each of the banner links
[ ] 4. 'About' is a link to *about.htm*
[ ] 5. 'Feedback' is a link to *feedback.htm*
[ ] 6. 'Advertise' is a link to *ad.htm*
[ ] 7. 'Awards' is a link to *awards.htm*
[ ] 8. 'Rings' is a link to *rings.htm*
[ ] 9. 'Copyright' is a link to *copyrite.htm*
[ ] 10. *fp_ad* frame loads with default ad
[ ] 11. The ad in *fp_ad* is a hyperlink to the advertiser's site
[ ] 12. *np_ad* frame loads with billboard
[ ] 13. Non-profit billboard performs correct transitions
[ ] 14. The ad in *np_ad* is a hyperlink to the advertiser's site
[ ] 15. *ad* frame loads with billboard
[ ] 16. For-profit billboard performs correct transitions
[ ] 17. The ad in *ad* is a hyperlink to the advertiser's site
[ ] 18. *main* frame loads with *test_d.htm*
[ ] 19. *title* frame loads with *titleframe.htm*
[ ] 20. Question mark displays at far right end of title bar
[ ] 21. Question mark is a link to *help.htm*
[ ] 22. Hover functionality over question mark
[ ] 23. *categories* frame loads with initial category list
[ ] 24. Category page size is correct
[ ] 25. No parent category is shown in initial list
[ ] 26. No child indentation is shown in initial list
[ ] 27. Categories with children are hyperlinks
[ ] 28. Categories with children have a "..." suffix
[ ] 29. Categories with links but no children are hyperlinks
[ ] 30. Categories with links but no children have no "..." suffix
[ ] 31. Categories with neither children nor links are not hyperlinks
[ ] 32. Both format of categories follow cascading style sheet
[ ] 33. Navigation hint prints at bottom of category list
[ ] 34. Clicking on a category leads to its children in same window
[ ] 35. Parent (clicked) category shows at top of children list
[ ] 36. Children are indented under parent category

[ ] 37. Parent (clicked) category follows CSS formatting

[ ] 38. Parent (clicked) category has "..." prefix

[ ] 39. Clicking on parent category returns to previous list

[ ] 40. Clicking on child category proceeds to its children

[ ] 41. Clicking on child category results in child showing as parent

[ ] 42. Clicking on new parent returns to previous list, with parent atop

[ ] 43. Clicking on original parent returns to list with no parent atop

[ ] 44. Hovering over category hyperlinks causes color change

[ ] 45. Moving mouse cursor away from hyperlink reverses color change

[ ] 46. Navigation bar paints properly

[ ] 47. Top-of-list icon is inactive and gray when at top of list

[ ] 48. Top-of-list icon is active and colored when not at top of list

[ ] 49. Previous-page icon is inactive and gray when at top of list

[ ] 50. Previous-page icon is active and colored when not at top of list

[ ] 51. Next-page icon is inactive and gray when at end of list

[ ] 52. Next-page icon is active and colored when not at end of list

[ ] 53. Top-of-list icon returns to top of list from subsequent levels

[ ] 54. Previous-page icon displays previous page, with first entry becoming final entry on the ultimate page

[ ] 55. Next-page icon displays next page, with final entry becoming first entry on the ultimate page

[ ] 56. Search bar displays properly

[ ] 57. Entering a phrase in the Find box and clicking "Find" displays list

[ ] 58. Unsuccessful searches are handled cleanly

[ ] 59. Categories not marked for "offer search", with no book recommendation, result in the book area being blank

[ ] 60. Categories marked for "offer search", with no book recomendation, result in the offer being made to search for a book title

[ ] 61. Categories with book recommendations but no cover image result in a generic icon offering a link to a recommended book

[ ] 62. Categories with book recommendations and a cover image result in the cover image being presented as a hyperlink

[ ] 63. Clicking the book search icon results in a new window and a search

[ ] 64. Clicking the generic icon for a recommended title goes to that title

[ ] 65. Clicking the cover image results in a new window and that title

[ ] 66. Clicking on a category results in associated links being displayed

[ ] 67. Clicking on a link results in a new window to that Web site

[ ] 68. Links and their descriptions are painted according to the CSS

[ ] 69. Clicking on the broken link icon after clicking on a link results in the correct link information being displayed (is a broken link application that's broken or that presents information that's broken like looking at yourself in a mirror in a mirror?

That's it for the main page; let's move on to the utility pages.

[ ] 70. The *About* page paints properly
[ ] 71. The navigation banner functions properly, especially the whale, which isn't functional on the main page navigation banner
[ ] 72. The *Advertise* page paints properly
[ ] 73. The link at the end of the *Advertise* page leads to the Puddleduck Press site
[ ] 74. The *Awards* page paints properly
[ ] 75. The link at the end of the *Awards* page leads to *nominate.htm*
[ ] 76. The *Rings* page paints properly
[ ] 77. The *Copyright* page paints properly
[ ] 78. The links on on the *Copyright* page function properly
[ ] 79. *blink.asp* generates the correct email message
[ ] 80. *blink.asp* generates the correct "thank you" message
[ ] 81. *helpmenu.htm* paints properly, with the explanation at the top
[ ] 82. *helpmain.htm* displays the graphic properly
[ ] 83. The hot spots in the graphic in *helpmain.htm* all function
[ ] 84. Each hot spot causes its related text to be presented at the top of the page in *helpmenu.htm*

Now, on to the Feedback pages

[ ] 85. *fbMenu.htm* paints the list of applications properly
[ ] 86. The list of applications are all links, pointing to the correct pages
[ ] 87. *fbMain.htm* paints properly
[ ] 88. The *click here* is a hyperlink that generates a mail dialog
[ ] 89. *General Comments* results in a form containing Name, Email, Comment, Contact Me and a Submit button
[ ] 90. Leaving Name, Email or Comment blank generates a message and a failed submit
[ ] 91. A successful submit results in a properly formatted email message
[ ] 92. *New Category* results in a form containing categories that function like the main page except that orphan categories aren't links
[ ] 93. The categories have radio buttons aside them

[ ] 94. The navigation bar beneath the categories functions properly

[ ] 95. *New Category* results in a form containing Name, Email, New Category, Comment, Contact Me and a Submit button

[ ] 96. Leaving Name, Email, New Category or Comment blank, or failing to select a category, generates a message and a failed submit

[ ] 97. *Category Comments* results in a form containing categories, Name, Email, Comment, Contact Me and a Submit button

[ ] 98. *New Link* results in a form containing categories, Name, Email, New Link, URL, Description, Comment, Contact Me and a Submit button

[ ] 99. Leaving New Link blank generates a message and a failed submit

[ ]100. *Award Nomination* results in a form containing Name, Email, URL, Comment, Submit button and the Award drop-down list box containing the four awards

[ ]101. Submitting each of the five types of feedback result in a properly formatted email message

So, it's a fairly lengthy list. Normally, if we had the time, the list would be twice as long, with many other items being tested. For one thing, we would perform this testing on two or three browsers. (Opera, a browser from Norway, is becoming a viable competitor to IE and Navigator.) We'll just test in IE here, since it contains a superset of the functionality (we don't send the category hover information to Navigator). Let's take the list in order.

14.2 Executing the Plan

[x] 1. Main page loads without errors

[x] 2. *banner* frame loads banner

We'll go into our browser and launch the Web page. The result is shown in Figure 14-1.

[x] 3. Hover functionality over each of the banner links

Next, we'll hold our mouse over each of the links on the banner. We're looking for a hint to appear above the link, the result of our exchanging the transparent image with one containing the hint. The results are shown in Figure 14-2 through Figure 14-6.

Figure 14-1   The Blowhole

Figure 14-2   *About* Hint

Figure 14-3   *Feedback* Hint

Figure 14-4   *Advertise* Hint

Figure 14-5   *Awards* Hint

Figure 14-6   *Rings* Hint

[x]   4. 'About' is a link to *about.htm*
[x]   5. 'Feedback' is a link to *feedback.htm*
[x]   6. 'Advertise' is a link to *ad.htm*
[x]   7. 'Awards' is a link to *awards.htm*
[x]   8. 'Rings' is a link to *rings.htm*
[x]   9. 'Copyright' is a link to *copyrite.htm*

We'll check these simply by holding our mouse cursor over the links on the banner and looking at what shows up in the browser's status bar. An example is shown in Figure 14-7.

Figure 14-7   Banner Link

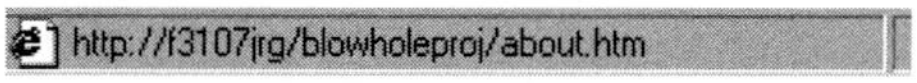

http://f3107jrg/blowholeproj/about.htm

[x] 10. *fp_ad* frame loads with default ad
[x] 11. The ad in *fp_ad* is a hyperlink to the advertiser's site

We can see in Figure 14-1 that the ad has loaded into the frame. If we hold our cursor over the ad we can see that it does link to the advertiser's site.

[x] 12. *np_ad* frame loads with billboard
[x] 13. Non-profit billboard performs correct transitions
[x] 14. The ad in *np_ad* is a hyperlink to the advertiser's site

Again, we can see that the non-profit ad banner loaded. Holding our cursor over any of the banner images and looking at the browser status bar shows that the advertiser's site address is in the link HREF. If we watch the banner for a while, we can see that the transitions work. An example of the effect is shown in Figure 14-8.

Figure 14-8   Non-Profit Banner Transition

[x] 15. *ad* frame loads with billboard

[x] 16. For-profit billboard performs correct transitions

[x] 17. The ad in *ad* is a hyperlink to the advertiser's site

We could see that the for-profit billboard loaded in the *ad* frame, and we can hold our cursor over it, like we did earlier, to check the link information. The different transitions are shown in Figure 14-9.

Figure 14-9   For-Profit Billboard Transitions

[x] 18. *main* frame loads with *test_d.htm*

[x] 19. *title* frame loads with *titleframe.htm*

[x] 20. Question mark displays at far right end of title bar

[x] 21. Question mark is a link to *help.htm*

[x] 22. Hover functionality over question mark

We can check-off 18-20 by looking at our page. We'll hold our cursor over the question mark to check-off 21, which will satisfy 22 too (see Figure 14-10).

Figure 14-10   Help Hint

[x] 23. *categories* frame loads with initial category list
[x] 24. Category page size is correct

Our category list does load with the initial list, that is, categories whose parent is 0. We can also see that six are being displayed at a time, the correct page size.

[x] 25. No parent category is shown in initial list
[x] 26. No child indentation is shown in initial list
[x] 27. Categories with children are hyperlinks
[x] 28. Categories with children have a "..." suffix
[x] 29. Categories with links but no children are hyperlinks
[x] 30. Categories with links but no children have no "..." suffix
[x] 31. Categories with neither children nor links are not hyperlinks
[x] 32. Both format of categories follow cascading style sheet
[x] 33. Navigation hint prints at bottom of category list

Items 25-33 can all be resolved by observation of the main page.

[x] 34. Clicking on a category leads to that category's children in same window
[x] 35. Parent (clicked) category shows at top of children list
[x] 36. Children are indented under parent category
[x] 37. Parent (clicked) category follows CSS formatting
[x] 38. Parent (clicked) category has "..." prefix

Clicking on *Aquariums* in the category list will allow us to satisfy 34-38 by observation (see). If we click on *Hobbyist*, then *Aquariums* again, we can satisfy 39-45. The sequence is shown in Figure 14-11 through Figure 14-14.

[ ] 39. Clicking on parent category returns to previous list
[ ] 40. Clicking on child category proceeds to its children

[ ] 41. Clicking on child category results in child showing as parent
[ ] 42. Clicking on new parent returns to previous list, with original parent atop
[ ] 43. Clicking on original parent returns to list with no parent atop
[ ] 44. Hovering over category hyperlinks causes color change
[ ] 45. Moving mouse cursor away from hyperlink reverses color change

Figure 14-11   Clicking on a Top-Level Category

Aquariums ...
Arts Literature ...
Conservation
Destinations ...
Exploration ...
Food

(more - use arrow button)

Figure 14-12   Clicking on a Child Category

...Aquariums
Hobbyist ...
Professional

Figure 14-13   Clicking on the Grandchild's Parent

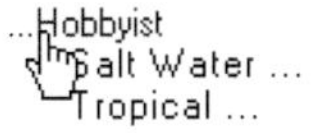

...Hobbyist
Salt Water ...
Tropical ...

Figure 14-14   Clicking on the Child's Parent

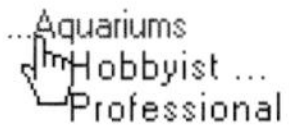

...Aquariums
Hobbyist ...
Professional

The next block of test items will be satisifed by noting the status of the navigation bar icons as we click the next-page arrow until we're at the last page, click the previous-page arrow until we're back to the first page, and then move to another page and click the home icon. We'll capture the status in a series of graphics in Figure 14-15.

[x] 46. Navigation bar paints properly
[x] 47. Top-of-list icon is inactive and gray when at top of list

[x] 48. Top-of-list icon is active and colored when not at top of list

[x] 49. Previous-page icon is inactive and gray when at top of list

[x] 50. Previous-page icon is active and colored when not at top of list

[x] 51. Next-page icon is inactive and gray when at end of list

[x] 52. Next-page icon is active and colored when not at end of list

[x] 53. Top-of-list icon returns to top of list from subsequent levels

[x] 54. Previous-page icon displays previous page, with first entry becoming final entry on the ultimate page

[x] 55. Next-page icon displays next page, with final entry becoming first entry on the ultimate page

Figure 14-15   Navigation Bar Testing

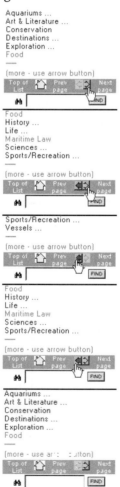

[x] 56. Search bar displays properly

[x] 57. Entering a phrase in the Find box and clicking "Find" displays list

[x] 58. Unsuccessful searches are handled cleanly

I'll put a keyword in the text box that should show up in various categories but isn't a category itself, *fin*. Also, to check the routine we wrote to strip quotation marks from the keyword, I'll put quotation marks around the keyword. The results are shown in Figure 14-16. Searching for a string that doesn't exist results in no categories being displayed, but also no navigation buttons are activated. There is a work-around, the browser's *back* button, so we'll note this as needing a later enhancement.

Figure 14-16   Testing the Find Dialog

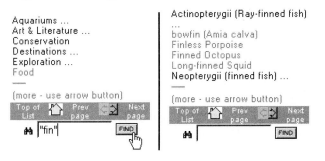

[x] 59. Categories not marked for "offer search", with no book recommendation, result in the book area being blank

[x] 60. Categories marked for "offer search", with no book recomendation, result in the offer being made to search for a book title

[x] 61. Categories with book recommendations but no cover image result in a generic icon offering a link to a recommended book

[x] 62. Categories with book recommendations and a cover image result in the cover image being presented as a hyperlink

[x] 63. Clicking the book search icon results in a new window and a search

[x] 64. Clicking the generic icon for a recommended title goes to that title

[x] 65. Clicking the cover image results in a new window and that title

We'll handle this testing by searching for known quantities. Having looked in the database, I know three categories that provide the three tests we need: Hobbyist Aquariums, Mammalogy and the Bering Sea. The results of these category selections are shown in Figure 14-17.

Figure 14-17   Testing the Book Logic

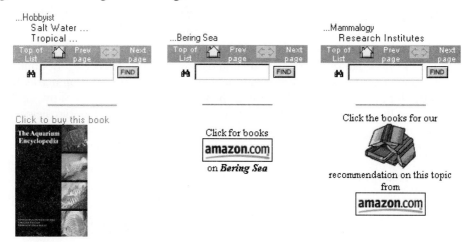

[x] 66.   Clicking on a category results in associated links being displayed

[x] 67.   Clicking on a link results in a new window to that Web site

[x] 68.   Links and their description are painted according to the CSS

We'll click on *Destinations* from the initial category list. We then receive one link in the main frame (see Figure 14-18). Clicking on it takes us to that site.

Figure 14-18   The Link Logic

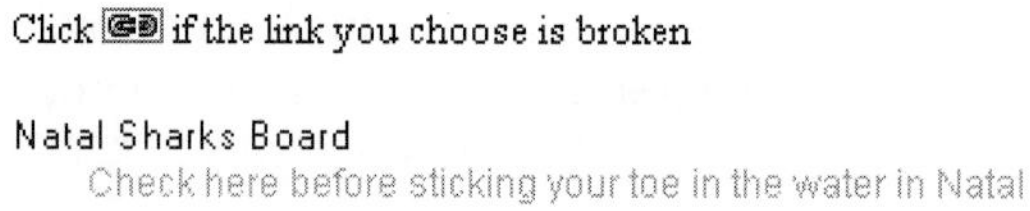

Click 🆖 if the link you choose is broken

Natal Sharks Board
Check here before sticking your toe in the water in Natal

[x] 69.   Clicking on the broken link icon after clicking on a link results in the
correct link information being displayed

We'll first click on the link, and the result is a new window being opened that takes us to that site. This shows that the information is getting through, and that *redirect.asp* is doing that part of its job. How about the data remaining in state? Clicking next on the broken link icon results in a new window with the contents shown in Figure 14-19.

Figure 14-19 Testing the Links

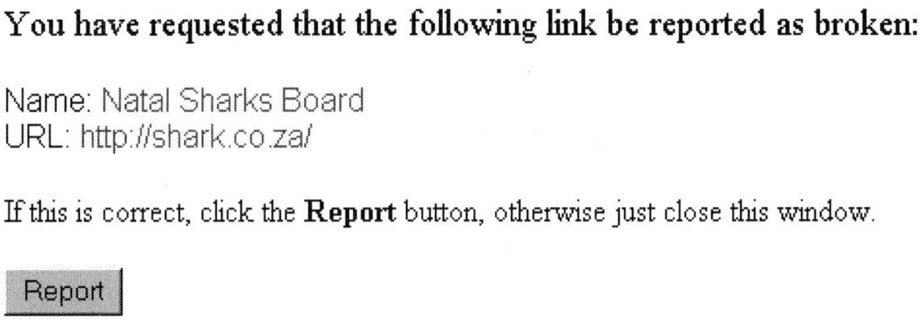
You have requested that the following link be reported as broken:
Name: Natal Sharks Board
URL: http://shark.co.za/
If this is correct, click the Report button, otherwise just close this window.
Report

Figure 14-20 The *About* Page

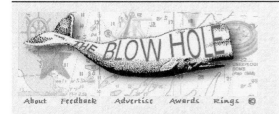

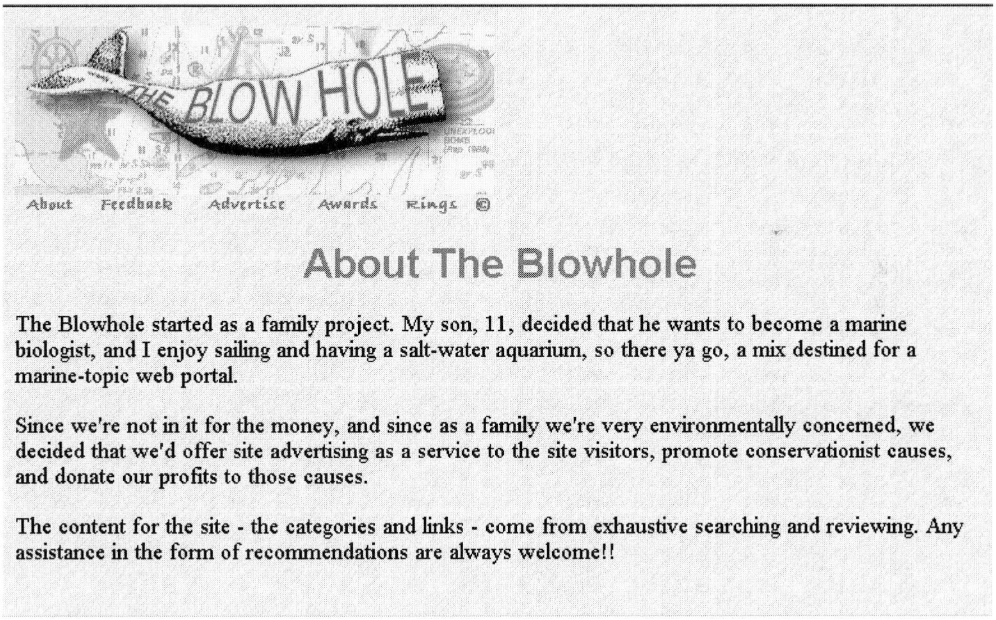

THE BLOW HOLE
About Feedback Advertise Awards Rings ©
About The Blowhole
The Blowhole started as a family project. My son, 11, decided that he wants to become a marine biologist, and I enjoy sailing and having a salt-water aquarium, so there ya go, a mix destined for a marine-topic web portal.
Since we're not in it for the money, and since as a family we're very environmentally concerned, we decided that we'd offer site advertising as a service to the site visitors, promote conservationist causes, and donate our profits to those causes.
The content for the site - the categories and links - come from exhaustive searching and reviewing. Any assistance in the form of recommendations are always welcome!!

[x] 70. The *About* page paints properly

[x] 71. The navigation banner functions properly, especially the whale, which isn't functional on the main page navigation banner

[x] 72. The *Advertise* page paints properly

Figure 14-21   The *Ad* Page

Advertising

The Blowhole is a **great** place to advertise.

- There is high exposure, and when people drill down to a category of interest, the audience is motivated. For example, someone seeing an ad for a sailboat manufacturer on a page listing links to sailboat manufacturers is more likely to "click through" the ad than someone interested in seashells seeing the same ad!
- With any ad you place you can select up to three categories for it to appear under!!
- Not only does your ad appear on the category page you select, but also on any category page with no purchased ads

There are three types of ads at The Blowhole. Each provides the visitor an opportunity to click the ad to be taken to a web page for the advertiser. Don't have a web page? That's okay, we offer that service to go with the ad. More on that later. Below is an example of each type of ad.

[x] 73. The link at the end of the *Advertise* page leads to Puddleduck Press
[x] 74. The *Awards* page paints properly

Figure 14-22   The *Awards* Page

This is the highest award offered by The Blowhole. It is bestowed upon sites that reflect excellence in all the categories listed below.

Presented to sites representing organizations that provide selfless dedicated effort to conservation

[x] 75. The link at the end of the *Awards* page leads to *nominate.htm*
[x] 76. The *Rings* page paints properly

Figure 14-23   The *Rings* Page

[x] 77. The *Copyright* page paints properly
[x] 78. The links on on the *Copyright* page function properly

Figure 14-24 The *Copyright* Page

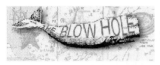

THE BLOW HOLE
Copyright Information
The pages and page elements on this site are all Copyright ©1998-1999 Puddleduck Press Inc. unless noted otherwise below. All Rights Reserved.
We'd appreciate any feedback you have . Feel free to drop by other Puddleduck Press sites - click here for a list.
This site created by a member of
THE HTML WRITERS GUILD
CREATED & MANAGED WITH Microsoft FrontPage
GET Microsoft Internet Explorer
Puddleduck Press
Contact the Webmaster

[x] 79. *blink.asp* generates the correct email message

[x] 80. *blink.asp* generates the correct "thank you" message

Let's go back and click on the broken link again, and this time we'll click on *Report*, note the screen we receive as a result, and check the email message we receive.

Figure 14-25 Reporting a Broken Link

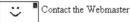

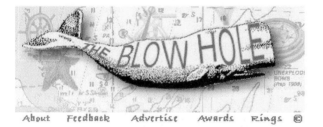

THE BLOW HOLE
About Feedback Advertise Awards Rings ©
Thank you for taking the time to provide us with your feedback

Figure 14-26   Broken Link Email

Subject: The Blowhole Broken Link

From: "feedback@theblowhole.com" <feedback@theblowhole.com>   Save Address

Date: Thu, 15 Apr 1999 00:48:50 -0700

To: info@theblowhole.com

The following feedback was received from The Blowhole Site

link: http://shark.co.za/
description: Natal Sharks Board

Reply   Reply All   Forward   Delete

[x] 81.   *helpmenu.htm* paints properly, with the explanation at the top

[x] 82.   *helpmain.htm* displays the graphic properly

[x] 83.   The hot spots in the graphic in *helpmain.htm* all function

[x] 84.   Each hot spot causes its related text to be presented at the top of the
page in *helpmenu.htm*

Figure 14-27   The *Help* Screen

Click items on the image below for a description.

The Logo

Clicking on the sperm whale logo will return you to the main page from all other p

[x] 85. *fbMenu.htm* paints the list of applications properly

[x] 86. The list of applications are all links, pointing to the correct pages

[x] 87. *fbMain.htm* paints properly

Figure 14-28   The *Feedback* Page

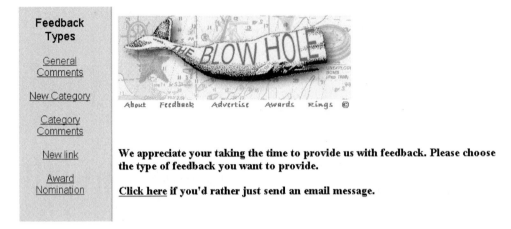

[x] 88. The *click here* is a hyperlink that generates a mail dialog

We can test this simply by clicking on the link. As long as we have mail capability, clicking should result in our receiving a screen for composing an email message.

[x] 89. *General Comments* results in a form containing Name, Email, Comment, Contact Me and a Submit button

Figure 14-29   General Comments

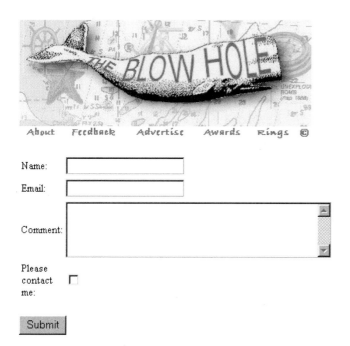

[x] 90. Leaving Name, Email or Comment blank generates a message and a
failed submit

Figure 14-30   — JavaScript Edit

[x] 91. A successful submit results in a properly formatted email message

Figure 14-31   General Comments Email

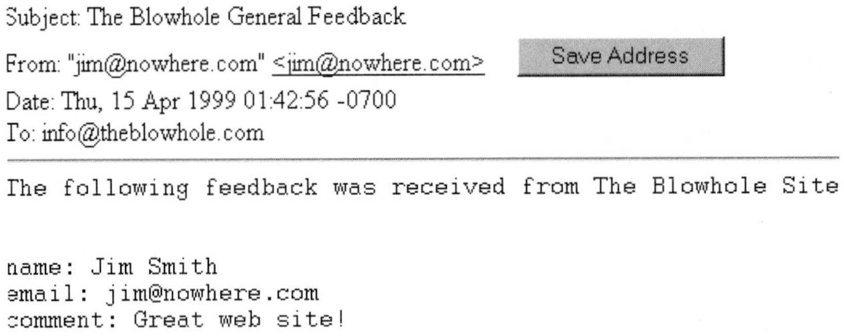

Subject: The Blowhole General Feedback

From: "jim@nowhere.com" <jim@nowhere.com>   Save Address
Date: Thu, 15 Apr 1999 01:42:56 -0700
To: info@theblowhole.com

The following feedback was received from The Blowhole Site

name: Jim Smith
email: jim@nowhere.com
comment: Great web site!

[x] 92. *New Category* results in a form containing categories that function
like the main page except that orphan categories aren't links

[x] 93. The categories have radio buttons aside them

[x] 94. The navigation bar beneath the categories functions properly

[x] 95. *New Category* results in a form containing Name, Email, New Category, Comment, Contact Me and a Submit button

[x] 96. Leaving Name, Email, New Category or Comment blank, or failing
to select a category, generates a message and a failed submit

Figure 14-32   New Category Form

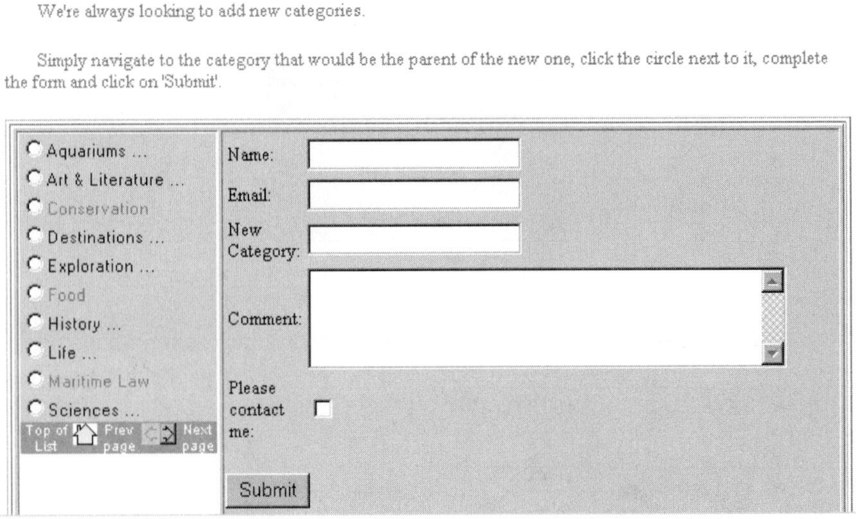

We're always looking to add new categories.

Simply navigate to the category that would be the parent of the new one, click the circle next to it, complete
the form and click on 'Submit'.

[x] 97. *Category Comments* results in a form containing categories, Name, Email, Comment, Contact Me and a Submit button

[x] 98. *New Link* results in a form containing categories, Name, Email, New Link, URL, Description, Comment, Contact Me and a Submit button

[x] 99. Leaving New Link blank generates a message and a failed submit

Figure 14-33 Category Comments Form

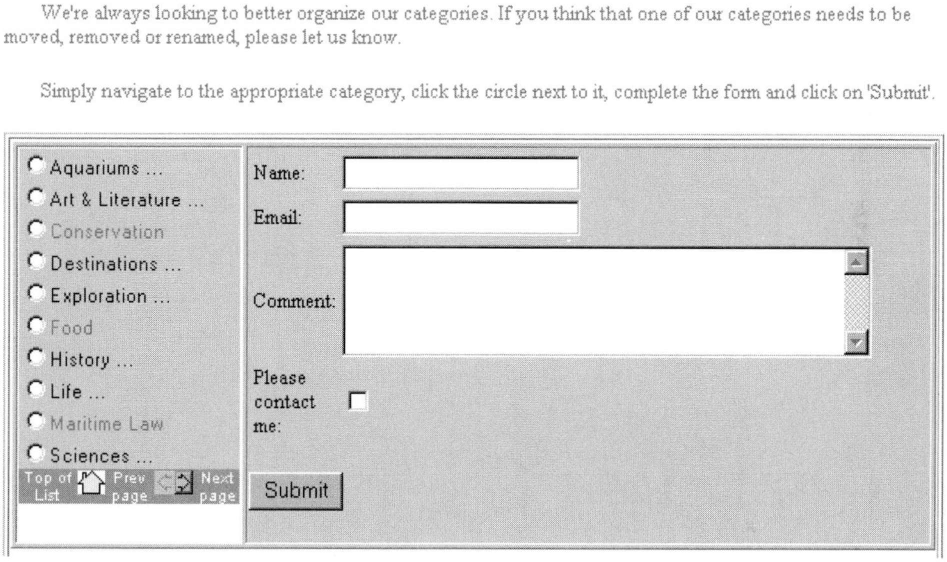
We're always looking to better organize our categories. If you think that one of our categories needs to be moved, removed or renamed, please let us know.
Simply navigate to the appropriate category, click the circle next to it, complete the form and click on 'Submit'.
Aquariums ...
Art & Literature ...
Conservation
Destinations ...
Exploration ...
Food
History ...
Life ...
Maritime Law
Sciences ...
Top of List
Prev page
Next page
Name:
Email:
Comment:
Please contact me:
Submit

Figure 14-34   New Link Form

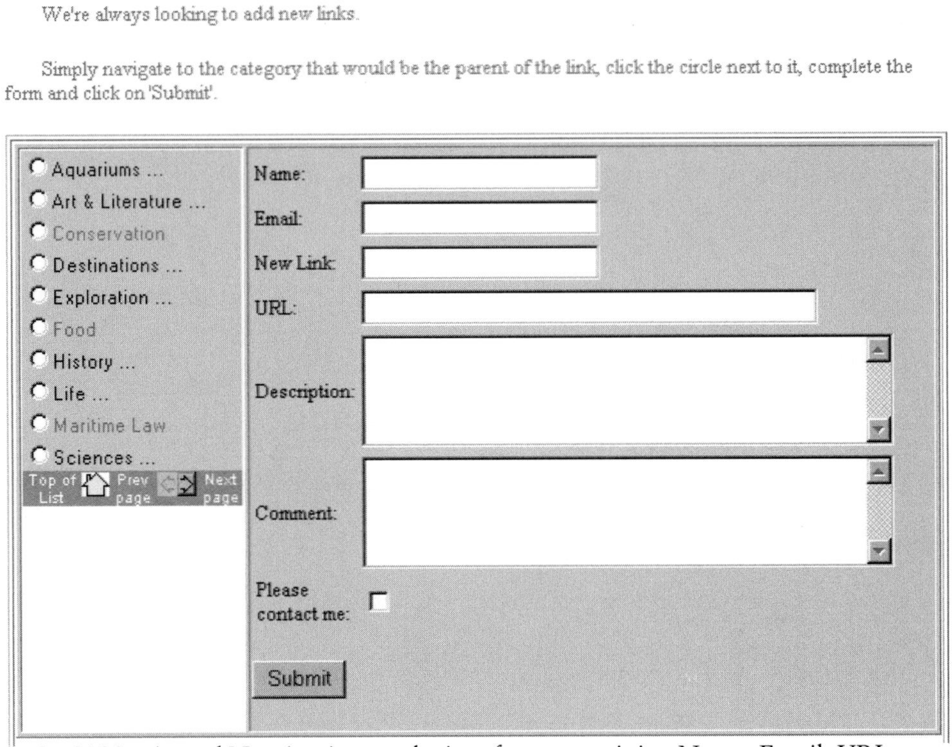

We're always looking to add new links.

Simply navigate to the category that would be the parent of the link, click the circle next to it, complete the form and click on 'Submit'.

[x]100. *Award Nomination* results in a form containing Name, Email, URL, Comment, Submit button and the Award drop-down list box containing the four awards

[x]101. Submitting each of the five types of feedback result in a properly formatted email message

Figure 14-35   Award Nomination Form

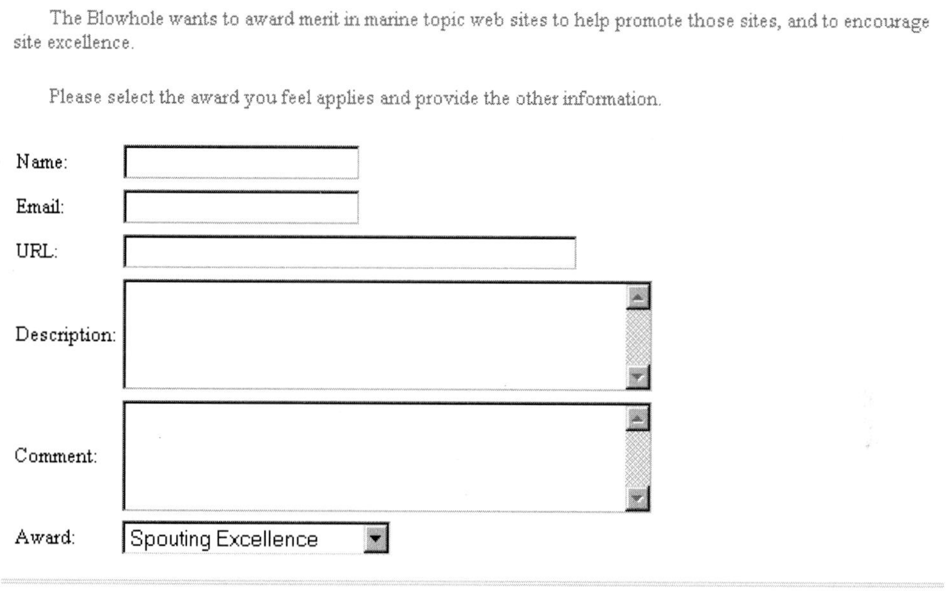

The Blowhole wants to award merit in marine topic web sites to help promote those sites, and to encourage site excellence.

Please select the award you feel applies and provide the other information.

Name:

Email:

URL:

Description:

Comment:

Award: Spouting Excellence

Figure 14-36   Five Feedback Emails

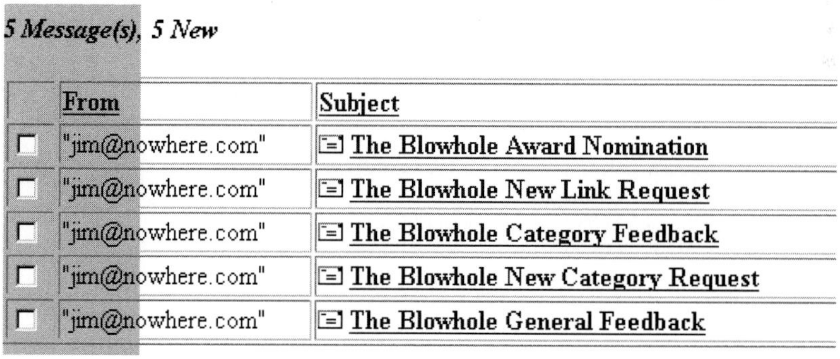

5 Message(s), 5 New

	From	Subject
☐	"jim@nowhere.com"	✉ The Blowhole Award Nomination
☐	"jim@nowhere.com"	✉ The Blowhole New Link Request
☐	"jim@nowhere.com"	✉ The Blowhole Category Feedback
☐	"jim@nowhere.com"	✉ The Blowhole New Category Request
☐	"jim@nowhere.com"	✉ The Blowhole General Feedback

Figure 14-37   Category Feedback Email

Subject: The Blowhole Category Feedback

From: "jim@nowhere.com" <jim@nowhere.com>   Save Address

Date: Thu, 15 Apr 1999 05:27:22 -0700
To: info@theblowhole.com

```
The following feedback was received from The Blowhole Site


cat:  100/Bays
name:  Jim Smith
email:  jim@nowhere.com
comment:  This category seems light on content
```

Figure 14-38   New Link Email

Subject: The Blowhole New Link Request

From: "jim@nowhere.com" <jim@nowhere.com>   Save Address

Date: Thu, 15 Apr 1999 05:29:25 -0700
To: info@theblowhole.com

```
The following feedback was received from The Blowhole Site

cat:  20/Conservation
description:  A site to sign up to sponsor a Lakota Sioux child

name:  Jim Smith
email:  jim@nowhere.com
newlink:  Circle of Children
url:  http://www.puddleduck.com/circle
comment:  This site does great things
```

Figure 14-39   Award Nomination Email

Subject: The Blowhole Award Nomination

From: "jim@nowhere.com" <jim@nowhere.com>   [Save Address]
Date: Thu, 15 Apr 1999 04:58:14 -0700
To: info@theblowhole.com

```
The following feedback was received from The Blowhole Site


name: Jim Smith
email: jim@nowhere.com
url: http://www.theblowhole.com
comment: Give yourselves an award!
description: Web portal for marine topics
award: Spouting
```

Figure 14-40   New Category Request Email

Subject: The Blowhole New Category Request

From: "jim@nowhere.com" <jim@nowhere.com>   [Save Address]
Date: Thu, 15 Apr 1999 05:22:55 -0700
To: info@theblowhole.com

```
The following feedback was received from The Blowhole Site


contact: ON
cat: 1/Aquariums
newcategory: Fish food
name: Jim Smith
email: jim@nowhere.com
comment: Fish need to eat too :-)
```

That takes us to the end of our testing. We did very well, and hopefully you have a very clear idea of what it is we've created. Now it's time to pubish the site. On to the final chapter.

CHAPTER 15

Going Live!

*I*t's been a long road to get to the point where we have working content, but there's nowhere for anyone to see it. Let's go through the steps necessary to bring our site up.

15.1 Selecting an ISP

You might be wondering why we need an Internet Service Provider (ISP) if we're going to have a Web hoster too. It's because Web hosters provide a home for your Web, but they don't provide *you* with any way of getting to that site. You need someone to provide you with a connection to the Internet. It can be your company (be forewarned, FrontPage does *not* work well through a firewall), or any dial-up ISP such as Mind-Spring. All you need from the ISP is a connection to the Internet so that FrontPage can establish a connection to your remote Web site.

15.2 Selecting a Web Hoster

The Web site needs someplace to live. It needs a home on a server available to the rest of the Internet. This service is provided by a Web hoster. Finding a Web hoster is not very difficult, but finding one that offers the right services at the right price can be.

Most Web hosters offer to host your Web site on a UNIX server. We don't want our site to be on a UNIX server, since it won't provide the services we're looking for, like ASP and ADO. We need to be hosted on an NT system. However, that's not the end of it, because there are a number of services that the hoster needs to provide to us. Following is a list of these services.

- Domain name hosting — the domain name, *theblowhole.com*, will be mapped to an account on one of the hoster's servers.
- NT hosting — the domain needs to be on an NT server.
- ASP — although ASP support is integrated into NT, we want to make certain that the server extensions have been installed.
- FrontPage support — this needs to be an account managed by FrontPage. File transfers will be done in this manner, as opposed to using FTP, the normal method.
- Data Source Name — the account should come with a data source name, which is needed so that the visitor can use one our pages in conjunction with our database.
- MS Access — this also should be integrated into NT.
- Disk space — it goes without saying that you can't have much of a Web site if you're not given storage space, but I'll say it anyway.
- Bandwidth — make sure that the amount of file transferring that is allowed per month is reasonable.
- POP mail — the account needs to be able to receive mail at xxx@theblowhole.com. They should offer a large number of POP accounts, or unlimited, so that you can set up more mailboxes if necessary.
- Server mail — some of the Web pages need to be able to *send* email.
- Statistics server — you need to know how active the site is. The plain fact is hit counters stink. They're worthless. Besides, one person can generate a couple dozen hits just by hitting your frames page and jumping around the site, what you want to know is how many *sessions* there were.

That's about it. Find all that and you're home-free.

15.3 Obtaining a Domain

We have a domain name, *theblowhole.com*, but how did we go about obtaining it? Domain names are controlled by InterNIC, a joint operation between the government and Network Solutions, although domain registration will be opened to four other registrars soon. Anyway, the first step in obtaining a domain name is checking to see if the domain is available.

We'll point our browser at www.networksolutions.com. There we will find a dialog box into which we put the domain we want to check on (see Figure 15-1). The search results, based on the "WhoIs" command, inform us that the domain name is not already taken [whew]. This is good news, because there are companies that actually buy up domain names and later auction them off. Domain information is public domain, so the information about the domain name we requested is presented to us (see Figure 15-2).

Each domain has three contacts, administrative, billing and technical. The technical contact is typically the Web hoster.

Figure 15-1   Visiting InterNIC

Figure 15-2   "WhoIs" Domain Name Information

```
Sorry, theblowhole.com is unavailable...


Registrant:
Puddleduck Press (THEBLOWHOLE-DOM)
    570 Leah Drive
    Powder Springs, GA 30127-4414
    US

    Domain Name: THEBLOWHOLE.COM

    Administrative Contact:
        Greenberg, Jeff   (JG3792)   jeff@PUDDLEDUCK.COM
        770-795-0365 (FAX) 770-795-0365
    Technical Contact, Zone Contact:
        Hostmaster   (ADM683-ORG)   hostmaster@CWSHOST.COM
        604-681-2414
Fax- 604-681-0659
    Billing Contact:
        Greenberg, Jeff   (JG3792)   jeff@PUDDLEDUCK.COM
        770-795-0365 (FAX) 770-795-0365

    Record last updated on 31-Jul-98.
    Record created on 31-Jul-98.
    Database last updated on 14-Apr-99 13:20:47 EDT.

    Domain servers in listed order:

    K2.CWSHOST.COM            209.153.208.101
    EVEREST.CWSHOST.COM       209.153.208.102
```

When you are ready to reserve a domain name, you'll need to obtain the IP (Internet Protocol) address of their primary and secondary Domain Name Servers (DNS), as this information is necessary for the domain name application.

15.4 Publishing your site

Once we have our Web hosting agreement, we can publish our Web site. We don't have to wait for the domain name to be active before using our account, but until the mapping is complete (typically several days to two weeks) we'll have to use the IP address instead. For example, in the address box of our browser we'd put:

```
http://xxx.xxx.xxx.xxx
```

We'll need some information from our Web hoster to use our account, namely a user ID and a password. We're going to use FrontPage to publish the site. FrontPage keeps internal information about the status of the site.

It's very important when maintaining a FrontPage site that you never use FTP to transfer files, because the FrontPage information can become corrupted.

If you only want to transfer a file or two, a valid shortcut is to open the *remote* Web in FrontPage (as opposed to your local copy), drag the file you want to transfer from Windows Explorer and drop it on the FrontPage Explorer window.

Anyway, let's take a look at the steps in publishing the Web site. First, we'll open the local Web site in FrontPage.

Once the Web is open, click on the *Publish* button. If it's the first time you've published this Web you'll need to tell FrontPage where to publish it to. In our case, it will be published to www.theblowhole.com.

There are a number of things that can go wrong in this phase. First of all, if your connection to the Internet isn't active, or if it times out (which can happen if your ISP's server is busy, for example) a screen will pop up asking you for FTP information. Cancel out at that point and try again. If your DUN (Dial-Up Networking) configuration isn't set for *Logon to Network*, you might receive a dialog screen stating that authentification failed.

Figure 15-3   Opening the Local Web

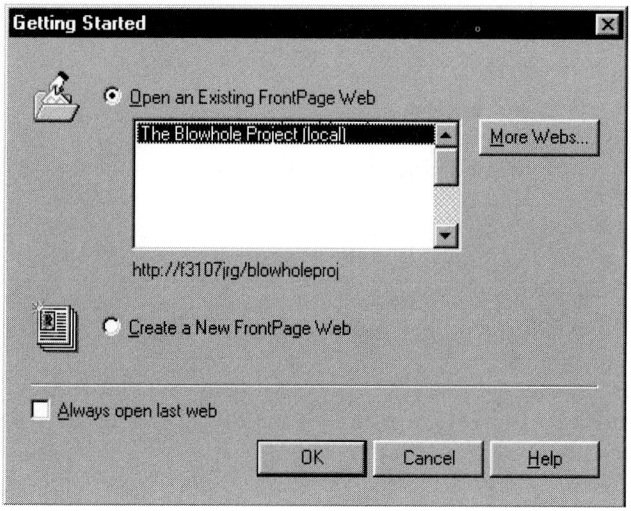

If none of those things goes wrong, and you provide the right user ID and password to connect to the remote site, you'll should see the following sequence of events:

- A list is created of the files on the remote Web.
- A list is created of the files on the local Web.
- The two lists are created.
- Files that are different are copied from the source to the destination.
- The internal records of both Webs are updated.

The first time you publish the Web, all the files on the local Web will be copied to the remote. From then on you can choose to publish only changed files. It's worth noting that you don't have to work in local-master mode. If space on your system is limited, or if it makes sense for another reason, you can open the remote Web on the Web hoster's server and make page changes directly to it via FrontPage.

15.5 Marketing the site

Once your site is up and ready, you need to let people know about it. There are many ways to do this, and none is the clear-cut "best" way to do it. One method is by submitting your site to search engines. You can do it yourself, or pay someone to do it, like SubmitIt.com.

Some search engines will eventually discover your site. There are many theories as to how best to structure your pages to be discovered. One method is through the use of meta tags, as follows:

```
<meta name="description" content= _
  "The Web portal for all matters marine">
<meta name="keywords"
  content="marine ocean sea fish inverts _
  crustaceans whale dolphin manatee porpoise _
  seal boat ship watercraft conservation reef _
  coral scuba snorkel walrus manta stingray">
```

Some search engines will use the contents of these tags to create their index entry, but not all do. Some use the page title, and some use words found in the body text on the page. It's a very unclear science right now, but certainly using the meta tags as well as placing some keywords in comments at the front of the page if they can't be put in the body will be helpful.

Another method is to submit information about your page to sites that give awards, like Starting Point, and to organizations that review sites, like the Hersch Web Site Observer.

Banner ads at other sites can lead people to yours, and organizations like Link Exchange make this process simple. Also, offering to link sites similar to yours if they'll do the same can help.

Purchasing ad space can help. Pricing for this type of space varies based on the number of imprints, or pages displayed with your ad, from low pricing at sites like The Blowhole, to much higher rates at the megasites like Yahoo.

Finally, you can purchase an email list and send out cold-call mail — spam. I can't offer any advice about how to get people to read it, except to tell you to be honest and keep the message very, very short.

And don't forget to have your Web address added to your letterhead, publications and business cards.

Epilogue

The idea was to get this site up and running as quickly as possible. Some design elements were foresaken in the process, and some were conceived during the course of the project and were not considered important enough to warrant a change order. All of these items can be addressed in the next version of this site. Below is a list of some of them.

- Database maintenance pages, for additions, modifications and deletions. Right now, adding categories, links, ads, etc., is done by using MS Access, making manual additions to the database, and then uploading the database to the remote server to overwrite the one that's there. Messy. There should be pages accessible only to The Blowhole staff to perform this maintenance.
- Write-to-database feedback pages instead of just email. When people enter feedback for new categories and links, the information should be written to a 'holding area' in the database, or to the existing tables but with a flag on the record, and await review by The Blowhole staff. This way the emails are minimized, and they're not rekeying information.
- Advertising ordering page. This one's obvious, there won't be much advertising if there's no way to order an ad.
- Advertising tracking (might require changes to the Billboard). Right now there's no way to track whether an ad is clicked. People actually going to the advertiser's site makes the advertising more valuable. This data needs to be tracked as well as how many times the ad was shown.
- More precise presentation control via DHTML and CSS-2. Once the major browsers support these standards, they can be used to improve the look and feel of the web site.

- Have categories in list show the number of children/links. It would be nice for the visitor if a category showed as "Destinations (34/245)," indicating that there are 34 child categories behind this category, and 245 links.
- Add an ad start-date to the database for advance orders. At this point ads are chosen if they haven't expired, but there could well be a need to load the information into the database prior to the date that the ad is to begin.
- Screen for generating email regarding ads about to expire. An automatic notification to the advertisers reminding them that their ad is about to expire, and perhaps include the statistical information (hits, click-throughs).
- Screen for generating emails to notify sites that they've been linked. This is a method of requesting a courtesy link from *that* site back to you.
- Create a text-only version of the site for those who use text-only browsers.
- Create a no-frames version of the site for those who don't like frames.
- Create test-mode logic, so that we're not constantly adding lines and removing lines from the code.
- Enhance the "find" logic to handle multi-word and Boolean searches, such as "shark NOT whale" to retrieve categories about sharks but not whale sharks.

Please use the feedback pages at The Blowhole to suggest anything else you think would make the site more useful.

The Web Site

The Web site we've created is fully functional and viable. There is, however, another section of the Web site for your use only. There you will find the following information:

- source code for the Web pages
- source code for the subroutine library
- source code for the Cascading Style Sheet
- source code and classes for the Dynamic Billboard applet
- links to other resources, such as Web hosting sites, ISPs and search-engine submittal sites
- all the graphics from the book, ZIP'd up by chapter number

The URL for the page is:

```
http://www.theblowhole.com/resources
```

You'll need a password to access the page — it is:

```
ireadit
```

Dynamic Billboard

B.1 DynamicBillboard

```
/**
 * @(#)DynamicBillboard.java
 * @version 1.51 04/06/97
 * @author Robert Temple (robertt@starwave.com)
 */

import java.awt.*;
import java.awt.image.ImageObserver;
import java.net.URL;

/**
 *    Applet which displays an image on an HTML page.  The image
changes to a
 *    new image after a delay.  This change from one image to the next
has
 *    some kind of special effect associated with it.  See the Bill-
Transition
 *    class for more information on these special effects.  Images can
have
 *    URLs associated with them.
 *
 * USAGE NOTE:
 *    The images this applet uses all must be the same size.  The size
of the
 *    applet must be the same size of these images.
 *
 *    HTML tag:
```

```
*    <applet code="DynamicBillboard" width="XXX" height="XXX">
*    <param name="delay" value="20000">
*    <param name="billboards" value="X">
*    <param name="bill0" value="XXX.gif,http://X.X.X/XXX.html">
*    <param name="bill1" value="XXX.gif,http://X.X.X/XXX.html">
*    <param name="bill2" value="XXX.gif,http://X.X.X/XXX.html">
*    <param name="bill3" value="XXX.gif,http://X.X.X/XXX.html">
*    <param name="transitions" value="4,ColumnTransition,FadeTransi-
tion,TearTransition,SmashTransition">
*    <param name="bgcolor" value="#FFFFFF">
*    <param name="target" value="_self">
*    </applet>
*
*    HTML tag NOTES
*    width - the width of the applet.  Must be the same size as the
images
*    height - the height of the applet. Must be the same size as
the images
*    delay - the time between images in milliseconds
*    billboards - the number of different BillBoards(images) that
you will
*              use
*    bill# - the image followed by the linking URL for a given
BillBoard,
*          starting with number 0.  this followed by a string that
will appear on
*          status bar when the mouse is over the billboard.
*          The image and URL should be separated
*          by a comma, *NO SPACES*
*    bill#... - this parameter should appear 0 to one less then the
value of
*          the "billboards" parameter.  Replace # with the Bill-
Boards
*          number
*    transitions - the number of classes that will be used as tran-
sitions,
*          followed by the names of these classes, separated by
commas
*          *NO SPACES*
*    bgcolor - OPTIONAL - the background color the applet will use.
The value is
*          similar to how one specifies the bgcolor tag in HTML.
*    target - OPTIONAL - the frame target the applet should goto
when the mouse
*          is pressed over the applet.
*       ## I hope that not too many people want different targets
for different
*          ## billboards
```

```
*
* DESIGN NOTES:
*    FAST CONTENT:
*    Java Applets take much longer to get to downloaded and displayed
then
*    most other things appearing on a HTML page under Netscape 2.0b4.
I
*    believe that most web surfers do not have the patience to wait
for most
*    applets to load.  Because of this I attempted to make this
applet load
*    and get content to the screen as fast as possible.
*
*    To accomplish this, The applet does little processing before
waiting for
*    the first image to be displayed on the screen.  This is unlike
most other
*    Java applet.  Most load all images and classes before showing
anything
*    but a gray box.
*
*    Later, the applet loads other images and classes only as they
are needed.
*
*    EXCEPTIONS:
*    I really would like to put more exceptions in the code, but I
did not
*    because I wanted the fastest possible loading of classes.  Hence
the
*    smallest bytecode
*
*    PUBLIC DATA MEMBERS:
*    A lot of data members are made public even though in good OO-
programming
*    they should not be.  This is done for the same reason as above,
bytecode
*    size.
*
*    Making data members protected, and then creating a function
that allows
*    read only access to this data increases the bytecode size.  Even
when
*    the one line function is made final, and the code is compiled
with
*    optimizations. :(
*/
public class DynamicBillboard extends java.applet.Applet implements
Runnable {
```

```
          /**  Array which holds all of the billboards */
          BillData[] billboards;

          /** Index into the billboards array of the current bill-
board */
          int current_billboard;

          /** Index into the billboards array of the next billboard
*/
          int next_billboard;

          /** Array of Strings which hold the names of the different
transition classes */
          String[] transition_classes;

          /** The main thread which drives the program */
          Thread thread = null;

          /** Current Image displayed on the screen */
          Image image = null;

          /**
           * The delay time from the completion of one transition to
the next transtion
           * Delay is initially set to -1.  This is used to check to
see if the
           * finish init function has been called before.  It has if
delay is
           * not -1
           */
          long delay = -1;

          /** Flag the keep track if the mouse is currently located
inside the applet */
          boolean mouse_inside_applet;


          /** The frame the applet will use as a target when going to
a new HTML document */
          String link_target_frame;

          /**
           * Initializes the applet.  Performs minimal work to get the
applet to the
           * screen ASAP.  The next method, finishInit completes the
initialization
           */
          public void init() {
```

```
        // Check to see if the user wanted a certain background
color
        String s = getParameter("bgcolor");
        if(s != null) {
        Color color = new Color(Integer.parseInt(s.substring(1),
16));
        setBackground(color);
        getParent().setBackground(color);
        getParent().repaint();
        }

        // Get the total number of billboards that the applet will
use &
        // Create an array to store the Data for each billboard
        billboards = new BillData[Integer.parseInt(getParame-
ter("billboards"))];

        // Chose a random billboard to start with
        current_billboard = next_billboard = (int)(Math.random() *
billboards.length);

        // create the BillData object for the first billboard
        parseBillData();
        }

        /**
        * Gets the applet parameter info about the
current_billboard, and creates
        * a new BillData object from this info.
        */
        void parseBillData() {

        // get the parameter for the next_billboard info
        String s = getParameter("bill" + next_billboard);
        int field_end = s.indexOf(",");

        // get the billboard's image
        Image new_image = getImage(getDocumentBase(), s.sub-
string(0, field_end));

        // get the billboard's URL link
        URL link;
        try {
        link = new URL(getDocumentBase(), s.substring(field_end +
1));
        }
        catch (java.net.MalformedURLException e) {
        e.printStackTrace();
```

```
        link = getDocumentBase();
        }

        // construct the new billboard
        billboards[next_billboard] = new BillData(link, new_image);

        if(image == null) {
        image = new_image;
        }
        else {
        // force loading of the image
        prepareImage(new_image, this);

        // create the image pixels
        billboards[next_billboard].initPixels(size().width,
size().height);
        }
        }

        /**
        * finishes the Initialization the applet
        */
        void finishInit() {
        // Make sure this is only called once, otherwise, when
        // a user leaves our page, and comes back, this gets
        // called again, and it messes things up.
        if(delay != -1) {
        return;
        }

        // Get the delay between transitions in milliseconds
        delay = Long.parseLong(getParameter("delay"));

        // read in the optional target parameter
        link_target_frame = getParameter("target");
        if(link_target_frame == null) {
        link_target_frame = "_top";
        }

        // get the number of transition classes that will be used
        String s = getParameter("transitions");
        int field_end = s.indexOf(",");

        // get the total number of transitions the applet will use
        int trans_count = Integer.parseInt(s.substring(0,
field_end));

        // get the transition classes that will be used
```

```
        transition_classes = new String[trans_count];

        for(--trans_count; trans_count > 0; --trans_count) {
        s = s.substring(field_end + 1);
        field_end = s.indexOf(",");
        transition_classes[trans_count] = s.substring(0,
field_end);
        }
        transition_classes[0] = s.substring(field_end + 1);

        // initialize the pixel data for the first billboard
        billboards[next_billboard].initPixels(size().width,
size().height);

        mouse_inside_applet = false;
        }

        /**
        * Called When the mouse moves over the applet.  Displays the
URL link in
        * the status bar.  Sets the mouse_inside_applet flag to
true
        */
        public boolean mouseMove(Event evt, int x, int y) {
        // show the URL on the status bar
        mouse_inside_applet = true;
        showStatus(billboards[current_billboard].link.toExternal-
Form());
        return true;
        }

        /**
        * Called When the mouse moves out of the applet.  Sets the
        * mouse_inside_applet flag to false
        */
        public boolean mouseExit(Event evt, int x, int y) {
        // clear the URL on the status bar
        mouse_inside_applet = false;
        showStatus("");
        return true;
        }

        /**
        * Called When the mouse button is released over the applet.
Goes to the
        * URL link
        */
        public boolean mouseUp(Event evt, int x, int y) {
```

```
          // go to the URL link of the billboard
          getAppletContext().showDocument(bill-
boards[current_billboard].link, link_target_frame);
          return true;
          }

          /**
           * Overide to prevent flickering
           */
          public void update(Graphics g) {
          paint(g);
          }

          /**
           * Called when the applet needs to be painted.  Draws the
image
           */
          public void paint(Graphics g) {
          g.drawImage(image, 0, 0, this);
          }

          /**
           * Called to start the execution of the applet.
           */
          public void start() {
          // there is not a next bill_board at this time...
          next_billboard = current_billboard;

          // need to set the current image
          image = billboards[current_billboard].image;

          // make the mouse appear as a link cursor when the mouse is
over
          // the applet
          if(getParent() instanceof Frame) {
          ((Frame)getParent()).setCursor(Frame.HAND_CURSOR);
          }

          if(thread == null) {
          thread = new Thread(this);
          thread.start();
          }
          }

          /**
           * Called to stop the execution of the applet
           */
          public void stop() {
```

```
        if(thread != null) {
        thread.stop();
        thread = null;
        }
        }

        /**
         * the main execution method of the applet
         */
        public void run() {

        // Get the first image to the screen ASAP
        while((checkImage(image, this) & ImageObserver.ALLBITS) ==
0) {

        try { Thread.sleep(600); } catch (InterruptedException e)
{}

        }

        // do the rest of the initialization required
        finishInit();

        // Index into the transition_classes array of the current
transition
        int last_transition_type = -1;
        // reference to the actual transition object
        BillTransition transition;
        // variable to hold the time of the next transition
        long next_billboard_time;

        while(true) {

        // Schedule the beginning of the next transition
        next_billboard_time = System.currentTimeMillis() + delay;

        // determine which billboard to display next
        current_billboard = next_billboard;
        if(++next_billboard >= billboards.length) {
        next_billboard = 0;
        }

        // Load the billboard if it has not yet been loaded
        if(billboards[next_billboard] == null) {
        parseBillData();
        try { Thread.sleep(120); } catch (InterruptedException e)
{}

        }

        // Randomly Determine the next transition to use, don't
```

```
include
        // the last transition in the random set, so that the applet
will
        // not use the same transition consecutively.
        int transition_type = (int)(Math.random() *
(transition_classes.length - 1));
        if(transition_type >= last_transition_type) {
        ++transition_type;
        }
        last_transition_type = transition_type;

        try {
        transition = (BillTransition)Class.for-
Name(transition_classes[
        transition_type]).newInstance();
        }
        catch(Exception e) {
        // NOTE: Was your class part of a package?  You might need
        // "package_name.XXX"
        e.printStackTrace();
        continue;
        }

        // initialize this transition
        transition.init(this, bill-
boards[current_billboard].image_pixels, bill-
boards[next_billboard].image_pixels);

        // get the current time and compare it against the next
scheduled
        // transition time.  If it is not yet time for the transi-
tion, wait
        // whatever time is needed.
        if(System.currentTimeMillis() < next_billboard_time) {
        try {
        Thread.sleep(next_billboard_time - System.currentTimeMil-
lis());
        }
        catch (InterruptedException e) {}
        }

        Graphics g = getGraphics();

        // loop through each frame of the transition
        for(int c = 0; c < transition.cells.length; ++c) {

        // show the next transition image
        image = transition.cells[c];
```

```
        // immediately paint the new image
        g.drawImage(image, 0, 0, null);
        getToolkit().sync();

        try { Thread.sleep(transition.delay); } catch (Interrupte-
dException e) {}
        }

        // the next billboard should be shown is its entirety
        image = billboards[next_billboard].image;

        // immediately paint the new image
        g.drawImage(image, 0, 0, null);
        getToolkit().sync();

        transition.flushCells();
        g.dispose();

        // if the mouse is currently is in the applet, show the new
link
        if(mouse_inside_applet == true) {
        showStatus(billboards[next_billboard].link.toExternal-
Form());
        }

        // clean up resources from the completed transition
        transition = null;

        try { Thread.sleep(120); } catch (InterruptedException e)
{}
        }
        }
}
```

B.2 BillData

```
/**
 * @(#)BillData.java
 * @version 1.51 04/06/97
 * @author Robert Temple (robertt@starwave.com)
 */

import java.awt.image.PixelGrabber;
import java.net.URL;
```

```
import java.awt.Image;

/**
 * The BillData class is used to store data about individual bill-
boards
 *
 * USAGE NOTE: Call initPixels before attempting to use the
'image_pixels[]'
 *    array.
 *
 * DESIGN NOTE: The initialization of the image_pixels is separated
from the
 *    constructor to allow the constructor to return in the fastest
time
 *    possible.  This is because the PixelGrabber required to ini-
tialize the
 *    image pixels waits until _all_ of the pixels have been delivered
by the
 *    image's ImageProducer before returning.
 *
 *    Because the DynamicBillBoard class attempts to get an image to
the screen
 *    ASAP upon startup, it is important to call the initPixel method
only
 *    after the first image is displayed on the screen.
 */
public class BillData {

        /** The URL of the page that this billboard will go to. */
        public URL link;

        /** The image that this BillBoard will show on the screen.
*/
        public Image image;

        /**
         * The pixels of the image of this BillBoard.  These pixels
are used by
         * BillTransition derived classes to create new images that
represent
         * transitions.
         * NOTE: The image pixel variable is initialized in the
initPixels method
         */
        public int[] image_pixels;

        /**
         * Constructor.  Initialize the link and image variables
```

```
 * @param link        value to set the link variable to
 * @param image    value to set the image variable to
 */
public BillData(URL link, Image image) {
this.link = link;
this.image = image;
}


/**
 * Used to initialize the image_pixels array variable
 * @param image_width        the width of the image variable
 * @param image_height    the height of the image variable
 */
public void initPixels(int image_width, int image_height) {

image_pixels = new int[image_width * image_height];

// Create a PixelGrabber to Get the Pixels of the image and
store
// them into the image_pixels array
PixelGrabber pixel_grabber = new PixelGrabber(image.get-
Source(), 0, 0,
image_width, image_height, image_pixels, 0, image_width);

try {
pixel_grabber.grabPixels();
}
catch (InterruptedException e) {
image_pixels = null;
}

}
}
```

B.3 BillTransition

```
/**
 * @(#)BillTransition.java
 * @version 1.51 04/06/97
 * @author Robert Temple (robertt@starwave.com)
 */

import java.awt.image.MemoryImageSource;
import java.awt.*;
```

```
import java.util.Hashtable;

/**
 * The BillTransition class is used as a base class for other tran-
sition
 * classes.  These other classes are what create transition cells
between
 * two individual billboard images.
 *
 * NOTE: This class is abstract.  Create subclasses from it.
 */
public abstract class BillTransition {
// Static Members

        /**
         * Holds static information which can be used on a per applet
basis for
         * applets of unique sizes.
         */
        static Hashtable object_table = new Hashtable(20);

// Instance Members

        /**
         * The actual images that are created by this transition.
The owner
         * uses these cells to transition from one billboard to the
next
         */
        public Image[] cells;

        /** The delay the owner should use to change from one cell
to the next. */
        public int delay;

        /**
         * Used to provide the Component which is needed to create
new images from
         * pixel arrays
         */
        Component owner;

        /** The number of cells to be created by this transition */
        int number_of_cells;

        /** The width of each cell */
        int cell_w;
```

```
          /** The height of each cell */
          int cell_h;

          /** The total number of pixels per cell */
          int pixels_per_cell;

          /** The pixels for the current billboard which is visible
on the applet. */
          int[] current_pixels;

          /** The pixels for the next billboard to be displayed on the
applet. */
          int[] next_pixels;

          /** A work canvas used to create cells onto */
          int[] work_pixels;

          /**
           * Used to initialize the transition right after it is cre-
ated.
           * @param owner the component to be used to create images
from cells
           */
          public abstract void init(Component owner, int[]
current_pixels, int[] next_pixels);

          /**
           * Called by derived classes to initialize the transition
and set
           * number_of_cells and delay
           * @param ownersets the variable: owner
           * @param number_of_cellssets the variable: number_of_cells
           * @param delaysets the variable: delay
           */
          final protected void init(Component owner, int[]
current_pixels, int[] next_pixels, int number_of_cells, int delay)
{
          this.delay = delay;
          this.number_of_cells = number_of_cells;
          this.next_pixels = next_pixels;
          this.current_pixels = current_pixels;
          this.owner = owner;

          cells = new Image[number_of_cells];
          cell_w = owner.size().width;
          cell_h = owner.size().height;
          pixels_per_cell = cell_w * cell_h;
          work_pixels = new int[pixels_per_cell];
```

```
        }

        /**
        * Called by derived classes to initialize the transition and set
        * number_of_cells.  Sets delay to 120 milliseconds.
        * @param ownersets the variable: owner
        * @param number_of_cellssets the variable: number_of_cells
        */
        final protected void init(Component owner, int[] current_pixels, int[] next_pixels, int number_of_cells) {
        init(owner, current_pixels, next_pixels, number_of_cells, 120);
        }

        /**
        * Used to create an actual Image from a pixel array
        * @param cell the index into the cell array to store the new image
        */
        final void createCellFromWorkPixels(int cell) {
        cells[cell] = owner.createImage(new MemoryImage-
Source(cell_w, cell_h,
        work_pixels, 0, cell_w));
        owner.prepareImage(cells[cell], null);
        }

        /**
        * clean up any resources associated with the cell images
        */
        final void flushCells() {
        for(int c = 0; c < cells.length; ++c) {
        if(cells[c] != null) {
        cells[c].flush();
        }
        }
        }
}
```

B.4 ColumnTransition

```
/**
* @(#)ColumnTransition.java
* @version 1.51 04/06/97
* @author Robert Temple (robertt@starwave.com)
```

```
*/

import java.awt.image.MemoryImageSource;
import java.awt.*;

/**
 * The ColumnTransition class changes one image into another by
drawing
 * increasingly larger columns of the new image onto the old image.
The
 * column sizes increases to the left, and the same pixels are
always drawn
 * on the left side of each column.  This makes the image appear to
be sliding
 * in from behind the old image.
 */
public class ColumnTransition extends BillTransition {
// Static Members
        /**
         * The total number of cells this transition will show on the
screen before
         * the new image is shown in its entirety
         */
        final static int CELLS = 7;

        /** The pixel amount a column show grow every cell */
        final static int WIDTH_INCREMENT = 3;

        /**
         * The maximum pixel size a column can grow to be.  This
determines how many
         * columns there will be, the width divided by this number.
         */
        // this number must be evenly divisible by the
WIDTH_INCREMENT
        final static int MAX_COLUMN_WIDTH = 24;

// Instance Members

        /**
         * The width of the last column, because the width of the
last column will
         * usually not be the same size as the MAX_COLUMN_WIDTH,
unless the width
         * of the image is evenly divisible by the MAX_COLUMNS_WIDTH
         */
        int rightmost_columns_max_width;
```

```
        /**
         * starting from the left hand side of the image, the pixel
that the last
         * column will start at.
         */
        int rightmost_columns_x_start;
        /**
         * the current size of the columns in pixels, the number of
pixels to
         * draw from the new images onto the old one in this column
         */
        int column_width = WIDTH_INCREMENT;

        /**
         * Used to initialize the transition right after it is cre-
ated.
         * creates cells
         * @param owner the component to be used to create images
from cells
         */
        public void init(Component owner, int[] current, int[]
next) {
        init(owner, current, next, CELLS, 200);

        rightmost_columns_max_width = cell_w % MAX_COLUMN_WIDTH;
        rightmost_columns_x_start = cell_w -
rightmost_columns_max_width;

        // copy the whole of the old image into the work pixel
array.
        System.arraycopy((Object)current_pixels, 0,
(Object)work_pixels,
        0, pixels_per_cell);

        // create all the image cells
        for(int c = 0; c < CELLS; ++c) {

        // give other threads a shot at the CPU
        try { Thread.sleep(100); } catch (InterruptedException e)
{}

        // draw the next cell into the work pixels
        NextFrame();

        // give other threads a shot at the CPU
        try { Thread.sleep(100); } catch (InterruptedException e)
{}
```

```
    // create the new cell image from the work pixels
    createCellFromWorkPixels(c);

    // make the column width wider for the next cell
    column_width += WIDTH_INCREMENT;
    }

    // we don't need the work pixels anymore
    work_pixels = null;
    }

    /**
    * Create the next cell in the work pixel array
    */
    void NextFrame() {

    int old_column_width = MAX_COLUMN_WIDTH - column_width;

    // iterate through each row of the image
    for(int p = pixels_per_cell - cell_w; p >= 0; p -= cell_w) {

    // iterate through each column of the image, except the
last
    for (int x = 0; x < rightmost_columns_x_start; x +=
MAX_COLUMN_WIDTH) {

    // copy one row of a column of the new pixels into the work
    // pixels
    System.arraycopy((Object)next_pixels, x + p,
(Object)work_pixels,
    old_column_width + x + p, column_width);
    }

    // now do the last column if we need to
    if(old_column_width <= rightmost_columns_max_width) {

    System.arraycopy((Object)next_pixels,
    rightmost_columns_x_start + p, (Object)work_pixels,
    rightmost_columns_x_start + old_column_width + p - 1,
    rightmost_columns_max_width - old_column_width + 1);
    }
    }
    }
}
```

B.5 FadeTransition

```
/**
```

```
* @(#)FadeTransition.java
* @version 1.51 04/06/97
* @author Robert Temple (robertt@starwave.com)
*/

import java.awt.*;
import java.awt.image.MemoryImageSource;

/**
* The FadeTransition class changes one image into another by draw-
ing
* a set of random pixels from the new image onto the old image each
cell.
* the number of pixels draw each cell is the same for each cell.
*
* DESIGN NOTE: This class uses a bunch of random number to fill in
the pixels
*   of each cell.  If found Java's random number generator too slow
for
*   this purpose, and wrote a really simple one.  The numbers are
not very
*   random, but it is very fast compared to Sun's.  The numbers gen-
erated
*   are more then random enough for my purposes.  Also the it only
generates
*   numbers between 0-7.  The only numbers we need
*
*/
public class FadeTransition extends BillTransition {

// Static Members

        /**
        * The total number of cells this transition will show on the
screen before
        * the new image is shown in its entirety
        *
        * DON'T CHANGE THIS NUMBER, the random number generator
will not
        * work because it only produces number between 0-7
        */
        private static final int CELLS = 7;

        /** Used by a very-pseudo random number generator */
        private static final int MULTIPLIER = 0x5D1E2F;

        /**
        * Creates a random array used later to create cells.
```

```
        * The FadeTransition class uses a two dimensional array
that holds indexes
        * a number of random numbers.  The first dimension is 8 ele-
ments in size,
        * one element for each Cell.  Each element in the second
dimension is 1/8
        * the size of
        */
        private static int[][] createRandomArray(int number_pixels,
int cell_h) {
        int total_cells = CELLS + 1;

        int new_pixels_per_cell = number_pixels / total_cells;

        // A multidimensional array that hold indexes into the work
pixel array
        // for every single pixel in the work pixel array.  The
first dimension
        // Holds the pixels for each cell, the other dimension is
the pixels
        // indicies.
        int[][] random = new int[total_cells][new_pixels_per_cell];

        // every cell will have the same number of new pixels draw
into
        // the image.  No more no less.  So keep track of the number
        // of random values added to each random cell, so that we
don't
        // try to add too many.  The array below keeps count
        int random_count[] = new int[total_cells];
        for(int s = 0; s < total_cells; ++s) {
        random_count[s] = 0;
        }

        int cell;
        int rounded_new_pixels_per_cell = new_pixels_per_cell *
total_cells;

        // inline random number generator starts here
        // *** read DESIGN NOTES above ***
        int seed = (int)System.currentTimeMillis();

        int denominator = 10;
        while((new_pixels_per_cell % denominator > 0 || cell_h %
denominator == 0) && denominator > 1) {
        --denominator;
        }
```

```
        int new_randoms_per_cell = new_pixels_per_cell / denomina-
tor;
        int new_randoms = rounded_new_pixels_per_cell / denomina-
tor;

        // create a bunch of random numbers and put them into the
        // array without checking to see if any particular array
        // is full.   Do this until it is possible that one filled
        // up.
        for(int p = 0; p < new_randoms_per_cell; ++p) {
        // Generate a random number between 0 - 7
        seed *= MULTIPLIER;
        cell = (seed >>> 29);
        random[cell][random_count[cell]++] = p;
        }

        // might as well as mix up the random number generator a bit
more
        seed += 0x5050;

        // give other threads a shot at the CPU
        try { Thread.sleep(150); } catch (InterruptedException e)
{}

        // generate the rest of the random numbers
        for(int p = new_randoms_per_cell; p < new_randoms; ++p) {
        // Generate a random number between 0 - 7
        seed *= MULTIPLIER;
        cell = (seed >>> 29);

        // if the cell this number is supposed to go in is
        // full, put it in the next cell
        while(random_count[cell] >= new_randoms_per_cell) {
        if(++cell >= total_cells) {
        cell = 0;
        }
        }
        random[cell][random_count[cell]++] = p;
        }

        // we only actually filled up the arrays part of the way.
        // now fill them up the rest of the way using the numbers
        // we already generated.  Also, we don't need to fill in
        // the numbers for the last cell, since at the last cell
        // we know that all the work_pixels would have been filled
        // in with pixels from the new image anyways.
        for(int s = 0; s < CELLS; ++s) {
```

```
            for(int ps = new_randoms_per_cell; ps <
new_pixels_per_cell;
                ps += new_randoms_per_cell) {

                int offset = ps * total_cells;

                for(int p = 0; p < new_randoms_per_cell; ++p) {
                random[s][ps + p] = random[s][p] + offset;
                }
                }

                // give other threads a shot at the CPU
                try { Thread.sleep(50); } catch (InterruptedException e) {}
                }

                // this cell is never actually used it is only needed pre-
viously
                // to make sure the random numbers where evenly distrib-
uted.
                random[CELLS] = null;

                return random;
                }

// Instance Members

                /**
                * Used to initialize the transition right after it is cre-
ated.
                * creates cells
                * @param owner the component to be used to create images
from cells
                */
                public void init(Component owner, int[] current, int[]
next) {
                init(owner, current, next, CELLS);

                // copy all of the current billboard's pixels into the work
pixels
                System.arraycopy((Object)current_pixels, 0,
(Object)work_pixels,
                0, pixels_per_cell);

                // get the random array for this sized applet from the
object table.
                int random[][] = (int[][])object_table.get(
                getClass().getName() + pixels_per_cell);
```

```
            // if the random array is not found, create it and put it in
the
            // object table.
            if(random == null) {
            random = createRandomArray(pixels_per_cell, cell_h);
            object_table.put(getClass().getName() + pixels_per_cell,
random);
            }

            // create all the image cells
            for(int c = 0; c < CELLS; ++c) {

            // give other threads a shot at the CPU
            try { Thread.sleep(100); } catch (InterruptedException e)
{}

            // draw in the pixels that the random array specifies for
            // this cell from the new image into the work pixels
            int limit = random[c].length;
            for(int p = 0; p < limit; ++p) {
            int pixel_index = random[c][p];
            work_pixels[pixel_index] = next_pixels[pixel_index];
            }

            // give other threads a shot at the CPU
            try { Thread.sleep(50); } catch (InterruptedException e) {}

            // create the new cell image from the work pixels
            createCellFromWorkPixels(c);
            }

            // we don't need the work pixels anymore
            work_pixels = null;
            }
    }
```

B.6 RotateTransition

```
/**
* @(#)RotateTransition.java
* @version 1.51 04/06/97
* @author Robert Temple (robertt@starwave.com)
*/

import java.awt.image.MemoryImageSource;
import java.awt.*;
```

```
import java.lang.Math;

/**
 * The RotateTransition class changes one image into another by making it
 * appear as if one image is rotating upward from below the other image.
 * it might appear as if the images are on a cube with the current image
 * facing you, and the next image on the bottom of the cube, but slowly
 * moving up to face you.
 */
public class RotateTransition extends BillTransition {
// Static Members
/**
 * The total number of cells this transition will show on the screen before
    * the new image is shown in its entirety
 */
final static int CELLS = 12;

// Instance Members

/** the current angle at which the billboards are rotated at */
double current_angle;

/**
 * Used to initialize the transition right after it is created.
 * creates cells
 * @param owner the component to be used to create images from cells
 */
public void init(Component owner, int[] current, int[] next) {
init(owner, current, next, CELLS, 180);

double angle_increase = (Math.PI / 2.0d) * (1.0d / (double)(CELLS + 1));

current_angle = angle_increase;

for(int c = 0; c < CELLS; ++c) {

// give other threads a shot at the CPU
try { Thread.sleep(100); } catch (InterruptedException e) {}

Rotate();
```

```
// give other threads a shot at the CPU
try { Thread.sleep(100); } catch (InterruptedException e) {}

// create the new cell image from the work pixels
createCellFromWorkPixels(c);

current_angle += angle_increase;
}

// we don't need the work pixels anymore
work_pixels = null;
}

/**
 * Create the next cell in the work pixel array
 */
final void Rotate() {
// calculate the portion of the top billboard that can be seen
double top_billboard_h = ((double)cell_h / 2d *
Math.sin(Math.PI / 2d - current_angle)) +
(double)cell_h / 2d;

// calculate the portion of the bottom billboard that can be seen
double bottom_billboard_h = ((double)cell_h / 2d * Math.sin(current_angle)) + (dou-
ble)cell_h / 2d;

// calculate the vertical location that the top billboard ends and the
// next billboard starts
int location = cell_h - (int)(bottom_billboard_h * Math.sin(current_angle));

// calculate the vertical adder to determine the vertical position
// to take pixels from the source image
float adder = (float)top_billboard_h / (float)location;

// the current vertical location on the source image to grab pixels from
float position = (float)cell_h - (float)top_billboard_h + adder - 1f;

// draw in the top billboard
for(int y = 0; y < location; ++y) {
```

```
System.arraycopy((Object)current_pixels,
(int)position * cell_w, (Object)work_pixels,
y * cell_w, cell_w);

position += adder;
}

adder = (float)bottom_billboard_h / (float)(cell_h - location);
position = 0f;

// draw in the bottom billboard
for(int y = location; y < cell_h; ++y) {

System.arraycopy((Object)next_pixels, (int)position * cell_w,
(Object)work_pixels, y * cell_w, cell_w);

position += adder;
}
}
}
```

B.7 SmashTransition

```
/**
 * @(#)SmashTransition.java
 * @version 1.51 04/06/97
 * @author Robert Temple (robertt@starwave.com)
 */

import java.awt.image.MemoryImageSource;
import java.awt.*;

/**
 * The SmashTransition class changes one image into another by drop-
ping the
 * new image onto the old one.  The old image appears to crumble
under the
 * weight of the new image.
 */
public class SmashTransition extends BillTransition {
// Static Members
```

```
/**
 * The total number of CELLS this transition will show on the
screen before
 * the new image is shown in its entirety
 */
final static int CELLS = 8;

/**
 * The old image will appear to be folded back and forth
under the weigth
 * of the new image falling on it.  This constant holds the
value of the
 * number of folds that will appear each cell
 */
final static float FOLDS = 8.0f;

/**
 * an array of white pixels used to fill in pixels where nei-
ther image will
 * appear in for a cell
 */
static int[] fill_pixels;

static void setupFillPixels(int width) {
if(fill_pixels != null && fill_pixels.length <= width) {
return;
}
fill_pixels = new int[width];
for(int f = 0; f < width; ++f) {
fill_pixels[f] = 0xFFFFFFFF;
}
}

// Instance Members

/** The amount of pixels to move the new image onto the old
image each cell */
int drop_amount;

/**
 * The index into the work_pixel array that the start of the
old image
 * current is at
 */
int location;

/**
```

```
        * Used to initialize the transition right after it is cre-
ated.
        * creates cells
        * @param owner the component to be used to create images
from cells
        */
        public void init(Component owner, int[] current, int[]
next) {
        init(owner, current, next, CELLS, 160);

        // ensure the fill pixel array is setup properly
        setupFillPixels(cell_w);

        // this cannot be reduced to 'pixels_per_cell / CELLS'
because there
        // is some rounding that is done in 'cell_h / CELLS'
        drop_amount = (cell_h / CELLS) * cell_w;

        // as above, the right half of this calculation cannot be
reduced
        // because of rounding
        location = pixels_per_cell - ((cell_h / CELLS) / 2) *
cell_w;

        for(int c = CELLS - 1; c >= 0; --c) {

        // give other threads a shot at the CPU
        try { Thread.sleep(100); } catch (InterruptedException e)
{}

        // create the next cell
        Smash(c + 1);

        // give other threads a shot at the CPU
        try { Thread.sleep(150); } catch (InterruptedException e)
{}

        // create the new cell image from the work pixels
        createCellFromWorkPixels(c);

        location -= drop_amount;
        }

        // we don't need the work pixels anymore
        work_pixels = null;
        }

        /**
```

```
 * Create the next cell in the work pixel array
 */
void Smash(int max_fold) {

// draw in the new image
System.arraycopy((Object)next_pixels, pixels_per_cell -
location,
    (Object)work_pixels, 0, location);

// calculate the height of the new image
int height = cell_h - location / cell_w;

// calculate the length of the lines to draw for the smashed
image
    int fold_width = cell_w - max_fold;

// variable used to store the current fold offset
float fold_offset = 0.0f;

// calculate the amount to add to the fold offset after
every line
    float fold_offset_adder = (float)max_fold * FOLDS /
(float)height;

// used to increment the src_y_offset defined below after
every line
    float src_y_adder = (float)cell_h / (float)height;

// used to determine the y-coordinate of the line to use
from the
// source image
    float src_y_offset = cell_h - src_y_adder / 2;

for(int p = pixels_per_cell - cell_w; p >= location; p -=
cell_w) {

System.arraycopy((Object)fill_pixels, 0,
(Object)work_pixels, p,
    cell_w);

System.arraycopy((Object)current_pixels,
    (int)src_y_offset * cell_w, (Object)work_pixels,
    p + (int)fold_offset, fold_width);

src_y_offset -= src_y_adder;
fold_offset += fold_offset_adder;

if(fold_offset < 0.0 || fold_offset >= max_fold) {
```

```
            fold_offset_adder *= -1.0f;
            }
        }
        }
}
```

B.8 TearTransition

```java
/**
 * @(#)TearTransition.java
 * @version 1.51 04/06/97
 * @author Robert Temple (robertt@starwave.com)
 */

import java.awt.image.MemoryImageSource;
import java.awt.*;

/**
 * The TearTransition class changes one image into another by making
it appear
 * as if the old image is covering the new image, and the old image
is torn
 * out from over the new image.
 */
public class TearTransition extends BillTransition {
        /**
         * The total number of cells this transition will show on the
screen before
         * the new image is shown in its entirety
         */
        static final int CELLS = 7;

        /** The number to start the x_cross variable at */
        static final float INITIAL_X_CROSS = 1.6f;

        /** The amount the x_cross number is divided by after each
cell */
        static final float X_CROSS_DIVISOR = 3.5f;

        /**
         * A number the cross product of the x and y values of a
pixel are
         * multiplied by to give a new x value
         */
        float x_cross;
```

```
        /**
        * Used to initialize the transition right after it is cre-
ated.
        * creates cells
        * @param owner the component to be used to create images
from cells
        */
        public void init(Component owner, int[] current, int[]
next) {
        init(owner, current, next, CELLS);

        // starting after the first row, Copy the new image into the
work pixels
        System.arraycopy((Object)next_pixels, 0,
(Object)work_pixels,
        0, pixels_per_cell);

        // copy all of the current billboard's pixels into the work
pixels
        System.arraycopy((Object)current_pixels, 0,
(Object)work_pixels,
                                            0, cell_w);

        x_cross = INITIAL_X_CROSS;

        // Create all the image cells, starting with the last cell.
Since each
        // cell progressively covers more and more of the old
image, we start
        // from the last cell to reduce the amount of drawing we
need to do from
        // cell to cell.  This is because the last cell covers the
least
        // amount of the old image.  So, after drawing the last
cell, we can draw
        // right over the work pixels, since we know that we will be
covering all
        // that the later cell (the one we had previouly drawn) drew
onto the
        // work pixels anyways.  So now we can just draw the pixels
of the new
        // image, and don't have to worry about drawing pixels from
the old image.
        // email me if this is not clear.  templer@db.erau.edu
        for(int c = CELLS - 1; c >= 0; --c) {

        // give other threads a shot at the CPU
        try { Thread.sleep(100); } catch (InterruptedException e)
```

```
        {}

            // draw the next cell into the work pixels
            Tear();

            // give other threads a shot at the CPU
            try { Thread.sleep(150); } catch (InterruptedException e)
        {}

            // create the new cell image from the work pixels
            createCellFromWorkPixels(c);

            // set the x_cross for the next cell
            x_cross /= X_CROSS_DIVISOR;
            }

            // we don't need the work pixels anymore
            work_pixels = null;
            }

            /**
             * Create the next cell in the work pixel array
             */
            final void Tear() {
            float x_increment;
            int p, height_adder;

            // p represent the current offset into the work pixels that
we are
            // drawing at
            p = height_adder = cell_w;

            // starting after the first row, draw all the rows, indi-
vidually into the
            // work pixels
            for (int y = 1; y < cell_h; ++y) {

            // the cross product will equal x_cross * x * y.  Since we
are gonna
            // have the same x_cross and y values for this row, calcu-
late it
            // x_cross * y  once for this row, so we don't have to do it
for each
            // pixel in this row.  For each pixel we will multiply this
value by x
            x_increment = x_cross * y;

            // This if-else structure is a speed optimization.  The
```

```
first block
        // draws the pixels, pixel by pixel.  The else block draws
the pixels
        // by copying sequences of pixels onto the work pixels.
        //##
        // A value of x_increment over 0.50 means that there will
never be two
        // adjacent pixels from the old image that will be copied
onto the work
        // pixels
        if(x_increment >= 0.50f) {
        float fx = 0.0f;

        // Adding x to a running sum of x_increment + 1 each time is
the
        // equivalent of x += x * x_increment, but it is faster
        x_increment += 1.0f;
        int x = 0;

        // draw in the pixels for this row until the end of the row
is
        // reached
        do {
        work_pixels[p++] = current_pixels[height_adder + x];

        // Adding x to a running sum of x_increment each time is the
        // equivalent of multiplying x * x_increment
        x = (int)(fx += x_increment);
        } while(x < cell_w);
        }
        else {

        float overflow = 1.0f / x_increment;
        float dst_end = overflow / 2.0f  + 1.49999999f;
        int dst_start = 0, src_offset = 0, length = (int)dst_end;

        while(dst_start + src_offset + length < cell_w) {

        System.arraycopy((Object)current_pixels, p + src_offset,
        (Object)work_pixels, p, length);

        ++src_offset;
        dst_end += overflow;
        p += length;
        dst_start += length;
        length = (int)dst_end - dst_start;
        }
```

```
        length = cell_w - src_offset - dst_start;

        System.arraycopy((Object)current_pixels, p + src_offset,
        (Object)work_pixels, p, length);

        }
        p = height_adder += cell_w;
        }
        }
}
```

B.9 UnrollTransition

```
/**
 * @(#)UnrollTransition.java
 * @version 1.51 04/06/97
 * @author Robert Temple (robertt@starwave.com)
 */

import java.awt.image.MemoryImageSource;
import java.awt.*;
import java.util.Hashtable;


/**
 * The UnrollTransition class changes one image into another by set-
ting a roll
 * which is the new image on top of the old image, and then unrolling
the new
 * image until it covers the old image.
 */
public class UnrollTransition extends BillTransition {
// Static Members
        /**
        * The total number of CELLS this transition will show on the
screen before
        * the new image is shown in its entirety
        */
        final static int CELLS = 9;

        /** array of three pixels used to fill in the right hand
side of the roll */
        static int fill_pixels[] = { 0xFFFFFFFF, 0xFF000000,
0xFF000000, 0xFFFFFFFF };

        /**
         * Creates a unroll array used later to create cells.
```

```
          * This array is used to determine how many verticle pixels
to unroll
          * the image for each cell.
          */
         private static int[] createUnrollAmountArray(int cell_h) {


         // The First line of the statement below determines that
average
         // amount each cell must unroll the image in order to com-
pletely
         // unroll the image during the transition.  Note that we add
one
         // to the CELLS count because the drawing of the whole next
         // image to the screen is part of the unrolling process too.
         // the second line determines the location the across the
x-axis
         // that this average will fall if the first cell starts at a
         // x point of 1.  This is why one more is added to cells
         // then the top.
         // The divide determines the slope of the line from (0,0) to
         // (x_avg, y_avg)
         // if you are confused here, don't worry, so was I...  but
         // it works...
         float unroll_increment = ((float)cell_h / (float)(CELLS +
1)) /
         ((float)(CELLS + 2) / 2.0f);

         int total = 0;
         int unroll_amount[] = new int[CELLS + 1];
         for(int u = 0; u <= CELLS; ++u) {
         unroll_amount[u] = (int)(unroll_increment * (CELLS - u +
1));
         total += unroll_amount[u];
         }

         // make sure we did not round our way to unrolling more of
the
         // image then there is to unroll
         if(total < 0) {
         unroll_amount[0] -= 1;
         }

         return unroll_amount;
         }

         /**
         * An array which holds the amount of verticle pixels to
```

```
unroll the image
        * each cell.
        */
        int[] unroll_amount;

// Instance Members
        /** The index into the work_pixel array that the start of
the roll is at */
        int location;

        /**
        * Used to initialize the transition right after it is cre-
ated.
        * creates cells
        * @param owner the component to be used to create images
from cells
        */
        public void init(Component owner, int[] current, int[]
next) {
        init(owner, current, next, CELLS, 220);

        location = pixels_per_cell;

        System.arraycopy((Object)current_pixels, 0,
(Object)work_pixels,
        0, pixels_per_cell);

        // get the random array for an applet of this height from
the object table.
        unroll_amount = (int[])object_table.get(getClass().get-
Name() + cell_h);

        // if the random array is not found, create it and put it in
the
        // object table.
        if(unroll_amount == null) {
        unroll_amount = createUnrollAmountArray(cell_h);
        object_table.put(getClass().getName() + cell_h,
unroll_amount);
        }

        for(int c = 0; c < CELLS; ++c) {

        // unroll the image
        location -= unroll_amount[c] * cell_w;

        // give other threads a shot at the CPU
        try { Thread.sleep(150); } catch (InterruptedException e)
```

```
{}

        // create the next cell
        Unroll(c);

        // give other threads a shot at the CPU
        try { Thread.sleep(100); } catch (InterruptedException e)
{}

        // create the new cell image from the work pixels
        createCellFromWorkPixels(c);

        // copy over the new image onto where the roll last appeared
        System.arraycopy((Object)next_pixels, location,
        (Object)work_pixels, location, unroll_amount[c] * cell_w);
        }

        // we don't need the work pixels anymore
        work_pixels = null;
        }

        /**
        * Create the next cell in the work pixel array
        */
        void Unroll(int c) {

        int y_flip = cell_w;

        // the offset is what makes the roll appear to be raised up
        int offset[] = new int[unroll_amount[c]];
        for(int o = 0; o < unroll_amount[c]; ++o) {
        offset[o] = 4;
        }
        offset[0] = 2;

        if(unroll_amount[c] > 1) {
        offset[1] = 3;
        }
        if(unroll_amount[c] > 2) {
        offset[unroll_amount[c] - 1] = 2;
        }
        if(unroll_amount[c] > 3) {
        offset[unroll_amount[c] - 2] = 3;
        }

        int offset_index = 0;
        int end_location = location + unroll_amount[c] * cell_w;
        for(int p = location; p < end_location; p += cell_w) {
```

```
        System.arraycopy((Object)next_pixels,
        p - y_flip + offset[offset_index], (Object)work_pixels,
        p, cell_w - offset[offset_index]);

        // draw in the right side of the roll
        System.arraycopy((Object)fill_pixels, 0,
(Object)work_pixels,
        p + cell_w - offset[offset_index], offset[offset_index]);

        ++offset_index;

        y_flip += cell_w + cell_w;

      }

      // cheesy way but kinda fast to make the roll appear more
3D.
      for(int x = location + cell_w - 1; x > location; --x) {
      work_pixels[x] |= 0xFFAAAAAA;
      work_pixels[x + unroll_amount[c]] &= 0xFF555555;
      }

    }
}
```

Index

Hewlett-Packard Computer Education and Training

Hewlett-Packard's world-class education and training offers hands on education solutions including:

- Linux
- HP-UX System and Network Administration
- Y2K HP-UX Transition
- Advanced HP-UX System Administration
- IT Service Management using advanced Internet technologies
- Microsoft Windows NT
- Internet/Intranet
- MPE/iX
- Database Administration
- Software Development

HP's new IT Professional Certification program provides rigorous technical qualification for specific IT job roles including HP-UX System Administration, Network Management, Unix/NT Servers and Applications Management, and IT Service Management.

In addition, HP's IT Resource Center is the perfect knowledge source for IT professionals. Through a vibrant and rich Web environment, IT professionals working in the areas of UNIX, Microsoft, networking, or MPE/iX gain access to continually updated knowledge pools.

http://education.hp.com

In the U.S. phone 1-800-HPCLASS (472-5277)